"Gillman's book is as rich and paradoxical
as Jewish assimilation itself,
for the author is at once telling a particularly Jewish
and a larger European story of aesthetic, cultural,
and sometimes even political engagement with tradition."

∎ ∎ ∎

WILLIAM DONAHUE, DUKE UNIVERSITY

VIENNESE JEWISH MODERNISM

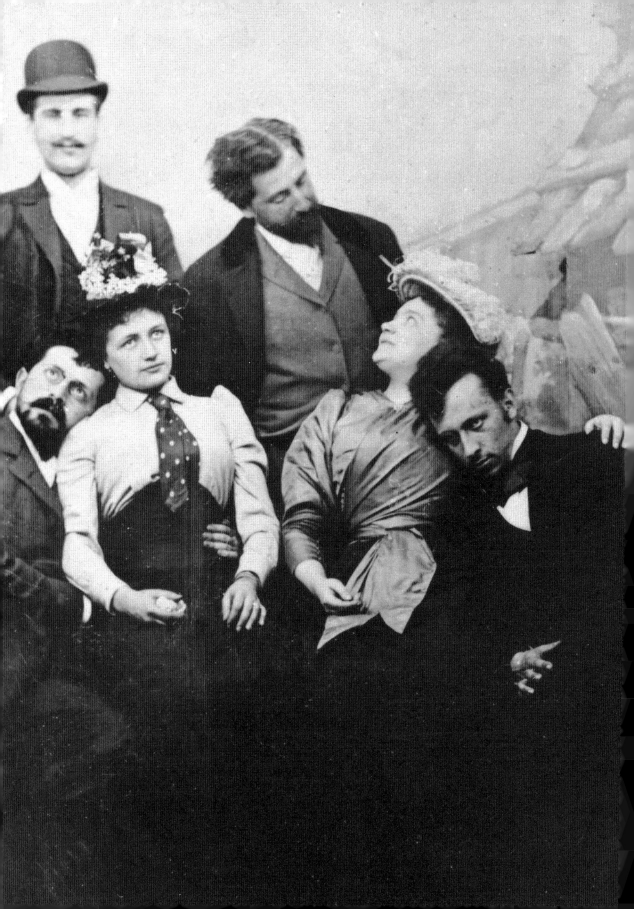

VIENNESE JEWISH MODERNISM

FREUD, HOFMANNSTHAL,
BEER-HOFMANN,
AND SCHNITZLER

ABIGAIL GILLMAN

THE PENNSYLVANIA STATE UNIVERSITY PRESS

UNIVERSITY PARK, PENNSYLVANIA

Library of Congress Cataloging-in-Publication Data

Gillman, Abigail, 1964–
Viennese Jewish modernism : Freud, Hofmannsthal, Beer-Hofmann,
and Schnitzler / Abigail Gillman.
p.   cm. — (Refiguring modernism)
Includes bibliographical references and index.
ISBN 978-0-271-03409-6 (pbk. : alk. paper)
1. Modernism (Literature)—Austria—Vienna.
2. Jews—Austria—Vienna—Intellectual life.
3. Austria—Civilization—Jewish influences.
4. Freud, Sigmund, 1856–1939—Criticism and interpretation.
5. Hofmannsthal, Hugo von, 1874–1929—Criticism and interpretation.
6. Beer-Hofmann, Richard, 1866–1945—Criticism and interpretation.
7. Schnitzler, Arthur, 1862–1931—Criticism and interpretation.
I. Title.

PT3828.V5G55 2009
830.9'89240436—dc22   2008029794

Frontispiece: Detail of figure 2, Young Vienna Circle, 1894.

CONTENTS

ILLUSTRATIONS

April 1919. By permission of the Houghton Library, Harvard University. MS Ger 131 (72).

20. Photograph from the Habima production of *Jaákobs Traum* in 1926: Leo Warschauer, in the role of Jaákob, sets free the slave Idnibaál, played by Czezhk-Efrati. By permission of the Houghton Library, Harvard University. MS Ger 131 (73).

21. Photograph from the Habima production of *Jaákobs Traum* in 1926: Benjamin Zemach in the role of the angel Samael. By permission of the Houghton Library, Harvard University. MS Ger 131 (73).

22. Sketch by Beer-Hofmann, "Old Castle Square in Bethlehem," the stage setting for scene 3 of *Der junge David.* By permission of the Houghton Library, Harvard University. MS Ger 131 (54).

ACKNOWLEDGMENTS

My first thanks go to Penn State University Press, and to four people at the Press who made this publication possible. I am grateful to Sandy Thatcher for his vision to place the book in a series devoted to "Refiguring Modernism." Eleanor Goodman treated my manuscript with care and enthusiasm from the outset. Cali Buckley patiently answered my many questions. John Morris was a meticulous editor and insightful reader.

A number of colleagues read all or parts of this book and offered valuable advice on substance and style. Dorrit Cohn was my first reader; her rigor and fondness for all things Viennese continue to inspire me. I am also very much indebted to Jeffrey Sammons, Liliane Weissberg, Judith Ryan, Catriona Macleod, Tom Kovach, Steve Beller, Ritchie Robertson, and Bill Donahue. In Vienna, I could not have had a better conversation partner than Konstanze Fliedl.

My three research assistants, Caitlin Zacharias, Elena Chardakliyska, and Allison Palm, were conscientious beyond the call of duty. I thank them for attending to countless details as I prepared the manuscript for publication. I thank Johannes Wich-Schwarz for assisting me with translations of Hofmannsthal and Beer-Hofmann, and Mary Bergstein for sharing her expertise in the visual culture of Vienna.

My research profited greatly from fellowships awarded me at critical points in my career. I am grateful to the Franz Rosenzweig Center for German Jewish Studies at Hebrew University, the Humanities Foundation at Boston University, the Österreichischer Austauschdienst, and the Institut für die Wissenschaften vom Menschen in Vienna.

At Boston University, I have been fortunate to be part of an intellectual community of the first order. Among many colleagues who have supported and inspired me, I thank Katherine O'Connor, Dorothy Kelly, Jeffrey Mehlman, Alicia Borinsky, Alan Smith, George Hoffmann, Irene Zaderenko, Nancy Harrowitz, Peter Hawkins, Susan Mizruchi, Steven Katz, and the late John Clayton. For her friendship and wisdom about so many things, I thank Deeana Klepper.

Nor could I have completed this book without the encouragement of my friends. Rebecca Steinitz, Mychal Springer, and Elena Sigman have been there for me from the start. No one has been more persistent than Julia Paley in reminding me that the process, and not only the product, is worth celebrating. My Boston friends—Judith Kates, Sharon Portnoff, Amy Ramdeo, Sharon Becker Jacobson, Sharon Cohen Anisfeld, Pamela Adelstein, Janet Segal, and Pamela Blau—enrich my life day after day. Though my friendship with Miriam Hasson *z"l* ended far too soon, Mimi's brilliance and love of learning are never far from my mind.

The Prince family—my second family—has supported me in more ways than I can name. I am fortunate to have in David, Erica, and Paul such inspiring models of intellectuality and creativity. Reva *z"l* would have been so pleased to add this book to her extensive library. I thank her for admonishing me so many times, and even in our last conversations, to keep working to achieve my goals.

My parents, Neil Gillman and Sarah F. Gillman, have nurtured my mind and my spirit for as long as I can remember. Their mutual passion for books and ideas, and their impeccable sense of rhetoric and style, set me on the course that led ulti-mately to the writing of this book.

I cannot pinpoint the moment when my younger sister, Deborah Gillman, became my role model. Though we have lived most of our lives in different cities, Debby's energy and understanding—together with the love of Danny and Judah Kass—sustain me in work and in life.

I also thank my children—Jacob, for his high standards and complete confidence in my success; Ellen, herself a budding writer, for understanding the challenges of a mul-titasking mother; and Livia, for her caring spirit and eloquence. I look forward to shar-ing more of the German Jewish experience with them in the years to come.

It is hard to overstate my gratitude to my husband, Michael B. Prince. Our fortuitous meeting on a Sunday morning in Harvard Square coincided with the beginning of my work on Jewish Vienna. Not only did he improve this book in innu-merable ways, he challenged me at every step to be a more ambitious scholar and writer, giving me also the time and the space in which to realize those ambitions. I dedicate this book to Michael, with all my heart.

Introduction

The Origins of Viennese Jewish Modernism

If one were to ask him: "What is still Jewish about you, since you have abandoned all of these common characteristics of your race?" he would reply: "A great deal, and probably the principal thing [*die Hauptsache*]." But he could not now express this existential quality [*dieses Wesentliche*] clearly in words. It will no doubt later become accessible to the scholarly mind. —Sigmund Freud, 1930

Another person need only defend his individuality—one of our own must first overcome the prejudice against Vienna, then that against Jewishness, and only then against himself. And it is the same with the Jew as with the Viennese: it is not simply the "others" who are against him, no; it is above all the Jew, the Viennese. —Arthur Schnitzler, 1908

This book brings together three cultural phenomena usually described separately: the breakdown of traditional modes of transmitting the past to the present; the development of European modernism; and the remarkable Jewish contribution to Viennese culture in the late nineteenth to early twentieth centuries. The crucible within which these phenomena interact is Vienna, 1890–1938. An array of works by four intellectuals—Sigmund Freud (1856–1939), Arthur Schnitzler (1862–1931), Richard Beer-Hofmann (1866–1945), and Hugo von Hofmannsthal (1874–1929)—exemplifies what I am calling Viennese Jewish modernism. The four would not likely have identified as Viennese Jewish modernists; most likely, all four were never in the same room together. Nevertheless, there is much to be learned by viewing them retrospectively as a circle unto themselves within Viennese modernism, itself a heterogeneous movement consisting of numerous intersecting cultural spheres and diverse trends.

The idea that "the whole structure of avant-garde culture in Vienna can be pictured as a series of intersecting 'circles'" has become a topos in the historiography of turn-of-the-century Vienna.[1] In many cases, the circles denote actual institutions, such as the Secession, established by a group of artists in 1897 under the leadership of Gustav Klimt, or the *Wiener Werkstätte* (Vienna Workshops), which Josef Hoff-mann and Koloman Moser opened in 1903. Vienna has always been famous for its coffeehouse cliques; less well known are the salons, such as the one organized by the Jewish journalist and salonière Bertha Zuckerkandl, which played a critical role in mobilizing the Austrian avant-garde.[2] In the aftermath of World War I, the circles proliferated.[3] Arnold Schoenberg founded the Society for Private Musical Perfor-mances in 1918, and the group of logical positivist philosophers that formed around Moritz van Schlick and met weekly between 1922 and 1936 became known as the *Wiener Kreis* (Vienna Circle).

Two circles are most relevant for our purposes. Schnitzler, Beer-Hofmann, and Hofmannsthal were central members of the most important literary association in turn-of-the-century Vienna, Jung Wien (Young Vienna), whose publications date from 1887 to 1902.[4] Hermann Bahr (1863–1934), a critic, editor, and writer, was the spokesperson for this informal circle of writers and journalists that met in the Café Griensteidl and that oriented itself toward French literary modes and against natu-ralism, which was the dominant mode in Germany at the time. Hofmannsthal, a six-teen-year-old student who published under the name Loris, was introduced to the group late in 1890. Schnitzler, twelve years his senior, had already begun to publish in literary periodicals; his first recorded impressions of Hofmannsthal were of a "sig-nificant talent . . . authentic artistry, unheard of for his age."[5] Beer-Hofmann, a thirty-four-year-old newly minted lawyer, also joined in 1890, and it was due to his friends' encouragement that he began to write creatively the following year. Other members included Felix Salten, Peter Altenberg, Gustav Schwarzkopf, and, for a brief time, Karl Kraus and Theodor Herzl (figs. 1–3).

In the same years in which the literati of Young Vienna were establishing their reputations, another circle was forming: that of Sigmund Freud and the psychoana-lytic movement.[6] Here, too, French influence played a key role, as Freud's experi-ence working with Jean-Martin Charcot in Paris in 1885–86 was a turning point in his shift from physiognomy to psychology. A number of Freud's foundational texts were written during these years, including the "Project for a Scientific Psychology" (1895), in which Freud elaborated his theory of memory; *Studies on Hysteria* (1896) together with Josef Breuer; and *The Interpretation of Dreams* (1900), containing the first descrip-tion of the topological model of the mind. In 1902, the year Freud was appointed to the University of Vienna, the *Mittwoch-Gesellschaft* (Wednesday Society) began meet-ing every Wednesday evening in Professor Freud's home to discuss his ideas and dis-coveries. In 1908, this circle became the Viennese Association of Psychoanalysis.

Viennese Jewish modernism connotes more than the intersection of these two historical circles, one literary, the other psychoanalytic; it describes the intersection of long-standing intellectual commitments of four creative minds. One can begin by not-ing the biographical commonalities. All four writers belonged to a generation of middle-class Austrians who were raised on the liberal humanism of the nineteenth century and who assimilated not so much into Austrian society as into German culture exemplified

1. In the Prater: Richard Beer-Hofmann, Hermann Bahr (standing), Hugo von Hofmannsthal, and Arthur Schnitzler (seated), 1895.

2. Prater excursion, Young Vienna circle, 1894: Hugo von Hofmannsthal, Arthur Schnitzler (standing), Richard Beer-Hofmann, and Felix Salten with two women (seated).

by Lessing, Goethe, and Schiller. They attended *Gymna-sium*, which was a prerequisite for university attendance, and were trained in professions in which Jews predominated: medicine (Freud and Schnitzler), law (Beer-Hofmann), and scholarship (Hofmannsthal).[7] They departed from these professions early on to become intellectual and artistic innovators. As literary artists, and in the case of Freud, as a scientist of the psyche, they sought to remain true to the enlightened, humanist vision, even as their society succumbed to political fanaticism and anti-Semitism in the 1880s and after. All four were of Jewish descent, their lives and careers a testimony to the "blessing of assimilation,"[8] but also to the sociological position that has come to be known as integrationism: their families were among the "Jews who were committed to the future of Jewish life and faith in the Diaspora but who rejected or dissented from the Zionist movement."[9] Lastly, all wrestled indirectly with the meaning of their Jewish heritage, in ways not recognizably Jewish and sometimes even anti-Jewish. Beer-Hofmann's *Der Tod Georgs,* for example, tells a story about the Jewish awakening of a classic Viennese aesthete, but fails to make explicit reference to Judaism. Sigmund Freud's *Moses and Monotheism* was read as a betrayal of Jewish interests; by

3. Lou Andreas-Salomé met with the Young Vienna group in the Café Griensteidl circle in 1895, and she vacationed with Schnitzler and Beer-Hofmann in Salzburg that August. Lou Andreas-Salomé, Arthur Schnitzler, and Richard Beer-Hofmann.

a similar logic, the Nazis thought that Arthur Schnitzler's most Jewish work, *Der Weg ins Freie* (The Road into the Open), was really an anti-Jewish novel, and they designated it the only book of his *not* fit for burning.[10] Hofmannsthal never identified as a Jew; yet, in turn-of-the-century Vienna, his invisible Jewishness was all too discernible. When he and Max Reinhardt founded the Salzburg Festival in August 1920, they were attacked in the local Christian and pan-German papers as Jewish interlopers from Vienna invading an Aryan region.[11] And in an entry on Hofmannsthal in the *Jüdisches Lexicon* of 1928, his lyric oeuvre was cited as depicting "the tragic situation of the modern cultural Jew [*Kulturjude*] who has lost his faith."[12]

Many other biographical affinities are pertinent. There are striking parallels in the medical training, early professional interests, and intellectual dispositions of Freud and Schnitzler.[13] Hofmannsthal and Beer-Hofmann make a natural pair in that both viewed art as a prophetic calling; both began writing in shorter genres and turned later to large-scale theatrical productions that they believed would inspire national renewal—for Austrians, or for German-speaking Jewry. Schnitzler and Hofmannsthal both died in their fifties, each having lived through the suicide of a child.[14] Beer-Hofmann and Freud reached old age and died in exile—Freud in London in 1939, and Beer-Hofmann in New York in 1945.

As important as these factual commonalities is the evidence of profound intel-lectual and emotional connections among the writers. In 1906, Freud wrote to Schnitzler acknowledging that he had long been aware of the "wide-reaching corre-spondence [*Übereinstimmung*] that exists between your conceptions and mine of some psychological and erotic problems."[15] Freud later used the term *Doppelgänger-scheu* (fear of encountering one's double) to explain why he had avoided making the acquaintance of his neighbor Schnitzler until 1922.[16] A similar ambivalence may have led Freud to wait until Beer-Hofmann's seventieth birthday, in 1936, to write a letter praising the author's work and noting the "many meaningful correspondences [*Übereinstimmungen*] between you and me."[17] There are equally important affinities with Hofmannsthal. In May 1911, Freud responded with great enthusiasm to a per-formance of *König Ödipus* (King Oedipus), most likely unaware that Hofmannsthal was the author of this psychoanalytically oriented adaptation of Sophocles' play.[18] The most direct link to Hofmannsthal was by way of the drama *Elektra,* performed in Vienna in May 1905, to which Freud devoted a special meeting of the Wednesday Society on May 24, 1905. The play had been criticized in the press for its fashionable infusion of modern psychology (mainly the theories of hysteria and sublimation) into ancient forms.[19] Though we don't know what was said at the gathering, it has been suggested that the drama and the conversations it provoked influenced Freud's decision to distance himself from the "Electra complex," as Carl Jung called it, in subsequent years.[20]

Hofmannsthal experienced something like *Doppelgängerscheu* when his two friends, Schnitzler and Beer-Hofmann, published works related to Jewish themes; in each case his negative reactions led to a breach in the friendship, after which Hof-mannsthal attempted to downplay or retract his response.[21]

The positive exchanges among the four writers also provide food for thought. In 1905, Beer-Hofmann dedicated a poem, "Der einsame Weg" (The Lonely Road), to Schnitzler. The poem, on a topic of intense mutual interest, loneliness, and its title a citation from Schnitzler's drama of the same name, was reprinted in the Jewish journal *Menorah* on the occasion of Schnitzler's death. The second of three "Vienna Letters" Hofmannsthal wrote for the American magazine the *Dial* (1922) contains a profound and detailed tribute to "Dr. Freud" as *the* central intellectual of Vienna, its "genius loci." "Vienna is the city of European music," wrote Hofmannsthal, "it is the *porta Orientis* [gate to the East] also for that mysterious Orient, the realm of the unconscious. Dr. Freud's interpretations and hypotheses are the excursions of the conscious *Zeitgeist* along the coast of this realm."[22] Perhaps the most moving hom-age is found in a very early letter Hofmannsthal wrote to Beer-Hofmann (1897): "I will never . . . ask of myself to draw out, from the weave of my being, the strains that you give me: everything would then fall apart. I know for certain that I am indebted to no one as much as to you."[23] These intimate exchanges begin to capture the range of interconnections, spoken and unspoken, known and unknown, among these four individuals.

The inclusion of Hofmannsthal and Freud in a quartet of Jewish modernists requires further explanation. Hofmannsthal, after all, was raised a Christian. The case for his inclusion here is not in the first place his Jewish ancestry, but rather the fact that this preeminent modernist poet was an artist of memory par excellence; the arc of his career reveals how a fascination with memory (personal, cultural, national) shapes a writer's artistic development.[24] I hope to demonstrate that it is in their treatment of memory and identity that the two works discussed in this book, a Jewish pantomime and biblical ballet, are surprisingly consistent with the compositions of his contemporaries. Hofmannsthal's life has long supplied a master narrative for understanding the epoch of Austrian cultural history that spanned his lifetime; these forgotten works comprise an untold chapter in that narrative.

Freud, whose personal artistic tastes were Victorian and who ignored much of the avant-garde art scene, would have been the least likely of the four to affiliate with something called Viennese Jewish modernism. Yet he is a central member of this group, the one who thought through the problem of cultural memory at its most fundamental level, as a problem of human memory. Two of Freud's theories about human memory are of vital importance to this study. The first premise was articulated in the letter to Wilhelm Fliess of December 6, 1896, and later developed in *The Interpretation of Dreams* (1900), *The Unconscious* (1915), *Beyond the Pleasure Principle* (1920), and "A Note on the Mystic Writing Pad" (1925). I refer to the notion that the conscious mind "is without the capacity to retain modifications and is thus without memory," as Freud writes in chapter 7 of *The Interpretation of Dreams*. "On the other hand, our memories—not excepting those which are most deeply stamped on our minds—are in themselves unconscious. They can be made conscious; but there is no doubt that they can produce all their effects while in an unconscious condition. What we describe as our 'character' is based on the memory traces of our impressions; and, moreover, the impressions which have had the greatest effect on us— those of our earliest youth—are precisely the ones which scarcely ever become conscious" (*SE*, 5:539–40; *SA*, 2:516). The second fundamental idea has to do with structure of the memory apparatus itself. As Freud wrote to Fliess: "As you know, I am working on the assumption that our psychic mechanism has come into being by a process of stratification: the material present in the form of memory traces being subjected from time to time to a *rearrangement* in accordance with fresh circumstances—to a *retranscription*. Thus what is essentially new about my theory is the thesis that memory is present not once, but several times over [*nicht einfach, sondern mehrfach*]" (emphasis in original).[25]

Though the model of memory becomes more sophisticated over the years, the basic assumptions remain. Our most potent, formative memories may never have entered consciousness. Those memories that we are able to retrieve are not fixed entities, akin to mental photographs. Memories are stored as traces or transcriptions in several layers of the mind. Over time, the memories move from more primitive to more advanced strata, and ultimately into language; repression is tantamount to the conscious mind's refusal to put memories into words. In the course of a lifetime, the process should occur automatically: the registrations or memory traces are "rearranged," "retranscribed," translated in later strata, as our understanding of our past develops and memories acquire different significance. When such a development would generate unpleasure, and a memory is repressed rather than translated, the result is what Freud calls "survivals" or anachronisms. Rather than enter the more advanced strata, the uncomfortable memories emerge in pictorial form in dreams, or they take the form of a neurotic or psychotic symptom. Freud later applies the term *fixation* to describe a relationship or attachment that persists in a primitive form, dictated by the rules of an immature self. The fact that even in healthy recollection the memory traces enter language only at a relatively "late stage" (only once they have become accessible to the preconscious mind) means that knowing our memories, expressing them "clearly in words," is no simple achievement.[26] Thus, psychoanalysis is committed to overcoming fixation and repression and to the pursuit of the most effective means of knowing the forgotten past, without which healthy existence is impossible. In sum: just as the Freudian self possesses no single, monolithic past—an idea memorably explicated by Jacques Derrida—so are human forms of memory destined to be stratified, complex, hybrid: not once, but many times over.[27]

These insights into memory are everywhere at play in the literary texts under discussion. There is one further sense in which Freud is relevant, and that is as a writer of cultural history whose compositional practices are similar to those of his three literary counterparts. In this book I wish to consider these affinities on a number of levels—as a shared concern with memory, as a shared wrestling with Jewish identification and Jewish sources, and as a shared practice of writers seeking to create new genres of cultural memory.

The argument of this book can be summed up in two points. First, Viennese Jewish modernism is a literary-historical construct that attempts to make sense of modernist experiments that link Jewish Vienna to European modernism. Most of the works under discussion here have been marginalized in one way or another, forgotten or branded as flawed. Taken together, they represent a variant modernism that is remarkably coherent in its conceptual and compositional principles.

Secondly, I argue that the optic through which these principles come into view is the authors' shared concern with memory. Writers of Jewish modernism sought to invent a Jewish countertradition through aesthetic means. The circumlocutions that mark Freud's famous Hebrew preface are symptomatic of the fact that a generation of German and Austrian Jews born into bourgeois, largely assimilated families in the second half of the nineteenth century lacked immediate access to Jewish traditions. The religious practices of their grandparents were anachronistic; the watered-down customs of their parents were perceived as "souvenirs" from the past, to cite Franz Kafka;[28] and new forms of engagement in Jewish culture were just being invented. History, which in the nineteenth century replaced religion as "the faith of fallen Jews," had by the twentieth century lost its power to shape the collective understanding of the past.[29]

That moment of history's losing its power to mediate is the starting point for the writers of Jewish Vienna (and, arguably, for all of European modernism after Nietzsche). If today, as Harold Bloom writes, "literature and ideology compete to occupy the abyss that Jewish memory has become," so too was this the case a century ago.[30] Theodor Herzl, the founder of political Zionism; Gershom Scholem, the German Jewish scholar who pioneered the scholarly study of Jewish mysticism, and Martin Buber, founder of neo-Hasidism, were the central "revisionists of Jewish culture and thought" in the German-speaking domain, but the term is equally pertinent in the case of four individuals whose approach to Jewish culture placed them, in many respects, on the margins of Jewish society.[31] They too found it necessary to resist the scholarly and artistic traditions that were their inheritance, and also to retranscribe, as it were, the formative episodes of the preeminent archive of Jewish memory, the Hebrew Bible. Their works render a fin de siècle modernism, backward-looking yet highly experimental.

VIENNESE JEWISH MODERNISM AND THE QUEST FOR FORM

The first epigraph to this introduction highlights the challenge that will be the central focus of this study, namely the search for a language in which to express those existential truths about the self, the collective, and the shared past.

My understanding of this quest for form in the Viennese milieu has been shaped in part by recent debates about collective remembrance in the United States and Europe in response to the Holocaust, the collapse of Communism, German reunification, and 9/11.[32] Although the late twentieth- and early twenty-first-century preoccupations with memory differ in important ways from the preoccupations of a century ago, clear similarities exist between the discourses of collective memory now and then.[33] Then as now, the experimental strategies of artists who have been charged with the task of commemoration run afoul of the expectations of the public. In the United States, in the last several years, two trends appear dominant: a minimalist aesthetic on the one hand, and a desire for individual commemoration on the other. The commitment to personal testimony and the individual story is exemplified by the Names Project AIDS Memorial Quilt and by Holocaust video archives.[34] Yet when it comes to memorial architecture, the preference is for abstract structures and countermonuments. The feat of the most popular American monument of the late twentieth century, Maya Lin's Vietnam Veterans Memorial, is that it managed to combine intimacy and abstraction. Lin's ability to balance tradition and experimentation has inspired many, but the consensus is that that her memorial remains in a class of its own. As I write this introduction, the design for yet another countermonument has begun to take root in the American national consciousness. In Michael Arad and Peter Walker's plan for the World Trade Center memorial, *Reflecting Absence,* negativity—the experience of loss symbolized by the "footprints" of the towers—predominates. Yet the counterpressure of a more traditional insistence upon figural representation, heroism, and continuity with the great nationalist monuments of the past remains strong. The fact that the memorial will include the names of every victim of 9/11 has not preempted the critique that the design lacks warmth, humanity, and "images of valor" such as one finds at the National Iwo Jima Memorial Monument.[35] Minimalist memory by nature frustrates those who seek a face-to-face encounter with the past, presence rather than absence, and an overwhelming evocation of national tragedy. The stakes could not be higher, and it remains to be seen whether *Reflecting Absence* will acquire the status of Maya Lin's "modern minimalist sublime."[36]

A more pertinent example of the quest for form can be found in present-day Austria. While researching this book in Vienna in 2001, I was struck by the ways in which contemporary initiatives to memorialize the Austrian Jewish past replicate the strategies of a group of writers who devised new forms of Jewish expression in Vienna one hundred years earlier.[37] The willed marginality I had noticed in the writers of Vienna 1900—their aversion to heroes, and their reliance upon mixed genres and experimental forms that were bound to frustrate audience expectations—seemed to be replayed in the most important efforts of the City of Vienna to come to terms with its Jewish past.

The reopening in 1994 of the Jewish Museum of Vienna (closed in 1938) in a mansion just a few steps outside the City Center was a milestone event. The museum's signature installation is the Historical Exhibit on the third floor. This installation is designed in such a way that every visitor must experience Austrian Jewish history as a work in progress, or, to paraphrase Freud, as a past *not yet* accessible. The interior of this gallery is bare, except for twenty-one glass panels arranged in an open square formation (fig. 4). Each panel contains a hologram reflecting either a period or a theme from Austrian Jewish history.[38] One is called *Out of the Ghetto,* another *Enlightenment,* and so on through a series of simulacra shimmering magically before the viewer's eyes: *Loyalty and Patriotism, Assimilation, From Historicism to Modernity, From Charity to the Social State, Zionism.* The images themselves, glowing in psychedelic red, yellow, and green, range from the familiar to the curious to the outright provocative: synagogues, Jewish ritual objects, the Ferris wheel in the Prater and other Jewish technological inventions, portrayals of Theodor Herzl, silver designed by Josef Hoffmann with a swastika motif, a bed quilt sewn by Empress Maria Theresa's Jewish seamstress, film canisters of *Some Like it Hot* (Billy Wilder was an Austrian émigré), yellow fabric imprinted with the black *Judensterne.* The fourteenth panel, titled *Fin de Siècle,* is overcrowded with traces of many luminaries: a pair of glasses (belonging to writer Karl Kraus), a podium light (used by composer/conductor Gustav Mahler), a playing-card case (designed by artist/composer Arnold Schoenberg), and other equally unexpected relics of poet Peter Altenberg, graphic artist Bertholde Löffler, theater director Max Reinhardt, architect Friedrich Kiesler, and, of course, Schnitzler and Freud. In this panel in particular, the installation's reliance on *pars pro toto* is most unsatisfying.

Why permit a museum charged with retrieving the rich and largely ignored history of Austrian Jewry to adopt the most fleeting of media to do so? No doubt

4. Now you see it, now you don't: twenty-one holograms displayed on glass panels make up the Historical Exhibit of the Jewish Museum of Vienna.

holograms, like other high-tech virtual media, are becoming ever more common in contemporary exhibitions—a symptom of the contemporary predilection for virtuality, interactive exhibits, and fabricated heritages.[39] The choice of an avant-garde form challenges the stereotype of Jewishness as unaesthetic, bookish, and associated with victimhood. But does it succeed as an *ars memoria?* The exhibit effectively renders Austrian Jewish history by denying the priorities of history itself—continuity, chronology, objectivity, and completeness. Holograms simulate haphazard recollection and subjective perception just as if these were empirically given on a somehow equal basis with the object of representation.[40] As such, they offer more than a nod toward avant-garde museology. They are intended as a provocation, above all, to the Austrian state's new Jewish agenda.[41] After so many decades of exclusion from the public sphere, the argument goes, and in light of the ongoing exclusion of Jewish history from the dominant narratives of Austrian history, suddenly to adopt a monumental stance toward Austrian Jewish heritage would be inappropriate, even offensive. But this kind of highly coded political statement comes at the cost of the museum's pedagogical mandate, not to mention the responsibility to do justice to a history that, for its victims at least, was anything but virtual. Holographic works do not so much remind their viewers or readers of what they have forgotten as stage an existential dilemma regarding the possibility of memory itself. This particular agenda is coyly alluded to in a declaration on the museum's Web site: "'Memory' is present on all four floors of the Jewish Museum Vienna. It is a key to Jewish culture and permeates the Museum right down to the smallest detail."[42]

Holograms are aesthetic constructs. In that sense, they are a good example of what is meant by a "genre" throughout this book. Like the makers of holograms, Viennese Jewish modernists deployed their aesthetic constructs to recombine history and memory in specific ways for specific purposes. They too were engaged in a fragmentation of the stable image of the past. They were allergic to the representation of heroes and shunned the type of political response represented by Zionism; instead, they refracted their consciousness of the Jewish question through fictions that undercut easy appropriation by one side or another. The risks they took are preserved in the negative reception each received, a point to which I shall return frequently in the following chapters. In these experiments it is unclear whether Jewish memory is preserved or thwarted: Hofmannsthal's pantomime started out with a Jewish cast, until the author expunged the Yiddish names; Professor Bernhardi, the hero of Schnitzler's Jewish drama, is Jewish in name only. With the notable exception of Beer-Hofmann's biblical trilogy, we find a concern more with the staging of Jewish memory than with the content of the Jewish past. It is this performance of memory as an aesthetic and political problem that will be the constant focus of the present study. Like a hologram, Jewish memory remains simultaneously present and absent in Vienna today: now you see it, now you don't. But such was also the case with Viennese Jews themselves over one hundred years ago, struggling over the meaning of their Jewish identity in a hostile environment. Then as now, it fell to the intellectual imagination to complicate the notion of seeing Jewishness, and to invent new forms of Jewish expression. The writers I discuss did not have lasers, but they did have a panoply of new and traditional forms of prose, drama, music, and dance that they combined and transformed in a spirit of vital experimentation.

MODERNISM AND MEMORY

It is my contention throughout this book that the quest for a usable past among Viennese modernists between roughly 1890 and 1938 intersects with the quest for answerable forms of recollection as a trans-European problem. The broad claim that modernism deploys memory *against* modernity has been understood in various ways. The focus on memory in philosophy, the social sciences, and aesthetics—one thinks of Friedrich Nietzsche, Henri Bergson, Maurice Halbwachs, Ernst Mach, William James, even Otto Weininger—was a reaction against the atrophying or rejection of traditional memory channels that, in earlier periods, had been grounded more solidly in social and religious forms. In the late nineteenth century, artists and intellectuals began to conceptualize memory as a means of restructuring the psyche to retrieve functions of personal memory as compensation for that which a mechanized and atomized society no longer guaranteed.[43] A second motive was the disenchantment with history. German modernists were particularly influenced by the critique of history as *Wissenschaft* (scholarship, science) advanced in Friedrich Nietzsche's "Vom Nutzen und Nachteile der Historie für das Leben" (On the Uses and Disadvantages of History for Life, 1874). One of Hofmannsthal's most angry poems, "Gedanken-spuk" (Simulacrum, 1890), bears an epigraph from Nietzsche: "Könnten wir die Historie loswerden" (If only we could be rid of history). These were years in which, as Hayden White has shown, hostility to history was widespread among early twentieth-century European intellectuals and artists, including Ibsen and Broch, Gide and Canetti, Camus and Sartre.[44]

Apart from these redemptive or compensatory aspects, the modernist turn to the past is a fundamentally ambivalent enterprise. Pierre Nora's characterization of the late nineteenth century as an age between memory (sacred, affective, living, magical) and history (secular, critical, reconstructive, prosaic) provides a framework within which to understand the modernist quest for the right forms of memory.[45] The tension as the modern artist experienced it comes into sharp focus as the psychological predicament of those whom Nora called "memory-individuals," upon whom the onus of recollection falls once collective forms of memory have disintegrated.[46] Memory individuals are solitary creatures, whose failure to sustain interpersonal connection is often a metaphor for their struggle to connect to the living past. They struggle in vain to anchor the significant moments in life—that which occurs naturally and spontaneously within a ritual community—by way of private strategies. An existential predicament results: the burden of recollection overwhelms them, estranging them from life in the present. At this point, they want only liberation from the past, even as they still crave the past. Memory individuals thus suffer paradoxically from too little and too much memory at the same time, a psychological conflict that (as I shall show) helps explain turn-of-the-century maladies such as aestheticism, the crisis of language, and epigonism.

While modernists initially turn to tradition to seek a refuge from the present, they soon find that this recourse has become obsolete. An archetypal moment in the Viennese milieu occurs when Anatol, Arthur Schnitzler's early dramatic hero (1893), declares, "I am searching for a sanctuary [Asyl] for my past." What Anatol has in mind is some place to store the accumulated mementoes of his erotic adventures. By the play's end, Schnitzler makes it patently clear that the refuge Anatol seeks is not *for* his past, but *from* his past, and the difference is decisive.[47] The fact that even the most amnesiac of Viennese aesthetes proves unable to leave the past behind is indicative of memory's new unpredictability—an experience Proust called *mémoire involuntaire* and Hofmannsthal likened to a bird's mysterious return to the dovecote. For the modern past is nowhere and everywhere; it "persists in germ cells and muscle tissue, dreams and neuroses, retentions and involuntary memories, guilt and ghosts."[48] In addition to trying to solve the conundrum of how to write in a virulently anti-Semitic culture, Freud, Beer-Hofmann, Schnitzler, and Hofmannsthal also testify to the tragic realization that "rather than being subject to our recapture, the past in fact malignantly captures us."[49] As a result, modernist mnemotechnics, the holograms of early twentieth-century Europe, tend to be ambiguous and provisional and, in this respect, "more an outgrowth of a dystopian modernity than its antidote."[50]

This book draws out the ramifications of these developments for the artist. The classical and medieval *artes memoriae* were thought to be "the auxiliary and assistant of natural memory," that which "comes solely from the gift of nature, without aid of any artifice."[51] Modernists have lost confidence in natural memory, in the rational mind and its myriad discourses—Freud's "klare Worte." "As though words could carry memories," writes the eighteen-year-old Franz Kafka in his friend Selma Kohn's album. "For words are clumsy mountaineers and clumsy miners. Not for them to bring down treasures from the mountains' peaks, or up from the mountains' bowels. . . . But there is a living mindfulness that has passed gently, like a stroking hand, over everything memorable. And when the flame shoots up out of these ashes, hot and glowing, strong and mighty, and you stare into it as though spellbound by its magic, then—"[52] In lieu of words, a sudden, spellbinding flame, then silence; in the absence of "history, community, tradition, the past, reflection and authenticity," the twentieth-century audience must contend with "fantasy, subjectivity, invention, the present, representation and fabrication."[53] The turn to the imagination is not in itself modern; Aristotle, in *De Anima,* wrote that when it comes to memory, "imagination is the intermediary between perception and thought," and Freud's discussions of the artistic imagination arrive at the identical conclusion. The holographic character of the literary works under discussion evokes this sense of an intermediary zone in which the writer transmits the past in a mischievous way, by defying legacies and refashioning traditions.

The most powerful turn-of-the-century analogy to this aesthetic experience may be found in the domain of psychoanalytic technique. Freud's description of the transferential situation repeats the same pattern, only now in clinical terms. As he documents in the paper "Erinnern, Wiederholen und Durcharbeiten" (Recollection, Repetition, Working Through, 1914), Freud came to believe that reenacting the past through transference, in the present tense, was more effective than verbal recollection in transforming a patient's unhealthy "compulsion to repeat" into a "motive for remembering." Above all, the therapeutic reenactment brings the patient's resistances into clear view:

We render [the compulsion to repeat] harmless, and even make use of it, by according it the right to assert itself within certain limits. We admit it into the transference as to a playground [*Tummelplatz*] in which it is allowed to let itself go in almost complete freedom and is required to display before us all the pathogenic impulses hidden in the depths of the patient's mind. . . . The transference thus forms a kind of intermediary realm [*Zwischenreich*] between illness and real life, through which the journey [*Übergang*] from the one to the other must be made.[54]

The work of art was, for the backward-looking modernist, a playground in which characters (in the case of *Der Tod Georgs*), an author (in the case of Hofmannsthal's pantomime *Der Schüler*), or an audience (in the case of the ballet *Josephslegende*) could make the journey from amnesia to self-knowledge.

Scholars in recent years have begun to view genres of memory, tradition, and history as vital sources of information about Jewish society.[55] Any attempt to understand the modern Jewish preoccupation with memory must consider that, from a certain perspective, "'memory' per se was not even an operable category" in premodern Jewish society.[56] As David Roskies has written,

Once upon a time, everything a Jew needed to know about the world was locatable in the Universal Jewish Encyclopedia known as *Mikra'ot gedolot* [the Rabbinic Bible]. The deep past, covenantal, codified at Sinai, was laid out in the Torah, Prophets and Writings; the surrounding commentaries provided the update. For greater convenience and affordability, the entire usable past was anthologized in the Five Books of Moses, the Five Scrolls, the Sabbath and Festival prayer books. . . . Local events were recorded in the communal *pinkas* [notebook]. Most of their contents were known by heart, through constant recital.

Traditional Jews mastered the shocks of history by "the restoration or recycling of memories already there; disassembling the present in terms of the eternal past."[57] To visualize such a process, one need think only of the Passover seder, the "quintessential exercise in Jewish group memory,"[58] as it integrates song, liturgy, Torah, rabbinic texts, body language, and food and drink into a ritual widely observed even among secular Jews.

It is beyond the scope of this introduction to trace the genealogy of Jewish memory from its role in biblical and liturgical texts to the ritual mnemonics developed in the medieval period and beyond. The specifically modern quest for a usable Jewish past—a past through which one might refract the challenges of modernity—began in the eighteenth century, with the Jewish Enlightenment or *Haskala* and the rise of Hasidic Judaism in Eastern Europe. As part of a complex pedagogical agenda, the *Haskala* promoted a return to the Hebrew language and the Hebrew Bible, both of which would form the linguistic and philosophical basis of an authentically Jewish national culture. In the nineteenth century, *Wissenschaft* became the new ideal, and with it, the Jewish turn to historical research; historical fiction soon became the predominant literary genre of Jewish high culture.[59] In the Hasidic world, by contrast, oral tales and wordless songs became the preferred genres of transmission. By the end of the nineteenth century, the quest for viable forms of Jewish memory intensified with the struggle between nationalistic and internationalistic solutions to the predicament of modern Jewish identity.

In the early twentieth century, the one who bridged the responses of Jewish religious culture and secular, literary society was himself an Austrian Jew, the philosopher Martin Buber (1878–1965). Of his many activities, the enterprise most relevant to this book is his attempt to create a German Jewish renaissance: a spiritual revitalization of Jewish life in the Diaspora. Buber drew the term *renaissance* from fourteenth-century Italy, from the writings of the most important nineteenth-century historian of the period, Jakob Burckhardt, as well as from Nietzsche and turn-of-the-century renaissancism. For Buber, the concept of a renaissance entailed "not the rejection of tradition but its resuscitation or respiritualization."[60] In this respect, Buber and his collaborator, the philosopher Franz Rosenzweig (1886–1929), broke with the nineteenth-century modernizers such as Leopold Zunz and the Verein für Cultur und Wissenschaft der Juden (Union for the Culture and Science of the Jews) and Ludwig Philippson, pioneer of liberal Judaism, who viewed themselves as "reformers" of and within the historical continuum. "By renewal," wrote Buber in 1909, "I don't mean anything gradual, an accumulation of small changes, but something sudden and awesome; not continuation and improvement, but return and revolution."[61] In what is perhaps his most strident statement of purpose, Buber avowed: "I shall try to extricate the unique character of Jewish religiosity from the rubble with which rabbinism and rationalism have covered it."[62] Like his secular Viennese counterparts, he reacted against the recent past in the name of a return to subterranean currents in the distant past, and his example played a defining role in the careers of Hofmannsthal and Beer-Hofmann.

Indeed, the central proponents of Jewish modernism were no less conflicted when it came to Jewish memory than their European modernist counterparts. The modernist tradition in Yiddish and Hebrew, with its emphasis on intertextuality as the dominant mode, is always already both backwards- and forwards looking.[63] Like the Austrians, for whom Enlightenment and modernization came relatively late, European Jews experienced the forces of Enlightenment, romanticism, modernism, political nationalism, and socialism in an exceedingly short period of time late in the nineteenth century. The first modern Hebrew and Yiddish writers, such as Chaim Nachman Bialik (1873–1934) and I. L. Peretz (1852–1915), were relentless advocates of modernization, though their work reckons everywhere with the attendant social and spiritual crises facing modern Jewry.

An unusually graphic description of the problem of memory appears in the preface to the autobiography of S. Y. Abramovitch (1835–1917), the Hebrew and Yiddish writer more popularly known by his pen name, Mendele the Book Peddler:

For some time now my pen has been trapped motionless between two contradictory opinions, like Muhammad's coffin which is said to be suspended between two magnets. While the one strives to attract it toward the past, the other tries to attract it toward what is happening now in our own time. These two forces are bickering within me like two shopkeepers that jump on the same customer and deprecate each other's merchandise. One says: "God save us from the new merchandise and the baubles that are now fashionable among Jews! Nothing that you see here is genuine. It's all a fraud: silver-plated clay, an empty shell; mascara, rouge, and jewels on the outside, filth, dirt, and muck on the inside. Nothing is authentic, nothing has any character of its own; everything is crude, like those dolls that seem to open their lips, beat a drum, blow a horn, sound a cymbal, and squeak, but only thanks to the key that wound up their spring. Forget them: here you have fine antiques, every one the work of our ancestors, and each with its own authentic value. . . ." The other one shouts: "Come to me! Look at my merchandise—what do you want with outmoded things from an age that is dead and gone? Do you think you're some kind of medium who can raise the dead? That's exactly why we are in so much trouble now: Jews are oblivious to the present; they attend only to the past."[64]

The almost sixty-year-old Abramovitch, writing in 1894, faced the identical quandary as did the writers of Jung Wien. Does the past offer fine antiques or outdated merchandise? Is the "modern" nothing more than a simulacrum, mascara and "silver-plated clay"? And what of a condition in which both options sound like the bickering of shopkeepers vying for the writer's attention? Abramovitch's trapped pen must be placed in its textual and biographical contexts. The nostalgia that prompted him to take up the form of autobiography set in only at the twilight of a long and defiant career as an arch-satirist. In a stunning gesture, the preface cited above depicts a charged confrontation between the writer Abramovitch and his own pseudonymous persona, Mendele the Book Peddler. It is of relevance to the methodological approach undertaken here that Mendele-Abramovitch's response to the bickering within his head takes the form of a generic hybrid: fictional autobiography.

In sum: if the Bible made Jews into a "people of the Book," and the people of memory par excellence, the Jewish modernist—following Israeli poet Yehuda Amichai—declares, "I want to confuse the Bible." This genealogy supplies the second framework for understanding Jewish modernism in turn-of-the-century Vienna.

VIENNA 1900, MEMORY SITE

I wish also to engage certain scholarly disputes as to the character of Viennese modernism. Narrowly defined, *die Wiener Moderne* was an avant-garde, cosmopolitan movement that peaked in the years 1890–1910, at the core of which were revolutionary changes in philosophy, plastic and visual arts, literature, and music.[65] Representations of Viennese modernism tend to emphasize discontinuity with tradition perpetrated by crises of subjectivity and language, by Machian neoempiricism, and by other political, sociological and philosophical forces. Certainly, this account captures part of the story. In his famous essay "Die Moderne" (1890), Hermann Bahr urged readers to "shake off the rotten past," to "open the windows," and above all to "be present." In Bahr's memorable formulation: "The past was great, often lovely. We want to dedicate somber funeral orations to it. But when the king is buried, long live the other king."[66] In line with this rejection of the past, artistic trends such as aestheticism, symbolism, and *Jugendstil* (art nouveau) removed the individual subject from the temporal flow altogether and created an alternative existence under the sign of art and artifice. In so many texts of the period, characters are redeemed not by memory, but by privileging the present, through fictional enactments of *Lebens-philosophie.*[67]

Much of the critical reception of Viennese Jewish modernism has been colored by the status of modernism as a cultural accolade for which German and Austrian writers competed. Whereas Bahr proclaimed the modernist accomplishment to be the "overcoming of naturalism," critics from Germany such as Michael Georg Conrad and Ottokar Stauf von der March accused the Viennese writers of being tainted with the very heritage they claimed to transcend. Their belatedness was equated with "physical and psychic decadence" of the French variety. The historicism epitomized by the eclectic architecture of Vienna's Ringstraße came to be seen as symptomatic of an epigonal age.[68] As Jens Rieckmann argues, this critique was part and parcel of a broader anti-Austrian and anti-Semitic agenda, whereby "Young Vienna = ungerman = semitic = decadent."[69] Understandably, the consensus has been that due to the extreme prejudice against Austrians and Jews by the forerunners of German modernism (i.e., the naturalists), only those writers who separated themselves from their ethnic (Austrian and/or Jewish) origins could elevate themselves to the status of European modernists.[70] To remain Jewish and also be modernist and Viennese would seem an insoluble conundrum.

The positive desire for the past in Austrian culture takes on great significance in the post–World War I period and tends be associated with nationalism, the theatrical mythmaking of Hofmannsthal's late works, the nostalgia of Stefan Zweig's *The World of Yesterday,* and Joseph Roth's *The Radetzky March.* This kind of literary memory is normally elegiac, theatrical, baroque, and Catholic (especially when perpetrated by Jews). It is neither modernist nor modern, nor is there anything necessarily Jewish about it.[71] Viennese modernism, in this scheme, is an international, nonreligious, nonaffective movement opposed to mythic thinking. Following the argument, the Jewish contribution is to be found in secular modernism on one hand and Zionism—a specifically Jewish movement—on the other. In the context of such schisms, it is not surprising that a modernism born of sensibilities that are at once liberal, Jewish, non-Zionist, and beholden to tradition falls through the cracks.

A number of recent books pave the way for a more integrated understanding of the period as characterized by what Thomas Kovach calls "traditionalist modernism."[72] Steven Scherer's *Richard Beer-Hofmann und die Wiener Moderne* and Konstanze Fliedl's *Arthur Schnitzler: Poetik der Erinnerung* interpret the oeuvres of Beer-Hofmann and Schnitzler as quintessentially modernist in their multifaceted philosophical responses to crises of memory and identity. Jacques Le Rider begins *Modernity and Crises of Identity* by noting that since modernization came late to Austria, "the modernist 'front' was less aggressive there than in other cultural centers. Viennese modernists recognized the authority of their precursors."[73] Le Rider describes a retrogressive strain within Viennese modernism that is skeptical, resigned, and almost postmodern in its "lack of confidence in modernity."[74] This backwards-looking modernism, in Steven Beller's view, is fundamentally liberal, informed by the Enlightenment, and possessed of a "particularly healthy skepticism against the spellbinding power that modernity exerts upon us."[75] Viennese modernist writers were under assault both from more extreme modernist tendencies, such as symbolism, impressionism, and aestheticism, and from more conservative and reactionary responses, such as historicism, *völkisch* ideology, and organic memory, which wedded the desire for memory to nostalgic and nationalistic causes. Fending off these mutually antithetical trends tended to destabilize cultural production. The texts I discuss both beckon to the past and strive to keep the past at bay, a practice that in many cases leads to perceptions of failure, even as it holds the key (in my reading) to the specific challenge of a modernist poetics of recollection.

THE JEWISH CHARACTER OF VIENNESE MODERNISM

I turn now to "the 'Jewish Question' about Viennese modernism."[76] Ernst Gombrich took an extreme position, arguing that the Viennese Jewish contribution to the arts was incidental. Stephen Beller's research makes possible a more nuanced portrait by providing a wealth of documentation about the Viennese Jewish middle class.[77] Beller concludes *Vienna and the Jews, 1867–1938* with the assertion that although the Jews were only one force among many within the European avant-garde, "it was indeed its Jews which made Vienna what it was in the realm of modern culture";[78] this view is grounded in statistics regarding the education, training, and professional activities of leading cultural figures of Jewish descent. While all of these elements contribute to the picture, it is also true that biography has been known to malfunction in the reception of this period; indeed, many of these cultural figures rejected biographical narratives of identity. Schnitzler once declined an invitation to participate in a Jewish authors' reading, claiming that there is no such thing as a Jewish author.[79] In a similar vein, Matti Bunzl argues that scholars have been unable to perceive the important affinities between the Zionist visions of Beer-Hofmann and Herzl because they are fixated on the fact that Beer-Hofmann never considered moving to Palestine.[80] And in the hologram *Fin de Siècle* in the Jewish Museum of Vienna, neither Hofmannsthal nor Beer-Hofmann is included, perhaps because Hofmannsthal did not regard himself as a Jewish writer and because Beer-Hofmann, an avowed Zionist, was too Jewish for this particular cluster.

In his analysis of the cultural codes built into the Salzburg Festival, Michael P. Steinberg asserts that the reification of Jewish culture is the "shared fallacy of philo-Semitic historiography and anti-Semitic historiography."[81] What he means is that contemporary approaches to the Jewish question tend to replicate the condition Schnitzler diagnosed, wherein "it is not simply the others who are against him, it is above all the Jews, the Viennese." As Sander Gilman demonstrates, many writers resisted this condition by actively engaging the cultural semantics of race and gender.[82] The challenge was, and remains, to allow the Jew to be seen as an individual, because even as anti-Semites view Jews as having any of a number of prescribed qualities, Jews view Jews in much the same way. Friends and foes alike participate in the same reification insofar as their arguments rely on a typing of the Jew.

In his preface to *Rethinking Vienna 1900,* Beller notes that political factors—the end of the Cold War, for example—have often determined how the Jewish aspect would be treated. An important recent development in the recuperation of the Jewish contribution to Viennese modernism was the reevaluation of Carl Schorske's thesis that the failure of liberalism produced a disaffected bourgeois liberal elite that invented a modernism that was fundamentally irrational and escapist in kind. In Schorske's influential study *Fin-de-Siècle Vienna: Politics and Culture,* Jewishness is primarily relevant to the case of Theodor Herzl; it plays no role in the interpretations of Hofmannsthal and Schnitzler, and only a minor role in the analysis of Freud. With the new understanding of Austrian liberalism put forth in the work of historians of the 1980s such as John Boyer, David Luft, and Peter Gay, as well as the publication of social and intellectual histories of Viennese Jews by Marsha Rozenblit, Robert Wistrich, and Ivar Oxaal, one can establish that the contribution of Jews and Austrians of Jewish descent was both predominant in modernism and continuous with the liberal tradition in significant ways. The question that remains to be asked is what exactly was Jewish about the modernism these Viennese Jews created.

VIENNESE JEWISH MODERNISM: GENRES OF MEMORY

The following chapters offer readings of key works by Viennese Jewish modernists. The book is arranged into three parts, moving from early to late productions, from private to public genres, from theoretical paradigms to mythic enactments. I begin with Sigmund Freud, not in order to view works of literature through a Freudian perspective, but to relate Freud's writings on culture to the larger phenomenon of Viennese Jewish modernism, of which he was himself a part. Freud's *Leonardo da Vinci and a Memory of his Childhood* (1910), "The Moses of Michelangelo" (1914), and *Moses and Monotheism* (1938) extend psychoanalytic technique into the writing of cultural history. Two deal with art and artists; two are about Moses; and *Moses and Monotheism* is sui generis as Freud's only "Jewish" book. Yet all three works relate to topics of central concern in this study; all, moreover, arise out of Freud's desire to invent a new genre of cultural remembering by refuting the constructions passed down in scholarly and religious sources. In these essays, Freud repeats a single strategy: he takes a cultural icon and strips away the layers of his identity to reveal a multilayered character. Though Freud takes pains to respond to the scholarly treatments of his subjects, his primary purpose is not to correct the historical record. It is to commemorate heroes in a way that is superior to history, because true to the hero's complexities and faults. Such commemoration is, at least in part, an imaginative enterprise, one best learned from artists. The holographic character of Viennese modernism—divided as to its heroes and hyperconscious about form—comes into sharp focus in Freud's writing on culture and religion.

Of all the works under discussion here, Hugo von Hofmannsthal's pantomime *Der Schüler* (1901), the subject of chapter 2, most vividly dramatizes the motives that gave rise to the Jewish modernist impulse in Vienna 1900: the desire of young writers, self-identified epigones, to resist the authority of the past, and the desperation of Viennese Jews to liberate themselves from the stereotyped Jewish body, as well as from a religion that had become nothing more than sterile mimicry or hypocritical posturing. The pantomime was first cast with Jewish characters, but their names were altered prior to publication. Suppressing his characters' Jewish origins may be interpreted as an act of self-censorship, but it can also be viewed as a provocation to consider the Jewish characters as shadows of Faust, Electra, and others, and a Jewish pantomime as an experiment that belongs in the tradition of Mallarmé's *Mimique* and the *commedia dell'arte*. A work as "minor" as *Moses and Monotheism* is "major," Hofmannsthal's pantomime, like the entire Freudian oeuvre, concerns the holographic staging of a forgotten past.

The works I discuss in Part 2 represent the most conscientious attempts by Beer-Hofmann and Schnitzler to rework conventional literary genres for the purposes of depicting contemporary Jewish affairs. Richard Beer-Hofmann's novella *Der Tod Georgs* (1900) was composed over a transformative phase in the author's personal and artistic development. This work poses a series of parallel questions. Can an individual's perceptions, sensations, and memories be made to cohere into what Henri Bergson called "duration"? Can a modern consciousness governed by chance associations find its way back from aesthetic detachment to ancestral Judaism? And, because Beer Hofmann experienced all of these questions simultaneously as problems of form, can discontinuous episodes and lyrical images combine to form a credible prose narrative? This ambitious literary experiment, and above all the Jewish conversion with which it ends, challenged contemporary readers to envision a psychological and spiritual trajectory that was virtually unimaginable for Viennese Jews in 1900.

Though he devoted his first novel, *Der Weg ins Freie* (1908), to the crises facing Viennese Jewry, Schnitzler did not see it as his duty to provide the much-needed solutions. His method was to conjoin a Jewish roman à clef, including a cast of characters based on his own acquaintances, with the typical plot device of a German bildungsroman. Schnitzler himself admitted that his hybrid novel was less than successful in aesthetic terms. Critics at the time and since have tended to agree. His long-awaited Jewish novel failed to produce the expected Jewish hero, but it did produce an answer to the *other* Jewish question—the question of how to talk about the destiny of the Jews without lapsing into ideological platitudes.

Nor is the protagonist of Schnitzler's second Jewish work, the drama *Professor Bernhardi* (1912), the kind of courageous leading man Schnitzler's audience had hoped for in the novel. Under attack for offending the Catholic Church, Professor Bernhardi has no desire to become a "medical Dreyfus." He does pride himself, however, on his excellent memory and unwavering humanism. But for the hero's experience of discrimination, Jewishness would be incidental to his character. Most confounding is the fact that despite its ostensibly tragic theme, Schnitzler called the play a comedy. Chapter 4 identifies Jewish tragicomedy as the genre of these two controversial experiments in Jewish writing.

Part 3 follows the trajectory of Viennese Jewish modernism into large-scale theatrical endeavors that have been neglected by critics and ignored by scholars of German-speaking Jewry. Hofmannsthal's ballet *Josephslegende* (1912), the subject of chapter 5, reveals that Hofmannsthal subscribed for a time to the premises of German-Jewish orientalism: the Orient represents the past that luckily still exists; modern Jews, even European ones, are Orientals; and the Jew can mediate Occident and Orient. As before, I am interested in explaining seemingly odd mixtures of cultural material: why is this focus on the orientalized Jew carried out through a *ballet* staged as pictorial scene? The title of this chapter, "mythic memory theater," captures Hofmannsthal's stated hope that an aesthetic rendering of the biblical story will foster an encounter between modern Europeans and their 'Oriental' roots—a belief central to his mature art of memory, and in particular, to his very next orientalist work, the opera *Die Ägyptische Helena*.

The final chapter concerns Beer-Hofmann's *Die Historie von König David* (1918–33), an unfinished dramatic trilogy composed in verse. The two parts that were completed, *Jaákobs Traum* and *Der junge David,* are seldom interpreted as anything more than a courageous morale booster, a timely retrieval of Jewish national legacies bequeathed to the German Jewish world in an age of rising anti-Semitism. Only the first, the prologue to the trilogy, has ever been acted. Both Hofmannsthal and Schnitzler found the play too chauvinistic for their own tastes. Hovering indeterminately between public performance and private lyric, the *Historie* exemplifies the phenomenon of modern Jewish countermemory, a phrase coined by Michel Foucault and drawn from Nietzsche. Beer-Hofmann identifies a moment in Jewish history, the ambiguous and ambivalent period between the reigns of a decrepit Saul and a youthful David, for sustained dramatic attention. As holographic technique, countermemory enters in when the viewer is forced to reassess the received history of the Jews (monumental, nationalistic) through the prism of David's struggle to achieve his rightful place in a time of decadence and political confusion. The fact that only Ruth, David's Gentile ancestress, makes his heroism possible reaffirms the role of the outsider in determining the future of the Jews.

∷ PART ONE

GENRES OF MEMORY

1 Freud's Modernism in *Leonardo da Vinci and a Memory of his Childhood* (1910), "The Moses of Michelangelo" (1914), and *Moses and Monotheism* (1938)

Everyone knows that Moses shattered the tablets of the covenant. The Bible tells us so. Yet in "The Moses of Michelangelo" Freud resists this knowledge, instead choosing to celebrate a sculpted image—the statue of Moses carved by Michelangelo for the grave of Pope Julius II—that denies this account. According to Freud's midrash on the image, Moses was on the verge of breaking the tablets when he felt them slip from his grasp and topple forward. This almost losing that to which he had devoted his life brought him to his senses and led him to secure them against his body. Moses regains his self-control, and the covenant is safe; but the tablets will remain forever in their accidental, upside-down position. Freud turns scripture on its head for much the same reason that Yehuda Amichai, in his poem "I Want to Confuse the Bible," enables Moses to enter the Promised Land after all. He claims that this version is superior to the story recorded in the Bible because it vivifies both the artist and the scholar's endeavor to record what is true about the psychic mechanism of inheriting and transmitting an almost-shattered past. Freud's modernism draws out the monumental implications that lodge in small adjustments and chance events, insisting all along that it is only being faithful to the plain view.

What I wish to emphasize in this chapter is Freud's connection to the literary figures of the Vienna circle through his counterscriptural, psychological readings of cultural figures. For Freud, the wisdom of unbreaking the tablets has to do with the overriding sense that human reality must be oppositional—that there are two sides to every story, even the most ancient of legends. Freud had already developed this conclusion about the language of dreams. In the essay "Über den Gegensinn der Urworte" (On the Oppositional Meaning of Primal Words, 1910), Freud took this perplexing characteristic of dream work as a touchstone for a meditation on the double-sided nature of words. Why is it the case that signs within dreams often represent, or are linked with, their opposites? Freud explained this phenomenon by way of two scholarly sources he came across, characteristically, by chance. In his research of ancient languages, the linguist Karl Abel arrived at the identical conclusion drawn by the English philosopher Alexander Bain, whom Freud cites: "The essential relativity of all knowledge, thought or consciousness cannot but show itself in language. If everything that we can know is viewed as a transition from something else, every experience must have two sides; and either every name must have a double meaning, or else for every meaning there must be two names" (*SE*, 11:153; *SA*, 4:232). The notion that primal words, as well as primitive images and concepts, have an antithetical character not only confirms Freud's observation about dreams, it also lends credence to one of the central dynamics of Freudian thought: the view that the most primal human relationships are rooted in conflict. What the mentally sick and mentally healthy have in common, since "we are all a little neurotic" (*SE*, 6:278), is that character is shaped from the start by conflicting feelings and desires that are resolved only to varying degrees.[1] That which is monolithic, unitary, in our character is infantile and by implication narcissistic. Driving the family romance is a process of differentiation that takes place only through conflict with one's primary love object. Much of Freud's conceptualization of inner life, like his discussions of memory, tells us that our most powerful and formative experiences have "two sides": one easily admitted to consciousness, the other repressed and unknown.

What are the implications of this agonistic view of character for Freud's interpretation of culture and cultural heroes? When Freud exhumes the tradition of the two Moses figures or Leonardo da Vinci's repressed feelings toward his mother, what he discovers is another form of the oppositional nature of primal words. To paraphrase Bain: if knowing our cultural heroes requires that we view them in transition from something else—from being forgotten to being remembered—then every hero must have two sides, "and either every name must have a double meaning, or else for every meaning there must be two names." By recuperating Michelangelo's conflicted Moses, renaming him, and splitting him into two historical personalities, the quest to commemorate Moses fulfills both of these requirements.

A double optic controls Freud's essays on artistic, cultural and religious figures. He himself names several motives for his unorthodox approach: to bring to light hidden traditions; to explain mysterious or controversial aspects of these famous personalities; to overcome fixation. But on a dynamic level, what Freud attempts is *to illuminate the object of analysis in the process of it becoming known*. That process—the expansion of psychoanalytic technique into cultural history—entails a new genre of commemorative writing. What does such a poetics of commemoration look like? Freud's analysis inevitably begins with a physical relic or material trace. These signs, the right hand of Moses in Michelangelo's depiction, or the mark of circumcision—function as metonymies for the double-sided, remembered-and-forgotten character of their subjects. When the aesthete scatters reality into episodes or particles, it is as a means of escape; when the novelist zeroes in on a single particle (such as the window in *Der Tod Georgs*), it is in order to trigger the eventual reconstruction of forgotten events. The trace in Freud's texts corresponds to a "survival" or screen memory: a relic of a past conflict that has been repressed and whose retrieval it serves to anchor. Freud relates his rhetorical gesture of focusing on visible details "from the refuse heap of observation" (*SE*, 13:222; *SA*, 10:207) to psychoanalytic technique, but this was also a widespread trend in the arts, made possible by new developments in photography. By a similar logic, Freud's cultural texts suffer from the same willed unreadability one finds in the prose experiments of the Viennese modernists. As accurate information, they are at times woefully insufficient, even wrong. As scholarship, they are contrarian. Freud believed most biographers, scholars, and religious communities were mired in fixation. And so his exegesis takes pains to contradict the sources and discourses upon which they inevitably rely. The flaws that render the texts suspect as scholarship also signal their counterhistorical, modernist dimension. They are holographic performances, if you will, aiming for a response that is not primarily cognitive but instinctive, experiential. Lastly, Freud's heroes infallibly have at least two sides: father and son; scientist and artist; Egyptian and Hebrew. Moses and Leonardo da Vinci are characters in the type of memory plots that obsessed turn-of-the-century Viennese writers. Walter Benjamin observed that Franz Kafka's characters are often physically deformed because they emerge from prehistory, from collective oblivion. In Freud's case as well, the text becomes a kind of psychic memory stage, onto which characters come into view still marked with the impermeable distortions common to all forgotten things, which is to say, indelibly marked by Freud's desire to portray the object of analysis as its own process of becoming known. Only at a late stage, at the end of *Moses and Monotheism*, does Freud name the method of these essays: to craft a genre that is able to do justice to tradition, if tradition is understood to be "die Ergänzung und zugleich der Widerspruch zur Geschichtsschreibung" (the supplement and at the same time the contradiction of the writing of history; *SE*, 23:68; *SA*, 9:517). To at once supplement and contradict what is known about the past, and by extension the present, was the ambition of the Viennese Jewish modernist.

"THE FATHER TOO WAS ONCE A CHILD"

Freud had enormous respect for those cultural figures he called "great men": Moses, Leonardo da Vinci, Goethe, and Beethoven. Rationalist that he was, he sought to identify as precisely as possible how they exerted their influence on him and on others, during their lifetimes and afterward. Yet he remained mystified by the impact of the hero, whose effect he had trouble putting into words. These cultural icons were no doubt Freud's own father imagoes, and his discussions of them are often mined for evidence of identification and countertransference. Yet in the last two decades, scholars have begun to ask what these essays about the "great man" can teach us about history, memory, tradition, and also trauma. Yosef Yerushalmi, Jacques Derrida, Cathy Caruth, Jan Assmann, and Richard Bernstein have all approached *Moses and Monotheism* as a self-conscious study in cultural history.[2] I too focus on Freud's construction of cultural memory. However, I wish to emphasize both the fundamental reliance of his rhetoric on the psychoanalytic understanding of human memory and as his recurring affinity with writers whom we now call "literary." I stress this affinity, not to describe the Viennese modernists as Freud's intellectual epigones, but on the contrary, to foreground his debt to the artistic imagination (in part by way of the specific artists da Vinci and Michelangelo) as he undertakes to invent his own alternative *ars memoria*. Rather than take *Moses and Monotheism* as a starting point, I begin with two other essays where Freud's modernism is more plainly in view. Most prominent in them is the enigma that runs throughout Freud's writings on art, culture, and religion: how does modern culture recollect its heroes once the genres traditionally used for such commemoration (biography, epic, history, scripture) have fallen into disrepute? When Freud comments, for example, that the genre of the epic has become extinct because its "determining cause no longer exists" (*SE*, 23:71; *SA*, 9:520), he provides a clue to his own project of inventing a new genre for cultural memory.

The modernist character of Freud's approach to cultural commemoration may extend most directly from his understanding of human memory as such. The texture of Freud's essays replicates the stratified character of the human memory apparatus. By allowing the reader to observe the great man not only as a child, but also alongside his posthumous lives in history and legend, and by representing the hero as a figure divided against himself, Freud recasts heroism, but also commemoration, as the shattering of fixation and the overcoming of resistance. These same motives inform Schnitzler's and Beer-Hofmann's evasive treatments of the Jewish hero. Literary forms that incorporate resistance within their boundaries apply yet another central insight of psychoanalytic technique, which holds that only by focusing on resistance can we make it possible for a truly salutary act of remembering to occur.

LEONARDO DA VINCI AND A MEMORY OF HIS CHILDHOOD (1910)

An exemplar of the Renaissance and a hero to German minds throughout the ages, Leonardo da Vinci was in many ways Freud's natural counterpart.[3] His genius extended equally to the domains of art and science; he sought to have art be accepted as a science in his day, an undertaking thought by many to parallel Freud's ambition for psychoanalysis.[4] The problem is that Freud's treatment of Leonardo emphasizes the rivalry between his subject's artistic and scholarly sides and exaggerates the incompatibility of art and science as modes of knowing the past. The agenda thereby served is an interpretation of a figure for whom artistic and scholarly activities represented radically different modes of relating to the world. Hence, two strong oppositions run through this essay: the opposition of art and science, and the opposition of productive and unproductive forms of remembering. These conflicts, one on the level of the story, the other on the level of its discourse, mirror one another. The first opposition shapes Leonardo da Vinci's quest to succeed as an artist and to overcome the circumstances of his childhood. The second corresponds to Freud's quest to know and pay homage to the great man. Both together lead Freud to refer to Leonardo, from the very outset, as an enigma: "Leonardo da Vinci (1452–1519) was admired even by his contemporaries as one of the greatest men of the Italian renaissance, yet in their time he had already begun to seem an enigma [*rätselhaft*] just as he does today. He was a universal genius 'whose outlines can only be surmised—never defined.'. . . *What was it that prevented Leonardo's personality from being understood by his contemporaries?*" (*SE*, 11:63; *SA*, 10:91; emphasis in original). Establishing the enigmatic nature of his subjects is Freud's consistent rhetorical starting point; it allows him, as it were, to map out what Walter Benjamin called the "blank spaces" in the minds of his readers. Partially to blame for this amnesia are the biographers. Disdain for biographers was a hallmark of modernism; the sentiment surfaces, memorably, in the opening pages of Oscar Wilde's dialogue "On the Critic as Artist" (1895), where Wilde's modern interlocutor, Gilbert, calls them "the pest of the age, nothing more and nothing less"; "the body-snatchers of literature."[5] In Gilbert's view, no one diminishes the great man more than biographers, literary societies, and pedants, who have no feel for the mystery of greatness. One who, like Freud, delights in the egocentrism of great men, he far prefers to encounter them by way of their letters and memoirs.

Similar sentiments recur throughout Freud's essay. The following passage bears clearly on the problem:

Biographers are fixated [*fixiert*] on their heroes in a quite special way. In many cases they have chosen their hero as the subject of their studies because—for reasons of their personal emotional life—they have felt a special affection for him from the very first. They then devote their energies to a task of idealization aimed at enrolling the great man among the class of their infantile models—at reviving in him, perhaps, the child's idea of his father. To gratify this wish they obliterate the individual features of their subject's physiognomy; smooth over the traces of his life's struggles with internal and external resistances, and they tolerate in him no vestige of human weakness or imperfection. They thus present us with what is in fact a cold, strange, ideal figure, instead of a human being to whom we might feel ourselves distantly related. That they should do this is regrettable, for they thereby sacrifice truth to an illusion, and for the sake of their infantile phantasies abandon the opportunity of penetrating the most fascinating secrets of human nature. (*SE*, 11:129; *SA*, 10:152)

Freud's psychological approach hopes to overcome the collective fixation on the great man by laying bare the mysteries of his human all-too-human nature. But what are these mysteries? In the case of Leonardo da Vinci, the riddle is how "the accident [*Zufälligkeit*] of his illegitimate birth and the excessive tenderness of his mother had the most decisive influence on the formation of his character and on his later fortune [*sein späteres Schicksal*]" (*SE*, 11:136; *SA*, 10:157). The inquiry "ascribes to accidental circumstances [*Zufälligkeiten*] of his parental constellation so decisive an influence on a person's fate" (*SE*, 11:137; *SA*, 10:158) . Stressing the influence of early environment on character is not the primary innovation here, as the emphasis on "milieu," the hallmark of naturalism, was common in contemporary scholarship.[6] The experiment is rather to factor in that which the biographers neglect: not only personal foibles, but also the role of chance in the shaping of character. Just as significant as the "accidents" of birth and parentage in Freud's account, if not even more signifi-cant, are Leonardo's chance encounters with a vulture and with a smiling model. That neglect of these accidents leads to immature forms of attachment such as ide-alization and fixation is a recurrent motif in Freud's writings. It so happens that fix-ation is precisely the condition that Leonardo da Vinci must overcome in order to paint his late masterpieces; he does so by way of a confluence of psychoanalytic tech-nique and creative genius that cuts close to Freud's own procedures. In effect, Freud allows his object of analysis to become known as he becomes known to himself.

In Freud's account, two gulfs (*Klüfte*) separate Leonardo from his contempo-raries and from us, one diachronic, corresponding to a period in Leonardo's life, and one synchronic, corresponding to a characterological mystery. The first gulf refers to a dramatic change that occurred during the second phase of Leonardo's life after he was forced to leave Milan: the "turning of his interests from his art to science [*von seiner Kunst zur Wissenschaft*]" (*SE*, 11:66; *SA*, 10:93). The second concerns the artist's apparent disinterest in sexuality, specifically in female sexuality. Why does Leonardo shun eros, both in life and in work? The answer to both riddles lies in unresolved, unconscious sexual feelings for his mother, dating back to early childhood.

Freud proceeds to divide Leonardo's life into three distinct phases. "The idea of a radiantly happy and pleasure-loving Leonardo is only applicable to the first and longer period of the artist's life" (*SE*, 11:66; *SA*, 10:93); the initial period was one of great artistic success. Yet increasingly Leonardo turns from art to scholarship, and it is this middle phase that catches Freud's attention. Freud describes with great rhetor-ical energy the origins of Leonardo's "double nature [*Doppelnatur*] as artist and investigator" (*SE*, 11:73; *SA*, 10:100). "He became an investigator [*Forscher*], at first still in the service of his art, but later independently of it and away from it" (*SE*, 11:133; *SA*, 10:155); "the scientist within him, once a servant to his art, rose up to oppress his erstwhile master" (*SE*, 11:77; *SE*, 10:104). Leonardo "investigated instead of loving" (*SE*, 11:75; *SA*, 10:102); "investigating has taken the place of acting and creating as well" (*SE*, 11:75; *SA*, 10:102); "Leonardo's researches had perhaps begun, as Solmi believes, in the service of his art," yet the desire for knowledge "swept him away until the connection with the demands of his art was severed" (*SE*, 11:76; *SA*, 10:103). Pas-sion "was converted to the urge to know [*Wissensdrang*]" (*SE*, 11:74; *SA*, 10:101).

In addition to the term *forschen*, Freud introduces the terms *grübeln* and *Grü-belzwang* to describe the obsessive intellectualizing that functions as a secondary defense against sexual thoughts and is most clearly characterized by its inconclusive researches.[7] Leonardo becomes a *Grübler* when, rather than repressing his libido, he sublimates it; research becomes a substitute for sexual activity. He undergoes a recur-rence of infantile craving for knowledge, thus exhausting himself with futile researches and activity with no resolution; he is unable to complete his paintings. "Because of his insatiable and indefatigable thirst for knowledge Leonardo has been called 'the Italian Faust'" (*SE*, 11:75; *SA*, 10:102). In sum, Freud diagnoses Leonardo's turn from art to science as a case of severe regression. The polarity is unmistakable: creativity, art, is progressive; scholarship, the discipline of the conscious mind, is regressive.

To understand the larger implications of this diagnosis, we need briefly to recount the biographical drama underlying the artistic one. Leonardo was an illegitimate child who lived for the first five years of his life alone with his mother before moving into his father and stepmother's house. Freud surmises that during those first five years Leonardo was subjected to excessive maternal affection; the absence of a father to curtail the normal phase of "infantile sexual researches [*Sexualforschung*]" (*SE*, 11:79–80; *SA*, 10:106) resulted in an unresolved Oedipal drama that left the artist overly attached to his mother, and thus unable to love any other woman. In the first phase of his adult life, as an artist, Leonardo creates without inhibition; as a productive man, he acts the father. "He who creates as an artist feels like the father of his work" (*SE*, 11:122; *SA*, 10:144). But when he turns to scientific research, Leonardo flounders; he no longer acts the father, just the fatherless child that he is. Emphasizing Leonardo's double nature highlights the fact that "the father too was once a child," as Freud would later write of Moses (*SE*, 23:110; *SA*, 9:556). The opposition can also be stated in terms of memory. The *Forscher-Grübler,* a modernist type, is stuck repeating an unresolved stage of childhood. The creative artist has a more mature relationship to the past. In Freud's scheme, Leonardo the artist must overcome the scientist within in order to triumph over his regressive tendencies.

In this construction of Leonardo's second period, Freud doth protest too much. Indeed, the pejorative depiction of Leonardo's researcher-identity is virtually reversed in the fifth chapter, when Freud takes up the artist's relationship to his father and to father figures. There, Freud celebrates Leonardo's intellectual achievements, and he attributes to Leonardo the quintessential rationalist tenet (cited by Solmi): "He who appeals to authority when there is a difference of opinion works with his memory rather than with his reason" (*SE*, 11:122–23; *SA*, 10:145). In this later section, intellect connotes the antithesis of a certain kind of (bad) remembering that is associated also with religion; Freud even admires Leonardo's refusal to submit to religious dogma or doctrine, and his disinterest in a personal divinity—virtues Freud liked to claim for himself. Reason, then, provides both Leonardo and Freud not only with a methodology, but also with a rhetoric of persuasion required to break time and again with past convictions—the antidote to an excessively pious memory. Scholarship, like science, comes to signify a healthy distance from authority and from the convictions to which faith, and more primitive mechanisms, hold us. By this stage in the essay, *Wissenschaft* has switched sides, so to speak: research was a trap for the artist, but it provides a framework within which change, even iconoclasm, can be exonerated, in contrast to religion, which allies itself firmly with memory, to its own detriment, and which always represents the ultimate "fixation" in the Freudian scheme. A remark at the conclusion of *Beyond the Pleasure Principle* captures the ambiguous role of scholarship in the Leonardo essay. "Only those believers who demand from scholarship a substitute for the catechism they have given up would blame the investigator [*Forscher*] for further developing or even changing his opinions" (*SE*, 18:64; *SA*, 3:372).[8]

The demotion of scholarship is only one of a series of digressions onto other texts, genres, and disciplines that comprise the middle phase of Freud's essay (chapters 2 through 5). These *grüblerisch* remarks are more strategic than substantive. In them, Freud engages the resistance to the kind of enlightened, artistic memory he is determined to bring to light. The long excursus on history writing is especially relevant in this regard; like the other digressions, it signals Freud's self-consciousness about the disciplinary and generic boundaries of his essay. Far preferable to history are the cryptic memory texts—a childhood memory, a shopping list, the late paintings, and a diary entry—that he enlists to solve different parts of the puzzle. These texts are communications from the past whose significance has been either missed or misread by biographers and art historians. The method is the same in each of the four chapters: Freud converts an apparently innocuous text into a meaningful source of memory about Leonardo's past. These fragments form touchstones in Freud's attempt to shift attention from hero worship—the "what" of Freud's ostensible subject—to the "how" of his psychocultural analysis, namely, how various sources transmit information about past events, and how they are, and are not, to be interpreted.

The contents of the first memory text, the childhood memory named in the essay's title, have been analyzed extensively.[9] Relevant to the present analysis of Freud's method is rather *how* he goes about constructing its efficacy as a mode of reading. He introduces chapter 2 with a dramatic claim: "There is, so far as I know, only one place in his scientific notebooks where Leonardo inserts a piece of information about his childhood [*Mitteilung an seine Kindheit*]. In a passage about the flight of vultures he suddenly interrupts himself to pursue a memory from very early years which had sprung to his mind" (*SE*, 11:82; *SA*, 10:109). Freud sets the stage by proposing that the memory intruded "suddenly." The chance occurrence conveniently mirrors the predestining role of chance in Leonardo's own account: "It seems that I was always destined [*vorher bestimmt*] to be so deeply concerned with vultures; for I recall as one of my very earliest memories that while I was in my cradle a vulture came down to me, and opened my mouth with its tail, and struck me many times with its tail against my lips" (*SE*, 11:82; *SA*, 10:109). Leonardo regards the chance encounter as a usable past, as it enables him to make sense of his destiny. Freud explains: "It was a vague suspicion that his researches and the history of his childhood were connected in this way which later prompted him to exclaim that he had been destined from the first to investigate the problem of the flight of birds, since he had been visited by a vulture as he lay in his cradle" (*SE*, 11:92; *SA*, 10:118). The trick that makes this interpretation possible is the transformation of the scrap of information (*Mitteilung*) itself. The strategy is to convert a one-dimensional document into a multilayered account, a straightforward testimony into a complex text woven of memory and fantasy.

This is often the way in which childhood memories originate. Quite unlike conscious memories from the time of maturity, they are not fixed [*fixiert*] at the moment of being experienced and afterwards repeated, but are only elicited at a later age when childhood is already past; in the process they are altered and falsified, and are put into the service of later trends [*verändert, verfälscht in den Dienst späterer Tendenzen gestellt*], so that generally speaking they cannot be sharply distinguished from phantasies. . . .

What someone thinks he remembers from his childhood is not a matter of indifference; as a rule, residual memories [*Erinnerungsreste*]—which he himself does not understand—cloak priceless pieces of evidence [*unschätzbare Zeugnisse*] about the most important features in his mental development. (*SE*, 11:82–84; *SA*, 10:109–11)

Freud's methodology extends from the logic that "memory is present not once, but several times over" in the psyche. Decoding the vulture memory leads Freud to claim that he has resolved the mystery of Leonardo's initial turn away from art: an early, highly erotic relationship to his mother, of which the memory is a highly-coded symbol, exacerbated by the absence of a father to curtail the Oedipal drama, caused Leonardo to turn so tenaciously to research. In the final lines of the chapter, the repressed idea will receive yet another translation, this time to solve a second enigma encoded in that same memory text: "'It was through this erotic relation with my mother that I became a homosexual'" (*SE*, 11:106; *SA*, 10:131).

Freud then turns to a second, even more innocuous text from the artist's diaries: a list of funeral expenditures for a woman named Caterina, which Freud takes pains to reproduce, as if for its rhetorical impact, in his own text. Why might Leonardo have preserved this shopping list in his diary? Biographers have absolutely no idea as to its meaning. Significantly, "the novelist Merezhkovsky alone is able to tell us who this Caterina was": Leonardo's mother (*SE*, 11:105; *SA*, 10:130). In Freud's view, the fact that such a trivial document was preserved signals its compulsive character. "What we have before us in the account of the costs of the funeral expenses is the expression—distorted out of all recognition—of his mourning for his mother [*die bis zur Unkenntlichkeit entstellte Äusserung der Trauer um die Mutter*]" (*SE*, 11:105; *SA* 10:130). The shopping list is another *Mitteilung* that proves to be a layered text— a distorted expression of mourning. Leonardo's repressed erotic feelings for his mother were "displaced onto trivial and even foolish actions" (*SE*, 11:105; *SA*, 10:130). The shopping list, then, is another kind of screen memory, a "compromise" between conscious and unconscious motives: "The opposition that came from the subsequent repression of this childhood love did not allow him to set up a different and worthier memorial [*Denkmal*] to her in his diary. But what emerged as a compromise [*Kompromiß*] from this neurotic conflict had to be carried out; and thus it was that the account was entered in the diary, and has come to the knowledge of posterity as something unintelligible" (*SE*, 11:106; *SA*, 10:131). In a stunning turn of phrase, the shopping list is raised to the status of a memorial; a provisional document is transvalued as a layered text evocative of the deepest of unconscious wishes.

At this juncture of the essay, as if to justify the exaggerated attention he has paid to two trivial memory texts, Freud sets up a pivotal analogy between these two distorted texts and the enterprise of history writing in ancient times. In a three-page digression, Freud attempts to argue that history is no less distorted than screen memories. The main argument is that history is "an expression [*Ausdruck*] of present beliefs and wishes rather than a true picture [*Abbild*] of the past" (*SE*, 11:82–83; *SA*, 10:110). Though Freud reminds us that history does contain a core of "historical truth," the audacity here concerns the demotion of history, the conscious memory text par excellence, to the status of a distorted text modeled on the indirection of displaced recollection. The awkwardly placed digression on historical method pertains both to Freud's own vacillations between scholarly and imaginative modes of inquiry, as well as to Leonardo's double identity as an artist and scientist. It serves as a pivot point from Leonardo's conflicted expressions to the texts that speak of inhibitions overcome and compromises reached: the masterpieces he paints during the third phase of his life.

Freud's reader is now in a position to understand the true nature of Leonardo's accomplishment. His art, we recall, was in a state of "decay," when the following transpired:

At the summit of his life, when he was in his early fifties . . . a new transformation came over him. Still deeper layers of the contents of his mind became active once more; but this further regression was to the benefit of his art, which was in the process of becoming stunted. He met the woman who awakened his memory of his mother's happy smile of sensual rapture; and, influenced by this revived memory, he recovered the stimulus that guided him at the beginning of his endeavors. . . . He painted the Mona Lisa, the "St. Anne with Two Others" and the series of mysterious pictures which are characterized by the enigmatic smile [*die Reihe der geheimnisvollen, durch das rätselhafte Lächeln ausgezeichneten Bilder*]. With the help of the oldest of all his erotic impulses he enjoyed the triumph of once more conquering the inhibition in his art. (*SE*, 11:133–34; *SA*, 10:155–56)

The chance encounter with a smiling woman affects Leonardo in much the same way as the taste of the madeleine affects Marcel Proust. The memory of his mother's "happy smile of sensual rapture" returns with such power that the artist in Leonardo is energized to tell about it: to allow the conflicting feelings and memories to rise to the surface, and to translate them into a series of paintings. The smile is enigmatic because it is multivalent; it fuses the contradictions of childhood—the loving and the destructive sides of the mother; the adult's eye and boy's gaze; erotic bliss and erotic deprivation—without sublating them. The smile is androgynous, appearing on John the Baptist, Bacchus, Leda, Saint Anne, and Mona Lisa del Giocondo. In contrast to the childhood memory named in the essay's title, which is an accidentally preserved trace of repressed erotic desire, and to the list of Caterina's funeral expenses—a more mature, still neurotic memory text—the painted smile represents healthy resolution.

Freud's interpretation of the Mona Lisa's smile reveals that the Leonardo essay is consistent with the approach of contemporary renaissancist mythmakers only up to a point. The pathography as a whole reflects the modern fascination with the artist-genius, and it also bears some resemblance to "experience aesthetics" (*Erlebnisäs-thetik*), the subjective, impressionistic criticism practiced by Pater, Wilde, Hofmannsthal, and others.[10] *La Gioconda* played an important role in the poetics of cultural memory at the turn of the century, when it attained the status of cultural icon, or what Ursula Renner calls a "Projektionsbild moderner Mythenbedürfnisse," an image onto which were projected the modern (male) desires for myths of feminin-ity.[11] The enigmatic smile, at once intimate and indifferent, beckoning and alienating, was the focal point or vanishing point of these projections; it was on this basis that Walter Pater, who (like Freud) links her to Saint Anne and also to the *Vampyr*, cre-ated the myth of the femme fatale. This "woman without qualities" made possible the quintessential aesthetic encounter qua memory encounter: unreachable as she was, she prompted a distinct sense of déjà vu. Freud was aware of this trend and outlines it in his essay. But does he himself partake of it? Mona Lisa's smile is no doubt a key element in Freud's reconstruction of the artist's life.[12] But is his primary motive "to interpret the psychology of the smile"?[13] The view that Freud "make[s] the interpre-tation of the smile the departure point of a psychoanalytic illumination of Leonardo da Vinci's art" contradicts the gist of Freud's interpretation and his method.[14] The smile represents the imagined interplay of biographical, psychological, and aesthetic matters. One might accuse Freud of mythmaking to the extent that he links Leonardo's narcissism and homosexuality to the androgynous faces in the portraits. Yet even if one construes the psychoanalytic treatments of homosexuality and female sexuality as myths, the portraits themselves, *La Gioconda* and *Madonna and Child with Saint Anne,* are not fodder for myth, and more important, the essay as a whole explicitly deflects that genre of cultural recollection. It does so by constructing the smile as a figure of compromise, rather than an icon—a mark of mature differentiation rather than fix-ation, of working through rather than repetition. It does so, moreover, by basing it all on a hologram: the chance correspondence of two smiles.

It is thus appropriate that Freud conclude the pathography with a fascinating paean to chance: the force that redeems us from rigid conceptions both of nature and of religion. "If one considers chance [*Zufall*] to be unworthy of determining our fate [*Schicksal*], it is simply a relapse [*Rückfall*] into the pious view of the Universe which Leonardo himself was on the way to overcoming when he wrote that the sun does not move" (*SE,* 11:137; *SA,* 10:158). In fact, Leonardo's triumph is indebted to two chance encounters: the early molestation by the vulture that prompted him years later to record and reconfigure his own destiny, and the fortuitous encounter with a smiling model that allowed him to reconnect with his mother as a source of inspira-tion. These are necessary, even logical stages in the artist's *Bildung.* The process that culminates in those paintings corresponds exactly to Freud's descriptions of how the imagination works in the essay "Der Dichter und das Phantasieren" (The Creative

Artist and Imagining) and elsewhere. The artistic imagination is the faculty able to reappropriate chance for the drama of memory, whereas such phantoms are inevitably ignored by those who are trapped in their fixations, who are captive to the catechism of necessity. The memory of past happiness *can* fill in a gap in the adult psyche; random occurrences *can* become triggers of growth, "sources" of destiny. The chance encounter becomes a metaphor for the enigmatic nature of human character as such. Freud's method in the Leonardo essay, if one can call it a method, is to solve one enigma with the help of another. Here, it is Freud's imagination that recombines traces from all periods in Leonardo's life, not in the service of hero worship, but in order to compose a meaningful and life-enhancing narrative. What prevents this *Denkmal* from turning into a reified portrait or myth is that it enacts the drama of its own methodological discovery. Like all of the texts discussed in this book, it is a distorted text, a negotiated compromise between different discourses, a composite of the probable and the possible. It harbors resistance, even failure, within its parameters, in the name of truth and knowledge. This is the final lesson that Freud claims to have learned from the artist:

Leonardo himself, with his love of truth and his thirst for knowledge, would not have discouraged an attempt to take the trivial peculiarities and riddles in his nature as a starting point for discovering what determined his mental and intellectual development. We do homage to him by learning from him. It does not detract from his greatness if we make a study of the sacrifices which his development from childhood must have entailed, and if we bring together the factors which have stamped him with the tragic mark of failure. (*SE*, 11:129–31; *SA*, 10:152–53)

UNBREAKING THE TABLETS: "THE MOSES OF MICHELANGELO" (1914)

"The Moses of Michelangelo" was originally inspired by a genuine artistic *Erlebnis.* Freud viewed Michelangelo's *Moses* in San Pietro in Vincoli, Rome, for the first time in 1901, and he returned to it on several occasions. During a three-week stay in September 1912, Freud visited the statue on a daily basis. The essay that he eventually published was just as much a product of careful research. Freud read Giorgio Vasari's *Lives of the Artists* (1568) in the 1890s, studied the work of art historians Jakob Burckhardt, Henry Thode, and many others, and also paid careful attention to published illustrations of the statue in his library and to photographic details he had specially commissioned.[15] And yet an aura of confusion has surrounded the essay since its very first appearance in 1914 in the journal *Imago,* a "Journal for the Application of Psychoanalysis to the Humanities" published by Freud himself. Three features of the original publication testify to the confusion. First, Freud published the essay anonymously; the byline reads, "By ***," and the sentence that follows the three stars is more a disclaimer than anything else: "Let me first say that I am not a connoisseur, only a layman." Nor did a curious footnote, found on the first page of the essay, help to clarify either the identity and motives of the author or the merits of the article. "The editorial board did not deny acceptance to this contribution, which strictly speaking does not follow the guidelines of the program, because the author, who is known to it, is close to analytic circles, and because his way of thinking [*Denkweise*] shows a distinct similarity with the methodology of psychoanalysis."[16]

The aura of confusion has led readers to personalize Freud's motives for writing this essay, and to understand Freud's intense preoccupation with Moses as a matter of personal identification or countertransference. Like Moses, Freud was a lawgiver; like Moses, betrayed by Aaron and the Israelites, Freud had to work through his rage over the recent defections of his followers (Jung, Adler, Steckel);[17] and like Moses, Freud founded a new movement and led his followers to the brink of the promised land—a secure future—that he could only glimpse, but not enter. In a letter of 1909, Freud wrote to Jung, "You will as Joshua, if I am Moses, take possession of the promised land of psychiatry, which I am only permitted to glimpse from afar."[18] Yerushalmi, who dissociates this first essay almost entirely from the late Moses texts, suggests that Michelangelo's Moses was a father imago and that Freud wrote the essay in order to liberate himself from guilt owing to his estrangement from religious observance.[19] Mary Bergstein, by contrast, suggests that Michelangelo's Moses represented an ideal Jewish father for this Hellenized Jew: "a muscular, classicizing figure, as strong and beautiful as the pagan river gods and the Laocoön of the classical sculpture."[20]

Whatever biographical issues may be in play, I concur with Ken Frieden's view that Freud's personal ambivalence is mainly of interest in light of "the distortions it produces in the work."[21] If the evidence of distortion is the clearest indicator of personal investment, then the real reckoning is less with Judaism as such than with the Hebrew Bible, the preeminent source of Mosaic memory. As he does in the Leonardo essay, Freud learns from the artist how best to transcribe the memory of the great man into a new (modern) stratum of collective memory. The resolution in this case, as in the previous essay, involves paying exaggerated attention to an involuntary occurrence. Here too, Freud attempts to solve one riddle with the help of another.

The enigma with which Freud begins this essay is the power of the aesthetic experience:

We admire [creations of art], we feel overawed by them, but we are unable to say what they represent to us. . . . I do not mean that connoisseurs and lovers of art find no words with which to praise such objects to us. . . . But usually in the presence of a greater work of art each says something different from the other; and none of them says anything that solves the problem for the unpretending admirer. . . . But why should the artist's intention not be capable of being communicated and comprehended in words like any other fact of mental life? (*SE*, 13:211–12; *SA*, 10:197–98)

Why does art move us so powerfully? And why is its impact so difficult to put into words? Why are even the greatest works of art "still unsolved riddles to our understanding" (*SE*, 13:211; *SA*, 10:197)? Freud's initial disclaimer that he is not a connoisseur anticipates his dismissal of the experts a few lines later. The connoisseur (like the biographer) knows too much (his opinions cancel each other out) and too little (since he is unable to communicate his knowledge to the layperson). As before, Freud's eventual interpretation draws both upon the naïve response to art and upon scholarly understanding in order to navigate a course of its own. Signaling the preoccupation with method is the fact that already in these first lines, the problem of language rears its head. The artist's motive cannot communicate itself to the viewer, art experts fail to communicate anything of use, and even the author of the present essay is unable to put his name to it. It is precisely by imitating the artist that Freud's discussion overcomes the initial crisis of language and, by harnessing the failures of innocence and experience, forges a "way back" from the mystery of the art to reality.[22]

Related to the difficulty of talking about art is the challenge of commemorating the great man. Here Freud's stance proves especially complex. It can be argued that Freud's interpretation transforms Moses from the servant of a jealous God into a Christian, turn-the-other-cheek type of hero. But if this was his primary intent, why then did he append a third section to the essay that seems to serve no purpose other than to remind the reader of Moses's origins in the Hebrew Bible? I submit that the Jewish Moses remains Freud's hero, and that the extreme measures taken here testify to the difficulties of paying homage to him in a way that challenges his codification in scriptural memory. The challenge is exemplified in an especially dramatic (and oft-cited) passage in which Freud identifies his role with that of the masses of idolatrous Israelites, the rebellious *Volk* toward whom the gaze of the seated Moses is directed (fig. 5).

No piece of statuary has ever made a stronger impression on me than this. How often have I mounted the steep steps from the unlovely Corso Cavour to the lonely piazza where the deserted church stands, and have essayed to support the angry scorn of the hero's glance! Sometimes I have crept cautiously out of the half-gloom of the interior as though I myself belonged to the mob upon whom his eye is turned—the mob which can hold fast no conviction, which has neither faith nor patience, and which rejoices when it has regained its illusory idols. (*SE*, 13:213; *SA*, 10:199)

Freud's primary identification here is not with Moses, but with the idolatrous mob. Just as the ancient Israelites replaced Moses with a golden calf, so does Freud's essay depose the biblical Moses in favor of a graven image—Michelangelo's statue—in order to argue that the artist has mediated a truth overlooked by countless generations of Jews.[23] In normative Judaism, replacing text with image is the ultimate idolatrous act. For Jewish modernists, idolatry serves the greater good of iconoclasm. As a human creation, the story only makes sense to Freud if Moses at the last moment drops, but does not shatter, the tablets. Scripture, the "sacred books of the Jews and their traditions as recorded in writing [*schriftlich niedergelegt*]," becomes the real idol,

5. Postcard, the Moses of Michelangelo. Freud sent a similar postcard to Ferenczi in 1913. He relied on postcards and photographs of the statue while writing his essay.

a text incapable of retaining the truth about Moses, which Freud will later call the tradition of Moses (*SE*, 23:7; *SA*, 9:459). To shatter this fixation *of* and *on* Moses—a kind of modern Jewish idolatry—Freud turns to art. His exemplar, the real hero in this text, is not Moses but Michelangelo.

Freud begins by citing a wide array of interpretations by German, French and English scholars to pin down the genre of the statue. The dominant view is that the statue depicts an actual episode in the life of Moses, namely his reaction upon seeing the Israelites dance around the golden calf (Exodus 33:19): "In the next instant, Moses will spring to his feet—his left foot is already raised from the ground—dash the tables to the earth, and let loose his rage upon his faithless people" (*SE*, 13:216; *SA*, 10:201). Freud cites several art historians in support of this "episodic" interpretation, two of them, Carl Justi and Fritz Knapp, at length. He agrees with their interpretations of some details—Moses's turned head and raised foot and the slipping tablets—but diverges from them on a critical point. Justi, Knapp, and others see the *anticipation* of an act (the lawgiver about to rise), but Freud sees the *completion* of an act (the lawgiver decides not to rise): an afterimage. The shift from before to after is phrased as a turn from a "historical figure [*Historienbild*]," an actual historical episode, to what Henry Thode, in his study of 1908, called a "character-type [*Charaktertypus*]." Thode's interpretation confirms Freud's empirical sense that this statue is not an incidental depiction of a man about to rise up in anger. "I was obliged to realize that something was represented here that could stay without change; that this Moses would remain sitting like this in his wrath forever" (*SE*, 13:220–21; *SA*, 10:206). Freud seems to have removed the statue from the domain of the episodic, and thereby from history, and placed it into the ahistorical realm of the *Charaktertypus.* However, Freud's memory texts are anything but timeless: he goes on to argue that any timeless significance lies paradoxically in the statue's temporal or narrative character—in its ability to portray not one gesture, but rather a sequence of gestures. The strategy entails turning visible traces into temporal traces, so as to correct those whom he accuses of "emancipating themselves from the visual image of the statue" (*SE*, 13:229; *SA*, 10:214). Freud's afterimage is composed of a series of distinct movements, an action and a reaction: the impulse to shatter the tablets and the overcoming of that impulse. Freud summarizes: "In his first transport of fury, Moses desired to act, to spring up and take vengeance and forget the Tables; but he has overcome the temptation, and he will now remain seated and still in his frozen wrath and in his pain mingled with contempt. Nor will he throw away the Tables so that they will break on the stones, for it is on their especial account that he has controlled his anger; it was to preserve them that he kept his passion in check" (*SE*, 13:229–30; *SA*, 10:214). The interpretation derives from two traces "from the rubbish heap, as it were, of our observation" (*SE*, 13:222; *SA*, 10:207). Freud first observes that Moses's right hand touches both the tablets and the beard. Why does the right hand cross over to the left strands of his beard, and why is only the index finger intertwined with the beard, creating a loop or knot effect? Also important is the small protuberance Freud spots on the underside of the tablets, which suggests to him that they are resting upside down and must have rotated from their original upright position. Putting these two traces together, Freud proposes the following pantomime: the seated Moses becomes distracted by the Israelites' orgiastic cries, turns his head to see them, and moves his hand leftwards to clutch his beard and body as he begins to rise up, at which point the tablets slip from his grasp, rotate forward 180 degrees, and nearly fall to the ground. Sensing the slippage "brings Moses to himself," and his right arm retreats and reaches back to steady the tablets, leaving one finger still enmeshed in the strands of his beard.

Moses's hand encapsulates the compromise that the statue as a whole embodies. "As our eyes travel down it, the figure exhibits three distinct emotional strata. The lines of the face reflect the feelings which have won the ascendancy; the middle of the figure shows the traces of suppressed movement; and the foot still retains the attitude of the projected action" (*SE*, 13:230; *SA*, 10:215). Freud locates in Michelangelo's Moses the identities of the two Moses characters he describes in *Moses and Monotheism*: Moses the Egyptian, who is impulsive, passionate, capable of breaking the tablets; and Moses the Midianite, who is capable "of the highest mental achievement that is possible in a man, that of struggling successfully against an *inward* passion for the sake of a cause to which he has devoted himself" (*SE*, 13:233; *SA*, 10:217). By claiming that Michelangelo immortalizes Moses not for his deed, but rather for his mental and psychological power, Freud does indeed universalize Moses; he removes him from the national drama, and he justifies this move in psychoanalytic as well as artistic terms. Moses's resistance is not sublimated or hidden, rather, it takes on material form; like the painted smile, or the small protuberance on the tablets, it remains in plain view. Freud attributes his method of inquiry to the Italian art connoisseur Ivan Lermolieff, the pseudonym of Giovanni Morelli. As Carlo Ginzburg has famously shown, when Freud stresses the affinity between Morelli's 1897 book and psychoanalysis—"[psychoanalysis], too, is accustomed to divine secret and concealed things from despised or unnoticed features, from the rubbish heap, as it were, of our observations" (*SE*, 13:222; *SA*, 10:207)—he identifies with a scientific method that sees minor details and unconscious gestures as the keys to the hidden core of character.[24]

An important question remains. Traces or no traces, is it not the case that the biblical Moses does shatter the tablets? How could Michelangelo blaspheme scripture in this way? To address this discrepancy, Freud appends a third chapter to the essay, the bulk of which is devoted to a discussion of the biblical account. Freud apologizes for citing "anachronistically" from the Luther Bible; it is of course scripture per se that functions as the anachronism in the course of this third chapter. Freud proceeds to cite Exodus 32.[25] The eighteen verses Freud cites (7–11, 14–20, and 14–35) begin with God instructing Moses to go down from the mountain because the people have sinned, and then telling him that he will destroy the people and make of Moses alone "a great nation." In verse 11, Moses begins to persuade God to spare the nation that

God brought out of Egypt. Freud omits verses 12 and 13, in which Moses carefully reasons with God, first with the canny "what would the Egyptians say . . . ?" and then by reminding God of promises made to the forefathers of Israel. In verse 14, God regrets the impulse to destroy the people, and in subsequent verses Moses comes down, learns a second time (from Joshua) of the people's rebellion, shatters the tablets (verse 19), burns the golden calf, argues with Aaron, leads the sons of Levi in massacring three thousand men, and then calls on God to spare the people or to "blot him out" of his book. God responds that he will not blot Moses out, and sends a plague upon the Israelites.

Too much scripture is included to convey the glaring lack of correspondence between text and image. After noting that the scriptural text has been "clumsily put together from various sources" and contains "glaring incongruities and contradictions" (*SE*, 13:232; *SA*, 10:216), Freud confirms that the statue "is not meant to record any particular moment in the prophet's life" (*SE*, 13:233; *SA*, 10:217) insofar as it is codified in scripture. The statue makes visible an internal, silent self-overcoming that the Bible fails to narrate. But then why quote scripture in the first place? Or more to the point, how does Freud want us to read this excerpt? And why does he preface this section of the essay by saying that he will at last "reap the fruits of [his] endeavors" (*SE*, 13:229; *SA*, 10:214)? The lengthy citation is not meant to support Freud's reading, but rather to highlight the disparity, or contradiction, between the biblical text (especially when viewed through the lens of modern scholarship) and the sculpted text. It is important to note that Freud reads scripture here through the enlightened lens of modern biblical criticism; he treats it as a secular, not a religious, memory text. Quoting scripture is not an exegetical practice, as it would be in a rabbinic text; its function here is rhetorical or ornamental. The verses appear only in the final section. They are not integrated into the interpretation; in fact, they are brought in tendentiously, only after Freud has completed his interpretation of the statue, as part of his second "endeavor." And they are quoted alongside four sketches Freud claims to have commissioned by an artist, but that he himself may have drafted from photographs, one of which accompanied his essay in *Imago* (fig. 6).[26] These rather inexpert sketches resemble "components of an animated cartoon or flip book";[27] yet they are meant to lend support to Freud's alliance with the artist in the endeavor of supplanting the biblical Moses, first with the Moses of Michelangelo, then with his own idiosyncratic, countertraditional reading thereof. Insofar as the sketches fill in Moses's movements leading up the moments, they comprise a new tradition, one that contradicts one account and supplements others. The artist is able to bring Moses to life for Freud, but the textual reminiscence must be killed off in the process.

At this point, the two agendas I have noted—aesthetic and commemorative, scholarly and imaginative—converge. Freud's identification is, at the very least, a double one: Moses and Michelangelo are both heroes, though their heroisms are at cross-purposes. Michelangelo's genius lay not in fidelity to the historical, the tradi-

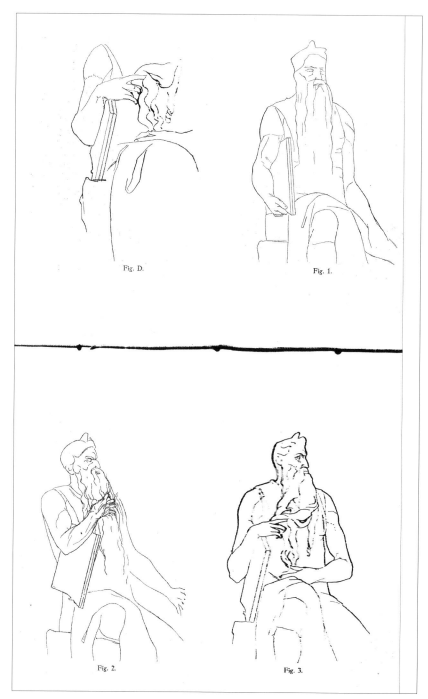

6. When Freud published "The Moses of Michelangelo" in the February 1914 issue of *Imago*, he included four cartoons to support his theory that the tablets as they appear (figs. D and 3) were originally sitting upright (fig. 1) before they slipped and rotated forward (fig. 2).

tional Moses, but in inventing a superior tradition of his own: "But Michelangelo
has placed a different Moses on the tomb of the Pope, one superior to the historical
or traditional Moses. He has modified the theme of the broken Tables; he does not
let Moses break them in his wrath, but makes him be influenced by the danger that
they will be broken and calm that wrath, or at any rate prevent it from becoming an
act. In this way he has added something new and more than human to the figure of
Moses" (*SE*, 13:233; *SA*, 10:217).

FREUD'S COUNTERSCRIPTURAL WRITING IN *MOSES AND MONOTHEISM*

In "The Moses of Michelangelo," Freud's approach to Hebrew scripture is at once idolatrous and iconoclastic: idolatrous from a traditional Jewish standpoint, because a
graven image is put forth as truer than scripture; iconoclastic from a modernist Jewish
angle, because Freud's premise is that by codifying or "fixing" a particular version of
the Moses story, scripture itself had become an idol. Two different types of fixation
(*Fixierungen*) come under attack in *Moses and Monotheism*. The first usage of the term
is neutral; it describes the codification of an oral tradition in writing, or what Freud
refers to as "Niederschrift." The second application is psychoanalytic and refers to an
attachment dictated by the rules of an earlier developmental stage. If scripture perpetuates the fixation of and on Moses, Freud's essays seek to reinscribe and retranslate
Moses's heroism into a fresh stratum of Jewish collective memory, one dictated by the
Jewish modernist imagination. Clearly, Freud did not fear offending the Orthodox
Jews, but he did fear that modern secular Jews had been blocked by a religious artifact
from knowing the more human side of Moses.

In the two texts I have already discussed, Freud takes a riddle as his rhetorical starting point. With the biblical Moses, however, since no obvious enigma presents itself, Freud constructs one. He begins by stating his intention "to deprive a
people of the man whom they take pride in as the greatest of their sons"—to eclipse
or block out Moses as we know him—and proceeds to offer a rationale for this
agenda (*SE*, 23:7; *SA*, 9:459). Not only have "national interests" wrested Moses from
the domain of "truth," but historians and scholars have fallen under the spell of the
Bible! "Science today [*die heutige Wissenschaft*] has become altogether more cir-
cumspect and handles traditions far more indulgently than in the early days of historical criticism" (*SE*, 23:7; *SA*, 9:459). Insofar as it sets itself up as a response to this
lapse, Freud's Moses project is an epigonal enterprise. History is not what it used to
be, and the first evidence of this is the persistent misunderstanding of the Hebrew
word for Moses, *Mosche*. Though numerous scholars agree that *Mosche* is an Egyptian word meaning "child," no historian, not even J. H. Breasted, has made the leap
from Moses's Egyptian name to his Egyptian origins. Freud deduces that the invin-
cibility of the Moses myth lies in the astonishing fact that religion and *Wissenschaft*
have allied with each other to shut out the truth about Moses's origins. In the face
of this alliance, Freud is moved to adopt the strategies of the old-fashioned, text-

critical *Wissenschaft* that was unintimidated by religious tradition. As we saw in the Leonardo essay, only *Wissenschaft* is powerful enough to challenge the religious view; if *Wissenschaft* itself has a blind spot, Freud must be an even better historian than the historians to illuminate it. Yet the alliance with classical historical scholarship proves to be short-lived. Later in the essay Freud switches sides in order to critique history writing, both ancient and modern, at which point *Wissenschaft,* with its limitations and fixations, comes to resemble the very same imperfect religious sources it opposed. In order to oppose the historians, Freud turns initially to literature, to the obsolete, yet still relevant genre of the epic. Epic writers know something about how to approach "the great man," and yet Freud is unable to cast his lot unequivocally with imaginative writing. The culmination of the rhetorical quest to commemorate Moses properly proves to be the notion of tradition, introduced in the last chapter of the section, dated "London, June 1938." Tradition is not an ideal type of transmission; traditions are broken, distorted, but at the same time undeniably true. What is most true about them, in Freud's eyes, is that they operate according to a logic that closely resembles how psychoanalysts believe unconscious memories become known to consciousness. "Tradition" proves to be the telos of a quest for form that begins with the deconstruction of Moses's identity and that proceeds by demoting the scriptural account of Moses and numerous other paradigms, one by one.

From Mosche to Moses

The name *Mosche* triggers Freud's analysis. Like the hand entangled in the beard or Leonardo's list of funeral expenses for Caterina, the trace is revealed to be a double-sided marker, a virtual screen memory. Freud introduces the name in Hebrew and then addresses the discrepancy between Moses's name and his identity.[28] Here again, the very procedure is revealing. Freud begins by faithfully quoting the etymology of the name *Moses* found in Exodus 2. He then deploys the *Jüdisches Lexikon,* a Jewish encyclopedia, to debunk scripture as offering nothing more than folk etymology. Lastly, he cites *The Dawn of Conscience* by J. H. Breasted to the effect that the name is widely known to be a common Egyptian word for *child.* The fact that the Hebrew name conceals an Egyptian word sets the stage for Freud's central thesis regarding the "original identity" of the Jewish and Aten religions; as a condensation of these Hebraic/Egyptian associations, the name *Mosche* encapsulates Moses's identity. Moreover, the rhetorical trajectory according to which Freud moves from a religious source to a Jewish scholarly source to the British scholarly source mimics the unraveling of the name itself: the reader is gradually led from legend to truth, from subjective, nationalistic memory texts to "objective" historical sources.

If historical truth is his goal, why does Freud refer to his subject in the way that the biblical narrator does, as "the man Moses" ("der Mann Moses," Hebrew "ha-ish Mosheh," Numbers 12:3).[29] The citation is not a sign of fidelity to scripture; the phrase is meant to signal Moses's status as a figure of Jewish memory, rather than a historical personality. Thus, the man Moses who "created the Jews" was himself created by the Jews and continues to be created by the Jews. Discrediting the biblical etymology of Moses's name is the first step in the process of exposing the cover-up. Since it is not only scripture, but also the normative religious archive that must in the process be rejected, Freud opens the second essay by dissociating his enterprise from that of the "Talmudists," or rabbinic exegetes.[30] In order to remember Moses properly, Freud must demote Hebrew scripture from the sole reliable source of Mosaic memory into an unreliable and distorted source of Mosaic memory.

Toward the end of the first essay, Freud denigrates "the traditions surrounding the heroic figure of Moses—with all their confusion and contradictions and their unmistakable signs of continuous and tendentious revisions and super-impositions" (*SE*, 23:16; *SA*, 9:467). In the second essay, Freud discusses at length the contradictory portrayal of Moses and corrects the various distortions to reveal the historical truth. Comparing Exodus 32:9 and Numbers 12:3, Freud writes that Moses "is often pictured as domineering, hot-tempered and even violent, yet he is also described as the mildest and most patient of men" (*SE*, 23:41; *SA*, 9:490); scripture has soldered two Moseses together. The description of Moses as "slow of speech," to note another example, encodes the fact that Moses spoke a different language; Aaron was not merely his spokesperson but also his translator. In sum: "No historian can regard the Biblical account of Moses and the Exodus as anything other than a pious piece of imaginative fiction, which has recast a remote tradition for the benefit of its own tendentious purposes. The original form of that tradition is unknown to us; we should be glad to discover what the distorting purposes were, but we are kept in the dark by our ignorance of the historical events" (*SE*, 23:33; *SA*, 9:403). From the vantage point of the historian, scripture is a piece of "imaginative fiction" politically motivated. Freud's own enterprise, always framed in the first-person plural, can be summed up as follows: "If we find means of recognizing the distortions produced by those purposes, we shall bring to light fresh fragments of the true state of things lying behind them" (*SE*, 23:42; *SA*, 9:491). The challenge is a matter of making out of these inconsistencies a consistent trend in which scripture "makes two into one" by collapsing dualities and condensing binary structures (events, characters) into unified or monolithic ones.

In Part 1 of the third and final essay, as he sets the stage for his discussion of tradition, Freud puts forth his most provocative image of biblical narratives thus far, likening them to mausoleums: "The poetically embellished narrative which we attribute to the Yahwist, and to his later rival the Elohist, were like mausoleums [*Grabbauten*] beneath which, withdrawn from the knowledge of later generations, the true account of those early things—of the nature of Moses and of the violent end of the great man—was, as it were, to find its eternal rest" (*SE*, 23:62; *SA*, 9:511). The image of a mausoleum foreshadows the still-to-be divulged hypothesis of Moses's murder. Striking is not only that the Bible has "buried" Moses, but that it does so in the manner of a mausoleum rather than a monument (*Denkmal*), the metaphor Freud chooses to describe Leonardo's list of funeral expenses for his mother. Like a decorative structure atop a tomb, scripture not only conceals, or lays to rest, the Mosaic religion, it beautifies or harmonizes a violent rupture. The mausoleum, moreover, evokes the *Urszene* of all mnemotechnics: the legend told by the Greek poet Simonides Melicus of how the art of memory first came into being after a roof collapsed upon a dinner celebration and the poet was able to name the dead by recalling their seating positions. In her study *Memory and Literature,* Renate Lachmann comments: "The primal scene of memory consists of bearing witness to *anatrope,* the plunge from life into death. It consists of the indexical act of pointing to the dead (the ancestors) and the iconographic act of transforming the dead into a concept of what they were as living people."[31] The Bible-as-mausoleum emerges out of Freud's imagination: it fulfills his wish that scripture-as-icon give rise to a new *ars memoria.* Comparing scripture to a stone structure recalls Freud's use of the Bible in the first Moses text, where a lengthy and discontinuous scriptural citation is relegated to the essay's final section in the manner of an afterthought, unrelated to the thrust of the inquiry. In *Moses and Monotheism,* text and image are again placed in opposition to one another. In "The Moses of Michelangelo," scripture-as-icon was supplanted by statue-as-text. Here the Hebrew Bible has become a burial place, to be supplanted by Freud's own unwieldy attempt to resurrect the Mosaic tradition from its long latency in Jewish collective memory.

Circumcision and Other Fossils

Mona Lisa's smile, Michelangelo's hand, Moses's name, and now Moses's circumcision: here, too, Freud garners prime evidence for his interpretation from a material trace. Freud may be at his most heretical when treating the psychohistorical origins of this most primal mark in Judaism.

The argument is as follows. Freud establishes with the help of Herodotus that circumcision is universally acknowledged to be an ancient Egyptian practice. If one assumes the biblical account to be true, why would the Jews leaving Egypt, who presumably wanted to free themselves from the past, have adopted this practice? Would it not instead keep "permanently alive their memory of Egypt" and thus be antithetical to the immanent national consciousness (*SE,* 23:27; *SA,* 9:478)? On the other hand, if Moses were an Egyptian, Freud reasons, imposing circumcision on his people would be a sign of his having chosen the tribe and having attempted to raise them to a status of a holy nation, namely, a people not inferior to the Egyptians. Circumcision (like the Hebrew name *Mosche)* becomes a mark of the originary identity between Egyptian and Jew. Like the biblical Moses and the monotheistic tradition he represents, the sign is not a Jewish original after all; it is derivative. The biblical account has distorted the truth. Like the character of Moses himself, the ritual of circumcision was perpetuated as a function of the compromise or merger at Kadesh that would ensure parity between two groups—those who experienced the Exodus (or inherited the memory thereof, such as the Levites) and those who merged with them.

From a normative Jewish perspective, the argument is sacrilegious. According to Genesis, circumcision is a sign of the covenant between God and Abraham and Sarah. Freud's transvaluation of circumcision reconfigures the vertical covenant as a horizontal interethnic partnership. Moreover, the physiological mark of Jewish difference becomes transformed into a mark of cultural pluralism, of the common origins and common holiness of Israelite and Egyptian, and later, a sign of the people's Egyptian heritage that the Israelites *chose* to retain. Older still than the Abrahamic circumcision was its function in primitive religion, where it served as a mark of submission to the primal father.[32] In this sense, circumcision is a *Zeugnis,* a piece of evidence. But Freud introduces a second term that stands out: *Leitfossil* (key fossil). "What happened in Kadesh was a compromise, in which the share taken by the tribes of Moses is unmistakable. . . . Here we may once again call on the evidence afforded by circumcision, which has repeatedly been of help to us, like, as it were, a key fossil" (*SE,* 23:39; *SA* 9:489). The concept of a fossil recalls the "survival," or *fuero,* in Freud's 1896 letter to Fliess—a memory that cannot be translated, and is retained in its immature form. "Thus an anachronism persists: in a particular province, *fueros* are still in force; we are in the presence of 'survivals.'"[33] Screen memories are another kind of fossil, "separate mnemic residues" that elude the amnesia that governs infancy. The concept of a fossil designates the status of circumcision within Freud's memory plot. Like Michelangelo's hand, the bodily mark is not only a relic from earlier epochs, it functions as a compressed capsule of an undisclosed truth that Freud alone is able to unwrap.

The dynamic of a key fossil connects to two other topics that *Moses and Monotheism* treats at length: religion as such (or Freud's view thereof), and its analog, the neurotic symptom. Religion, like all delusions, is a "core of truth" wrapped around with "errors." This core is a kind of fossil, a relic primarily constituted by its pastness, which emerges into the present. Because it is both true and delusional, belonging to the past and yet undeniably of the present, one can speak of its compromise character. The language of compromise formation also emerges in Freud's lengthy discussion of neurosis, which he calls the "better analogy" for explaining how religious traditions operate in the collective memory.[34] Within society, religion can be said to be a fossilized domain, out of touch with "laws of logical thinking" and "the demands of the real external world" (*SE,* 23:76, 77; *SA,* 9:525). The word *fossil* recurs once more, in the final essay: "And yet in the history of religion—that is, as regards the return of the repressed—Christianity was an advance [*Fortschritt*] and from that time on the Jewish religion was to some extent a fossil [*Fossil*]" (*SE,* 23:88; *SA,* 9:536). In what sense is Judaism a fossil in the history of religion? Judaism fixes, in an ossified and nonrational form, an experience that cannot be expressed: the traumatic memory of the murder of Moses, and the eventual compromise, which together form the "essential substance" of Judaism. Christianity, by openly acknowledging a tradition of murder, guilt, and atonement, is "progressive" because it communicates that which Judaism refuses to admit to collective consciousness.

The requirement for retranscribing not only the sign of circumcision, but the fossil that is the Jewish religion as such, is a new, hybrid genre of religious memory that is able to register multiple dualities and divisions, from the double nature of Moses himself to the composite character of the Jewish nation. Freud situates his findings at the juncture of religion and *Wissenschaft*, history and epic, scholarship and art, Christianity and Judaism, Hebrew scripture and modernist poetics. By staging his rescue from one discourse by another, Freud tries to gives the impression of crossing a river by moving from stone to stone. Yet the recombination is strategic; in fact, he himself is placing the stones, building the bridge back to the past and into the future—a creative undertaking held together not so much by key fossils as by the will to create a more enlightened scripture, one true to the oppositional character of Judaism itself.

A Genre of and for the Jews

In a letter to Arnold Zweig dated September 30, 1934, Freud describes the genre of his own literary experiment. "Faced with the new persecutions, one asks oneself again how the Jews have come to be what they are and why they have attracted this undying hatred. I soon discovered the formula: Moses created the Jews. So I gave my work the title: *The Man Moses, a Historical Novel*."[35] As might be expected, Freud's self-diagnosis is double-edged. The text is historical in that Freud's purpose is to discover "what really created the particular character of the Jew" and to offer "the solution to a problem, still current today," namely, the condition of modern European Jewry.[36] The text is novelistic (and modernist) in that Freud constructs a fictional narrative on the basis of a series of double-sided, Egyptian-Hebrew traces. However, Freud elsewhere denies the straightforward generic affiliation. In the unpublished introduction of 1934, rather than argue for his application of the genre historical novel, Freud rejects the two commonplace understandings of that genre. He points out that a historical novel normally has one of two priorities: either to "affect the emotions" or to "aspire to historical truth." But Freud claims to be "neither an historian nor an artist" and to subscribe to neither goal. Thus, the work is a historical novel only in an idiosyncratic—holographic—sense.

One would be entitled to curtail the attempt [to gain knowledge of the person of Moses] as hopeless, were it not that the grandeur [*Grossartigkeit*] of the figure outweighs its elusiveness and challenges us to renewed effort. Thus, one undertakes to treat each possibility in the text as a clue, and to fill the gap between one fragment and another according to the law, so to speak, of least resistance, that is—to give preference to the assumption that has the greatest probability. *That which one can obtain by means of this technique can also be called a kind of "historical novel," since it has no proven reality, or only an unconfirmable one, for even the greatest probability does not necessarily correspond to the truth.* Truth is often very improbable, and factual evidence can only in small measure be replaced by deductions and speculations.[37] (emphasis added)

The historical novel is normally thought of as a cross between truth and fiction. Yet the binary is precisely what Freud wants to deflect, for the same reason that Martin Buber, in the preface to his study *Moses* (1947), rejects the distinction between history and saga, and that Arthur Schnitzler composed a "two-in-one" German-Jewish novel, yet resisted lending it symmetrical structure. These modernists believed the opposition between fact and fiction itself had become a fixation, a spurious approach to cultural recollection, even as the imperative to relate the events of the past to present-day concerns grew more compelling. Literary forms were needed to facilitate this more cagey refraction of the past through the present.

In "Der Dichter und das Phantasieren" (The Creative Writer and Imagining), Freud described an intricate process by which the imagination is able to fuse recent and earlier experiences in order to produce what he called a "Zukunftsbild," an image of, or for, the future. The bottom line is that the imagination, because not beholden to chronology, manipulates the events of the inner life in such a way as to fulfill a wish. In Freud's terms: "So past, present and future are threaded, as it were, on the string of the wish that runs through them all."[38] *Moses and Monotheism* reads like a wishful amalgam of past and present concerns, of memory and history, of numerous discourses, disciplines, and genres. Freud resists each one as an independent enterprise, yet he draws upon them all partially and imperfectly. The first principle of this new genre of Jewish memory is its commitment to compromise. Compromise understands itself as the mirror image of distortion, of the less mature hybrid work. Thus, Leonardo's shopping list was a "distorted" monument to his mother, since it testified to unprocessed feelings of ambivalence, whereas the late paintings—such as *Virgin and Child with Saint Anne,* where the bodies of the two mothers appear fused together—result from ambivalence turned productive. Compromise is progressive, not regressive; it is the modus operandi of fathers, and of artists. Freud's essays take numerous distorted texts as their touchstones, texts that turn out to be, like dreams, distorted in fairly legible ways. However, Freud does not use the term *distortion* to describe what he sees as "the essential outcome, the momentous substance, of the history of the Jewish religion"; he uses the notion of compromise. Freud will claim to have tracked down the numerous compromises that yielded what came to be known as "the man Moses and the monotheistic religion," but as a practitioner of cultural memory writing in an artistic mode, he invents compromises of his own.

A particularly strained compromise, by now familiar from the other essays, is the one forged between scholarship and art. The tension in *Moses and Monotheism* takes the form of his nearly simultaneous critique of history and epic, even though both evidently inspire him and both supply him with rhetorical authority. Modern history is faulted for its dialectic of enlightenment. In a critique that echoes almost verbatim that of Nietzsche, Freud argues that the historian, for all his objectivity, is a memory individual. The innumerable causes he discovers disarm him; the material proves uncontrollable, "frightening," and forces him into a series of defensive tactics such as "Zerreißung" (rupture) and oversimplification, which in turn produce artificial polarities such as truth and fiction. The result is a discourse that imposes a wholly impersonal understanding of the past. For Freud's purposes, the most glaring flaw in the historical record is its failure to pay homage to heroes.[39]

Epic poets are shortsighted for the opposite reason. Like the biographers who figure in the Leonardo essay, epic writers are primarily motivated by nostalgia for a "golden age": "Long-past ages have a great and often puzzling attraction for men's imagination. Whenever they are dissatisfied with their present surroundings—and this happens often enough—they turn back to the past and hope that they will now be able to prove the truth of the unextinguishable dream of a golden age. They are probably still under the spell of their childhood, which is presented to them by their not impartial memory as a time of uninterrupted bliss" (*SE,* 23:71; *SA,* 9:520). But this childlike quest for a blissful past is the antithesis of Freud's undertaking. Epics prove to be epigonal genres, though in one important respect they are able to render the past usable: retrieving a heroic past is another way of creating an image of and for the future.

If all that is left of the past are the incomplete and blurred memories which we call tradition, this offers an artist a peculiar attraction, for in that case he is free to fill in the gaps in memory according to the desires of his imagination and *to picture the period which he wishes to reproduce according to his intentions.* One might almost say that the vaguer a tradition has become the more serviceable it becomes for a poet. We need not therefore be surprised at the importance of tradition for imaginative writing, and the analogy with the manner in which epics are determined will make us more inclined to accept the strange hypothesis that it was the tradition of Moses which, for the Jews, altered the worship of Yahweh in the direction of the old Mosaic religion. (*SE,* 23:71; *SA,* 9:520)

The filling in of gaps in memory is what the artist has in common with the psychoanalyst; this mission does not apply to the scholar or historian. (Freud goes on to note that epics incorporate a period of latency, though he does not introduce this term until he presents his "psychopathological analogy" to the genesis of neurosis and in particular of traumatic neurosis.) Yet Freud proceeds to reject the epic as a model for two reasons that bring his own methodology into sharp focus. First, he upholds the principal distinction between artistic and religious memory. Artistic memory (*Dichtung*) is too "free," too unconcerned with fidelity to the past. Freud allows that anyone who undertakes to convey religious memory is subject to *Treue,* fidelity to the past. Freud distances himself from imaginative literature, not as a scholar, but as one who, by a strained circumnavigation, turns out to be loyal to religious tradition and does not claim to invent tradition. The second critique of the epic is that it is finally an unpsychological genre, too "rational," unable to convey the essentially compulsive character that Freud associates with the resurrection of forgotten experiences. This notion is commonplace in the early twentieth century, where the novel is deemed "modern" and psychological (Lukács).

Despite his admiration for artists, they are not Freud's primary authority here (as they were in the prior two essays). Despite his well-known admiration for rational intellectuality, Freud comes down hard on rational approaches to memory. Despite his well-known disdain for religion (and disregard for the metaphysical side of the same), he struggles throughout the essay to discover a sense in which religion is valid or true. Once Freud has considered and rejected the approaches of religious writers, historians, and poets, he is in a position to make his primary contribution to our understanding of "the one man Moses, who created the Jews" (*SE*, 23:106; *SA*, 9:553). This insight is not only a matter of asserting that the first Moses was an Egyptian and that the repressed memory of Moses's murder formed the basis of Judaism. Freud is equally interested in how it was possible for this episode to disappear from the sources, elude mention in scripture, live on to become even more powerful over time, shape the essential character of the Jewish people, and finally emerge from oblivion and resurface in the present day and present context. This ultimate expression of Mosaic memory, which is also the genre that best captures the remembered-forgotten character of all that is most important in life, is "tradition." Tradition, as Richard Bernstein elucidates it, operates in ways exactly parallel to unconscious memory in the case of the individual.[40] The concept of tradition pays homage to the enigma of memory: the sheer force of characters who endure, and past ideas that resurface, and the wholly unpredictably ways in which they do so. Allying himself with the tradition of Moses enables Freud to approach not only Mosaic monotheism, but also all religion, from the perspective of unconscious memory rather than conscious transmission; most importantly, it legitimates his own counterscriptural writing, even granting him a type of irrefutability that he refers to as "historical truth."[41] Religion, like all that which returns from oblivion, "exercises an incomparably powerful influence on people in the mass, and raises an irresistible claim to truth against which logical objections remain powerless." Freud wrote that approaching religion as a historical rather than material phenomenon allowed him to move beyond the "essentially negative valuation of religion" articulated in *The Future of an Illusion.*[42]

Tradition, by definition, has a hybrid character: Freud provocatively describes it as "the supplement and contradiction" of the official record. Traditions behave sometimes like poets and at other times like historians, combining truth and fiction in ways that neither the historian nor the artist would recognize. The tradition of "a single great god," for example, is "a completely justified memory, though, it is true, one that has been distorted. An idea such as this has a compulsive character: it *must* be believed. To the extent to which it is distorted, it may be described as a *delusion* [*Wahn*]; in so far as it brings a return of the past, it must be called the *truth* [*Wahrheit*]" (*SE*, 23:130; *SA*, 9:575; emphasis added). Tradition interweaves objective and subjective realities in ways that are justified and, if not actually true, then virtually so. In this respect, and as others have noted, the faculty of belief—though not in the normative sense—returns into Freud's text through the back door. As Yerushalmi

writes, "The return of the repressed is the Freudian counterpart to biblical revelation, both equally momentous and unfathomable, each ultimately dependent, not
on historical evidence, but on a certain kind of faith, in order to be credible."[43] But
the ramifications of tradition surpass its contribution to religious history. Tradition
is Freud's third term in the way that the faculty of the imagination surpasses and
links conscious and unconscious forms of recollection. But the concept also hearkens back to the very early hypothesis that consciousness and memory are incompatible within one and the same system, and suggests that the fascination with the
incommunicable truths that a group manages to transmit over time, through indi-
rect channels, resonates in other domains of Freudian inquiry. The same dynamic
led to the invention of transference in the psychoanalytic context, as well as to the
investigation into the mystery of art.

A tradition that was based only on communication [*Mitteilung*] could not lead to the compulsive character that attaches to religious phenomena. It would be listened to, judged,
and perhaps dismissed, like any other piece of information [*Nachricht*] from outside; it
would never attain the privilege of being liberated from the constraint of logical thought. It
must have undergone the fate of being repressed, the condition of lingering in the unconscious [*des Verweilen im Unbewußten*], before it is able to display such powerful effects on
its return, to bring the masses under its spell, as we have seen with astonishment and hitherto without comprehension in the case of religious tradition. (*SE*, 23:101; *SA*, 9:548)

Lastly: in what sense is Freud's tradition of Moses "the supplement and at the
same time the contradiction of the writing of history"? This paradox gets to the heart
of what makes tradition the prototype of Freud's modernism. Freudian tradition is
an imperfect form of compromise—a minor compromise, in just the way that
Michelangelo's Moses statue and Leonardo da Vinci's late masterpieces are monumental compromises. Traditions, it turns out, are not unlike scripture and history
after all; they are distorted, though not because subject to "distorting tendencies"
[*entstellende Tendenzen*] such as political, nationalistic, and pietistic influences, which
delegitimize the codified accounts. The legacies that elude this process are far more
probable in Freud's eyes than those written sources. Yet tradition too is subject to
changes and disfigurements; it is "vulnerable to being crushed," "incomplete," and
"fluid," naturally distorted, or innocently so (*SE*, 23:69; *SA*, 9:518).[44]

In this chapter, I have extended my inquiry into the construction of memory
in fin de siècle Vienna to the province of Freudian psychology, where the cultural
issues receive their most theoretically nuanced and far-reaching formulations. Like
Moses and Monotheism, the works I discuss in subsequent chapters respond to dilemmas of collective identity through generic experimentation. Hofmannsthal and Beer-
Hofmann also retrieve heroic figures from Hebrew scripture; Schnitzler's Jewish
characters, while situated in the historical present, likewise take a counterideologi-
cal stance to the question of Jewish destiny. Though each of these works was written

prior to Freud's Moses book, I have placed the latter work first, since it displays in the most extreme way tendencies common to all: the awkward consolidation of a new genre of Jewish discourse out of extant scholarly modes and artistic forms; the compulsion to resist tendentious interpretations and to frustrate or undermine the expectations of readers; the problematization of Jewish heroism; and, in the cases of Schnitzler and Beer-Hofmann, the eschewal of a Jewish nationalist ethos in the name of liberal humanism.

2 Hofmannsthal's Jewish Pantomime

Der Schüler (The Student, 1901)

In this way, in pure gestures, the true personality comes to light.
—Hugo von Hofmannsthal

The facts are these: I connect with Judaism through the person of my paternal great-grandfather, born in 1759. Whose son early on [became] a Christian—following a highly natural tendency, a tendency that at the beginning of the nineteenth century was virtually the only possible one in order to step out of a seclusion that was no longer imaginable, into the domain of what was viewed as the human, the universal—in Mailand got married to a young person from an ancient bourgeois Mailander family (in prior centuries, an aristocratic one). Out of this Roman admixture, if you want to pursue it further, some things in the style of my works may be explained—my father, the son of these two, married the daughter of a Viennese notary, who was the son of lower Austrian farmers; the family has lived in the same village for countless centuries. My mother's mother, lastly, was the daughter of a Swabian who had migrated to the Donau, an innkeeper who descended from a craftsman (blacksmith) from Ulm. . . .

These aforementioned facts, which I assume are more or less known, were perhaps unknown to you and may alter the direction of your thoughts. Or perhaps not; we live in an increasingly confusing world, and the sense of responsibility about what we describe as "spiritual connections" is so weakened that even this is possible. In that event, I remain utterly vulnerable. . . .

My position as artist in the contemporary world is infinitely precarious. One can view my entire oeuvre as a difficult, strange self-affirmation.[1]

The facts triggering Hofmannsthal's statement of the facts are these: in 1922, the Jewish literary critic Willy Haas (1891–1973) contributed an essay on Hofmannsthal to Gustav Krojanker's anthology *Juden in der deutschen Literatur* (Jews in German Literature).[2] Haas took the "nowhere and everywhere" approach to Hofmannsthal's oeuvre, arguing that Jewishness, though nowhere explicit, was everywhere implicit.

Die Ahnentafel des Dichters Hugo von Hofmannsthal.
Von Arthur Czellitzer, Berlin.

Im Juli 1929 folgte der sprachgewaltige Dichter seinem heißgeliebten Sohne in den Tod. Sein Wunsch, in einer Mönchskutte bestattet zu werden, zeigt die Innigkeit, mit der er dem Katholizismus sich verbunden fühlte; und doch war er im Mannesstamm einer jüdischen Familie entsprossen, die sich in zahlreichen Persönlichkeiten um das Judentum Österreichs und besonders das Wiener wohlverdient gemacht haben. Die nachfolgende Tafel soll die Blutmischung seiner Abstammung klarstellen:

Isaak Löw¹) Hofmann — Reserl²) Schefteles — Anton von Rho³) — Cäcilia Bossi — Fohleutner — Schmid

August Hofmann⁴) seit 13.VIII.1833 geadelt als H. Edler von Hofmannsthal — Petronella von Rho — Dr. iur. Lorenz⁵) Fohleutner — Josefine Schmid

Hugo H. von Hofmannsthal⁶) — Anna Fohleutner

Hugo H. von Hofmannsthal
1874—1929

¹) Isak Lör Hofmann wurde 1763 in Prostiebor bei Pilsen geboren; die Hofmanns stammten aus der Fürther Gegend, wo sie, in dem Dorfe Preifeld schon im 17. Jahrh. nachweislich sind. Als junger Mann kam er über Prag nach Wien, erwarb dort als Großkaufmann Reichtum und Ansehen. Großzügig und unternehmungslustig führte er die Seidenkultur ein und erntete als kaiserliche Anerkennung das Adelsprädikat mit einem Wappen, das auf seinen besonderen Wunsch die Gesetzestafeln von Sinai enthielt. Er starb in Wien 1849 als Vorsteher der Israelitischen Kultusgemeinde; seine zahlreichen Kinder heirateten in angesehene Adelsfamilien wie die Wittgenstein, Grafen Rasumofsky, Freiherrn v. Burian, v. Schey, Karabacek u. a. Einer seiner Söhne war Dr. Ignaz H., geboren 22. Mai 1807 in Wien, der als Arzt des israelitischen Spitals, als Präsident der israelitischen Taubstummenanstalt und der Kultusgemeinde und hochherziger Freund der Armen in Wien noch heute unvergessen ist. Dessen Enkel ist der Pazifist und Eherechtsreformer Dr. iur. Emil von H., geb. 30. Dezember 1884 zu Wien.

²) Reserl wurde 1770 zu Prag geboren als die Tochter des dortigen Kaufmanns Wolf Schefteles; ihre Mutter stammte aus Königswarth bei Marien-

bad, wo ihr Vater Joel Baruch und seine Vorfahren als Metternichsche Schutzjuden saßen.

³) Anton von Rho lebte in Mailand als Sproß einer alten lombardischen Familie, zu der Gerhardus de Rho gehörte, ein Historiker des 17. Jahrhunderts. Auch die Bossi waren eine altangesehene Mailänder Familie.

⁴) August v. H. (1815 in Wien geboren, 1881 daselbst gestorben) wurde dem Judentum abtrünnig und heiratete 1839 das Mailänder Edelfräulein Petronella von Rho.

⁵) Dr. iur. Lorenz Fohleutner war Notar und Advokat zu Wien.

⁶) Hugo (der ältere) v. H. war Direktor der österreichischen Bodenkreditbank.

Die jüdischen Familien von Zülz O.S. 1725.
Von Bernhard Brilling, Breslau. (Forts.)
II.

In meinem ersten Artikel über die Zülzer Juden (vgl. 1928 Nr. 3, S. 72—76 dieser Zeitschrift) brachte ich das Verzeichnis der jüdischen Hausbesitzer nebst den ihrer jüdischen Mieter. Es war ursprünglich nur ein reines Namensregister (das nur aus den Unterschriften zu den Steuererklärungen bestand), aus dem ich eine Art Zülzer jüdischer Prosopographie (d. h. Zusammenstellung aller eine gewisse Person betreffenden Notizen) zu machen versuchte. Wenn dort nämlich z. B. nur Nathan Perlhefter angegeben war, so gab ich selbstverständlich alles Material, das mir über diese Person zur Hand war, bei. Der erste, nun bereits veröffentlichte Teil enthielt die Oberschicht der Gemeinde, nämlich die 34 Hausbesitzer (zwei Häuser waren außerdem im Besitz der jüdischen Gemeinde). Unter diesen Hausbesitzern finden sich natürlich diejenigen Persönlichkeiten, die Unter bekleideten und politische Verhandlungen führten (wie z. B. Jacob Gerstel Nr. 117) und diejenigen, die die schlesischen Münzen mit den benötigten Metallen belieferten, die zur Messe nach Leipzig fuhren, und endlich diejenigen, die schon Träger eines berühmten Namens waren, wie die Perlhefter (-Bruck) und Sachs. Unter diesen Hausbesitzern gab es 8 nachweisbare Münzlieferanten; 2 dieser Hausbesitzer hatten sogar noch neben ihrem Haus in der Judenstadt auch eine Wohnung (man würden heute „Filialen" sagen) in der Christenstadt gemietet; es waren dies ein Tabak- und Salzhändler, sowie ein Kaufmann, der mit Leinwand, Schleier und Wollzeug handelte (es handelt sich um die Hausbesitzer Nr. 135 und 121).

Diese jüdischen Hausbesitzer hatten natürlich nur jüdische Mieter, die wir bei den betreffenden Häusern bereits in der ersten Liste mit angegeben haben. Ihre Zahl betrug 23, unter denen sich der „Judendoktor" sowie drei jüdische Schulmeister befinden. Diese 23 Familien bildeten zusammen mit den 38 bei Christen wohnenden jüdischen Familien die untere Schicht der Gemeinde, die die niederen Berufe stellte. Unter ihnen befindet sich niemand, der die Münze beliefert, noch jemand, der auf der Leipziger Messe erscheinen kann (eine Ausnahme bildet der Gewürz- und Tabakhändler Löbel Markus, Hsnr. 11, der 1753 auf dieser Messe anwesend ist.) Es sind die Juden, die in allen Lande als „Kober" oder „Puttenträger" ihren Lebensunterhalt erwerben mußten — ein Beruf, den wir unter der Bezeichnung „Medine-Geier" (= Landgeber) kennen. Die jüdische Gemeinde in Zülz umfaßt nach dem vorliegenden Kataster 1725 also 95 Familien,

7. The newsletter of the Society for Jewish Family Research illustrated Hofmannsthal's family tree. The article begins: "In July 1929, the powerfully eloquent poet followed his dearly beloved son into death. His wish to be buried in a monk's cowl shows his affection for Catholicism; and yet, on the male side of the family he sprang from a *Jewish* family." Jüdisches Museum der Stadt Wien, Bibliothek.

Hofmannsthal took issue with this interpretation. In the letter cited above, he defends himself by recounting family history, as if, by localizing a certain strain of the past, he could contain or delimit its significance—just the opposite of what Haas had done. Yet these certainties give way to expressions of vulnerability and precariousness. The more details he provides, the clearer it becomes to him that the hard facts of history—dates and geography—are scarcely able to supply a foothold for identity in the contemporary world, let alone to shield him from the misuse of biography by those determined to typecast him. A striking example of the Jewish territorialization of Hofmannsthal's biography is the spate of articles that appeared in the Jewish press shortly after his death devoted not to the career, but to the Jewish lineage (fig. 7). No wonder Hofmannsthal had asked to be buried in a monk's cowl.

It is perhaps inevitable that the relevance of Hofmannsthal's work to the politics of Jewish identity at the turn of the century has remained an open question. The almost complete exclusion of explicitly Jewish themes from his literary oeuvre, critical writings, and correspondence, has done its share to forestall inquiry into how Jewish concerns influenced Hofmannsthal and vice versa. Though it has become commonplace to acknowledge the author's Jewish ancestry, scholars have been unable to offer a plausible reading of the literary oeuvre in terms of Jewish concerns without resorting to one of the two essentialisms mentioned earlier: either Jewishness is expressed by virtue of racial affiliation or it is nowhere to be found. The exception remains Hermann Broch's classic essay of 1947, reissued in 1964 and again in 2001, which constructs the author as an exemplary product of second-stage Jewish assimilation.[3] Hofmannsthal's dominant reputation remains "repressed, one-quarter Jewish." In the *Yale Companion to Jewish Writing and Thought in German Culture* (1996)—the latest episode in the genre initiated by Krojanker—the entry on Hofmannsthal is titled "Hugo von Hofmannsthal Worries About His Jewish Mixed Ancestry," and the news remains biographical, even though the object of biography was a literary subject.[4]

Two scholarly initiatives of the 1990s provide important inroads into the largely uncharted territory of Hofmannsthal's Jewish consciousness. Jens Rieckmann's 1993 article brings hitherto unknown evidence from the author's early unpublished letters and diaries confirming that the young writer was preoccupied with his Jewish heritage, an issue Rieckmann locates somewhere on that psychic continuum "between consciousness and repression."[5] These texts disclose ambivalence wholly typical of assimilated Viennese Jews—anger at anti-Semitism, for example, alternating with antipathy toward "typical" Jewish traits—but they also contain some surprises. In the course of a letter written when he was only thirteen, Hofmannsthal describes in empathetic tones the predicament of emancipated Jewry at the end of the nineteenth century—the circumstances of his own family history. Hofmannsthal bemoans the fact that once the European Jews were prohibited access to channels of intellectual betterment ("geistiger Aufschwung"), they were driven to improve their lot in material (or materialistic) ways, squandering in the process their spiritual-ethical legacy. Regarding his own Jewish legacy, a single negative association predominates: Jewishness bequeaths a decadent mode of thinking ("Reflexion"; "jüdische Denkungsweise") that is detrimental to life and to that most precious of neo-romantic capabilities: the capacity for "experience" ("Erlebnis").[6] Only after 1899, Rieckmann speculates, does Hofmannsthal repress these concerns, driven by the need to promote a modernist ethos (and to cultivate an authorial image) that was strictly German and untainted by decadence and epigonality.[7]

While Rieckmann's findings provide important new documentation, Michael P. Steinberg's *The Meaning of the Salzburg Festival* (1990) addresses a methodological impasse in Viennese cultural studies. In Steinberg's view, lack of evidence is not the primary obstacle to a straightforward consideration of Hofmannsthal's religious position(s); what is lacking is a conceptual model of identity adequate to the range of options facing Viennese artists and thinkers. Steinberg criticizes the tendency to reduce Jewish identity—a "crucial and ambiguous" part of their lives—to a range of quantifiable or deterministic traits (such as "one-quarter Jew"). He proposes that a recuperation of what it meant to be a Jewish artist during this period (or a Jew pure and simple) requires a theoretical redirection: "In discussing Austrian intellectual culture between 1890 and 1938 we need to identify two intersecting spectra: the spectrum from the critical, avant-garde, or revolutionary to the conservative, and the cultural and religious spectrum with Jewishness as the position least integrated into mainstream society, Protestantness as the middle position, and Catholicity as the most integrated position."[8] In light of the double code, Steinberg reads Hofmannsthal's development from the alienated, modernist poet of the Chandos period into the nationalist, collectivist author of *Jedermann* and *Das Salzburger große Welttheater* as accompanying a turn from a Jewish to a Catholic aesthetic. The artistic metamorphosis can then be seen to parallel a transformation in Hofmannsthal's ethnic/religious identity, while reminding us that for him, as for others, the motive was not primarily religious, but reflective of the "desire to participate in public forms of meaning, to adapt their minds, intellectually and spiritually, to the dominant culture." Thus is born the paradoxical phenomenon Steinberg calls "the Catholic culture of Austrian Jews," exemplified by the creation of the Salzburg Festival plays.[9]

Steinberg's call for "a model . . . that can interpret the relations of ambiguous but intense patterns of intellectual and cultural production by stressing questions of meaning and avoiding assumptions of deterministic causality" is a good first step in understanding what, beyond genealogy, constitutes a writer's Jewishness.[10] To this twofold "cultural and religious spectrum," however, I would want to add a third variable, namely, the literary and journalistic forms of communication that these Jewish writers selected and combined. For these writers, including Freud, the medium was the message, because all media were understood ahead of time as embroiled in the polemics of anti-Semitism and incipient nationalism.

If any medium could hope to fend off the inevitable, it was the ballet-pantomime, a form Hofmannsthal discovered on a trip to Paris in 1900 and enthusiastically embraced.[11] This chapter concentrates on the pantomime that came to be called *Der Schüler.* It was published in the November 1901 issue of *Neue Deutsche Rundschau,* the literary periodical of the Fischer Verlag, and performed the following year in Vienna and Berlin.[12] The original manuscript, dated September 1901 and titled "Pantomime," is cast for Jewish characters of Eastern European origin, or *Ostjuden.* The Jewish pantomime became a site of Hofmannsthal's own resistance, a disburdening that he then had the burden of covering up. Hofmannsthal retracted twenty-three hundred copies of the text published to accompany the pantomime performance prior to distribution.[13] A more provocative retraction occurred even before its appearance in the periodical: Hofmannsthal doctored the characters by changing the two explicitly Jewish figures, "der Rabbi" and "der Bocher" (Yiddish: the student) into "ein gelehrter Alchimist" (a learned alchemist) and "der Schüler." The omission of Jewish names is the only difference between the manuscript and published versions of the work. One might argue that, while this erasure masks the most conspicuous evidence of the figures' Jewish origins, it is on another level an ironic gesture, for it leaves the characters in the performed pantomime otherwise unchanged—a fact that may explain why the author went on to retract the piece in toto. Add to this erasure the further one of adopting the minor genre of pantomime and then avoiding any discussion of it in correspondence, and all the seeds of forgetting are in place: criticism has by and large excluded *Der Schüler* from consideration, and of the few who do consider the text, none has incorporated the Jewish version into his or her reading.[14]

The pantomime quite literally enacts the disappearance of Jewish themes. Written originally with Jewish characters, *Der Schüler* became, under its author's editing, a text without Jewish characters and no ostensible connection to the Jewish question. Its holographic character is expressed quite openly in its Italian epigraph: "Scaramuccio non parla, et dice gran cose" (Scaramouche does not speak, and says much). The genre invoked by the epigraph is the improvisational theater called *commedia dell'arte,* which was popular in the sixteenth through the eighteenth centuries. Scaramuccio was an adventurer, identified by his black velvet mask and black garb. Hofmannsthal found the citation in a 1694 French collection called *Le theatre italien,* though as Karin Wolgast notes, he could have easily written it himself.[15] In this performance, the black-masked adventurer is the poet who described his status as a writer of Jewish origins in modern times as "infinitely precarious." The advantage of looking closely at this minor text is to be able to observe better the tactics by which Jewish concerns are both encoded and concealed in Jewish writing throughout the modernist tradition. In the case of *Der Schüler,* Jewish modernism provides both tradition and countertradition, and in the case of the author's biography, the "supplement and the contradiction" of the bare facts. The competing ethnic and cultural tendencies the pantomime incorporates refuse to coalesce into a single story; indeed, the combination of a German text, Italian genre and epigraph transmitted through a French source, and Yiddish-speaking characters reminds us of the most striking diary entry cited in Rieckmann's article: "What if the sum total of my inner developments and struggles were nothing more than agitations of my inherited blood, rebellions of the Jewish blood-drops (Reflection) against the Germanic and Romanic, and reactions against these rebellions?"[16] Jewish, Romanic, Germanic: each heritage played a significant role in the poet's early life. The paternal great-grandfather, Isaac Löw Hofmann (1759–1849), began life as a yeshiva *bocher* (student) in Prague and rose to become a leader of the Viennese Jewish community, a silk manufacturer and philanthropist who, upon his ennoblement by Emperor Ferdinand in 1835, received special permission to place the decalogue on his coat of arms. His portrait hangs today in the Jewish Museum of Vienna. Also important is the fact that Hofmannsthal married a Jewish woman, Gertrude Schlesinger. His paternal grandmother, Petronella von Rho, was an Italian Catholic, and his dissertation (1898) and *Habilitation* (1901) were in the fields of Romance philology and literature. German, of course, identifies Hofmannsthal's primary cultural endowment (*Bildung*) and all that makes him a poet in his own right. Indeed, *Der Schüler* not only bears the imprint of each of these legacies, its plot mirrors the turbulence of their interaction in the poet's psyche: "rebellions . . . and reactions against those rebellions."

A PANTOMIME IN ONE ACT

The key to the work's unique status within Hofmannsthal's oeuvre and to its status as a formative work of Viennese Jewish modernism is his creative deployment of the pantomime genre. Not quite poetry, not quite drama, the pantomime marks Hofmannsthal's transition from the "lyric decade" to the performative works of the middle and late periods, in particular to the dramas of 1903–5. A liminal form in many respects, pantomime represents an artistic strategy by which the modernist— and his audience—can disengage from the predetermining narratives of identity, be they ethnic, religious, or cultural, and reconnect with them in a more self-conscious and productive way. Hofmannsthal explicates the strategy ten years later in his essay *Über die Pantomime* (On Pantomime); it can be summarized by the following paradox. In a pantomime, as in dance, the unspeakable becomes the condition of creative expression; form allows the Jewish and non-Jewish versions to intersect and inform one another. This condition enabled Hofmannsthal to unburden himself of a story that was highly sensitive for personal and political reasons, to transgress a taboo, to "say much without speaking." But it also enabled him to do something even riskier. The versatility of the genre makes *Der Schüler* a richly allusive work, one that, upon closer examination, reveals itself embedded in a range of intertextual narratives: European, Jewish, German. Moreover, far from being anomalous in the Hofmannsthal canon, the pantomime echoes key motifs from the lyric decade and anticipates much that is to come, above all in the drama *Elektra* (1903). A transitional work in more than just the formal sense, the pantomime establishes Hofmannsthal's role in Jewish modernism and the reach of that singular performance in the "non-Jewish" oeuvre.

Der Schüler—my summary will conflate the manuscript and published versions—opens on a cold winter night in a proverbial "windowless, vaulted room," where the Rabbi (or Alchemist) sits hovering over his folios, mumbling, his hands restlessly moving from book to book.[17] He suddenly discovers that three books contain "das gleiche" (the same thing). This revelation prompts a triumphant conclusion: "Now I am great. Now I am in a position to blow the breath of life through my lips. My shadow, who cowers behind me, who lies in wait here behind my chair, I can breathe into him the breath of life. Here it is written. Now I shall do it" (55).[18] With the help of a magic ring, the Rabbi succeeds in animating his shadow, who wears a beard and hat like his own. Momentarily stunned, the Rabbi commands the shadow to kneel. When the shadow obeys, he declares, "I am no longer human, now that I have done this," and proceeds to dance about the room for joy (56).[19] The final interaction brings an even greater pleasure: the shadow kisses his feet.

The first pantomime ends when the Rabbi's raven-haired daughter, Taube, enters the room. Taube dispels the narcissistic hallucination by turning on the light and chastising her father's "Grübeln und Lesen" (brooding and reading), until she herself becomes trapped in his conceit. Her father revels in her beauty, her "beautiful hands," and lasciviously fondles her hair, "a fleece in which one can wrap oneself when it is cold outside" (57).[20] This fantasy is dispelled in turn by the arrival of the Bocher (or Student), who no less than the shadow and the daughter proves to be at the Rabbi's mercy. He is weighted down by books carried under each arm, but unlike his mentor, he finds no correspondence between them, and laments, "the two books do not agree" (57). A related complaint follows later: "All these books here, and these here, and those there are dead to the heart, they nourish only the brain! In the brain, wishes, desires, dreams are gathering, yet no lustful feelings flow to the heart, no surging of joy to the heart! My heart withers!"(59)

In response to his student's accusation that the two books do not agree, the Rabbi places them on the table and performs the following demonstration:

This (*he points with the right hand to the book lying to his left*),
Refers to that! (*Here he points with his left hand to the book lying to his right.*)
And this here (*his right hand pages forward through the book on the left*),
Can be explained by this here (*his left hand opens to a place in the book on the right*).
Thus, the two are in total agreement.
Now do you understand? (58)

The Rabbi's parodic gesticulations, like the incestuous fondling of his daughter, confirm the corruption of the generational chain. In both cases, guilt is written on the Rabbi's hands. By crossing his hands, the Rabbi simultaneously bequeaths and withholds the textual legacy—the knowledge he appears still to command. At the point when truth becomes displaced from the book onto the body (pantomime), and teaching, from the heart to the hands of the hermeneut, transmission from past to present devolves into malicious parody and worse.

A third pantomime follows, this one again directed at Taube. After the Rabbi loses patience with his disciple, he turns to his daughter and, moving his hips suggestively, commands her to dance for him. "Tanz mein Kind, tanz für deinen Vater!" (58) Taube refuses to dance, but the Rabbi hypnotizes her with the magic ring and she begins to dance wildly, playing with her hair "as if with a veil" until her father tells her it is enough. The Bocher, now cast the role of spectator, doubles over in pleasure. When permitted to stop, the panting Taube staggers offstage into her own room. The Bocher then begins to plead for the Rabbi's ring, not to marry Taube, ironically, but to control her "if only for one hour." It is when his teacher tells him to go study that the Bocher scorns books and learning, and continues to importune his teacher, kissing his feet and garment.

The next scene, an encounter between the tortured Bocher and the daughter, conveys the extent of the Bocher's plight. *He:* "I love you, I do, it is I who desires you,

I!" *She:* "You? You—me? Fool!" *He:* "Why not me? Why not me?" *She:* "Your hair is disgusting. Your eyes are red-rimmed. Your hands are too dirty!" The Bocher tears at his hair madly, gnaws at his fingers. Taube remarks: "Your body is too ugly for me!" and runs to her room (60–61).[21]

The remainder of the plot bifurcates into two separate pantomimes of resistance against the Rabbi, which then coincide, by sheer accident, to bring about the self-destruction of the two young resisters. Taube and the Bocher each conspire to escape. The daughter attempts to send a letter she has written; this is a gesture with larger implications in canonical daughter plots, as we shall see. The letter is ostensibly addressed to a rival suitor, and thus the Bocher refuses to deliver it for her. Since the Rabbi has appointed a blind maid to guard her door, Taube masquerades as her father in order to escape and post the letter. "She imitates, by leaning on a cane, the old man's wearisome shuffle, coughs, stamps on the floor with the stick" (63). Meanwhile, the Bocher enlists a red-bearded tramp to murder the Rabbi and procure the magic ring. Significantly, he reaches this fatal decision by way of a series of signs. He turns first to the dice. "What shall I do?" cries the Bocher. "I'll throw the dice. Six means life, one means death." Thrice in a row the Bocher throws a pair of ones. "I'll wait for one further sign. *Looks around in grisly anticipation. Suddenly, the pendulum stands still. His face exudes demonic joy.* I am only carrying out his destiny. And she will belong to me!" (64).[22] But when Taube returns from her errand, the Bocher and the tramp mistake the disguised Taube for her father and kill her in his stead. Believing initially that their plan has succeeded, they prop up the corpse in the Rabbi's chair and dance wildly, "like two demons," around the room (65). When the Bocher realizes their mistake, he turns on the tramp; the pair flee just as the Rabbi returns from the "evening service" (65). The Rabbi likewise mistakes Taube for his own shadow; he sees it sitting at his desk, "animated by a higher force," and dances around the effigy, circling it three times before leaving the stage. The viewer is left with an exact replica of the opening tableau. The libretto concludes on an ironic note: "The figure, immersed in the holy book, appears not to have noticed him, and he disappears in awe into the alcove, leaving behind the mute reader" (66).[23]

A daughter's corpse, a father's shadow, a reader struck dumb: untangling the many layers of this final impression alone encapsulates the challenge of interpreting a work at once so rich in literary allusion—to Lessing's *Nathan der Weise,* Goethe's *Faust,* Wilde's *Salomé*—and yet also sui generis. A pantomime that spurns books, yet draws upon the literary canon to do so, is a qualified rebellion at best. However forceful the message of the plot (that disburdenment and escape are the only desirable routes for the young), the imperative of the genre (to uncover a silent plot lurking behind the written plot) is more powerful still. Hofmannsthal's Italian epigraph makes exquisite sense. In proclaiming its own duplicity, the motto proves to be prescriptive, and it challenges the reader/spectator to enter into this thicket of duplicitous behavior. *Der Schüler* calls for an interpretive strategy that accounts for the double intention expressed in its epigraph and literalized in its plot. To do otherwise would be to grant the racist optic the last word. Locating a redemptive intention to this work entails reversing Hofmannsthal's cover-up: reuniting the Jewish and non-Jewish versions, restoring to the characters their Jewish shadows, and to the Jewish characters their European counterparts, in the interest of reminding ourselves of what Hofmannsthal tried so hard to forget.

THE TAINTED PANTOMIME

When Daviau calls *Der Schüler* "as pessimistic, indeed as nihilistic a work Hofmannsthal ever created," he takes the bait, as does Wolgast when she speculates that the work was retracted because it was simply too violent. This is the message the pantomime would have sent had Hofmannsthal retained the Jewish names—the interpretation he halfheartedly tried to cover up. It goes like this: By staging the final vignette as a visual reprise of the first, Hofmannsthal conveys that the three interlocking escape initiatives we have witnessed are equally futile, that the three *do* contain the same thing. The Rabbi can no more escape his shadow than Taube can escape her daughterhood or the Bocher, his books. The nihilistic interpretation is driven by its racial dimension: Jews who attempt to escape their shadows only bring destruction upon themselves.

Why would a writer betray his own people in this way, unless he was, like Otto Weininger, a self-hating Jew? Every racist culture treats its victims as types, as if they were players in a pantomime, and in turn-of-the-century Vienna, no body was as discursively predetermined as the Jewish body. *Der Schüler* plays upon the stereotype of Jewish discourse as pantomimic in a pejorative sense: a language that is not only accompanied by physical gestures, but in itself illogical, a mere trick of association like the Rabbi's crossing of the hands. Thinking disintegrates into a mindless clamor; minds imitate bodies and cripple them as a result. The familiar caricature of the male Jewish scholar, complete with tubercular cough, limping gait, and frenetic gesticulations, is one that, in light of Hofmannsthal's diary entry, we can assume he took seriously. The shadow who "cowers and lurks" at the Rabbi's side represents the outward projection of the diseased Jewish physique. Even when Hofmannsthal purges the "Alchimist" of his rabbinic lineage and appends an Italian epigraph to the pantomime, the tainted pantomime abides: in the Rabbi's *pilpul,* the Bocher's hand-wringing, the daughter's incestuous masquerade—in the numerous motifs of empty mimicry, blindness, and deception, which lead inexorably to a violent outcome. That the Jews self-destruct because they have so thoroughly introjected the image of their own impotence and self-hatred represents the tragic part of what a character in Schnitzler's Jewish novel *Der Weg ins Freie* calls "the tragicomedy of contemporary Judaism."

But for Hofmannsthal, as for Schnitzler, the generational rage driving the stereotypical Jewish plots runs deeper than racial politics. Schnitzler makes this clear by composing his Jewish novel as a hybrid of a German bildungsroman and a Jewish roman à clef, and Hofmannsthal does the same by overlaying an Italian-German pantomime over a Jewish one. In Schnitzler's novel, the crippling of the young generation is embodied in Georg and Anna's plot. *Der Schüler* depicts children foundering because of the narcissism of the father, who is himself an epigone. Epitomizing this crisis are the moments when communication lapses into mimicry, and resistance into parody. The force of violence that causes difference to collapse into identity surfaces throughout the German modernist tradition, as for example in Franz Kafka's *Der Prozess* (The Trial), where the artist Titorelli's three identical landscape portraits stand for the gruesome realization that the three possible resolutions to Josef K.'s trial all amount to the same thing: no way out. The parallel to the three paintings is the initial correspondence among the Rabbi's three books. The pantomime implicitly blames the fetishization of text culture for the Rabbi's physiological decline and moral degeneracy. His intellectual inquiry, *grübeln,* involves reading with the hands rather than the heart, and this leads us to suspect that the "identity" he discerns is not about divine revelation or inspired knowledge. In contrast to the benevolent father of Lessing's ring parable, the Rabbi refuses to transmit the ring—symbol of material wealth, spiritual sustenance, and mystical power—to his living heirs; he uses it rather to disable them. When the Rabbi dances in the opening vignette, it is only because the degenerate self has been exorcised. But one generation's shadow becomes the next generation's dybbuk: a disembodied spirit that, in the classic Yiddish folklore, takes possession of the innocent. Both the Bocher and the daughter are trapped within the Rabbi's narcissistic plot, denied the means to become characters in their own right. The Bocher appears to suffer from the condition Hofmannsthal referred to as a "jüdische Denkungsweise": an overly reflective disposition that stifles vitality. However, he is no less representative of the generation of "wandering encyclopedias" whom Nietzsche diagnoses in *Vom Nutzen und Nachteile der Historie für das Leben* (On the Uses and Disadvantages of History for Life) as suffering from a rift between intellect and spirit. Moreover, what if both of these afflictions—one Jewish, one German—in fact have a common genesis? The Bocher carries the heavy tomes in frostbitten fingers but has no access to the hermeneutic code or to the ring; thus, his impotence degenerates into depravity, and his resistance plot, into farce, since in resisting the Rabbi, he ends up imitating him by victimizing Taube, the object of their mutual desire. Taube's attempt to escape the patriarchal economy leads her to mimic the father in a similar way: to abuse the Bocher and to clothe herself in the very shadow her father has expelled. Though her masquerade allows temporary escape from daughterly destiny—more on this later—it unwittingly delivers her into her next role, that of the scapegoat. Such generational rage surfaces frequently in Hofmannsthal's early oeuvre, though seldom with such lethal consequences.

The Rabbi's self-disburdening is a primary transgression that creates an economy of guilt that demands retribution. The exorcised shadow self retaliates by causing the daughter's sacrifice. Precisely that which the Rabbi believes to have been discarded or repressed is visited upon the next generation. This collapsed and contorted revenge cycle begins when the father commands his daughter to dance. Her debasement links her symbolically to the shadow; she becomes the second figure for the father's destiny, now thought to be fully under his dominion. The consequences of exorcism/creation become clear. The father-daughter dyad is defined by violation but also by guilt; as in the case of Herod and Salome, the incestuous dance makes explicit the father's guilt relation to his offspring. Guilt appears to be repressed as the father exercises his new powers, believing he has been liberated from the constraints of genealogy and generation. But *Herrschaft* (dominion) only leads to *Verschuldung* (indebtedness), as Hofmannsthal later wrote. The father experiences *Verschuldung* in the final scene, when he encounters the daughter/daemon from which he believes to have been liberated, unaware that she is his dybbuk, much as he turns out to be hers.

THE PURE PANTOMIME

The Jewish pantomime as tainted pantomime speaks loudly and says little. Where, in all of this, can one detect an alternative interpretation? The roots of a subversive reading lie in a conception of the pantomime genre that seems at first glance far removed from the tainted pantomime: the modernist valorization of gestic language and dance as a superior, even redemptive, ancient-modern genre. Hofmannsthal himself wrote about pantomime in this way, and he did so in part under the influence of Stéphane Mallarmé. In the theater sketch "Mimique" (The Mime, 1891), Mallarmé attempts a brief phenomenology of pantomime based upon the experience of watching a performance of *Pierrot Assasin de sa Femme* (Pierrot, Murderer of His Wife). Pantomime represents something truly ideal: "a medium, a pure medium, of fiction."[24] This pure fictionality is "a perpetual allusion without breaking the ice or the mirror": what Derrida calls a sign with no referent, an imitation without an original, a "speculum with no reality."[25] The unshattered mirror, a barrier that Mallarmé enigmatically calls "a hymen (out of which flows Dream)," creates, above all, the illusion of immediate meaning. Body language transpires in a liminal space: "between desire and fulfillment, perpetration and remembrance: here anticipating, there recalling, in the future, in the past, under the false appearance of a present." As he writes in *Ballets,* "écriture corporelle" (corporeal writing) becomes a trope of emancipated discourse: the "poem disengaged from the apparatus of the scribe."[26] Bodies, unlike words, are able to narrate without having to commit to tense; they are beholden neither to scripture nor to history. For Mallarmé, in sum, pantomime communicates freely, even when the story it tells is about imitation.[27]

Hofmannsthal's essay "Über die Pantomime" (On Pantomime, 1911) carries on Mallarmé's utopian vision of dance and pantomime, while introducing, in true Viennese form, an explicit psychological dimension.[28] This paean to pantomime was not occasioned by a live performance, but by a text from second-century Greece, Lucian's dialogue "On Dance," whose aura it palpably conveys. Rather nostalgically, Hofmannsthal, via Lucian, calls pantomime an "Urgenre"; he extols the idiom of bodies as a remnant of a heroic age, a means of expressing "that which is too great, too general, too near, to be captured in words."[29] "The language of words seems to be individual, is in truth generic; that of bodies seems general, but is in truth highly personal."[30] The magic of pantomime, then, is in part a matter of reception. Body language can yield the most intimate expression, whereas speech vitiates the individual into the banal. Corporeal language can render the universal comprehensible and meaningful to each individual; verbal communication appears to be personal, but ends up being "generic." The impact of bodies and that of words are thus at cross-purposes. But Hofmannsthal notes a further impact that hearkens back to Lucian: through the experience of watching a pantomime, one may truly fulfill the Delphic imperative "Erkenne dich selbst" (Know thyself), only Hofmannsthal modifies the classical dictum by noting that the self-knowledge acquired by the spectator goes beyond the rational. Pantomime dramatizes, and in so doing facilitates, what Hofmannsthal calls "Entladung," the literal disburdening of the psyche. "It is a person just like us, who moves before us, but more freely than we ever move, and nonetheless, the purity and freedom of his gestures express the same thing that we express when, twitching, self-conscious, we disburden our inner fullness."[31] Hermann Bahr expressed the same thought in a contemporaneous review,[32] and Freud also understood the power of pantomime (understood as reenactment during analysis) to reacquaint us with parts of the self that are inaccessible to the conscious mind. Viennese modernists revive an ancient conception of pantomime to meet a modern, psychological need. The free movement of the dancer does not dramatize escape from memory after all, but promotes instead a vicarious release of the spectator's own inhibitions, thereby allowing for a deeper kind of self-knowledge. Bodies are not merely free signifiers, as in Mallarmé; they imitate souls that "reveal" or "disburden" themselves in nonverbal ways.

The notion of corporeal writing as a medium through which one is able to fulfill the delphic oracle (or the modern equivalent thereof) seems dubious in light of the genre's reliance on stock figures. Is not this "perpetual allusion" of necessity stuck in tradition, its allusive power limited by its narrow cast of characters—Harlequin and Hanswurst, Scaramuccia and Pierrot, Bocher and Rabbi—caricatures that ground the spectator even more deeply in his or her own prejudices? When modernists ascribe to gestic language this double power to promote self-liberation and self-discovery, they confirm what Robert Storey has claimed of the French pantomime tradition as a whole, namely that it fuses probability and chance, convention and improvisation. Though the repertory of themes and characters was the same, the stories were typically "plotless," liberated "from the logical demands of realism," and unconcerned with destiny or final outcomes.[33] It is in light of this tension that Hofmannsthal's ingenuity becomes clear. Pantomime almost subordinates its figures to the restrictions of their personae, but not quite. Hofmannsthal's choice of genre reflects his own desire to resist these (and other) restrictions—to tell a story that is in the end about bodies attempting to remove themselves from the racist pantomime that is Vienna, 1901. The acts of exorcism and futile escape in *Der Schüler* represent the laughable attempts of stock types to escape the tainted pantomime by discarding their very typehood.

Can *Der Schüler* possibly inspire an epistemological *Erlebnis?* Are there grounds for seeing in Hofmannsthal's pantomime the type of redemption he finds in Mallarmé and Lucian? Was Hofmannsthal justified in retracting the published pantomime, and did he hope thereby to make possible a liberated and liberating theatrical performance? And what remains once the tainted pantomime and the pure pantomime cancel each other out? I have already noted that, text or no text, *Der Schüler* inhabits the very literary traditions it appears to reject; I refer to its striking intertextual accomplishment. The Rabbi, daughter, and Bocher are not simply types trying to become characters; in fact, they already represent many well-known characters from German and Jewish literature. It is on an intertextual level that the pantomime bears out Hofmannsthal's ancient/modern assertion that pantomime might become a means of challenging its audience to "Know thyself." Just as racial typecasting is in the eyes of the beholder, so is the power to replace typing with more complex recognitions of identity and difference. The Jewish non-Jewish pantomime invites this recontextualization by calling to mind the affinities between works not traditionally in dialogue with one another.

A pantomime that is about resistance to identity takes its cues from the behavior of those whom the arbiters of culture (that is, male, Christian culture) have deemed most vulnerable: Jews and daughters.[34] The father-daughter pair stands at the center of two separate plots that mimic one another, not only because Taube ends up appropriating her father's physique, but also because both portray attempts at self-transformation.[35] In the remainder of this chapter, I trace the constellations of literary characters related to the Rabbi and the Jewish daughter.

A JEWISH FAUST

Hofmannsthal's Rabbi-alchemist belongs in the Faust tradition—an intertext both Daviau and Wunberg explore at length. In the poem "Gedankenspuk," published ten years earlier, the sixteen-year-old Hofmannsthal had sought to evict Faust from his imagination. But this Rabbi yearns to become Faust, able-bodied man of culture, gentleman of the canon. At the core of Goethe's Faust myth is the exchange of scholastic pursuits for erotic desire. But here it is the Bocher who raises the Mephistophelian objection, "all these books . . . are dead to the heart." Here the fatal pact entails not a lapse into sensuality but an initiation to a realm of mystical potency that frees the Jew from his dysfunctional body. Erotic experience is only accessible once books *and* bodies are transcended. The particular configuration of Faustian motifs acquires coherence if we posit such a character as a "Jewish Faust." A Jewish Faust is vulnerable, not only to the devil—"the spirit that always negates"—but also to his own internal mechanisms of self-denial.

An important precedent for this Jewish Faust is the protagonist of Heinrich Heine's *Der Doktor Faust: Ein Tanzpoem* of 1846–47. Here, too, a Faust text inhabits the genre of ballet, albeit with extensive commentary. The ideas of *Faust* as ballet and the devil as a dancing female were present in Heine's "dance-poem" from its inception. Mephistopheles has become the ballet dancer Mephistophela, "dressed in the customary gauze-and-leotard costume and fluttering about in the most insipid pirouettes."[36] Although Heine does not identify his Faust as Jewish, Jeffrey Sammons suggests Heine identified with this "maladroit gull of his own desires and . . . ultimately doomed *Schlemihl.*"[37] Heine's Faust must learn to dance a pas-de-deux in order to win his beloved.[38] The dance motif has well-known ideological implications in Heine's oeuvre. The bear Atta Troll knows that Jews cannot dance, "since the sense of style, of the rigorous sculpture of movement, is lacking in that race."[39] Dance—a sign of refinement and a dionysiac counterforce to religious asceticism—became for Heine a preeminent symbol of the liberating role of sensuality.[40] Read by way of Goethe and Heine, Hofmannsthal's pantomime can be understood as an allegory of failed acculturation. The Jewish Faust, alter ego of the canonical Faust figures, longs for social acceptance and strives for cultural refinement and grace. Hofmannsthal's Rabbi strives only *to become* Faust.[41]

If the Rabbi were simply an alchemist, the first scene could be read to parallel Faust's invocation of the macrocosm and Earth spirit, or as a show of generic or "godless" mysticism widely treated in the period. A Faust pantomime cast for Eastern European Jews at the same time evokes a countertradition: that of the golem legends, highly popular among neo-romantic German writers in the early twentieth century.[42] Confirming this allusion is a small notice in the Zionist newspaper *Die Welt* stating that an upcoming performance of a work by Hofmannsthal would be cast with Jewish actors and set in the Prague Jewish ghetto.[43]

"Golem," most simply defined as an external human form, refers both to a corpus of mystical and magical Jewish texts as old as the sixth century and to a popular folkloristic tale that became widely known in the nineteenth century. According to the legend, the correct combination of alphabetical letters and the secret name of God empowered great Rabbis or righteous men to animate an artificial anthropoid in emulation of the divine creator. The techniques and symbolism of this extraordinary practice received much study and speculation and were on occasion attempted. Hofmannsthal's Rabbi accesses an esoteric realm of creative power by juxtaposing not letters, but books, to free himself from the limitations of his humanness: "I am no longer human, now that I have done this." Like other parallel golem legends and tales of late Romanticism, this version combines elements of alchemy or magic and the animation of an automaton. Romantic is both the desire to intervene in life processes and the inexorable failure—tragic or ridiculous—of such attempts. The one who attempts to control the creative act ends up himself a powerless golem.

And yet one powerful message of this legend is that a text culture *can* be productive; that letters themselves are powerful vessels of life and death. The Rabbi undergoes a psychological transformation that empowers him to (a) dance, and (b) exercise dominion over others. The act of creating a golem, one might say, renders memory creative. Its premise is that mastery of text-based secrets can bring about a liberating encounter with fate, and the most sublime mimetic act can lead to supreme self-exaltation. For the golem, a symbolic alter ego, is controlled exclusively by the will of the creator. Hence according to Gustav Meyrink's golem novel, the creature that is pure *physis,* without will or memory, becomes a speculum through whom the ghosts of the ghetto, the chain of generations, can be viewed: "One can recognize thousands of ancestors in its features."[44] At the same time, even in the golem myth one sees that the past cannot be conjured with impunity. The shadow-golem ultimately wreaks havoc by functioning like a dybbuk, the spirit of a dead person that cleaves to an innocent soul.[45] Like a repressed memory, a dybbuk seeks refuge in the bodies of the living, cursing whomever it possesses. The logic of this inversion (disembodied spirit/soulless body) may be a testimony to the racial codings of the day. Taube's dybbuk, unlike that of Leah in S. Y. Ansky's famous play *The Dybbuk: Between Two Worlds* (1914), is the Jewish male physique. The repulsion she feels for the Bocher amounts to an act of self-hatred that indirectly brings about her own death. Within the tainted pantomime, as noted, Taube is doomed because she mimics her father's false disburdenment and, absorbing his dybbuk, must live out its fatal destiny.

Whether an echo of a kabbalistic practice or an evocation of Eastern European Jewish lore, the Rabbi's exorcism is tantamount to a radical and ecstatic invocation of divine creative fire, a mystical *Erlebnis* in the truest and most dangerous sense. A set of terms from Hofmannsthal's own self-criticism regarding phases of psychological/spiritual maturation explains the logic by which the Rabbi's mystical *Erlebnis* plays itself out in a need to dominate. Among the numerous notations in the autobiographical fragment *Ad me Ipsum* we note the following antinomies: "Duration/Time, Being/Becoming. The I as Being and the I as Becoming."[46] The first term within each set refers to the subject's mode of life in what Hofmannsthal called "Preexistence," when one is immune to fate and historical contingency, and sees "only totalities," refusing to acknowledge otherness of any kind. Preexistence culminates (in this scheme) in an act of creative magic.[47] For Hofmannsthal's audience, then, the spectacle of self-disburdenment conveyed not only the perpetuation of Jewish typecasting, but also a release of spiritual energy through psychological catharsis, a symbolic escape from history, or, more exactly, from the pejorative roles history has designated the Jew. The dancing Rabbi casts off a body that limps, that sits and studies, that walks only with a stick. Liberation from a "shadowed existence" entails emancipation from the identifiably Jewish body, from the restless hands paging frantically through book after book, looking not to find something new, but only the same thing again. The lamed one learns to dance; *grübeln* yields a supernatural event, an access out of the mundane into the vertical axis of existence; books become sources of mystical experience; destiny has been transcended. When Hofmannsthal fuses these two alchemists into a single character—Dr. Faust, and his ethnic counterpart, the Jewish mystic —he effectively interlaces the mythic responses of two distinct cultures to the same dilemma.

THE JEWISH DAUGHTER RESISTS

To these intertextual links to both the Faust traditions and the golem legend must be added those standing behind Taube's pantomime of resistance. Taube dances; she writes a letter; she dons her father's clothes; she leaves the father's house. This archetypal sequence conforms to a "daughter plot" throughout Western literature. The parameters of the daughter plot manifest themselves in a constellation of interrelated motifs and behaviors that stem from a central dynamic. In these tales, in which the ethnic distinctions blur even more dramatically, protagonists move from victimization and compliance to disobedience, though they often sacrifice their lives in the process.[48]

Taube's Yiddish name offers the first clue to a literary genealogy that traces back to the earliest Jewish daughter scapegoat: the biblical Jephthah's daughter (Judges 30). The novella *Jephthas Tochter* (Jephthah's Daughter, 1878) by Salomon Mosenthal—an author whose widely produced play *Deborah* Hofmannsthal was moved to write about in the 1890s—provides a variation on this tragic theme.[49] Mosenthal's story recounts the fate of the dark-haired young Täubchen (Yiddish: little dove), whose father, Tobias, an indigent widower, despairs of earning the money to pay back his patron, Wolf Breitenbach. Caught on the road in a whirlwind storm one night, Tobias swears an oath to God to give his daughter in marriage to the older man. "'Almighty God,' he stammered, if I come through this alive, I *menadder* [Hebrew: vow] to offer Wolf Breitenbach my child in marriage and ask his forgiveness,'" to which the narrator adds, "He did the only thing he could do; like the devotees in the Temple, he sacrificed a dove [*Täubchen*] to the Lord."[50] Taube, in the tradition of Täubchen and the biblical Jephthah's daughter, is sacrificed in the (financial) interest of her father.

Other texts, such as a ballad called "Die Judentochter" (The Jew's Daughter) provide the bare outline of the Jewish daughter's pantomime of resistance.

> There was an old Jewess
> A grim, yellow hag;
> She had a lovely daughter;
> Her hair was beautifully plaited
> With pearls, as many as she wanted
> For her wedding dress.
>
> Oh dearest, dearest mother
> How my heart aches;—
> In my flowered dress
> Oh, let me stroll for a while

On the green heath
Until I reach the blue sea.

Good night! Good night, dear Mother,
You will never see me again;
To the sea I wish to walk,
And should I also drown;
It must baptize me today;
It is raging far too strongly![51]

Resisting destiny takes the Jewish daughter on a course away from the trappings of social role (braids, dress, pearls) and from her origins (yellowed mother)
out into the exposure of the elements (green heath, blue sea). The timing of her
escape is critical: the violent storm is a figure for the disruptive liminal moment
between past (mother) and future (impending marriage), and therein lies the opportunity for breaking out via an ambiguous act of drowning/baptism. Two longer versions of this ballad interject a dialogue between the daughter and a scribe (*Schreiber*)
that gives further insight into her motives. In the version published in *Des Knaben
Wunderhorn*, that dialogue is interposed between stanzas two and three, revealing
that the daughter turns to death only as a last resort, when baptism is named as the
condition of her marriage.[52] In Bettina von Arnim's poem, "Die Judentochter," the
daughter expresses her desire to remain with the scribe—a wish that he rebuffs:

"Oh Jewess, dearest Jewess,
Indeed that cannot be!
Were you to have been baptized,
I would want to buy you a ring
You should be my beloved."

"Oh scribe, dearest scribe,
Write my mother a letter,
Write you and me together,
Write to her in the name of God,
I wish to be a Christian."

"Oh Jewess, dearest Jewess,
Indeed that cannot be!
It would be a disgrace for me
In the eyes of all Christians,
If I wanted to marry a Jewess."[53]

Freedom for the Jewish daughter involves entering into a covenant with a Christian
God and a Christian husband. Bettina von Arnim's version links liberation to writ-

ing: the repetition of the imperative "Write" (*Schreib*) emphasizes that she desires a scriptural, that is, legal and/or religious conversion of status, not a blind flight from norms and roles. The scribe-suitor wants a baptized bride, but cannot take on the role of liberator. Her version has a slightly different ending than the others: after proud farewells to both scribe and family, the Jewish daughter turns defiantly to the ocean, but the poem ends triumphantly, omitting any reference to death.

The canonical prototype for Taube's behavior is Jessica in Shakespeare's *The Merchant of Venice*. In contrast to her Christian counterpart, the loyal Portia, Jessica is determined to escape her father's house and his heritage. Here too the plot involves the practical problem of leaving home unnoticed. On the night of her departure, Shylock warns his daughter to stay indoors and not be drawn out by the masked merrymaking of Christian neighbors.

But stop my house's ears, I mean my casements
—Let not the sound of shallow foppery enter
My sober house.[54]

The father's house, a space sealed off from the world, personifies the daughter's status.

Well, Jessica go in;
. . . .
Do as I bid you, shut doors after you.
Fast bind, fast find,
A proverb never stale in thrifty mind.[55]

After Shylock exits, Jessica responds: "Farewell, and if my fortune be not crossed, / I have a father, you a daughter, lost."[56] Jessica's heroism involves crossing in another sense, as she escapes by cross-dressing—a betrayal Shylock anticipates, even as he confines Jessica.[57] Jessica sends a letter to Lorenzo via her father's servant; the rival suitor is present in *Der Schüler* only as the implied addressee of Taube's letter, though he plays an important role in Ansky's *The Dybbuk* and in Hofmannsthal's ballet *Der Triumph der Zeit* (The Triumph of Time). Masquerading as her own father suggests that Taube choreographs her own pantomime of resistance by attempting to redeem a legacy that has gone corrupt, by placing the father's golem—his diseased physiognomy—into service.

In nineteenth-century novellas such as Achim von Arnim's *Die Majoratsherren* (The Estate Owners, 1820), Heinrich Heine's *Florentinische Nächte* (Florentine Nights, 1837), and Wilhelm Raabe's *Holunderblüte* (Elderblossoms, 1865), dance signals the transformation whereby parentless daughters reconnect with inner sources of autonomy, often in the face of impending violence.[58] The most prominent dancing daughter of the fin de siècle was Oscar Wilde's Salomé. Like Taube, Salomé is reluctant to dance and is fully aware of the incestuous nature of her stepfather's request. "It is strange that the husband of my mother looks at me like that. I know not what it means. In truth I know it too well."[59] Salomé chooses to unveil nonetheless, mocking those who seek to control her visually. Subverting the extant power dynamic allows Salomé to avenge her mother's suffering. Taube dances Salomé's dance before the gaze of both her father and the Bocher.

Taube's face is transfigured, she shakes her hips, stamps her feet in dance, plays with her loosened hair as with a veil.

. . . .

Master: Now that's enough.
Taube stands, as she regains her composure, purple-red, with eyes lowered, breathing heavily. The student at the door devours her with his gaze.
Master: Now go my child, go rest.
Taube staggers, like one released, into her chamber.[60]

Hofmannsthal underscores the intensity of the dance as a moment of self-abandonment (*Auslösung*). Despite her apparent pliability, she is in fact on the verge of escaping male control by stepping out of her role in their plot. Dance has a hypnotic effect on the male voyeur, rendering him momentarily impotent. In the tales of Arnim, Heine, and Raabe, male protagonists recount their experiences watching the dancing women and testify to their bewilderment, fascination, and repulsion.[61] Although the reader's access to the inner experiences of these dancers is filtered through the male perspective, it is nonetheless noteworthy that each is depicted entering a protected (inaccessible) space of self-recollection as a prelude to autonomous behavior.[62]

This is true as well for the female protagonists who are arguably Taube's most immediate precursors. In three works that Hofmannsthal composed almost contemporaneously with *Der Schüler*—the drama *Die Hochzeit der Sobeide* (Sobeide's Wedding, 1897),[63] the pantomime *Der Triumph der Zeit* (The Triumph of Time), and a short dialogue entitled *Furcht* (Fear)—he conjoined motifs of daughterhood, dancing, and memory. Sobeide, whose oriental name links her to Taube and to Salomé, is forced to dance for her father's creditors, and ultimately to marry one of them; she resembles in this respect the mad Esther of Arnim's *Die Majoratsherren* and the heroine of Arthur Schnitzler's *Fräulein Else* (1924). Sobeide's husband eventually grants her freedom, symbolically, by telling her he has canceled her father's debts, but the liberation comes too late, and she takes her own life by jumping from the tower. In *Der Triumph der Zeit,* a dark-haired daughter voluntarily dances for her father, but later goes on to dance the maenadic dance before her secret lover; accompanying her dance is a monologue that confirms this daughter is able to dance her way out of destiny, succeeding where Taube and Sobeide do not.[64] An even more sustained attempt to describe the experience of dance from the vantage point of the dancer herself appears in *Furcht*, a dialogue between two courtesans in the genre of Lucian's courtesan dialogues. Laidon, the elder of the women, envisions the essence of dance much as Mallarmé does, as a primitive and pure form of expression and disburdenment. What prevents dancers from actually dancing this dance is fear. "[Fear] holds the strings from above that are attached to the middle of our bodies, and pulls us here and there and makes our limbs fly."[65] Fear turns free dancers into marionettes, characters back into type figures. Laidon is desperate to communicate the experience of being gripped by fear to her naïve younger partner. "Can you be happy for just one moment? . . . Can you forget yourself, be rid of all fear, be rid of that shadow that darkens the blood in your veins?"[66] Given the series of dancers we have tracked, it is evident why here of all places, in a dialogue between two courtesans about fear, Hofmannsthal chooses to voice this crucial question.[67] Is it possible to resist the claims of memory with impunity? Can one ever release that shadow darkening the blood in our veins? "You jump here and there: do you flee from yourself? You imitate the gestures of animals and trees: do you become one with them? You climb out of your robe. Do you climb out of your fear?"[68]

In the essay "On Pantomime," Hofmannsthal writes that pantomime could transport spectator and actor alike to a place beyond convention and role; the physical release of the one mimics the psychic catharsis of the other. In a series of fictional works that incorporate dancing daughters, Hofmannsthal conveys the opposite: the suspension of mimesis and the inversion of the power dynamic, however short-lived.

ELEKTRA: TAUBE REINCARNATE

The crisis of memory confronting the characters in *Der Schüler* is very much present in Hofmannsthal's later works: in *Elektra* (1903), the two Oedipus dramas of 1905, *Ariadne auf Naxos* (1911), and *Die Ägyptische Helena* (1924). It is no doubt the first of these protagonists, Elektra, who is most visibly trapped between past and future: physically and psychologically possessed by the memory of her father's murder, she is nonetheless paralyzed, unable to perform the deed that would avenge his death and liberate herself from history. The drama's memory thematics have been treated at length, as has the dance motif.[69] Taube's story may provide the missing link between Elektra's dancing (a motif absent from Sophocles' *Electra*) and her quest for deliverance from the father's dybbuk, around which the plot as a whole revolves. When Hofmannsthal goes on to rewrite *Der Schüler* as *Elektra,* pantomime evolves into drama (and eventually into opera), and the Jewish cast metamorphoses again, from modern Europeans into mythic Greeks.

Elektra too accords with the archetypal daughter plot. Hofmannsthal structured the one-act play as a series of encounters between a daughter and her "spectators," her mother, sister, and brother, who, thanks to Elektra's vigilance, have been allowed to forget the past. Her mother's repressed guilt manifests itself in agonizing dreams. Her sister Chrysothemis knows she must move on if she is to marry and bear children; her brother Orest, like other brothers of traumatized daughters, is free to escape the household and return at will. Why is only Elektra stuck? In the dialogue with Orest, it becomes clear that her obsession is not a rational desire for justice, but that she, like Taube, has become possessed by the father's shadow, which has trespassed into the daughter's domain.

> Jealous are
> the dead: and he sent me hatred, hollow-eyed hatred for a bridegroom.
> I had to let the fearful one, one who breathes
> like a viper, come over me into my sleepless bed; he forced me
> to know what happens between man
> and woman.[70]

Agamemnon's ghost has become Elektra's dybbuk. Elektra's unkempt hair, like Taube's, is the mark of the father's defilement. In Elektra's words, "this sweet shudder / I had to sacrifice to the father."[71] When Orest consummates the long-awaited act and murders Ägisth, Elektra regains the ability to dance, and dance she does, maenad-like, moments before her collapse: "a nameless dance, in which she marches forwards."[72] Elektra, like Taube, Sobeide, and the more famous Fräulein Else, cannot outlive her own liberation. Hofmannsthal's Elektra may have her ancient roots in Sophocles, but she is also the Jewish daughter in a less objectionable ethnic guise: Taube reincarnate.

In *Der Schüler,* Taube's drama of resistance lasts barely a moment. Yet if we recollect it in slow motion, we can notice that it differs in an essential way from the plots of the Rabbi and the Bocher. While the men metamorphose from lame readers to equally ineffectual dancers, Taube moves in the opposite direction: from dancing to texts, not to read them, but to write them. All three figures dance, but only Taube's dance foments action; the male dancing is delusional, a symbol of patriarchal guilt but also of the feminization of the Jewish male. Even as they dance, the men remain her spectators, her imitators, her shadows. Taube is the only character who, in the spirit of Nietzsche, demonstrates that writing "with one's feet" can create new incentive to write with one's hands.[73] No wonder, then, that this pantomime pitting youth against age, text against dance, fake hermeneutic against spontaneous expression, leads to the ritual sacrifice of the daughter. Taube's dance, rich in intertextual allusion, triggers a different kind of pantomime altogether: a metamorphosis from type to author. In the larger cultural and biographical terms I have been suggesting, the daughter's dance points to an artistic strategy that couples conscious disinheritance with creative expression, and that corresponds most closely to the net impact of the work as a whole.

CAN YOU ESCAPE YOUR FEAR?

Hofmannsthal's pantomime was an experiment with a new kind of artistic response. It amounts neither to repression nor expression, but to a temporary, tentative suspension of extrinsic pressures in favor of exposing an inner drama. The history of the text's genesis and (non)reception leads one to conclude that Hofmannsthal managed to "have it both ways" with *Der Schüler,* to write and not write this story at the same time. The allusions to classical texts of the German and European tradition provide the backdrop for placing racially typed characters on the stage, and moreover, grant him the legitimacy of "high" culture at the same time that the piece, written in a low genre, suggests not only the rejection of "text" culture as such but of all literary precursors in favor of mystical creative experience. The genre of pantomime enabled Hofmannsthal to avoid the media and discourses more common to his Jewish contemporaries. At the same time, however, he openly trades on the stereotype that Jews are hyperthinkers and communicate through gestures, succumbing to the dictates of a climate in which physiognomical characteristics tell all. Lastly, even as he was able to activate various strands of his lineage and spiritual heritage, and thereby, perhaps, come to "know himself," the work has remained in the shadows of all that we know about its author.

I have sought this pantomime's significance by reversing the stages of its evolution and restoring its Jewish shadow, by realigning body script with manuscript and with literary subtexts. The liberating moments in *Der Schüler* take place beyond the visible parameters of the pantomime itself. But it was Hofmannsthal's belief that fragmentary gestures can release the memory of correspondent texts that trigger limitless associations in the minds of spectators whose response is not dictated (as it would be in drama) by the cognitive content of dialogue. The ideal viewer of such a work would moreover experience the very blurring of Christian and Jewish sources that Hofmannsthal had to combine in his own life; whatever the conflicts and contradictions may be between them, the pantomime rehearses the possibility of their correspondence. The fact that the alchemist was a rabbi in his former life, or that Elektra descends from Taube and from Salomé, reminds us that the conundrums of Jewish identity, and of modern identity, are in essence quite similar.

The pantomime's intertextual dimension further exemplifies the tendency of modernism to render identity "not once, but many times over." In lieu of the primal scene, one returns to a series of formative episodes drawn from culturally antagonistic narratives that are nonetheless interreferential, related to one another as different translations of one's character. The opposite position is represented by Hofmannsthal's Faustian Rabbi, for whom multiplicity collapses into singularity, and who must gloss the textual disagreement at all costs. By this same logic, he fails to notice that his shadow is also his daughter's corpse.

Hofmannsthal returned briefly to the pantomime genre again in 1910 and 1911 to compose *Das fremde Mädchen* and *Amor und Psyche;* he also wrote three pantomimes intended for inclusion in *Das Salzburger große Welttheater* during the years 1922–28 that were neither performed nor published. But it is fair to say that the pantomime of 1901 serves as a formal way station for the dramatic and operatic works to come. It is not only Taube's corpse, but the letter she writes—a legacy deposited offstage—that represent the reach of this work. This letter, the writing of disinheritance that becomes the daughter's death sentence, prefigures the letter Lord Chandos writes to Francis Bacon: a letter that emerges "from the grave" less than one year later, eventually to become Hofmannsthal's modernist manifesto. What would it mean to view *Der Schüler* as a first draft, a precursor text of "The Chandos Letter"? If nothing else, the letter's program likewise derives from the incongruity between message and diction, plot and genre; its writer envisages "a language . . . in which someday, perhaps, I will answer in the grave to an unknown judge," a language in which the silenced give testimony.[74]

If Hofmannsthal's work has not been permitted to speak to the predicament of Jewish identity at the fin de siècle, it is in part because we lack a model for conceptualizing the interaction of European modernism and Jewish modernism that would be adequate to his case. At this point we stumble into the central challenge of modernism itself: how to express crises of identity while dodging the pitfalls of both mimetic (essentialist) and antimimetic frameworks of meaning. Mallarmé saw in pantomime a liberated sign. For the traditionalist-modernist Hofmannsthal, body language became a site where spirit and body commune, a medium of a new kind of self-knowledge. Both poets value pantomime's extraordinary, even heroic pathos. Both praise the genre in lyrical language that strives to sublimate the distinction between tenor and vehicle in the attempt to render the effects of body language via written prose. Pantomime foregrounds the unpredictable relationship between mind and body, text and life, past and future, ranging from the mimetic to the parodic. The consummate genre of mimesis, a pantomime can nevertheless offer release through an array of intertexts that configure anew the volatile rapport between memory and life.

▪▪ PART TWO

HYBRID PLOTS, VIRTUAL JEWS

3 How a Viennese Modernist Becomes a Jew

Beer-Hofmann's *Der Tod Georgs* (The Death of Georg, 1900)

Say whatever goes through your mind. Act as though you were sitting at the window of a railway train and describing to someone behind you the changing views you see outside.
—Sigmund Freud, "Further Recommendations in the Technique of Psychoanalysis: On Beginning the Treatment" (1913)

In an interview in New York City shortly before his death, Richard Beer-Hofmann offered an intriguing reminiscence about the composition of his first important work, *Der Tod Georgs.* "It is written in a purely associative manner [*rein assoziativ*], as when you simply push a button, and one thing leads to another."[1] It was a strange admission, not only because of the slow pace of composition—the work took over six years to complete—but also given that the novella ends with the aesthete's conversion back to the religion of his forebears, Judaism. The way back may be difficult at any time, but under the cultural conditions that led Beer-Hofmann and others into the modernist aesthetic of impressionism and empiricism, this finding of a determinate solution through random associations makes the Jewish aesthete's return all the more remarkable.

In turn-of-the-century Vienna, association was both a predicament and a solution. A novella composed associatively is written from the standpoint of one who no longer makes necessary connections between thoughts, only associations suggested by the moment—one who remains detached, even when matters of life and death are at stake. Yet at a certain point, the position becomes untenable. As the author described it: "Because there is precisely that question regarding the involvement in life. One has the sense that he can no longer take part, because with every step he would take, so much, so many possibilities and seeds to a different life would be destroyed. But then, when he stands still, all that grows immediately under his feet withers away. The book grows out of this irresolvable dilemma."[2] Unable to stand still, yet unable to progress: if the aesthete is to participate in life—let alone become a Jew—the writer must find a way to divert the modernist impulse back towards the ethical. How then should he consolidate chance occurrences into a teleological narrative? And in the case where the conclusion to this narrative (like that to any spiritual journey) is both unforeseen and somehow inevitable, how should he convey that the transformation is at once an outgrowth of the aesthete's natural tendencies, as well as a wholly unexpected turning point, an *Erlebnis* or epiphany? This is where Beer-Hofmann's evocation of associative writing proves illuminating—not as modernist cant, but as a key to a particular literary experiment.

Association had become the aesthete's stalemate (and it became the sticking point for many of Beer-Hofmann's critics). But it also supplied a logic of mental progress and psychological growth, as when Freud instructed his patient to "say whatever goes through your mind," give yourself over to the arbitrary stream of impressions, feelings, and memories, believing that only in this way could true progress be made. The key difference is that in the first case, association is the mechanism of a mind given over to surface perceptions and superficiality, and in the second, it is the operating principle of the

8. Richard Beer-Hofmann.

remembering mind: the mechanism whereby perceptions and words connect with images and episodes within the temporal flow. The difference corresponds to that between the novella's two main characters at the outset of the story. Paul, the narcissist, believes that making connections of any kind is beneath him. "When he spoke he thought he could see the face of his words, which had been distorted and made weak and low by the strenuous service they rendered to the everyday."[3] Georg's words, by contrast, are so potent that they have the power to conjure the memories that become lost in "the gray mass of days, just slipping away" (80).[4]

Georg will not influence Paul's conversion in any direct way, but rather indirectly, by dying while a guest in his home. The shock of this unexpected death leads Paul to adopt Georg's stance in life, to repudiate his narcissistic ways, submit to the laws of nature, and lastly, to discover his Jewish roots. It is well known that the author's own Jewish awakening, inspired by marriage and fatherhood, as well as by the appearance of Theodor Herzl's *The Jewish State* in 1896, corresponded to the period of the novella's composition (1893–99) (fig. 8).[5] The Jewish vision that Beer-Hofmann came to develop was at once enlightened, historically attuned, and deeply spiritual (thus altogether atypical for a middle-class Austrian Jew), and it bore fruit in the dramas discussed in chapter 6. What remains to be understood about *Der Tod Georgs* is that the story of how the aesthete becomes a Jew encodes the quest of a Viennese modernist to become a Jewish writer. These parallel transformations are difficult to track, since they transpire for the most part on an almost microscopic scale, within the aesthete's mind.

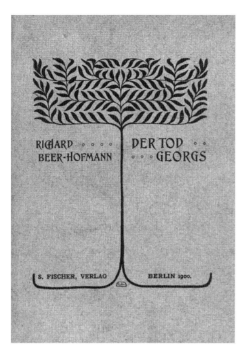

9. Cover of the first edition of Beer-Hofmann's *Der Tod Georgs*, 1900.

THE NEGATIVE RECEPTION OF *DER TOD GEORGS*

Among the literary works produced by the avant-garde writers of *Jung Wein* in the fertile years 1890 through 1900, *Der Tod Georgs* has long been regarded as a flawed gem: an exemplary, defective work (fig. 9). Even as readers have admired Beer-Hofmann's lyrical prose and technical virtuosity, they have also concluded that a disagreeable effect arises from prose drawn too taut between its prodigious lyricality and the demands of a sequential narrative. The consensus has been that *Der Tod Georgs* lacks what Hermann Bahr called "Notwendigkeit," inevitability. The chief complaints are two: first, that the modernist inclination to mix poetry and prose with no discernible plot beyond a shifting from image to image, leitmotif to leitmotif, fails to support any kind of teleological plot; secondly, that the leap into faith is unpersuasive. "Everything slips away, dissolves, and evaporates," writes Hermann Bahr in his *Feuilleton* review of 1900: "one thing flows into the other, nothing possesses form."[6] To justify the seeming disparity between the text's poetry and its plot, contemporary readers postulated a rift between novelistic content and lyric form. Schnitzler's reaction, "there's much more poetry in the book than . . . reason," parallels the view of Lukács and others that the book failed to advance any clear political purpose.[7] The most prevalent trope for conveying the novella's form—the pearl necklace—was first used by Alfred Gold in his review in *Die Zeit:* "every part is trimmed, measured, and toned, as if it should have its own shining effect."[8] The image highlights the degree to which questions of association and the interrelation of the parts mystified the critics. Schnitzler felt hoodwinked by the conclusion; Jewish contemporaries generally were displeased with the ethnically grounded climax, though, as we shall see, their response to Beer-Hofmann's poems and biblical dramas was overwhelmingly positive.[9] Later interpreters have also found it highly implausible that Paul's solipsistic mind could achieve such a dramatic transformation, arguing that a genuine conversion would mandate a shift from the controls of impressionistic feeling (*Stimmung*) to those of cognitive understanding (*Erkenntnis*).[10] Because the conversion is abrupt and not accompanied by any behavioral change, critics such as Rainer Hank argue that the denouement was intended as nothing more than a further *Stimmung,* and Paul's Judaism, "aestheticism in another guise."[11] Hank echoes Beer-Hofmann's contemporaries when he notes that the work intentionally ends in "aporia," with Paul no longer an aesthete, and not yet an authentic collectivist. Scheible too is on target when he calls the conclusion "at once true and illusory."[12] It is worth noting that Rainer Maria Rilke, an admirer of Beer-

Hofmann, felt that the "one hundred poems" did add up to a cohesive narrative.[13] Almost alone among Beer-Hofmann's recent readers, Walter Sokel sees a unifying theme in the protagonist's gradual development of an ethical conscience.[14]

My purpose here is not to defend the work against charges of aesthetic failure. My goal is to better understand the logic driving Paul's transformation: the logic by which all that precedes the final discovery—Georg's death, the poetry/prose hybrid, and the exaggerated attention to Paul's mental processes—both does and does not anticipate the novella's conclusion. Analyzing the author's poetics of association requires an interpretive zoom lens, and the focus on the minutiae of Paul's mind may seem overly detailed. But this is a work in which the broad strokes convey next to nothing about its significance, let alone what recommends it as an exemplary work of Viennese Jewish modernism. To depict a protagonist whose imagination is as myriad as his activities are vacuous, the author applied the principles of a burgeoning literary psychologism, which no longer conceived of plot in terms of action, conflict, and dialogue, but rather sought to render the minutiae of psychic life.[15]

The novella opens on the night when Paul has received Georg as a visitor in his summer home (and Georg has already gone to bed). During that night, Georg dies in his sleep. Inexplicably, the reader is diverted from this event by Paul's elaborate dream: a lengthy account of a woman's sickness and death as experienced by her narcissistic husband. The remaining incidents are unrevealing: Paul, now a survivor in life as in the dream, escorts Georg's body by train to the burial (also unnarrated). In the final chapter, months later, Paul goes walking in a park. The novella's real intrigue is psychological and expository. Beer-Hofmann presents a narrator who appears to know all there is to know about his protagonist. That he can depict both the conscious and unconscious minds as knowable entities testifies to the reification of Paul's inner life. The narrative lens never deviates from him, alternately capturing his activities from the outside through third-person narration and, more often, slipping into his mind via what was then an innovative blend of psychonarration and narrated monologue.[16] Paul's train of thought as he drifts off to sleep at the end of chapter 1 follows the chain of sensory impressions: "How moonlit the room was! And that thing on the wall was the black shadow of the window cross. Georg slept in there. The foliage of the lime tree in front of the window looked like a grille.—What kind of a fragrance was the wind bringing in through the opened window? Did it come out of the garden? Or was it from the freshly mowed meadows on the mountains?— He slept" (15).[17] The text appears to weave inside and outside seamlessly together, and lodged within these sensory impressions, seemingly incongruous, is a reference to Georg, who has already absented himself. In such subtle ways does the narrator convey that he is adroitly positioned to know more about the narcissist than the latter knows about himself. But two episodes intrude "out of nowhere" to undermine both the narcissist's self-assurance and the reader's security. Georg's premature death creates the first disruption, and the discovery that Paul is after all a Jew creates the second. These episodes stand at opposite ends of the religion/decadence divide: the one is an untimely event; the other is all about a permanent (though forgotten) feature of one's identity. Taken together, these episodes cast Paul's return to Jewishness as the necessary outcome of a long and detailed process of recollection triggered by Georg's death. Bridging two unexpected events is a chain of associations, in the course of which lyric gives way to prose, the sterile remembering of fixed images gives way to the verbalization of repressed childhood memories, and the mind only able to make connections in visible space—the sensationalist condition theorized by Ernst Mach—becomes suddenly vulnerable to relationships in time and through time. Recollection redeems the aesthete, not only by reminding him of what he had forgotten, but also by providing a new, temporal logic of association and integration—a literary enactment of theories of Mach, Hering, Freud, Bergson—whereby one might forge a connection with that which eludes perception: a dead friend, memories from childhood, even a transcendent God.

IN THE MIND OF THE MEMORY INDIVIDUAL

Paul, the prototypical aesthete, has lost his memory, which is not to say that the past has no significance; on the contrary, "he saw nothing without ancestors" (42).[18] Paul experiences the past as both a burden and a void. He obsessively traces the "ripening" of a crystal glass, while cringing at the face of a newborn baby, "distorted as an old man's face and laden with the burden of memories, and dragging itself along with chains that shackled it to bygone things"(42).[19] His recollection is typically misguided. "Stubbornly he followed the traces of all things back in time, until their ways merged indissolubly with the ways of all life" (42).[20] Most comfortable in the world of objects, Paul finds human connection overly taxing. In the final chapter (after Paul's recovery), the narrator recalls precisely how an artificial relationship to the past had enabled him to keep his distance from living people:

> Past things, and what was around him every day, had been equally close to him. With feverish hands he had pulled close to himself actions that had grown cold long ago, of which only a faint and fading glimmer shone across the centuries to the living, and he had kept away from himself with outstretched fingers the still-trembling destinies of living people who surrounded him, who strode the earth at the same time as he, until both— the dead and the living—seemed to be equally distant from him, as on the same stage, playing themselves in the manner of shadows.[21] (118–19)

This passage details both the affliction and the adaptive strategy of the modern type whom Pierre Nora christened the memory individual. The affliction first arises from the inability to keep past and present in their correct mental grooves. The past is too remote, leading Paul to grasp at the cold residue with feverish desperation. Existence in the present poses the opposite threat, that of *drängen*, of suffocation. The intimacy of "still-trembling destinies" provides no relief for the narcissist who shuns interpersonal connection. Unable to order past and present diachronically, the aesthete synchronizes them in fantasy, and so transforms his memory into a theater of shadows. The aesthete is born when an artistic pose becomes the prime strategy for bringing temporal disorder under the dominion of (mental) space.

The aesthete's misguided recollection resembles that of other turn-of-the-century type figures such as the *Grübler* or brooder. Sigmund Freud described *grübeln* as a secondary defense in which unresolved intellectual energy becomes channeled away from sexuality onto innocuous or purely speculative matters; Leonardo da Vinci regresses into *grübeln,* in Freud's account, when his scientific investigations cease to serve artistic production. Walter Benjamin diagnoses a similar condition in the *Passagen-Werk:* "His case is like that of someone who had already grasped the solution of the great problem, but then forgot it. And now he broods not just over the issue, but over his past thinking about it."[22] Beer-Hofmann's aesthete is also related to Baudelaire's *flâneur,* the city-dweller who relishes chance encounters but is freed from responsibility and enduring commitment.

Flâneur, Grübler, aesthete, memory individual: Paul's inchoate experience of temporality lies in the fact that he experiences reality as Ernst Mach defined it, as a stream of discrete sensations and elements. Hermann Bahr, the writer most responsible for conveying Machian empiricism into Viennese literary life, believed that Mach had conceptualized reality as experienced by the modern writer.[23] To one who beholds the world by way of a Machian optic, any and all inherent principles of distinction and causality vanish. Writes Bahr: "All distinctions have been dissolved here; physics and psychology flow into one another, element and sensation are one, the I dissolves itself and everything is merely an eternal tide which seems to stop here, and to flow more quickly there, everything is just movement of colors, sounds, warmths, pressures, spaces and times, which appear on the other side, here by us, as moods, feelings, and wills."[24] Perception reduces cause and effect to simple contiguity, collapsing any rationale for determining the coherence of sensations or elements that goes beyond the accidental and experiential. Thus, one lives amidst "a discontinuous multiplicity of elements, inert and juxtaposed."[25] Paul's impressionistic optic, referred to as *gleiten* (sliding), can neither penetrate surfaces nor discern causality, controlled as it is by what Gotthart Wunberg has called a "Vergessenszwang" (compulsion to forget).[26] His gaze reduces a landscape, a person, a book to its material attributes, and only repetition or "horizontal correspondence" manages to rivet his attention to a single image. At one point, two women strolling in the park appear to him as figures moving aimlessly—*irren, gleiten* (straying, wandering)—through a maze: "They stood still in front of one of the great sandstone urns that surrounded the plaza, unsure into which alley they should go. In the sunless, foggy air their figures appeared to be without form, seemed to be only shadows projected from invisible bodies upon the gray, stony mass of the urn. They detached themselves from it, were covered by broad tree trunks, reappeared behind them, and seemed, as if caught behind the black, unyielding net of thin hedges, more and more to lose their way" (119).[27] Woman, like any object, becomes utterly fungible:

initially reduced to an insubstantial phantom, she then appears to be a relief figure emblazoned on a stone urn; then, released again, she becomes a creature trapped in the black hedges of the landscape. By imagining that the figures proceed as through a maze, without will, Paul's own mind is free to impute any logic he wishes to the sequence of impressions before his eyes.

Beer-Hofmann goes on to expose the mental activities that yield such modes of perception: "Then the rings, which usually would anxiously chain one thought onto the other, detached themselves—and his thoughts strode as a sleepwalker over bold, unsupported bridges which bent themselves vertiginously" (11).[28] The mind as a chain again evokes the rhetoric of associationism. In the case of one for whom all connections provoke anxiety, the chain comes undone and thoughts wander as if sleepwalking, free of the need to connect one impression to the next. Here as elsewhere, the architectonic analog for the aesthete's mind is the labyrinth. Life in a labyrinth becomes a never-ending succession of atomized episodes that are both temporally and spatially self-contained.[29]

The *locus classicus* of the labyrinth happens to be Paul's favorite book: *The Thousand and One Nights*. This work fanned the orientalist fantasies of generations of European writers, and it was reissued in German in 1907 with a sentimental introduction by Hofmannsthal (discussed in chapter 5). Orientalist motifs such as the arabesque and labyrinth, as aestheticist writers of the fin de siècle appropriated them, endowed the anarchic experience of time and space with an aura of inexorability. Paul fantasizes about such an existence: "Their lives moved in winding and labyrinthine ways, peculiarly connected with other lives. What appeared to be a dead end, led to the goal" (18).[30] The exotic appeal of the labyrinth lay, in Paul's words, in "the impossibility of getting lost," as if Machian reality, when raised to an absolute in the form of an aesthetic, ceased to be alienating and paradoxically generated a new guiding principle.[31]

A POETICS OF ASSOCIATION

In letters to Schnitzler and to Hofmannsthal of 1898, Beer-Hofmann mentions reading Mach's *Popular-Scientific Lectures,* and many have noted Beer-Hofmann's incorporation of Machian empiricism.[32] When Beer-Hofmann fails to narrate transitions in the plot, replacing them with symbols of rupture and continuity, death and birth, sleeping and awakening, that become moments of interpretive crisis for the reader, he uses Mach in the service of a larger experiment. The novella introjects the labyrinth in order to dispel its aura, to expose it as nothing more than an asylum from the past, and ultimately to replace it with images of duration and integration. Numerous symbolist leitmotifs, such as the color red, the fish, and the female form, are introduced in the manner of lyric ornaments, only to become associated with events that disorient Paul (and the reader) and catalyze the memory quest. As transitional symbols, they serve as tangible markers of Paul's internal development.

The window is perhaps the most conspicuous transitional symbol in the text.[33] The first three chapters begin—and both the first and second conclude—with Paul attending to windows. The window functions both metonymically to signify Paul's openness within the text, and metaphorically, as a sign for the memory individual's false consciousness. The glass barrier symbolizes the aestheticist's sterile interaction with reality conceived of as surface: as line art (*Jugendstil*), atomized elements (Impressionism), or illusory extensions of his person (narcissism). On the opening page, a friend passing by calls up to Paul's window, inviting him to come for a walk; Paul leans out, but refuses the summons—he is "too tired." This is the only dialogue in the entire novella. But the window functions simultaneously as a figure of the Paul-Georg relationship. While in the reader's mind Paul's character becomes associated with glass, in Paul's memory Georg is associated early on with the *Fensterkreuz*, a cross-shaped divider configuring the isolated panes, an image that also anticipates the noncoincidental evocation of Jesus at a critical point in the text. On the eve of his arrival, Georg sits facing Paul with his back to the window. The resulting visual image of Georg's face at the crux of the cross window, a light illuminating his head like a halo, becomes permanently imprinted in Paul's memory.

With Georg's arrival, other forces begin to encroach upon the surface of the narcissist's existence, evoking sensations that he cannot ignore. A lengthy dream, above all, presages the psychological crisis. Within the dream, Paul sits at his wife's deathbed and begins to feel vaguely culpable. At one point, he looks out the window to the still lake. He observes, characteristically, the reflection of the mountains and the light on the surface of the water. Suddenly a "blood-red" fish jumps through the surface. Paul realizes that the scene has changed irrevocably, and he can no longer see the surface for the depth. "The earlier picture was lost" (57).[34] This jumping fish recurs on multiple occasions to signify the innate ability of living things to bridge various strata of existence. Beer-Hofmann's red fish transvalues a common symbolist ornament into an omen of disruption and change, and by the same logic, the lake has replaced the window as a figure for Paul's mind. (In this scene's recapitulation in the last chapter, two women symbolically feed fish in a fountain graced, appropriately, by a statue of a mermaid; a figure of perceptual disruption becomes an emblem of reintegration.) The change is dramatized when, moments before his wife dies, Paul absentmindedly puts his fist through the window, angry at the rowdy children playing in the adjacent garden. Shocked at his uncharacteristic outburst, Paul stands frozen, "hearing" only the drops of his blood dripping to the floor, and when his wife's nursemaid cries, "Jesus—she's dying!" he can only watch immobile as his wife breathes her last, after which her body topples over the side of the bed and hits the floor with a thud.[35] At this moment Paul wakes up, causing a dramatic interruption for the reader. Suddenly, the reader's experience corresponds with Paul's. For the time that has supposedly passed has not passed; the plot events never transpired as plot. Like Paul, the reader is coerced into a position of retrospection—forced to resist the *Vergessenszwang*, to retrace his or her steps, rather than proceed. Paul acknowledges this new development upon awakening. Groping about for the words to define his premonition about the dream's impact, he comes up with the adjective "gleich-gültig" (insignificant), which he had applied to the conversation with Georg. Dreams, however, contain "nothing insignificant" (*nichts Gleichgültiges*), they harbor the possibility of self-knowledge. In a dream, one is potentially no longer a *Nachtwandler* (sleepwalker), following disengaged associations. Dream time contains "no empty hours that were merely the bridges to expected richer ones; and nothing that stood worthless by the wayside, and that one passed with indifference. All things had turned their faces to him—he was incapable of ignoring them; they existed for his sake, and he was not able to disconnect their destiny from his own. He stood up and went to the window" (65).[36] From this point on, dream and fact interweave, uniting the reader with Paul's psychic condition, even while releasing the desire to escape that condition and understand what's "really" going on. The aesthete likewise begins to interweave perceptions and dream images, facts and memories, in his quest to understand Georg's death and his own life.

The next window is found in the train carrying Georg's body to burial with Paul accompanying the coffin. Paul at first keeps the compartment window and curtains firmly shut to avert any further social interaction. As the train begins to move, Paul feels relieved (*erleichtert*). He opens both window and door, the wind enters, his head sinks back, and he begins to succumb to exhaustion. The train begins to lull him to sleep—his third act of going to sleep thus far. But again, the unforeseeable interferes. Semiconscious, he hears a tinkle of glass, a sound that he cannot block out. "From where was it coming? It seemed to come from up close; in irregular intervals it resounded again and again in his drowsing and woke him up. He sat up" (70).[37] The noise of an empty wine bottle rattling around in the baggage net above his head triggers an astonishing association: "Only for a moment did he follow the greenish glittering of the bottle, which was rolling back and forth; then his thoughts were far away from it, and he had to think of Georg's coffin, which stood alone in the baggage car, unsettled by the thrust of the train or maybe hurled into a corner when the train passed joltingly over a switch" (70).[38] Rather than dismiss the annoyance, Paul thinks of Georg's corpse, "rigid and defenseless," packed in the coffin "as in a box, only packed more shoddily and carelessly than an object."[39] How could Georg, Georg of all people, have been transformed into such an object? Fearing that he too is a mere piece of freight, Paul distances himself from his friend by establishing two essential contrasts: that between Georg as he was (human) and Georg as he is (*Ding*), and between himself (alive, in motion) and his friend (dead, in motion). Dead bodies are tossed about randomly, defenselessly, in nets; he, on the other hand, progresses forwards with surety.[40] Paul perceives the annoyingly irregular motion of the bottle, the net in which it is trapped, and the susceptibility of the corpse, as the opposite of the train's predictable course. Gliding along on iron tracks, above the hectic and contingent flurry of everyday existence, the train follows its predestined path, carrying Paul along with it. "Every incidental and capricious feature of the country road seemed to have been removed from his path. His path ran in an unavoidable manner" (71).[41] Paul feels most immune to contingency precisely when he is most vulnerable to it.

THE MEANING OF GEORG'S DEATH

To understand Georg's transformation, in Paul's mind, from inanimate corpse into a figure of living memory, one must first understand the strategic role of his death. A brief comparison of *Der Tod Georgs* with contemporaneous death stories by Hofmannsthal and Schnitzler proves instructive. Hofmannsthal's verse drama *Der Tor und der Tod* (The Fool and Death) appeared in 1893; Schnitzler's study of dying, a novella called *Sterben* (Dying), was published in 1894.[42] In Hofmannsthal's baroque treatment of this theme, Death himself appears on stage, as do the already deceased, to confront Claudio in his final hour. *Sterben* depicts dying naturalistically, as a drawn-out occurrence that allows readers and characters alike ample time for reckoning with mortality. Georg's death comes not at the point of closure, to fulfill expectations previously generated, but rather midway: a novelistic *Wendepunkt* (turning point) that introduces the unexpected and thereby instigates a different plot altogether. Like the other works, Beer-Hofmann's story dramatizes the refutation of decadent aestheticism by staging a protagonist's psychological rebirth in response to mortality.[43] Yet while *Der Tor und der Tod* and *Sterben* portray direct encounters with the spectacle of death, the author refrains from narrating the death event. Situating death at the midpoint, as an unforeseen and unseen turn of events, Beer-Hofmann conjoins the act of reckoning with death with a parallel process of learning how to remember the deceased, or remember at all. If death as the terminal event in the novel confers meaning and totality along a diachronic axis, as Peter Brooks has argued, the unnarrated death is subversive; it is nowhere and everywhere.[44] Like Paul, the reader must learn how to absorb Georg's death without any perceptual record of the event. The reader must rely on Paul's ability to speak of Georg and ultimately, to remember him. Georg's gradual coming into view as a character is thus a marker of the aesthete's new powers of recollection and narration. Beer-Hofmann's method relates to Freud's tactic of representing a figure in, or as, the process of his becoming known.

It is in part for this reason that I have referred to *Der Tod Georgs* as a novella, where others have classified this work without explanation as a short novel or *Erzählung*. Beer-Hofmann had published a volume of two novellas in 1893, but supposedly resisted generic classification in this case. On my reading, the work creatively employs many formal trademarks of the nineteenth-century German novella: concentrated symbolic artistry, a *Grenzsituation* (liminal situation) involving a death event, a subversive turning point, and the requisite "incredible event that has occurred."[45] The title connotes not a happening in time and space, but a forgotten or omitted episode in a story. Mnemotechnic plots operate semiotically, as Umberto Eco and Renate Lachmann have claimed, and in texts that argue for recollection, memory itself becomes the text's structural and semantic referent.[46] Georg is the first sign in this text: the absent referent whose retrieval configures Paul's (internal) plot, and the projected embodiment of all that Paul lacks—transitional logic, temporal consciousness, and organic life. The novella fulfills, in its final episode, an additional qualification of the quasitraditional, quasimodern mnemotechnical text as Lachmann defines it. What begins as a ritual act of memorializing the dead is shown to contain within it the germ of new, memory-based paradigms of cultural understanding.

Georg's character, not only his absence, qualifies him as a sign of Paul's lost past. Georg was a doctor by profession. His treatments involved restoring to his patients their most important experiences as lived memories, like a therapeutic brew. "Like precious goods in buried treasuries of kings who had taken flight, it had rested for a long while, until Georg's word had lifted it up. . . . Hot and sweet and fragrant as a sleeping potion, all this offered itself to the dying; and they stood there, these things, with open eyes, their faces turned to him, as if the last hours had called them by their true names" (80).[47] Georg is an artist of memory in the Freudian tradition. His profile matches the criterion of late nineteenth-century memory researchers, who held that only a collaboration of physiologist and psychologist could infiltrate the mystery of memory.[48] Georg scrutinizes a human face to discern both organic and spiritual destiny; he knows that body and soul form a totality. "Just as the eyes of the artists touch upon all things and ask the form for its destiny—where it had come from and what would become of it—so would his questioning eyes rest upon people suffering"(74).[49] Closely attuned to the myriad ways in which death shapes the body from within, and knowing that the source of the physical affliction also contains the psychological cure, Georg (like Freud, the writer) seeks the key to the past in the smallest bodily gestures and the subtlest features of the human physique: "Out of sick people's own lives, receding behind them, Georg found for them relief. He let the children they had begotten sit at their bed—and children's children. . . . Georg's words lured memories long since banished by life, until they floated back with light, quietly flapping wings, and came to sit at rest at the bedside" (76).[50]

The logic by which the artist of memory catalyzes the aesthete's transformation is articulated in theoretical discussions of memory with which Beer-Hofmann was intimately familiar. Scientists and psychologists in the late nineteenth century regarded memory as the underlying substance unifying inner life. In 1870, Ewald Hering, a proponent of the theory of biologically inherited memory, phrased it thus in a widely acclaimed public lecture to the Viennese Imperial Academy of Sciences entitled "Über das Gedächtnis als eine allgemeine Funktion der organisierten Materie" (On Memory as a General Function of Organized Matter): "So we realize that it is to memory that we owe almost everything we are and have, that ideas and concepts are its work; every perception, every thought, every movement is sustained by it. Memory connects the countless individual phenomena of our consciousness into a whole, and as our body would disperse into an infinite number of atoms if it were not held together by the attraction of matter, our consciousness would, without the binding power of mem-

ory, shatter into as many fragments as there are moments."[51] Where the force of tradition no longer holds, memory becomes the binding power of consciousness, able
to unite and carry over the isolated perceptions, ideas, and movements of mental life.
Without memory, consciousness would shatter into "as many fragments as there are
moments," a good description of the state of Paul's mind at the start of the book. Like
Theodulé Ribot in France, Hering became the most widely cited German-language
source on the subject of "organic" or biologically inherited memory.[52] Even Ernst
Mach, in *Beiträge zur Analyse der Empfindungen* (The Analysis of Sensations, 1886),
cites Hering's findings in order to describe the preservative element (*Erhaltungsten-
denz*) that he too considered the defining characteristic of organic life.[53] In later essays,
such as "Leben und Erkennen" (To Live and to Know, 1906), Mach consistently
describes memory as the faculty that allows human beings to acquire knowledge and
modify instinctual behavior patterns.[54] Through memory, the past *does* have influence. "So what is memory?" asks Mach. "A mental experience [*psychisches Erlebnis*]
leaves mental traces, but also physical traces."[55] Mach states that recollection, defined
as the preservation of memories and the associational paths guaranteeing their reawakening, distinguishes organic from inorganic life as "the basic condition of developed
mental life."[56] Though Mach claims not to understand this mystery, he espouses Hering's theory that memory fuses—not only figuratively, but chemically—physical and
mental life. Memory traces, which he elsewhere refers to as "a bundle of individual
memories," do not remain static in an internal storehouse, as the self is not a static,
material entity. Rather, they enter in and, more importantly, alter the flow of matter
and energy, thus influencing the course of life and, in consequence, the response to
every new stimulus.[57] Mach also theorizes that older memory traces play a key role in
shaping what he called *Vorstellungen* (representations).[58]

Beer-Hofmann's approach to redeeming the aesthete is reminiscent of Freud's
view that overly rational approaches to the past require correction, whereas the imagined past—vividly manifest in art—is a composite of new impressions with earlier
scenes that the mind has retained. By conducting his reader into the depths of the
memory individual's mind, Beer-Hofmann's narrator is able to trace Paul's ideas and
images back to progressively earlier periods of his life. Beer-Hofmann's poetics of
association obeys the dictates of the artistic imagination as Freud conceptualized it,
by providing a "way back" from space into time, from fixation to a more nuanced
knowledge of the past. But whereas Freud valorizes the artist as such, Beer-Hofmann,
by virtue of his aspirations to transcendent rather than material sources of continuity, eventually renounces the aesthetic impulse.

ENTERING DURATION; REMEMBERING GEORG

The incidental association of the glass bottle with Georg's body epitomizes the reify-
ing tactic of the aesthete's mind. Paul has already referred to his own mind as a tightly
woven net in which "everything was inextricably knotted together. What had once

been, stood upright next to him like the living" and became suffocating (42).[59] Georg, on the other hand, has already become "like grain in dry storage," essentially forgotten (26).[60] Paul is stunned into wakefulness by the thought that the dead Georg has metamorphosed, not simply into a *Ding,* but into numerous fragments, hard shards scattered in Paul's mind like the inanities the friends exchanged the night before. Like Orpheus, Paul turns back to gather the fragments in an attempt to reconstitute Georg as a living memory.

The train is more than a metonymic figure for Paul's ensuing memory journey: encompassing his entire being in its motion, it signifies an existential change of state. Train travel, more so than any nineteenth-century invention, was a symbol of the modern revolution in the "culture of time and space" and the dramatic psychological and epistemological consequences it brought.[61] While many poetic accounts of the impact of railway travel stress the perceptual revolution it brought about, Paul's perceptual capacity becomes altered in precisely the opposite direction: he perceives the landscape less impressionistically and more reflectively. Being subjected to ongoing, sensorimotor stimulation challenges Paul's instinct to control reality from a distance.

At the onset of the journey, Paul has thus far reacted only to "der Tod, nicht Georgs Tod" (death, not Georg's death) (70). He senses that a certain response still eludes him; his natural inclination is to postpone mourning. "Maybe only later would he be able to mourn him" (71).[62] Mourning a loved one, writes Freud, entails determining not *who* has died but *what,* with respect to one's own inner life, has been lost.[63] In Paul's case, the loss entails the very capacity to recollect at all. Yet the aesthete does not believe that the potential for such authentic recollection exists.

The first step amounts to the awakening of "slumbering" neural paths of association that are, as William James writes, the "condition of recall." "But be the recall prompt or slow, the condition which makes it possible at all (or in other words, the 'retention' of the experience) is neither more nor less than the brain paths which *associate* the experience with the occasion and cue of the recall. *When slumbering, these paths are the condition of retention; when active, they are the condition of recall*"[64] (emphasis in original). Recollection is analogous to travel, according to George Poulet, as both create rapport with that which is absent.[65] Similarly, inscribing the dead into memory is the psychological correlative to burial. When the narrator gives notice near the close of the chapter that Georg was "eingegraben" (engraved), and later that he was "begraben" (buried), he acknowledges that the journey serves a double purpose, namely to engrave Georg in Paul's mind prior to burying him in the ground (104). Occasioned by the need to bury a dead friend, the train ride creates a dialectical experience of progression and regression, remembering and forgetting, that is a trademark of modern aesthetics. In the privacy of his compartment, alternately looking out the window and sitting back to reflect, Paul not only struggles to reconcile an untimely death, but fixates on his deepest fear: the seeming impossibility of retention over time. This reflection occurs because the train symbolically projects Paul into the temporal continuum, or that which Henri Bergson conceptualized as duration. Duration signifies life in the "concrete present" as opposed to the "ideal present."[66] The concrete present eludes spatialization, for it is an "undivided whole," a sensorimotor experience of having "one foot in my past and another in my future."[67] Existence as duration moreover connotes a dimension in which the past continually, ceaselessly grows within the self.[68] A passage from Bergson might supply an epigraph for this section of *Der Tod Georgs:* "We shall never reach the past unless we frankly place ourselves within it. Essentially virtual, it cannot be known as something past unless we follow and adopt the movement by which it expands into a present image, thus emerging from obscurity into the light of day."[69] Paul must enter duration in order to reconnect with memory in the temporal continuum.

Under the original terms of Georg and Paul's friendship, Georg, not Paul, personified duration. Their initial meeting is an intersection of two opposing energies. One has a destiny, he arrives and departs; the other represents *Ruhe,* inertia.[70] By the train trip in the third chapter, the friends are still together, but they have traded destinies. Georg, a ripening fruit who was not meant to die, has assumed the destiny of Paul, an aesthete trapped in stasis and detachment. What can one make of the fact that the coffin-maker brought a coffin too small for the body, other than the fact that the coffin bearing Georg had been designated for Paul's symbolically slighter frame?[71]

During the train trip, Paul's initial thoughts explicitly identify Georg with his (Paul's) own past, but also, for the first time, with a type of dialogical remembering radically unlike his own. He comes to this by realizing that Georg's death will finally sink in at the point later in life when he looks for a partner in reminiscence: "and later, much later, when his eyes, which then would no longer be hoping for much, would search for him, who like himself, had called this summer 'youth,' and in whose cool aging, memories would be drawn up hot and sweet when he said to him: 'Do you still remember?'" (71).[72] In the context of recollecting the life and work of the artist of memory, Paul conceptualizes the difference between himself and Georg as a distinction between two experiences of temporality. The first assumes that just as time can be measured in *Abschnitte* (sections) like clock time, so life can be contained and controlled through conscious memories that become vessels for life experience only after the fact. Satisfaction arises only at intervals separated by meaningless spans of empty time. "What lay in between had only been an empty path, and was it only at the end points that one stood still, and in what one had achieved, felt with pleasure the contents of one's life?" (61).[73] The flow of life is inherently meaningless, but one can bestow sense by standing apart and gaining distance from the flow—just as Paul does by imagining a spectacle of the dead and the living playing on an inner memory stage. If meaning is only to be found at resting places, terminal points, then death would provide the ultimate finale. The alternative view regards experience as unquantifiable: "Or was he one of those who knew that their life flowed, and that water did not stand still in order to look at itself? Those who knew that you couldn't contain it in jugs in order to stare into the flood caught within and say to it: '*You* are my life'... and who knew that hidden thinking became, inside us, breath and sound and words that tremblingly parted from our lips, and resoundingly returned to us, and, face to face with our thoughts, stood there like our double [*Doppelgänger*], frozen in fear" (73).[74] One cannot store memory as one might gather water in a vessel, but must instead *believe* that although the past remains hidden from view, it infiltrates (and unites) physical and mental life. The ability to associate between the visible and the invisible will ultimately enable Paul to acknowledge a transcendent God. The prerequisite for this type of relationship is not an escape from temporality, but the acceptance of life as duration.

This apparent digression in Paul's chain of retrospection in fact represents the beginning of a shift to Georg's style of recapturing the past. Whether or not the aesthete can be content with such an intangible conception of *Besitz* (possession) has yet to be determined. For now, Paul persists in his attempts to recapture Georg, and struggles to resist the desire to hold on and demolish the other by the familiar tactics of reification. The second turning point occurs when Paul, for the first time, manages to articulate a recollection of his last meeting with Georg that goes so far beyond the banal expressions that had surfaced thus far that it reads like a prose poem:

Georg had turned his back to the window, and his cheeks, tanned brown by the sun, were framed in a bright light. Georg's deep voice sounded full and calmly reverberated, softly enwrapped by the warm and light rain, as from the distant beating of wings of endless flocks of birds. They hadn't spoken with one another for a year; they talked about more or less trivial things, and their words aligned themselves in a monotonous and similar fashion, like the high windows with shutters closed in the heavy dusk of old palaces; but they knew: if one of the windows opened, then outside would lie brightly as a shining outspread landscape—their friendship. And now it was over; gone as quickly as the signs that you fleetingly write with your finger on glass clouded with breath.[75] (86–87)

Paul's recollection is marked by the unresolved tension between figures of depth and duration (voice; open window; land; friendship) and of surface and transience (words; closed windows; evanescent signs; glass). He observes all of this as from a third dimension altogether. Paul's acoustic memory still fails to retain Georg's words, but does recall a sonorous voice reminiscent of eternity. Like an angel (or a Christ figure), Georg brought the outside in, the far near, the perpetual into the fleeting. Paul intimates the hidden dimension beneath the surface of the *Nebeneinander*, namely "friendship," a limitless, bright expanse. Windows shut can also be open; the referential dimension abides. However, Paul at this stage still assumes that such intimacy is as transient as the sign traced on the steamy mirror. In the absence of true interpersonal connection, the hermeneutic fails; Georg has not yet been buried. "And he felt, amidst all the sorrow awakened by Georg's death, the joy of his own being-alive shamelessly rejoicing" (87).[76] Georg's death has awakened Paul to life—though not yet to the faculty by which living beings retain the dead. As a reflection of this wondrous emotion, Paul proceeds to map the feeling onto the landscape, looking out of the train window and seeing the barely visible signs of nascent life.

Paul then dives in even deeper. No longer content to feel wind in his hair, "he leaned far over the window ledge, and bent his body toward the wind." He suddenly feels driven to animate the wind with his voice: "For a moment he felt face to face, as if in a mute struggle, with the wind; then he had to speak, and he heard his own voice brightly cutting through the rattling of the train. 'Wind,' he cried, 'wind,' and it felt like good fortune that his breath moved through his lips and gave the wind its name, and forced it, the strong one, to carry along the echo of its name for a stretch" (89).[77] Years later Beer-Hofmann wrote: "Each thing only exists for us when we have named it."[78] Paul hears his own voice resonate and imagines it to be a bridge connecting his inner life with the external world. He notes that voice has duration, and the act of naming empowers him. By wresting from the wind its proper name, he vanquishes the power it had exerted over him in the past. Moreover, hearing his own voice above the ongoing noise corresponds to his own posture leaning out the window: his obtruding form bisects the path of wind and train and diverges at a right angle from the course along which he is being borne. Thus Paul himself bursts into duration, this time willingly. From this point on, Paul's struggle to recollect Georg's life translates into a struggle to narrate Georg's death and thereby integrate the unknowable into the stream of his own consciousness, with moderate success. The thread of attempted dialogue again falls slack. "Paul closed the window; then he stepped back into the compartment" (90).[79] Again: at stake in this struggle to narrate death is the capacity to know the unknowable, to derive, as if logically, the transition or bridge between the two inherently unbridgeable states. Encoded in this desire to interpolate the missing link (that which likewise is a blank space within the novella) is the wish to solve the riddle of the missing transitions that plagues the aesthete.

THE CIRCUIT CLOSES

Distinct perception is brought about by two opposite currents, of which the one, centripetal, comes from the external object, and the other, centrifugal, has for its point of departure that which we term "pure memory." —Henri Bergson

Paul returns to Georg via a distinctly new pathway. "As the train went around a bend, he saw the last car. Georg was lying inside it. Paul remembered how he had last seen him" (102).[80] When Paul looks out of the window and sees the car carrying Georg's body as the train bends around a curve, then associates to their last meeting, his own eyes close the circuit by means of which the friends will be reunited. This experience runs counter to Paul's earliest assessment of the train motion, when he was struck by the disparity between the thing-like, uncontrolled rattling of Georg's body and his own regular, unvarying motion along steel tracks—a contrast that made connective recollection inconceivable. But as he now perceives the last car, the common force moving both him and the dead Georg becomes an image of their abiding connection. The certainty about Georg's presence reflected in the words "da drinnen war Georg" echoes the night of chapter 1, when Paul harbored Georg in his own domain. Yet at this later moment, the two are united on Georg's terms—in motion, rather than at rest. Paul is now able to associate the visible trace with the absent, lost partner. This moment concludes a journey that looks alternately outside and in, matching external stimuli with dormant memory traces. The circuit begins to run both backwards and forwards: to harmonize those two operations—perception and recollection, *vorstellen* and *erinnern*—that in the memory individual had become desynchronized.

What makes this possible is a pair of associations that have no clear trigger in the text and that are qualitatively different from Paul's recollections of Georg. Paul unearths two traumatic childhood memories that function as primal scenes. He recalls standing before a toy store window on one particular winter morning. As Paul turns to leave the store, a sound draws his attention upwards to a collection of masks hanging high on the wall. "The ugliness of old age was gathered here in horrific distortion" (96).[81] The masks strike him as the consummate image of forgetfulness, "because mouth and eyes were merely holes, *incapable of storing the traces of experiences*" (102; emphasis added).[82] The description actually conflates the elderly peasant faces Paul glimpses from the train window and the masks in that toy store window into a frightening symbol of organic disintegration and reification. The face hardens ("versteint") into a larva, as the self becomes reduced to a surface incapable of retention. Habit wears down the body like a machine: "The smile had distorted itself through repetition; because it was granted continuity by life itself, it had become ugly" (97–98).[83] The notion that growing old severs life from dynamism illustrates aestheticism's dangerous affinity with its contrary, namely a mechanistic conception of organic life, whose premise is that life can be calculated just like the progress of inanimate objects.[84] Paul brands time the villain: "What, *what* had happened to them? . . . But every day had stolen from their selfhood" (99, 100).[85] While this passage is often interpreted as an introjection of traditional aestheticist cant, within the memory quest it fulfills a different purpose: it becomes a primal scene, a psychological cause, rather than a symptom. Beer-Hofmann suggests, in a word, that Paul's alienation from life in duration originated in a primordial fear of self-loss, traceable to the early fear that his face too would come to resemble that toy mask. The fact that he is able to retrieve this traumatic memory persuades Paul that he possessed powers of retention that he had never known. Paul begins to realize that memory offers a road into the open: an escape from the escape. Of the faces glimpsed in the landscape, he notes: "Many things he had passed by without much thought, but his memory, without the consent of his will, had retained them" (97).[86] Memory conserves and preserves irrespective of will. What feels transient does abide in a part of one's self that has no connection to visual centers of control. The train ride gives the character psychological depth. Recollection, in turn, alters Paul's mechanism of perception, allowing him to see the train as a figure for that closed circuit which we call memory: the *Rückweg* by which he might return to Georg, and to his own past.

Once life has been reconceptualized within duration, ancestral origins beckon. Yet it is not that simple. The final episode in Paul's memory quest, in which he testifies to his Jewish ancestry, is not entirely continuous with all that has preceded it. Paul's Judaic "grand récit," as Le Rider calls it, amounts to the statement that, even for Jews who know it not, Jewishness is an inalienable part of the self.[87] This alone was enough to establish Beer-Hofmann's reputation as a Jewish author. But it also addresses the broader question formulated by Jens Rieckmann: "the question of which forces— intellectual, cultural, social, or exclusively 'racial'—play the most significant role in the formation of identity."[88] In this respect, what was most problematic about the turn to Judaism is not its substance, but the fact that Beer-Hofmann stages the return of Jewishness via the blood in Paul's veins.

The epiphany is prefaced by Paul's request for a sign that would guarantee him future access to the evening's discoveries. "But what sign was given to him to show that this was not transient inside him, that this was not able to leave him?" (132).[89] The narrator responds: "But what this evening hour had given him, remained, always and only in him; not just comparable to the blood in his veins—it was his blood itself that had spoken to him, and to listen to it—this was what this hour had taught" (132–33).[90] The move from "comparable to blood" to "blood itself" suggests that Paul's past at long last has become present, and that the quest for signs, mnemotechnics, genres, narratives is over. But the turn to blood also evokes the essentializing certainty of organic, racial memory. Paul continues:

Because over the life of those whose blood passed through him, justice [*Gerechtigkeit*] had stood like a sun, but they were not warmed by its rays, nor had its light shone for them, and yet, before its blinding light they raised their trembling hands, reverently throwing a shadow upon their sorrow-filled brow.

Ancestors, wandering . . . astray; everyone against them. . . .

And behind them all a people, not begging for mercy, wrestling to obtain the blessing of their God; wandering over oceans, not held up by deserts, and always suffused by the feeling of the just God like the blood in their veins: their triumph–God's triumph, their defeat–God's verdict, they themselves determined to bear witness to his power, a people of saviors, anointed with thorns and chosen for suffering. And gradually removing their god from sacrifices and incense, they raised him high above their heads, until, no longer a battle god of shepherds, he—a guardian of all law—stood invisible over transient suns and worlds, shining over all. And he too was of their blood.[91] (133–34)

The blood imagery framing this narrative transmits to Paul his ancestry and, equally important, the legacy of worshipping a transcendent God. The centrality of transcendence establishes that the sheer experience of recollection has trained Paul to appreciate the invisible and unforeseeable aspects of existence. This God, like these ancestors, is present to Paul as the remembered Georg can be present; the channels of recollection correspond to those of belief. The memory quest is revealed to be the threshold marking a transition from aestheticism to belief.

Does it turn the aesthete into a Jew? The conclusion could not but disappoint those hoping to see the author's burgeoning Zionism in play, even as such an expectation holds the text to a standard it does not rightly claim for itself. Beer-Hofmann's Jewish hero does not turn into another Theodor Herzl—the prototype of a (self-stylized) aesthete-convert to Zionism, and a good friend of the author—but neither did his creator. Nor does the author end up inventing something like a Jewish *Jugendstil*—a literary analog to a design of Ephraim Moses Lilien (1874–1925), in which a Torah ark, Jewish star, and Hebrew inscription are framed by the classic motifs of art nouveau (fig. 10). Judaism comes to Paul, after all, not in the way of a political awakening or a religious conversion, but as an intimation of ancestral connection. Scheible and Hank interpret Paul's enduring social isolation following the "conversion" as a critique of bourgeois liberalism's inability to provide viable answers to the Jews of prewar Austria—an issue with greater ramifications for the author than for Paul.[92] On the other hand, critics like Le Rider who regard Paul's conversion as the individual's dionysiac submergence into the mystical totality of life err in the other direction, by denying memory, time, and history any influence on the conclusion.[93] More to the point is Hank's suspicion that Paul's Jewishness may be nothing more than "aestheticism in another guise." Is it real or virtual? Will it endure? These are questions the novelist has been posing all along, and not only about Jewish identity.

In this respect, how one interprets the conclusion hinges upon how one understands the turn to blood as a source of Jewish memory. At issue in the move from a cognitive process to blood memory is the passage from quasispiritual, quasipsychological sources of selfhood, which require reflection and self-analysis, to a purely somatic source. The effort to distill out the "blood" component from identity held currency not only among German and Austrian nationalists but also among a particular sector of Zionists.[94] Though Jewish nationalism was not immune to such chauvinism and biological rhetoric, it is fair to say that insofar as Jewish intellectuals themselves co-opted this discourse, they did not do so necessarily in the spirit of self-hatred; heeding one's blood was a metaphor for unearthing the inalienable Jew within. Still, if Paul's new powers of association culminate with the assertion that identity is finally a matter of one's blood heritage or organic, inherited memory, does this imply a retreat, not only from conscious choice and from will, but also from the very process of regaining self-knowledge? Does the climax of Paul's memory quest render the very act of recollecting obsolete?

Paul's connection to his Jewish ancestors bears an important caveat, namely that he cannot, as they did not, directly perceive the source of his destiny, just as surely as the mermaid statue shields her eyes. I suggest that this looking away mitigates against the objectionable aspects of blood memory. The fact that *erkennnen* (recognition) becomes paired with *nichtverstehen* (nonunderstanding) can be interpreted as an argument for a blind acceptance of fate; yet it must also be viewed in

10. Jewish artist Ephraim Moses Lilien's (1874–1925) illustration for a collection of ballads features a classic *Jugendstil* design (vines, flowers, female forms) framing a Torah ark with the tablets of the law, Jewish star, and candelabra. Inscribed in Hebrew is the illustrator's name: "Ephraim Moses son of Jacob Ha-cohen Lilien from the loyal sons of Zion." Private collection, Providence, R.I.

the context of the novella's progressive refutation of aestheticism or narcissism. The ambivalence arises from the author's attempt to stretch the organic model to enable Paul to access one further facet of his identity (ancestry), while simultaneously tempering that model so as to preempt its extremist misappropriations (racism). The organic model of memory does not offer as enlightened a resolution as is desirable, and Beer-Hofmann capitalizes on its rhetorical allure. But it generates a narrative that, when closely analyzed, appears to argue the opposite of a chauvinistic or essentialist position.

The narrative engendered by the blood contradicts the organic memory model in three ways. First, it acknowledges the presence of a transcendental signified: a God/sun who ordains the destiny of all created beings, body and soul. Second, it subordinates the discourse of organic memory to *Gerechtigkeit* (justice), a multivalent concept whose repeated occurrences toward the end of the novella emphasize the innate affinities between (and interdependence of) nature, metaphysics, and ethics. The word itself intrudes from a different register, "as if it had fallen from the sky, heavy and like iron, and now lay as something alien amidst his thoughts" (118).[95] Yet it connotes the principle of continuity that Paul (and the reader) have sought all along: an ethos of inalienable destiny equally characteristic of a river's natural flow and the miraculous outpouring of water from a rock. "Everything went its just way," the text notes, "fulfilling every law . . . that slept in its seed, awakening" (126).[96] For a path to be *gerecht,* it need only obey its own internal logic.[97] This is the aspiration of a literary poetics of association, and of the technique of free association in psychoanalysis. Out of the same confidence, Paul's ancestors could accept all twists of fate as implicitly (though not empirically) justified, and worship the divine embodiment of this ethos. *Gerechtigkeit,* a sign after all, signifies constancy in the absence of signs and continuity in the face of randomness.

Lastly, when Paul narrates the legacy attributed to his Jewish ancestry, he recounts a peculiar allegory of a people who *exorcised* the essence of their *Volkstum:* who took the powerful experience of their own inner destiny, released it from its particularistic roots, and elevated it into a universal principle. "And gradually . . . they raised God high above their heads, until, no longer a battle god of shepherds, he—a guardian of all law—stood invisible over transient suns and worlds, shining over all." Paul's narrative relies on biblical motifs and a scriptural idiom, but it gains distance from the biblical account by describing how the people themselves invented transcendence, namely by turning the parochial, immanent God of Genesis "who struggled with shepherds" into a transcendent, universalistic force, from whom one had to avert one's gaze.

Paul's myth alludes to an exchange between God and Moses in Exodus 33:18–23, in which Moses asks to behold God's presence. "And God answered, 'I will make all my goodness pass before you, and I will proclaim before you the name Lord, and the grace that I grant and the compassion that I show. But,' God said, 'you cannot see My face, for man may not see Me and live.'" Then follows the remarkable gesture that finds its way into Paul's theology: God offers to shield Moses with his "hand" as he passes by. "Then I will take My hand away and you will see My back; but My face must not be seen." *Der Tod Georgs* is nowhere more Jewish than when it centralizes the moment at which the face-to-face becomes excluded from the human-divine encounter.

By shielding their eyes, Paul's ancestors relinquished the temptations of aestheticism and chauvinism in a single moment. It is this gesture above all that leads the protagonist, even as he becomes acquainted with an immediate source of selfhood, to emulate his forebears and effectively surrender control once again—this time to an even greater memory plot, "a great, solemn circling, measured from primeval times on," reaching back to the Bible and to the creation of the universe (130).[98] By the same logic, I suggest, Beer-Hofmann nowhere calls these people Jews. Is it an act of evasion (or exorcism) on his own part, comparable to Hofmannsthal's erasure of his characters' Jewish names? Does he wish to stress that what the protagonist associates with his Jewish ancestry is a legacy that originated prior to, and runs deeper than, the *Volk* itself? A negative interpretation of this omission would attribute it to cowardice; a positive interpretation would read that the ancestral legacy is finally about the promise of memory "itself"; it falls short of offering a rational argument for justice (and even less, for conversion), but neither is it a conduit of blind determinism.[99] That a contemporary reader might be able to appropriate a Jewish legacy without the burdens imposed by *Jewishness* squares with the anti-ideological bent of the Viennese Jewish modernists. In sum, it is not just Paul who needs to relinquish empirical certainty about who is a Jew and why.

CONCLUSION

Even as Paul learns to remember previously forgotten and inaccessible facets of his being, at each step this new competence stops short of guaranteeing absolute selfknowledge—from such absolutes one must, so to speak, shield one's eyes.[100] Both are essential components of Beer-Hofmann's poetics of memory.

In 1943, Beer-Hofmann wrote an introduction to the memoir *Paula: Ein Fragment* in which he testified that composing a memoir presented the artist with a unique challenge. This genre, he felt, could not properly be called *Dichtung,* since it demanded that the artist surrender his will and free choice altogether to compose the memory text, for, in his words, "Memories—which do not submit to the strict order of time—are often capriciously—and yet perhaps, unconsciously, obeying a hidden law—ordered."[101] The notion of a hidden law, as I claimed at the outset, is capriciousness or "automatic writing" raised to the second power. Experiencing the sheer willfulness of his own memories while composing his last work leads Beer-Hofmann to postulate an inscrutable law governing its pathways—to favor law over contingency—and it may have been what lead him to a new understanding of the process by which his first major work was composed as well. The mystery of involuntary memory in literature had by this time crystallized in Marcel Proust's *À la recherche du temps perdu,* and there are clear reasons why a French reviewer wrote that Beer-Hofmann's novella of 1900 prepared him to encounter Proust. Yet in the late 1890s, rather than aestheticizing the *mémoire involuntaire,* Beer-Hofmann goes the opposite route: he uses involuntary memory to escape from the aesthetic labyrinth, into temporality and ancestral heritage—a passage that requires submission even as it promises *ranken,* a lifeline stretching backwards and forwards. While one might consider this solution retrograde from the vantage point of high modernism, as a strategy for salvaging the disunited subject of the fin de siècle it marks a distinguished chapter in its own right.

4 Anatomies of Failure

Jewish Tragicomedy in Schnitzler's *Der Weg ins Freie* (The Road into the Open, 1908) and *Professor Bernhardi* (1912)

I intercede for no one just because he happens to descend from the same family as I. . . . I was never someone's comrade just because he happened to occupy the same rank as I, never someone's classmate because he happened to be in the same class as I. . . . I don't feel solidarity with anyone because they happen to belong to the same nation, the same class, the same race, the same family to which I belong. It is exclusively my choice to whom I wish to feel related. —Arthur Schnitzler, "Bekenntnis"

For the first time the label Jew, which had so often frivolously, derisively, and contemptuously crossed his lips, began to appear to him in a completely new, as it were darker sense. A presentiment of this people's mysterious destiny, that somehow expressed itself in everyone who sprang from this origin, began to dawn in him; not less in those who tried to escape from it like a disgrace, an injury or a legend that didn't concern them, than in those who stubbornly referred back to it, as to a fate, an honor, or a fact of history which stood fast and immovable. —Arthur Schnitzler, *Der Weg ins Freie*

If anyone was equipped to produce the prototypical work of Viennese Jewish modernism, it was Arthur Schnitzler. A self-described "Austrian of Jewish descent writing in the German language," Schnitzler felt there was no intrinsic contradiction among the three facets of his identity; exactly how to communicate that feeling was another matter. "I am a Jew, an Austrian, a German. It must be so, because I feel insulted in the name of Judaism, Austrianness, and Germany whenever someone says something bad about one of the three."[1] What led Schnitzler to feel at home as a German-speaking Austrian Jew ran deeper than cosmopolitanism. Schnitzler's commitment to the land and the city of his birth led him to declare, even after the Lueger era (1897–1910): "We . . . experience the fate of this country as deeply as others do, perhaps even more deeply. How rooted we are with the land that gave us birth! What do the citizens matter, the diplomats, the monarchs? The land! The homeland!"[2] This sense of rootedness notwithstanding, Schnitzler was averse to any form of determin-

11. Arthur Schnitzler, with handwritten dedication to Joseph Chapiro.

ism, as he states in "Bekenntnis" (Confession), quoted above in the first epigraph. Yet he was all too aware that history had rendered that position obsolete. Schnitzler's enrollment at the University of Vienna in 1879 coincided with a dramatic rise in nationalism and Jew-hatred in student circles; throughout his career, he was subject to anti-Jewish attacks, censorship, and other indignities, among them the charge that Jews are temperamentally unable to produce great literature or to understand the Viennese mentality. To fend off these types of attacks, and at the same time to remain true to himself: these were the primary motives that gave rise to Schnitzler's experiments with Jewish writing (fig. 11).

The endeavor was especially pressing because unlike Beer-Hofmann or his friend Felix Salten, Schnitzler opposed both cultural and political Zionism.[3] He resisted attempts to honor him as a Jewish writer,[4] and he declined invitations to Zionist gatherings, which led to an undeserved reputation in Jewish circles as an assimilationist. As a writer, however, he allowed a well-drawn defense of Zionism to find its way into his first novel, which led the Zionists to appropriate him as a spokesman for their cause. Schnitzler did give a reading before the Prague Zionist group Bar Kochba in 1911. Yet his focus was upon creating a livable inward state, not a Jewish nation. As Robert Wistrich writes:

[Schnitzler] had seen with his own eyes how swiftly his Austrian fatherland could turn into an "enemy land" for the Jews, in spite of their economic prosperity and civic equality. He had never believed that polemics, apologetics, or political agitation by Jews could radically alter this situation. Yet he remained stubbornly attached to Vienna and the liberal cosmopolitan traditions of the late eighteenth-century German Enlightenment. Hence his sceptical individualism sought bravely to reaffirm the autonomy of the inner self in an age of collectivist ideologies such as nationalism, Darwinian racism, anti-Semitism, militaristic Imperialism, and even Zionism, which might threaten its integrity.[5]

This view of things did not allow Schnitzler much "Spielraum," as Egon Schwarz notes, which explains his reputation for public silence on political matters in general, as well as the fact that direct discussion of Jewish issues is largely absent from his extensive dramatic and novelistic oeuvres.[6] Yet two works, the focus of this chapter, concern themselves directly with the cultural, political, and psychological status of

Austrian Jews. The novel *Der Weg ins Freie* (1908) and the play *Professor Bernhardi* (1912) share more than a thematics of Jewish concerns; in their "failure" with readers early and late, their conscious crossing of forms and genres, and their provocation to consider the "Jewish question" anew, they respond to the situation by offering anatomies of failure: works that on formal and thematic levels are all about a hopeless hybridity failing to cohere in the well-made story or political program. These texts are prime expressions of the phenomenon described throughout this book under the heading of Viennese Jewish modernism. "The tragicomedy of contemporary Judaism" (*Die Tragikomödie des heutigen Judentums*) is simultaneously their theme and structure (*Road*, 113; *Weg*, 146).

THE EARLY RECEPTION OF SCHNITZLER'S JEWISH WORKS

The artistic sensibilities that made Schnitzler an important German modernist also worked against his reception as a Jewish writer. The long-awaited first novel *Der Weg ins Freie* and the controversial drama *Professor Bernhardi* both portrayed Viennese Jews parrying anti-Semitic insults large and small and searching for solutions, whether psychological, cultural, political, or religious, to the untenable conditions of life in an increasingly hostile society. On this level, Schnitzler's works were realistic, transparent: his acquaintances easily recognized the real-life counterparts behind his characters and plots. Yet the early reception history tells a different story. Despite their seeming engagement with Jewish issues, both works failed even with readers sympathetic to the Jews. Historian Richard Charmatz, damning *Professor Bernhardi* with praise of the author's reputation, delivered this judgment in 1912: "From you, most honored Herr Doktor, I expect *the* Austrian drama, the work that should sharpen our understanding and bring comfort to generations. Is the creative artist not lured by the dilemmas that have long been posed by the existence of our state, problems that are today more prevalent than ever? Has there not in Austria awoken a longing, a *Sehnsucht*, precisely now, to use the pen as a sword and thereby ennoble it?"[7] Schnitzler, of course, was aware of not having used his pen as a sword. As we shall see, the whole question of swordplay—of Jews dueling against Christians to preserve their honor—is a constant theme in both novel and drama. But what is remarkable about both works are the artistic lengths to which Schnitzler went to resist the duel: to frustrate the expectations of readers and viewers who expected a Jewish writer of Schnitzler's prominence to take a stand and show the "road into the open."

The author's close friend Gustav Schwarzkopf complained that the main character in *Der Weg ins Freie* failed to develop. He added that there was no clear connection between the plot (the story of a young Christian baron who has an affair with a Catholic girl, gets her pregnant, and ends the relationship after a stillbirth) and the treatment of the *Judenfrage*.[8] Minnie Benedikt, an early romantic interest of the author's and the daughter of the editor of the *Neue Freie Presse,* told him that she was bothered by the unflattering portrayal of her in the person of Else Ehrenberg, and, Schnitzler noted, was "very opposed to the treatment of the Jewish question (like most Jews, from what I hear)."[9] The primary indicator that the Jewish novel failed to champion the Jewish cause was the absence of "heroic Jews." Journalist Anton Bettelheim felt that the novel failed to tackle the Jewish question "with sufficient courage."

Dr. Bettelheim . . . complained about my novel that the "Jewish question" was not tackled with sufficient courage. I responded that until now I had heard mainly the opposite—and anyway, I am not here to "tackle questions," but to depict figures, people, who take this or that stance to questions. When he realized how silly he sounded, he came back to this after some digressions to say what he had meant: "I had neglected to depict the heroic Jews." Who? I asked. He responded: Friedjung. I: "Yes, he is a very talented man, but what makes him a heroic Jew?" He holds fast to Judaism, he isn't baptized. "And you miss such characters in my novel? Is Leo Golowski less heroic than Friedjung?" To such audacities is an otherwise intelligent person brought by hypercriticism, grudges, and partisanship.[10]

If Schnitzler's tone sounds exasperated, it is because the hero Bettelheim recommends, Heinrich Friedjung (1851–1920), was a German nationalist who argued in favor of annexation up until the moment when Jews were written out of the "German race" in 1885, in the wake of the Linz Program, which Friedjung himself had coauthored. Schnitzler is being somewhat disingenuous when he recommends, as an alternative, his own character, Leo Golowski (modeled on Theodor Herzl). For, as we shall see, one of the primary effects of Schnitzler's deformation of novelistic and dramatic conventions was the eclipsing of heroes and heroism; the treatment of Leo Golowski's duel epitomizes this strategy. Dueling—what Schnitzler is being accused of not doing in his public agency as a man of letters—enters these texts as a figure, not for the contest between right and wrong, but for the tragicomic status of Jews in Vienna, whose plight may be more accurately represented by the fate of the hapless baron and his Catholic mistress than by the Jew who takes destiny into his own hands. But such subtlety was lost on early readers. They expected a writer of Schnitzler's stature to take sides, and for this purpose they awaited a recognizable hero who would show the way. What they got instead was a Christian aesthete (Georg in *Der Weg ins Freie*) and an apolitical doctor who goes against the Catholic Church and then steadfastly refuses to grant that there was any political calculation in his action (Dr. Bernhardi in *Professor Bernhardi*).

The withholding of a program would bring Schnitzler a kind of success that was anathema to him: these two works dealing with Jewish themes were vulnerable to cooptation by almost every ideological camp. The liberal papers the *Neue Freie Presse* and *Die Zeit* found the novel to contain a fully accurate depiction of Viennese Jewish society. The Zionist paper *Die Welt* praised it as a pro-Zionist novel. The left-wing *Arbeiter-Zeitung* identified with the novel's socialist heroine, Therese Golowski, and attacked Schnitzler for dealing only with upper-class Viennese Jews. The right-wing anti-Semitic papers such as *Das deutsche Volksblatt* read it as an anti-Jewish novel because the plot ultimately removes its hero from the Viennese Jewish milieu, which is shown to be decadent and ingrown, and sends him to Germany.[11] It is a sign of the times that a book many regarded as an important Jewish novel was one the Nazis opted not to burn in 1933. Works of Schnitzler's with no explicit Jewish content were considered *more* Jewish in the eyes of the Nazis.

From the standpoint of Jewish cultural studies, a failed aesthetic is no less interesting than a successful one, especially when the cultural pressures defining success and failure are so clearly at work in deforming efforts at European literature into the odd productions of Viennese Jewish modernism. The reviews provide part of the picture of the early reception; Schnitzler's own expressions of fear of artistic failure in writing both novels and dramas also help fill in the author's anticipation of what it would it mean to be a Jewish writer. His thoughts, gathered from numerous diary entries, can be summarized as follows:

- He wanted to write "the great Viennese novel" or no novel at all.[12]
- He pictured his novel as next in the line of great German bildungsromans: Goethe's *Wilhelm Meister,* Keller's *Der grüne Heinrich,* Mann's *Buddenbrooks.*[13]
- He feared that a Jew is incapable of writing great drama.[14]
- His attraction to the real situation of Jews brought him also to the roman à clef, yet he feared that its sensational aspect would diminish his artistic achievement.[15]
- He realized that as a novelist he really had no adequate solution to the gathering threats to Jewish existence. He was divided between the view that "security is nowhere, other than in me," the phrase he chose for the book's motto, and the less hopeful conclusion, which he admitted to himself in his journals, that "security is nowhere."[16]

Variations on these hopes and fears could be repeated for each of the authors treated in this study. In his usual crystalline way, Franz Kafka sums up the Jewish writer's predicament: "The impossibility of not writing, the impossibility of writing German, the impossibility of writing otherwise."[17]

The drama *Professor Bernhardi* also met with a hostile early reception. It was banned by the Austrian censors in October 1912, before its first production at the Deutsches Volkstheater, due to its "allegedly 'distorted' depiction of Austrian public life."[18] Yet the view that the play "betrayed Austria" and was "polemically anti-clerical" was countered by the complaint that the play lacked any political commitment whatsoever.[19] The liberal press could not decide. While *Der Morgen* and the *Neue Freie Presse* praised the play for taking a moral stance (above politics), Robert Hirschfeld of the *Neues Wiener Tagblatt* wrote that, regardless of its moral stance, the play offended the "inner censor" because it was artistically flawed. When the play was first performed in Berlin in November 1912, it was attacked for its weak hero, and the same was true in later reviews of the published play in Austria. Paul Goldmann, an old friend of Schnitzler's and a Dreyfusard who had fought a duel in

Paris, expressed the common opinion when he linked the weak hero to a flaw in Schnitzler's own constitution: "It is regrettable that Professor Bernhardi won't fight; and it is regrettable that the writer only touches upon the major problem that his material posed for him."[20]

Schnitzler was obsessive about recording such comments and collecting reviews, and he often responded, either in print or on his own furiously marked-up copies.[21] His retorts are often revealing of the tortured cultural logic standing behind these literary experiments. The irony of having written a comedy, only to have it vilified as either too polemical or not polemical enough, was not lost on him. "Some can't get past the idea that I have written a political play, the others, that I haven't written such a play."[22] Another interpretation he believed diminished his achievement was the autobiographical one, made public by Georg Brandes in an article in the journal *Merkur*.[23] Brandes claimed that a play based upon personal insult risked being interpreted as polemic rather than poetry.[24] In what has been regarded as an act of willful forgetting, Schnitzler denied the charge that the plot had any relation to the defamatory campaign against his father, Dr. Johann Schnitzler, who founded a polyclinic much like Bernhardi's Elizabeth Institute.[25] Although he wrote about his father's experiences in detail in his 1904 autobiography *Jugend in Wien* (My Youth in Vienna), he insisted that the plot of his Jewish drama was purely fictional and that only someone with no feeling for art would regard it as motivated by a vendetta.

In responding to his critics, Schnitzler did not hesitate to name the odd genre of his experiment: "*Bernhardi* is not a political play [*Tendenzstück*], nor does it want to be one, neither in its particulars nor in the general sense. If one must categorize it, I would prefer to have it be viewed as a character comedy [*Charakterkomödie*]."[26] Schnitzler's response was along similar lines to that of Ludwig Hirschfeld, a critic for the *Neue Freie Presse*, who attempted to locate the drama's significance in its numerous discussions. "You call *Professor Bernhardi* a spirited dramatic discussion. That is not entirely true. *Professor Bernhardi* is not a dramatic discussion, but rather a character comedy, whether spirited or not is not for me to determine." Any play contains discussions, Schnitzler writes; yet the essential "material of poetry [*Dichtkunst*] and the value of drama"—that which elevates true drama above a theater play—is "the word and only the word . . . that which is unlearnable and barely able to be grasped"—the unutterable message lying beneath the surface.[27]

Just as we find Schnitzler expressing doubts that he could live up to the standards imposed by the great European novel, so, as a dramatist, he feared failure. His diary records the following exchange with his wife Olga about modern drama:

On the occasion of Schönherr's "Family" conversation with O. about the dramatic.[28] It is denied to me (probably to all Jews) to write an absolutely good drama. This requires one thing: "to make one's peace with circumstances" [*sich innerhalb des gegebenen zu beruhigen*]. Worldviews such as those expressed in the third act of *Ruf*[29] (and also in the fifth act of *Charolais*)[30] offset the dramatic. The hero of drama must proceed within the existing laws.

Kerr specifically likes (only) the third act of *Ruf* ("with a promising future" [*Zukunftsträchtig*]). The dramatist may be heavy with pasts, but he should never promise the future.[31]

The point, of course, is not whether it is true that the successful dramatist must be at peace with circumstances. Rather, the interesting question is why a Viennese Jewish writer would come to this conclusion. Schnitzler did not subscribe to the postmodern view that marginality is a potential source of strength; he experienced it as detrimental to his work. Marginality brought with it a tendency to engage in polemics ("worldviews") to the detriment of dramatic art. Further, the hero of the drama must appear to be motivated by fraught circumstances ("heavy with pasts") and not by idealized resolutions pulled out of the hat ("promise the future"). For Schnitzler, the aesthetic criteria of successful dramatic art made it impossible for an overtly Jewish dramatist to succeed. Any and every representation of the Jewish question would be seen as polemical from the outset, as the reception history proves. These fears, albeit born of an insecure temperament, proved to be an accurate assessment of the cultural dynamics of reception: the perception of futility shaped the Jewish works Schnitzler did write. Bernhardi's character has long been "a chief bone of interpretive contention. Is he weak, or a man of principle?"[32] It was precisely by refusing to provide definitive answers to this type of Jewish question that both works were able to respond to another Jewish question, namely, what literary strategies can do justice to the tragicomedy of contemporary Judaism?

TOWARD AN AESTHETICS OF DETACHMENT

Schnitzler was convinced that the most defeating consequences of anti-Semitism were the reaction formations to which it gave rise—hypocrisy, self-deprecation, social posturing—and he consistently attacked these poses in others. He identified three particular attitudes arising out of the anti-Semitic milieu: "Snobismus," those (like Hofmannsthal) who assimilated to the extreme and attempted to curry favor with the mainstream (also called "Jewish anti-Semites"); "Renegatentum," Jews who were baptized or became German nationalists (such as Karl Kraus and Alfred Polgar); and the "Esoi Juden," Jews who lacked respect for other Jews.[33] Many of his recorded perceptions about the "so-called Jewish question," as he referred to it, revolve around the insight that Jew-hatred—a visible societal crisis—and Jewish self-hatred—an invisible, psychological dilemma—were inextricably bound together. An autobiographical fragment from 1912 reads: "It was impossible, in particular for a Jew who was in the public eye, to disregard his Jewishness, as the others didn't do this, not the Christians and *even less so the Jews*. One had the choice of being viewed as insensitive, obtrusive, insolent, or as sensitive, bashful, and paranoid."[34] Jews who escaped the stereotypes imposed upon them by the majority culture were no less trapped. Yet the comment that directly follows contains a clue as to how an author might position himself above the fray: "And even if one guarded one's inner and outer pose to the degree that one was neither of these, it was impossible to remain fully unaffected, just as it would be impossible for a person to remain impassive, who, though he had his skin anesthetized, was forced to watch with wakeful and open eyes as unclean knives tear, cut into it, until the blood comes."[35] This passage calls to mind the stance of the "enlightened" European explorer in Franz Kafka's *In der Strafkolonie* (In the Penal Colony), who declares: "I can neither help nor hinder you."[36] It suggests a path that many Jewish writers appear to have taken: the stance of the detached observer who, because numb to his own pain, is able to testify to the violence being inflicted on himself and his people. Here is the point of Schnitzler's duel.

The first step in Schnitzler's aesthetics of detachment was to invent hybrid forms that would forestall any impression that the author was taking sides, and then, when pressed, to deny that form had any significance whatsoever. A second central strategy was to forfeit the Jewish hero, and moreover, to select as protagonists virtual Jews rather than real Jews. This tactic forced readers to question who is a Jewish character and why, and thereby to mistrust their fixed assumptions about Jewish identity as such. These two tactics evoke the discussion of minor literature in Gilles Deleuze and Félix Guattari: "The three characteristics of minor literature are the deterritorialization of language, the connection of the individual to a political immediacy, and the collective assemblage of enunciation."[37] Though the full relevance of these strategies will become clearer in what follows, a few general points can be made at the outset. The brief account of Schnitzler's early reception already suggests the importance of rhetorical "territory," with each reader claiming Schnitzler's text as his or her own, even as the text itself does its best to subvert easy appropriation. The novel's own struggle for form extends from Schnitzler's personal crisis of self-expression; it in turn affects almost all members of the novel's young generation.[38] The second trait is also relevant. Deleuze and Guattari elaborate: "The second characteristic of minor literatures is that everything in them is political. In major literatures, in contrast, the individual concern (familial, marital, and so on) joins with other no less individual concerns, the social milieu serving as a mere environment or a background. . . . Minor literature is completely different; its cramped space forces each individual intrigue to connect immediately to politics. The individual concern thus becomes all the more necessary, indispensable, magnified, because a whole other story is vibrating within it."[39] The Jewish milieu of *Der Weg ins Freie* does not simply provide an innocuous backdrop for Baron Georg von Wergenthin. Both Georg and Professor Bernhardi are at once implicated in and detached from the intense confusion and contradictions of Jewish Vienna; the Jewish story vibrates within them. As to the third point, the disappearance of the individual subject in favor of collective enunciation: though the Jewish collective in the novel is comprised of many voices and political stances, the potential for any one to develop from a type into a character is severely restricted. Even characters who attempt to break out—Heinrich Bermann becomes a creative writer, Bernhard Stauber pursues a medical career, and Leo Golowski fights a duel— are powerless in the greater scheme of things. One of the most radical experiments of *Professor Bernhardi* was to construct an "assemblage" out of friends and foes alike, none of whom attain three-dimensionality as characters. Even so, it is important to note that in Schnitzler (if not in Kafka), virtuality accords characters a measure of the humanity that reality denies them.

A final strategy, closely related to the sinking of the hero, is the writer's persistent need to undermine "serious" sources of inevitability (*Notwendigkeit*), knowledge, and destiny in favor of comedic and contingent forces (*Zufall*). In the unpublished "Confession" with which this chapter opens, Schnitzler proclaims his refusal to endow life's accidents with predestination: "I don't feel solidarity with anyone because they happen to belong to the same nation, the same class, the same race, the same family, to which I belong." Throughout his writings, chance supplies a potent alternative to the vicious dialectic of racial determinism and political correctness.

With these three strategies—hybridization of form, withholding of heroism, overreliance on chance—Schnitzler failed to respond to the question that so obsessed his public. But as we shall see, adopting an aesthetics of detachment also enabled him to call attention to the human drama underlying it all. In other words, these two experiments were motivated neither by ambivalence nor skepticism, but by the challenge of translating the humanistic position into an enlightened poetics. Buried within *Der Weg ins Freie* is an apt metaphor for a method that seeks to expose the fleeting similarities of polarized communities and characters whose destinies ultimately oppose one another. In a rambling letter Heinrich writes to Georg in Italy, he reports that their friend Gleißner has a new sport: "he plays with human souls" [*er spielt mit Menschenseelen*] (*Road,* 161; *Weg,* 209). Gleißner's psychological pastime has two complementary goals: to turn an innocent girl into a depraved one and a prostitute into a saint. The experiment comes home to roost in the final chapter, when Georg spots Gleißner at the opera sitting with a strange woman by his side. Georg wonders: which of the two types is she, the innocent one on the road to depravity or the prostitute en route to sainthood? Of course he cannot tell: "Halfway through the process [*in der Mitte des Wegs*] they would look just about the same" (*Road,* 261; *Weg,* 335). The wisecrack contains the wisdom of Schnitzler's hybrid experiments. Playing with human souls was also Schnitzler's pastime, his aesthetic *Spiel.* But playing with souls allowed him to be true to the human side of things, to foreground the uncanny similarities that underlie incompatible communities. While the titles of both Jewish works create desire for ultimate solutions, the plots refocus our attention on that which transpires midway, *in der Mitte des Wegs,* to victims and heroes alike.

"BUT HAVEN'T YOU WRITTEN TWO BOOKS?" THE FORMAL ENIGMA OF *DER WEG INS FREIE*

By all accounts, the most serious flaw marring the reception of *Der Weg ins Freie* is its enigmatic, two-in-one structure. "But haven't you written two books?" wrote Schnitzler's good friend, the Danish critic Georg Brandes, in a letter of 1908. "The relationship of the young Baron and his mistress is one matter, and the new condition of the Jewish population of Vienna because of anti-Semitism is another one that, it seems to me, has no necessary relation to the first. The mistress is not Jewish."[40] Most recent interpreters echo Brandes's critique of the novel's bifurcated structure, viewing it as a work that attempts to do two different things, neither with great success. "A novel of development without development: it is also, however, a novel of society without social interconnectedness" writes Russell A. Berman.[41] On the basis of structure alone, *Der Weg ins Freie* denies both its characters and its readers the redemption that the title promises.[42] "His novel depicts the end of liberalism and the psychological compromises that individuals are required to make. . . . We have reached the end of the road; only Schnitzler is not willing to acknowledge, as the Zionists do, that this road was ultimately a dead end."[43] The reading I offer here is not an attempt to suggest that the dead end is actually a way out. My purpose instead is to deepen the enigma, so as to better understand its cultural logic.

The first step is to note that the novel's two subplots inhabit two different prose genres. The Jewish plot is a *Zeitroman,* a genre with early nineteenth-century origins that typically foregrounds the social, political, cultural and or religious affairs of the present day. Within the turn-of-the-century Jewish *Zeitroman,* devoted to "depicting a colourful gallery of contemporary Austrian Jewish types confronted with the problems of Jewish identity under Catholic anti-Semitic rule,"[44] the absence of a central protagonist is not remarkable. Schnitzler includes a cast of secondary characters modeled on his Viennese Jewish contemporaries.[45] Young and old, male and female, these characters represent all positions between the "Scylla of anti-Semitism and the Charybdis of Zionism,"[46] with the exception of the *Ostjuden,* who are present only by allusion. While these characters have minor subplots, the *Zeitroman*'s main components are conversation, debate, and retrospection. Schnitzler also employs a shifting narrative lens for the "discussion novel," which fosters the impression of a multifaceted yet static social portrait rather than a developing story.

Both framing and interrupting these political discussions are scenes that comprise a second subplot, the "novel of development."[47] This plot relates a year in the life of Freiherr Georg von Wergenthin, a twenty-seven-year-old aristocrat and budding composer with distinct aestheticist predilections, starting with his reentry into social life following the death of his father two months earlier. Georg begins seeing Anna Rosner, the daughter of Catholic bourgeois parents, who is likewise musically inclined and whom he has no intention of marrying. A child is almost immediately conceived; the pair travels to Italy for the duration of the pregnancy and returns to the outskirts of Vienna, where Anna delivers a stillborn son. The infant's death marks the end of the affair; Georg takes a position as *Kapellmeister* in Detmold, and the novel's final chapter describes his first visit back to Vienna after a three-month absence. Although the bildungsroman proceeds chronologically, Georg's plot is largely shaped by accidents. Georg's father dies unexpectedly; the pregnancy is unexpected, and the stillbirth, even more so; the position that opens up in Germany is due to another "sudden death."

Chance is more than a leitmotif; it is the very motor of Georg's existence. The profound challenge Schnitzler sets up for Georg is to transvalue these random occurrences as purposeful ones, or in other words, to see them as points along "a mysterious but sure line" (eine geheinmisvolle und sichere Linie) (*Weg*, 11; *Road*, 6).

How does the story of a Viennese baron and his mistress, a rather banal story on its own terms, bear any real relevance to the agon of Jewish Viennese intellectuals? Conversely, what real impact do the profound life struggles of these Jewish *Zeittypen* have upon Georg's predicament, and do they contribute in any way to his development? The absence of a moral outcome is especially glaring in that such an expectation is built in to both the *Zeitroman* and bildungsroman genres. Writes J. M. Hawes: "The novel thus leaves us, as it leaves its protagonists, 'vater- and heimatlos' in the broadest sense. Just as they cannot discover the 'Heimat' of an ethically comprehensible world, we are left without a reliable concluding voice. Any doubt as to whether this is a structural feature of the text is dispelled by the way in which it continually juxtaposes polar opposites, with no indication of which alternative, if either, is to be read as authoritative."[48] Compounding the structural difficulty is the fact that Georg, the figure charged with linking the two subnovels, is so weak. Schnitzler states unequivocally, in his response to Brandes, that the burden of the novel's unity rests squarely on Georg's shoulders.

Most esteemed Mr. Brandes, you are right that my book contains two novels, and that, from an artistic standpoint, the connection may lack absolute necessity. Even during my work I always felt that it would come out this way—but I could not, or did not, want to help myself. Because as carefully as I composed the book, it just became itself, while I wrote it. . . . The relationship between Georg and his mistress was always just as important to me as his relationship to the different Jews of the novel—I managed to depict a year in the life of Freiherr von Wergenthin, in which he attains clarity about all kinds of people and problems and also about himself.[49]

Schnitzler does not deny that he has composed two separate novels; he even agrees that the connection lacks inevitability ("absolute Notwendigkeit") from an artistic perspective, going so far as to claim that the book, like Anna's and Georg's progeny, "just became itself, while I wrote it." The letter leaves no doubt that both plots are of equal importance and that both serve the same purpose: the enlightening, not of the Jews, but of Georg.

Rather than clarify things, the author's comments only exacerbate the enigma. On a superficial level, Georg's role is self-evident. A hinge figure, he drifts freely and frequently in and out of two worlds: one private, apolitical, Christian, and ultimately Germanic; the other social, highly politicized, Jewish. On a typical day, he will spend time with Anna; attend a Jewish salon; leave to escort Anna home; then go on to a café to meet his Jewish friend Heinrich Bermann. Georg's perspective, conveyed by an admixture of narrated monologue and interior monologue, is as dominant as it is limited. His profoundly ineducable nature, his self-absorption, and above all his apathy toward the dilemmas of his far weightier Jewish counterparts make it difficult to see what might qualify him for this important role. The enigma of *Der Weg ins Freie* is not only why Schnitzler composed the novel in this way, but why he himself views the very lack of necessity—embodied by Georg—as necessary.

All of this puts even more pressure on our dilettante protagonist, a figure who, despite having no political engagement whatsoever, contains the key to the novel's cultural politics. The questions remain: Why does this forgettable character bear the weight of Schnitzler's grand attempt at nothing less than "the total depiction of an epoch"?[50] Why might the "great Viennese novel" need to be a hybrid of a Jewish *Zeitroman* and a German bildungsroman?

In an examination of the bildungsroman in European modernism, Franco Moretti suggests a framework within which the internally unstable text can be construed as a positive chapter in the bildungsroman tradition. The conventional view has been that Georg's character is unfit for *Bildung* in the classical sense.[51] Yet I would identify Schnitzler's novel, as Moretti does Kafka's *Amerika,* as marking a turning point in the history of the genre. It stands between two more recognizable literary formations: on the one hand the "well-functioning bildungsroman, and the Long Nineteenth Century of Conrad and Mann; on the opposite side, erratic and unsteady structures, and the modernism to come of Rilke, Kafka and Joyce."[52] What arises in the interim is a literary failure when judged by the standards of either terminus: "the sort of thing that occurs when a form deals with problems it is unable to solve." The problem *Der Weg ins Freie* cannot solve is the nonintersection of Jewish and Christian communities; the best it can do is translate the sociopolitical problem into a generic one. A further sign of failure, according to Moretti, is a disjunctive relationship between "kernels" and "satellites," between the hero and his world.[53] "What really happened when the nineteenth-century episode fell apart, then, was that narratives could concentrate either on kernels or on satellites: the late bildungsroman chose the former, and modernism, the latter."[54] Rather than choose one or the other, Schnitzler constructs two plots—a kernel plot and a satellite plot—that are all but incompatible, or, in his own words, whose connection lacks "absolute inevitability." His motive for doing so is to depict the failure of the Christian-Jewish encounter on a formal level. Schnitzler has the Jewish world supply the constant, the satellite; Georg is a kernel, yet his point of view dominates. The very factors that render Georg the weak link between two nonintersecting genres are thus a measure of the work's simultaneous failure and success.

SCHNITZLER'S VIRTUAL JEWS

If destabilizing the form of the Jewish novel was Schnitzler's most visible strategy, a second priority, to undermine assumptions about Jewish identity, inspired a radical experiment in characterization of Christians and Jews alike. In casting the lead figures in both novel and drama, Schnitzler went out of his way to build expectations of Jewish types, only to replace them with virtual Jews: proxies whose very divergence from the expectation—a Catholic mistress for a Jewish one; a passive activist for the "Jewish" cause—drew attention to their failure to live up to a heroic conception. Virtual Jews are characters who observe Jews, mimic Jews, learn from Jews, "happen to be Jewish" (in the case of Bernhardi), or who happen not to be Jewish (in the case of Anna and Georg). Here it is the last part of Georg Brandes's question that provides the key to Schnitzler's method: why, against every expectation, did Schnitzler make the female victim, Georg's mistress, a Catholic instead of a Jew?

Schnitzler took up this very question in his response to Brandes in a letter dated April 7, 1908. Why couldn't he cast the mistress as a Jew? "I could not. The figure of Anna appeared to me from the very start as incontrovertibly Catholic. I finally had no intention of proving anything, neither that Christians and Jews don't get along, nor that they are able to get along—I wanted rather to represent, without bias, people and relationships I have observed (whether in the outside world or in fantasy makes no difference)."[55] The difficulty of representing Jewish themes and characters is that everything is "loaded" in advance. Placing a Jewish-Christian couple in the foreground, for instance, especially a couple that loses a child, would immediately lend itself to a political reading—namely an allegorical critique of Jewish assimilation and intermarriage.[56] At the same time, by admitting that he opted *not* to depict a Jewish-Christian couple, Schnitzler acknowledges that ideological considerations *did* influence him. There would appear to be no out. He even withheld the heroes, characters who might have helped heal the *formal* breach between *Zeitroman* and bildungsroman. Schnitzler sacrificed formal cohesiveness and inexorability of plot in order to preserve the illusion of ideological indifference, and the appearance of neutrality was carefully planned. Early drafts of the novel contain both more explicit anti-Semitic discourse and more pointed Jewish propaganda than the final version.[57] Marc Weiner, in analyzing the role of Wagnerism in the text, points out that the conductor of the two performances of *Tristan und Isolde* that Georg attends had to have been Gustav Mahler. Omitting this detail was consistent with Georg's own mind-set, in this case, repression of the heroic Jew. To have highlighted the heroism of a Jew would have violated Schnitzler's artistic principle of representing things as they are!

Yet even virtual Jews cast shadows, and Anna's Jewish shadow haunts *Der Weg ins Freie*. Most reviewers wanted her to be Jewish; the *Times Literary Supplement* even wrote that she was Jewish.[58] Anna resembles the Jewish characters, above all, in her excessive devotion to Georg. "Anna was destined to become a mother" is one of the novel's central motifs, and it is a destiny she fulfills, both by babying Georg and by becoming pregnant by him. Georg, who never recovered from his own mother's early death, is of course drawn to just this aspect of her character. Anna parts company with the novel's Jewish mothers in being what Theodor Fontane in *L'Adultera* calls a "cold" rather than a "warm" Madonna. The account she gives of her erotic awakening is about renouncing rather than surrendering to sexual feelings. Anna's sobriety is nowhere more in evidence than in the scenes following her child's stillbirth. She recovers much more quickly than Georg, as the loss puts to rest any doubt that the relationship is over. Her final reported gesture is to place Georg's farewell roses on the baby's grave.

Anna's characteristic loyalty (*Treue*) is also coded Catholic, as it is unlike that of the novel's two Jewish daughters, Else Ehrenberg and Therese Golowski.[59] Therese, a radical socialist, is the character most clearly associated with self-sacrifice, and Anna admires her: "I admire all people in general who are willing to risk so much for something that is really none of their concern. And when it happens to be a young lady, a beautiful young lady like Therese . . . I am only all the more impressed" (*Road*, 21).[60] Yet Therese's sacrifice is politically motivated and self-aware—what the novel calls "überklug" (conceited)—and in these respects, coded Jewish. Anna's decision at the end of the second chapter to cast her lot with Georg "with the firm resolution to accept all happiness and sorrow that lay in store for her"[61] is a pathetic attempt to imitate the conviction she admires in her Jewish counterparts. Anna's sacrifice is religious, because absolute, and the fact that she is a lapsed Catholic makes her fate even more dire than it might have been. In her cyclical trajectory from daughterhood to aborted motherhood back to daughterhood, the Catholic Anna becomes the novel's true victim, one who only happened not to be Jewish, but who ultimately learns the lesson of Jewish survival: the virtue of detachment. That Anna is both predestined for and denied motherhood epitomizes Schnitzler's representation of principal figures, and the same strategy will be at work in *Professor Bernhardi*. It is as if the relation between major and minor dramatis personae has been reversed and the heroes have been ushered to the wings.

That this approach to characterization was at cross-purposes with any perceived Jewish agenda is amply illustrated by the Nazis' decision to withhold the book from the flames. The approach was consistent, however, with Schnitzler's purpose as a novelist: "I wanted . . . to represent, without bias, people and relationships I have observed." Schnitzler needed Anna to stay Catholic in order to show that there are other kinds of victimization at work in Viennese society, for instance the ostracism of women who become pregnant outside marriage. He also evokes, through negation, stories of successful integration on one hand and family life on the other. Georg refuses to marry Anna, where he might have done the right thing and recognized that his possible salvation lay through her. In Beer-Hofmann's early novella *Das Kind* (The Child, 1892), the secular Jewish protagonist is inspired by the faith of his Catholic girlfriend at the moment when he also overcome by guilt due to the death of their child. Though the emotion is short-lived, the protagonist begins to recollect long-forgotten liturgical phrases in the hope that they will restore his own lost faith.

Unsurprisingly, the same skewed approach to characterization shapes the representation of Georg. Georg inherits the contours of his personality from Anatol, Schnitzler's first aesthete. Georg is Anatol writ large: we observe his repeated and pathetic rationalizations, paranoia, sentimentalism, and full-blown narcissism. But

we are forced to take Georg seriously in large part because Anna does, and by extension, and even more remarkably, because the Jews do. The Jews mentor him,
although he is profoundly uneducable, welcoming him again and again into a Jewish circle. However predictable, Georg's behavior is not reducible to typology alone,[62]
for Schnitzler gives us intimate access to his thought processes. Furthermore, he
makes Georg endure a chain of traumatic events—in particular, the deaths of his
father, mother, and son.[63] Whereas Anatol obsessed over fidelity in love, Georg must
reckon with fidelity toward a (symbolically doomed) family, to the *Generationskette*
linking fathers and sons. In the novel's code, family and home are stabilizing loci of
Jewish identity for the younger generation.[64] I have argued elsewhere that Georg's
existential struggle to move beyond his experience of life as a random sequence of
unrelated episodes and to embrace Anna amounts to a Jewish *Bildung*, in particular
since Georg's Jewish contemporaries are his prime mentors in this quest.[65] Coming
to terms with his own childhood memories (above all with the trauma of his mother's
death) in anticipation of becoming a father makes his a virtually Jewish plot.

All told, however, Georg's function in the Jewish domain is utterly confusing.
Schnitzler goes to extreme lengths to preempt two expected interpretations of Georg's
psychological detachment from the Jews (and just about everyone else except himself). He is neither an obvious ally nor a visible foe; neither an anti-Semite nor a true
partner in dialogue; "I can neither help, nor hinder you." The Jewish characters are
drawn to him but doubt he understands them. His is the optic through which the
reader views Jewish experience; yet his gaze is voyeuristic and partial. Heinrich is the
first to tell Georg that his daemon, his deepest purpose, is to be a passive observer.
Georg has little appreciation for this insight until late in the book, when he attends
the opera. A performance of Wagner's *Tristan und Isolde* triggers this recognition,
reported as follows:

At such moments, of all his relationships to this beloved art, only one remained: to be able
to penetrate it with deeper understanding than any other person. And he felt that Heinrich
had spoken the truth as they walked through the dew-damp forest together: it was not creative work—but the atmosphere of his art alone that was necessary for him to exist; but he
was not condemned to failure like Heinrich, who was always driven to grapple, to shape, to
defend, and for whom the world always fell to pieces and slipped through his creative
grasp.[66] (*Road*, 264)

In diverting his male lead from confrontation with real issues of the day, Schnitzler
also removed from his fiction a potent ideological weapon, as employed by Herzl
and others—to portray heroic action in the name of a program for the future (namely
Zionism). What we gain is a patient, psychologically intuitive character study of the
reluctant anti-Semite. On one of the very first occasions when the topic of Jewishness
arises in his presence (and in the novel), Georg manages to conceal his irritation with
a "pleasant smile": "He felt that there had been absolutely no reason for the older

Doctor Stauber to give him official notice of his relation to Jewry. He knew it quite well anyway and didn't hold it against him. He didn't take it ill in general; but why did they always start talking about it themselves? Wherever he went, he encountered only Jews who were ashamed of being Jewish, or those who were proud of it and were worried that someone might think they were ashamed" (*Road*, 26).[67] Georg turns from the substance of the remark ("all Jews are related") to its type ("official notice of his relation to Jewry"). We then see his mind take the logical next step by typing the individual through his remark—hence the move from the singular to the plural ("why do they always start talking about it themselves?"). The reader learns that in Georg's experience there are two types of Jews: those who are too Jewish, and those who are not Jewish enough. In both cases, Georg perceives a disjunction between actual identity and public identification, between reality and rhetoric. Those who are too Jewish need to bend over backwards in denial; those who are not Jewish enough need to overcompensate for their lack of commitment. The response as a whole exemplifies how a detached anti-Semitism emerges. Georg's gaze reduces all Jews, no matter how different, to a single stereotype, even as it faithfully incarnates Schnitzler's own frustration with the myriad forms of Jewish posturing he witnessed.

TOWARD A THEORY OF JEWISH TRAGICOMEDY

As *Der Weg ins Freie* closes, Georg and Heinrich give up their idea of collaborating on an opera. Heinrich, incapable of writing the third act, abandons the libretto for a hybrid genre, "politische Tragikomödie." Tragicomedy, a form historically allied with perspectivalism, tells it like it is; it counters the view of those looking for heroes and victims. The genre is mentioned on two other occasions as well, both times to offer an ironic perspective on Jewish public behavior. Heinrich defines "the tragicomedy of contemporary Judaism" by way of the well-worn anecdote about the Polish Jew sitting next to a stranger on a train, who comports himself perfectly until he discovers that his traveling companion is also Jewish, at which point he stretches his feet out on the seat across from him. Heinrich's interpretation of the joke—that the intimacy that exists among Jews precludes mutual respect—and Georg's retort, that Heinrich is a worse anti-Semite than any Christian he knows—lead to one of the most heated discussions of Jewish identity in the novel. Later, news of Leo Golowski's duel becomes the hot topic of conversation. Golowski goes further than any other character in aggressively challenging destiny when he kills his anti-Semitic lieutenant in a duel, then manages to obtain a pardon from the Kaiser for this act of murder! The "heroic" incident arouses mainly skepticism; one response is that if the practice of dueling became widespread it would likely kill off the entire Jewish male population. Leo's sister Therese goes so far as to object to her brother's release from jail, on grounds that the duel is "a disgusting dueling act [*Duellkomödie*] . . . a [grisly], state-condoned gamble of life and death" (*Road*, 277).[68] Therese's tragicomic insight is that the Jew who behaves heroically is often nothing more than the victim or player in someone else's game, in this case a game of honor that had been denied to Jews in advance. Heinrich's joke, in suggesting that one need only scratch the surface of the Jewish character to discover his very unheroic core, is a variation on the same theme. These jokes trade on a tragicomic condition: Jews can be their own worst enemies, and nowhere more so than when they become players in the public sphere. Schnitzler captured it perfectly in a journal entry of the same year: "Another person need only defend his individuality—our kind must first overcome the prejudice against Vienna, then that against Jewishness, and only then is it his turn. And it is the same with the Jew as with the Viennese: it is not simply others who are against him, no, it is above all the Jew, the Viennese."[69] Dueling has no place in such a world. Dueling epitomizes a clash of cultures, but also the redemptive illusion that one might actually salvage one's honor or rectify injustice in an outright contest.[70] Thus, duels abound in tragedies, where the collision of incompatible value systems is often at stake. In Vienna in the 1890s, the Jewish national student organization Kadimah became a dueling fraternity. By the same logic, unfought duels abound in Schnitzler's tragicomedy, and they may even be its signature motif. Professor Bernhardi refuses to fight a duel yet all the while is provoked into one, in much the same way that the writer cannot either engage in politics or be viewed as not engaging in politics. It is as a reminder of these refusals that the language of formal dueling proliferates in the play: Bernhardi's colleague Pflugfelder speaks of obtaining *Genugtuung* (satisfaction).[71] Shortly thereafter, a newspaper article advocates exacting *Genugtuung* from the Jews by Vienna's Christians (*PB*, 221). Standing behind this taunting of the Jew into a duel (or of the dramatist into writing a political play) is the cultural subtext of the Waidhofener Resolution of 1896, in which German nationalist fraternities declared that Jewish students were "without honor or character" and ineligible to duel.[72] Schnitzler knew of other reasons why the Jews were not *satisfaktionsfähig,* not eligible to duel. His oft-cited prophecy of 1897, "it will soon be time to write the tragedy of the Jews," is more of a red herring than is normally assumed.[73] Schnitzler was constitutionally unsuited to tragedy. His distrust of absolutes and of all collectivist visions, philosemitic and *völkisch* ideologies, good guys and bad guys alike, meant that whatever Jewish writing he produced, it would not be the last word on the subject of Jewish destiny, not a solution, but rather something ambiguous, impractical, and utterly realistic: Jewish tragicomedy. First in the novel and then more directly in the play, Schnitzler stresses the ability of art to capture the tragicomic condition of European Jews.

Schnitzler does intimate, at critical moments, an awareness of that which lies beyond the scope of tragicomedy. When Georg himself gains this recognition, the moment is noteworthy—and I have offered it as one of the two epigraphs to this chapter: "For the first time the name Jew, which had so often frivolously, derisively, and contemptuously crossed his lips, began to appear to him in a completely new, as it were darker sense. A presentiment of this people's mysterious destiny, that somehow expressed itself in everyone who sprang from this origin, began to dawn in him

(*Road,* 83).[74] Georg's habitual typing of Jews lapses into a momentary insight—one that seems to be forgotten soon after. On the heels of the passage above, Georg observes, "Heinrich, who insisted that he belonged here, resembled in form and gesture some fanatical Jewish preacher, while Leo, who wanted to move to Palestine with his people, reminded him in profile and demeanor of the busts of Greek youths he had once seen in the Vatican" (*Road,* 83).[75] I have already argued that Schnitzler wanted his readers to observe the process of rhetorical detachment as it deforms even a well-intentioned intellectual's view of the Jews. But it is by no means the case that Georg's detachment disqualifies him as a source of insight.[76]

Georg's relation to the Jews plays out a reversal of the usual story of Jewish acculturation. Georg, a Christian, circulates within the Jewish world, observes the Jews, and, for a time, becomes a cipher for Jewish experience. Georg even begins to model his behavior on that of the Jewish characters. When Georg at last confesses feelings of guilt and remorse over his treatment of Anna, Heinrich tells him, "Nothing like that would ever have occurred to you in your life, if you hadn't been associating [*verkehren*] with a character like me, and if it weren't sometimes your way, not to think your own thoughts, but rather those of someone else who was stronger—or weaker than yourself" (*Road,* 296).[77] Georg admits that the Jews are often in advance of his own thoughts: "These people knew everything before he did himself" (281).[78] The direction of imitation is reversed: the assimilatory narrative whereby Jews leave the ghetto by mimicking non-Jews is replaced by a novel in which a clueless Christian aesthete must imitate his Jewish friends in order to regain his humanity.

This reversal provides an implicit critique of Herzl's *Das neue Ghetto* (The New Ghetto, 1894) a work Schnitzler knew intimately. Herzl's play allegorizes the failure of German-Jewish assimilation. It depicts the *Verkehr* between Jews and Christians as unilateral and ultimately futile. The hero, Jacob Samuels, sheds his ghetto identity by imitating a Christian friend:

He was more than a friend to me, he was also the "Christian fellow-citizen" who liked to associate with me [*der gern mit mir verkehrte*]. It was so flattering—despite everything, we still have something of the ghetto inside us. Gratitude, when we are treated just like everyone else. For that I wanted to thank him by modeling myself on him, adopting his habits as much as possible, speaking his language, thinking his thoughts . . . and he abandoned me, he just abandoned me.[79]

Schnitzler found this sort of writing one-sided and heavy-handed. He offered instead the story of a weak aesthete who is drawn into and resists a Jewish circle. Georg and the Jews have something essential in common. Both are on the road to self-actualization, though, like the saint and the prostitute, they begin at opposite ends of that same road. Georg is rooted in Viennese society, but can he become a father? The Jews are rooted in family, but can they achieve social and political self-determination? These two quests intersect on the level of plot, if not of form. Georg and Anna are in limbo, suspended between childhood and motherhood, with little power to alter their fate. Just as the fact of her becoming pregnant is not reported, only alluded to, so does Anna's pregnancy, once it becomes visible, impose a marginalization that is in part justified (social), in part invisible (psychological). On one hand, she is required to leave Vienna; at the same time, everyone knows of her condition, and it is assumed that she will return once the child is born and take up her life as before. For a period of time, both Georg and Anna (though Anna more acutely) are in exile. The Jewish collective is likewise in limbo, facing a predicament that is tragicomic because both visible, social (anti-Semitism) and invisible, or psychological (self-hatred). Jews are both at home and in exile in Vienna; whether amidst *Fremde, Feinde,* or *Freunde* (strangers, foes, or friends) is uncertain. This internal confusion vibrates in Georg's and Anna's plot. In fact, the two are never more "Jewish" than when they return from Italy, only to be absorbed into a makeshift Jewish family. Dr. Stauber is Anna's doctor, her confidante, indeed, her substitute father; Frau Golowski, the novel's most warmhearted Jewish mother, serves as her nurse, attendant, and ersatz mother; Therese Golowski actually finds the house in which Anna will deliver the child; Else Ehrenberg later offers to adopt and raise the baby. That the Jews embrace Georg and Anna as two of their own for the duration of their trial suggests that the minor and major predicaments are one and the same. The hybrid novel that cannot be reduced to the sum of its parts thus served as a prism for an author to present both an accurate view of Jewish relations with the Christian world and a tragicomic tale of misdiagnosis: a culture that needs Jews will reject them; Jews who need and helped create Viennese culture will deny their immediate heritage for a distant one. Like the saint and the prostitute, they begin at opposite ends of the road and look pretty much the same in the middle.

SCHNITZLER'S AUSTRIAN TRAGICOMEDY: *PROFESSOR BERNHARDI*

In *Professor Bernhardi,* completed in 1912, Schnitzler clearly responded to the criticism that the earlier novel, with its large cast of Jewish characters, failed to provide an identifiable Jewish hero. Bernhardi is a Jewish doctor who heads the Elisabeth Institute, a medical polyclinic that relies on patrons and government subventions for financial security. The viewer is taken in medias res into an average day at the clinic, broken by a sudden confrontation between Dr. Bernhardi and a Catholic priest, whom the nurse has summoned, as per protocol, to administer last rites to a young girl. The girl is on the threshold of death, but she is in a state of drug-induced euphoria, fantasizing that her lover is about to arrive and take her away. The priest insists upon his obligation to administer last rites, but Bernhardi won't allow it, not because he fears this will hasten her death—she is past all hope—but because the appearance of the priest at her bedside will shock the young girl out of her blissful state. If he cannot prolong her life, he wants at the very least to preserve her "final dream." Sure enough, when the girl is told of the priest's arrival, she asks, crestfallen, "Am I really to die?" and dies.

In the four remaining acts, Bernhardi is persecuted by his colleagues at the clinic, by the Church, and by right-wing politicians in parliament. He is ultimately tried in court and jailed for his offense against state Catholicism. As in the Jewish novel, the action is reported and discussed in hindsight, rather than directly portrayed in real time. Acts 1 to 3 consist mainly of conversations among doctors, as attempts are made to convince Bernhardi to apologize and prevent a public scandal. The turning point toward the end of act 3 is the news that parliament has voted to prosecute Bernhardi for *Religionsstörung,* interfering in religious matters, despite the pledge by Bernhardi's former colleague Flint, now Minister of Education, to prevent this outcome. Before his colleagues can vote whether to suspend Bernhardi and pre-empt the withdrawal of funds from the clinic, he resigns as director. Act 4, set at Bernhardi's home, depicts conversations of a different sort: with his lawyer and with supporters who urge him to become a "medical Dreyfus"—a heroic role he vehemently resists. Bernhardi submits to the circus, maintaining throughout the unlikely view that there is nothing either political or tendentious about his affair. Another revelation occurs when the priest comes seeking conciliation, to confess in private that which "God would not permit [him] to say publicly," namely, that he believes Bernhardi did the right thing. In Act 5, Bernhardi has just completed a two-month term in prison and is more celebrated than ever. When evidence is brought to light that would clear Bernhardi's name, however, he will have no part of a new trial. With the news that the prince has reinstated him as his personal physician, the comedy ends with the symbolic assurance that Austria under the Habsburgs remains an asylum for its Jewish compatriots.

Schnitzler's technique of literary hybridization plays out on the level not of form, but of theme. The biographical scandal that appears to have provided the impetus for the play actually comprises two separate affairs, as Elizabeth Loentz notes: "the public political struggle between the Catholic church and medical science, which invokes the Wahrmund affair but is further complicated by Bernhardi's Jewishness;[80] and the internal politics (the hiring of a Catholic candidate over a better-qualified Jewish one) of a clinic that Schnitzler's father had founded, which, though supported in large part by Jews, was increasingly dominated by an emergent anti-Semitic faction."[81] But the most obvious crossing is of personal and political concerns. Bernhardi insists, "My affair is purely personal" and "I want to have absolutely nothing to do with the people who want to make a political affair out of my private business" (*PB,* 266, 267).[82] His attempt to separate politics from personal life is itself politically charged. It runs counter to the conservative view, expressed by the character Dr. Ebenwald, that "Today in Austria, all personal matters must conclude in the political domain" (197).[83] It also parts company with the moderate position, represented by the journalist Kulka, that "many personal affairs carry the seed of the political within them" (266).[84] Once again, Schnitzler opted to conjoin two plots and then cast as his hero someone who claims the two need have no connection. The dispute over whether Bernhardi's act is personal or political reaches its apotheosis when Flint, the weakest of all the characters from a moral standpoint, offers the following gloss on Bernhardi's "martyrdom":

"I hope you don't think that your martyrdom impresses me. Yes, if you had undergone these difficulties for something great, for an idea, for your fatherland, for your faith—difficulties which have long since been rectified by your small triumphs—then I would have some respect for you. But I see in your behavior—as I am an old friend, allow me to be frank— nothing but a tragicomedy of egotism [*Tragikomödie des Eigensinns*], and permit me to question whether you would have persevered with the same consistency if people were still being burned at the stake in Austria today."
Bernhardi: *stares at him for a while, then begins to applaud.*[85] (*PB*, 286)

Bernhardi's farcical applause conveys that Flint has gotten it right: he has identified the genre, tragicomedy. Only whereas Flint views it as the tragicomedy of an egoistical Jew, Schnitzler presents it as the tragicomedy of Jewish life in Vienna at the turn of the century. The provocation is to consider whether or not there is something great (heroic) at stake in preventing the "reterritorialization" of a single deed by friend and foe alike. In his mission to hold fast to the original (in)significance of his decision to confront the Catholic priest, Bernhardi is a minor hero in the Deleuzian sense.

As was the case in *Der Weg ins Freie,* failures of form become an explicit theme in the text. The play parades before us a range of forms and genres that might clear Bernhardi from his difficulties. Pressed to defend himself in Act 2, Bernhardi realizes that "the form of the so-called explanation" ("die Form der sogenannten Erklärung") already puts him on the defensive and runs counter to his nature (*PB*, 192). Bernhardi allows himself to be persuaded by Drs. Cyprian and Löwenstein to write an apology so that "in this way, a form will be perhaps be found" ("so wird sich vielleicht eine Form finden lassen") (192). We see him scribbling the apology in his notebook. But when Dr. Ebenwald interrupts him with an alternative "Modus" by suggesting that Bernhardi make amends with the clinic board by voting to fill an opening with the non-Jewish Dr. Hell in place of a better-qualified Jewish candidate, Bernhardi not only rejects that scheme but tears his own apology to pieces. Acts 3 and 4 make clear that neither in parliament nor in the doctor's own sphere nor in the courtroom will the proper form of reconciliation be found. When the setting shifts to Bernhardi's home, where he circulates among his supporters, the expectation is that people are speaking the same language. Yet the discourse of the Jewish lawyer Goldwasser has been contaminated by pragmatism and opportunism. Even the initiative of the liberal journalist Kulka, champion of personal freedom, who wishes to put his newspaper at Bernhardi's disposal, is rebuffed. The telegrams arriving from Freemasons and others who would champion Bernhardi as a "medical Dreyfus" are viewed as equally wrongheaded. When the priest turns up unexpectedly at the house with his own confession and apology, viewers might expect that the deus ex machina heralds a peaceful resolution. But the priest's goodwill evaporates when it becomes clear that Bernhardi is not the forgiving and forgetting sort. In the final act, Bernhardi's desire to exonerate himself by writing a book is short-lived. He decides to confront Flint in person. But Schnitzler shows us a conversation also permeated by politics and rhetorical trickery. What Bernhardi calls a betrayal, Flint denotes with the musical term *Kontrapunkt,* the notion of compromise without bad conscience, which retroactively justifies Flint's unexpected turn against Bernhardi in his speech before parliament. What Bernhardi calls a "Wortbruch" (breach of one's word), Flint calls a "Wendung" (idiom) (285). This total failure of language and form all but convinces us to accept Flint's diagnosis that Bernhardi's character is ultimately at fault.

In this sense the work is indeed a "character comedy." And that is the description Schnitzler gave of it when asked to defend the work's hybrid form: "I have written a character comedy that plays in medical, and to some extent, in political circles, not a tendentious play that seeks to depict the conflict between science and the church, nor, as you believe, to settle the dispute between two religions. It was not my intention . . . to resolve a question. . . . I feel that my job is to create people, and I have nothing to prove other than the diversity of the world [*die Vielfältigkeit der Welt*]."[86] The comedy Schnitzler contrives is that whereas the doctors he typically represented remain on the sidelines, even while their patients self-destruct, Bernhardi is forced onto center stage to adopt a public stance and to play a role that goes against his nature.[87] He is at his best in private conversation, and, though he can be adept at verbal sparring among his medical colleagues, in the public sphere (as when testifying at his trial or when being interviewed by journalists) he tends to fall mute. He refuses to enter the ring, to appeal his case (in act 4), to seek a pardon or official redress, or to ask for a new trial (in act 5).[88]

Yet the function of Schnitzler's comedic hero is to draw attention to a tragic situation: there is no way out of being judged and typed if one is a Jew. The tragicomedy Schnitzler perpetrates is to make clear that even if Bernhardi were to take up the gauntlet and agree to fight, the contest has been rigged from the start. The drama's compelling contests—doctor versus priest; science versus religion; "Gotteshäuser—Krankenhäuser"—are always already triangulated by a nebulous politics (or rather, a parody thereof), to the point where the plot is no longer about right versus wrong action but about whether or not it pays to act at all. The entire assemblage, consisting of friend and foe, extending from church to media, has been contaminated by politics, just as politics has been infected by anti-Semitism. Personifying the contamination of politics is Minister Flint, Bernhardi's friend from medical school days. Flint is associated with forgetfulness: with the power to "tread on corpses" if need be. For Flint, forgetting is not a natural matter, it is principled; one is obligated to forget in the name of higher ends. By this logic, Bernhardi recollects, Flint once withheld the correct treatment for a patient who subsequently died, so as not to contradict his superior and potentially endanger his career. Politics provides him with the opportunity to turn his character flaw into a professional asset.

What *is* tendentious about the work is that here, even more than in the hybrid novel, Schnitzler sought to challenge societal and aesthetic norms regarding Jewish behavior in the public sphere by way of an unorthodox approach to characterization. Schnitzler noted in 1918 that, of all his works, "I like myself nowhere more than in Bernhardi,"[89] and Bernhardi is nowhere more himself than when he comments: "I refuse to be "seduce[d] . . . into playing a role that I don't like, to which I am barely suited, if only because it is nothing more than a role" (*PB,* 268).[90] Put to the test, Bernhardi becomes a Job figure, as one group after another attacks or defends what it takes to be his "position," while he all the while refuses both provocation and comfort. The achievement of *Professor Bernhardi,* one might say, was not the construction of the heroic Jew, but rather the construction of a hero who happens to be Jewish. Dr. Löwenstein first makes the association: "'To be perfectly clear, no one would attempt [to turn a completely innocent incident into an affair] if Bernhardi didn't happen to be a Jew" [*wenn Bernhardi nicht zufällig ein Jude wäre*] (182).[91] Bernhardi does not act in the name of Jewish belief or honor when he bars the priest from his patient's threshold. His is an instinctive humanism, but his accidental Jewishness is what endows the act with meaning and provides the impetus to dramatic action. Although Bernhardi's opponents on both sides try to endow his deed with necessity, Bernhardi stubbornly denies the claim:

Bernhardi: . . . My affair is purely personal . . .
Löwenstein: But—
Kulka: Many personal affairs carry the seed of the political in them. Yours—
Bernhardi: That is an accident for which I am not responsible. I belong to no faction and I do not wish to be preoccupied with any one.[92]

By associating Bernhardi's defiance of the Church with contingencies of personality rather than decisions of reason, Schnitzler introduces a modernist spin on the traditional opposition between rationalist and believer that one finds in works of the Faust tradition and G. E. Lessing's early plays *Der Freigeist* (The Freethinker) and *Die Juden* (The Jews) of 1749. *Die Juden* attempted to enlighten the public via theater by placing a virtuous character on stage who would then be unmasked as a Jew. Schnitzler reverses the Enlightenment motif, as Bernhardi's Jewishness is the mask that prevents his conduct from being understood. Rather than prompt the audience to see Bernhardi as a real Jew, Schnitzler constructs him as a virtual Jew, one who provokes the audience to look past his Jewishness by perceiving it as a character trait void of necessity.

This strategy extends directly from Schnitzler's understanding of how identity does and does not shape allegiances and behavior. In the 1904 "Confession," which provides the other epigraph to this chapter, Schnitzler sets forth articles of his own peculiar faith: "I don't feel solidarity with anyone because they happen to belong to the same nation, the same class, the same race, the same family to which I belong. It is exclusively my choice to whom I wish to feel related."[93] Choice might be rational and enlightened, or on the other hand it might be motivated by whim, *Zufall.* It cannot be systematized, only depicted. Of course, as we have seen in *Der Weg ins Freie,* Schnitzler was vitally interested in "a fact of history which stood fast and immovable," namely the survival of the Jewish people. In this respect, he cannot be identified with Bernhardi's position. In another undated observation found in his *Nachlass,* Schnitzler reinterprets chance as "the necessity that lies beyond the line that we, primarily, observe" ("die Notwendigkeit, die außerhalb der von uns hauptsächlich beobachteten Linie liegt").[94] These positions are incommensurable in strict philosophical terms, yet they are shared elements in the anatomy of Schnitzler's Jewish tragicomedy, and no doubt also of his identity: "No less strongly than you do I believe to feel what I owe the German Volk. But even if I thought I owed everything I possess to Germanness, in total neglect of my racial membership (a notion which to me appears to be contestable), the thought would occasionally force itself upon me, how much Germanness itself owes to the cultural and ethical achievements of Judaism, as far back as its history reaches, and I would also feel to some degree indebted to my ancestors."[95]

Much as Schnitzler refused to detach his Jewish from his German heritage, so do *Der Weg ins Freie* and *Professor Bernhardi,* by their complex hybridity of structure, prohibit us from treating their Jewish elements in isolation, as an oasis of facticity within a fictional universe.[96] Problematization of form, radical questioning of the Jewish character, and a determined, if perverse, attachment to life's paradoxes and contingencies are the basic elements comprising Schnitzler's tragicomic method. The approach was virtually unrecognizable to his contemporaries, to whom it added up to little more than a cowardly response to urgent matters. They were unable to understand the logic of a Jewish novel that portrays a panorama of Jewish characters but puts forth as its dominant plot the trite tale of a Viennese baron and his Catholic mistress. In the second instance, they were unable to grasp the function of a drama that appears to be "about" an anti-Semitic scandal but that forfeits its opportunity to become the next *Nathan der Weise.* That the approach was consistently applied in both *Der Weg ins Freie* and *Professor Bernhardi* suggests that, different as they are, the two form one statement.

EPILOGUE: SCHNITZLER VERSUS HERZL

Both of Schnitzler's Jewish works are written in opposition to the approach Theodor Herzl adopted in his play *Das neue Ghetto,* a work that may be most famous for the impression it left on another anti-Zionist, Sigmund Freud.[97] Schnitzler's involvement with the play antedated its production. Herzl, a journalist living in Paris, entrusted Schnitzler, whose early stories and plays he greatly admired, with the task of circulating the manuscript to prospective theater producers under the pseudonym Albert Schnabel. The play became a bond of friendship between the two men, whose letters during these years are filled with mutual admiration. Relevant here is Schnitzler's antipathetic reaction to the main character of a play—an activist named Jacob Samuel—that he otherwise found quite praiseworthy ("natural," full of "genuine life"). "Jacob still seems to me to be the palest. What shimmers too strongly through his skin is that which already powerfully expressed itself in the course of the drama—the idea of the play. The basic mistake of nearly all modern heroes?"[98] Schnitzler found Samuel too transparent, and he urged Herzl to tone him down so as to allow his motives to emerge "freely." (Schnitzler may have recalled that Herzl had disliked the ending of *his* play, *Das Märchen* [The Fairytale, 1891], because no one dies at the end.) For similar reasons, he found the death scene in *Das neue Ghetto* most unsatisfying. Samuel's dying words, which justify the duel by way of the logic of martyrdom as a meaningful response to anti-Semitism, ring false for Schnitzler.[99] "Let him rather die wordlessly," Schnitzler advises, and he belabors the point. "I also don't like the 'Jew with the wounded honor'—give your Jacob more inner freedom— this won't detract from the basic idea, and the character will be more sympathetic. Don't you think? . . . And above all, don't let your hero die so submissively."[100] Schnitzler's ideal hero—or ideal Jewish hero—would die an understated death rather than a martyr's death. In his view, characters with "inner freedom" are ultimately more sympathetic than those whose identities are overdetermined. As we have seen, Schnitzler took this philosophy one critical step further when casting characters for his own Jewish works. The Jewish condition "vibrates" within the tale of a Viennese baron and his Catholic mistress, and by the same logic Bernhardi, though he holds his ground on moral matters, opts for silence rather than the sword. Just as Bernhardi claims that his last words are "seldom different from his first ones" (*PB*, 267), so does his silence endure until the end, to the point that when he attempts at long last to write a book about his persecutions, he gives up, as his numerous grievances seem suddenly irrelevant, but for the issue of *Willensfreiheit* (freedom of will): the power to transform a series of accidents, not into a predestined course, but rather into a road into the open (292).

Schnitzler's critique had little impact on Herzl, who did not hesitate to refer to *Das neue Ghetto* as "a sermon for Jews" ("Judenpredigt") delivered not in the synagogue but rather "in the freedom of the theater"—a motive that justifies, even necessitates, the "redemptive impact" he sought, not to mention the subordination of artistic to political aims. "Yes," Herzl writes to overcome another friend's objections: "Yes, it is a play about Jewish politics. And what I want approval for is not the play, but the Jewish politics."[101] Schnitzler came to just the opposite conclusion.

The opposition "Schnitzler versus Herzl" boils down to the irreconcilable contest between tragicomedy and tragedy. And yet halfway along, *in der Mitte des Wegs,* each was able to acknowledge the other. In one of their first letters, Herzl not only pays homage to Schnitzler but, with rare humility, voices a sentiment that would recur frequently in later correspondence: regret that he was not Schnitzler, a genuine *littérateur*. "If you will be steadfast, not let yourself be diverted by the theater rabble and by the critic-rascals—if you will be—what I unfortunately was not—true to yourself, you will become Alkandi, whose song everyone must sing, whether they want to or not. You have a sweet voice in your throat, my dear Schnitzler; don't coarsen it for God's sake. Be true to yourself."[102] Herzl makes reference to the artist-genius of Schnitzler's very first play, *Alkandis Lied*, when imploring him to "become Alkandi"—to achieve monumental fame by remaining true to his artistic aspirations.

The corresponding tribute on Schnitzler's part is a diary entry made shortly after Herzl's death, based upon the report of Hermann Bahr's final visit with Herzl: "The strangest thing (not surprising): this person, world-famous, wanting to found countries, mourned by millions when he died—Jews in Odessa closed their shops when the death notice came—were driven out of the synagogue by Cossacks—this man talked on this Sunday, on his deathbed, mainly about how unjust it was that he, a first-rate artist, was considered an artist of the second rank."[103]

▪▪ PART THREE
▪▪

PERFORMING
THE HEBREW BIBLE

5 Mythic Memory Theater and the Problem of Jewish Orientalism in Hofmannsthal's Ballet *Josephslegende* (Legend of Joseph, 1912)

Lie with me! —Potiphar's wife to Joseph (Genesis 39:1)

In a letter to Richard Strauss of June 23, 1912, Hugo von Hofmannsthal solicited the composer's participation in his newest project: a biblical ballet, to be staged by the most innovative ballet company of the twentieth century, the Ballets Russes. "Together with Kessler, who has a truly productive, vivid imagination, I have composed a short ballet for the Russians, 'Joseph in Egypt,' [featuring] the episode with the wife of Potiphar, the boyish Joseph naturally for Nijinsky, the most extraordinary human being on stage today."[1] Strauss agreed to compose the music for what would be his only ballet (Opus 63; he called it a "Symphonic Fragment"), though dance had been central also in the operas *Salome* (1905) and *Elektra* (1909). Legend has it that the plot had been conceived by Hofmannsthal and Count Harry Kessler, the German writer and diplomat, over a midnight Paris dinner at the Restaurant Larue on June 5, 1912, following the premiere of *L'après-midi d'un faune*. Also at dinner were some of the most creative theatrical minds of day: Sergei Diaghilev, ballet master of the Ballets Russes; Max Reinhardt, the prominent theater director from Berlin; and Jean Cocteau, the French poet, who had also written for the Ballets. Kessler and Hofmannsthal put finishing touches on their libretto while walking in the Tuileries Gardens the following morning.[2]

The one-act ballet *La Légende de Joseph* premiered in Paris on May 14, 1914, and then in London, where the company had a second core audience and a generous patron (fig. 12). The May–June 1914 season was an ambitious one, with five premieres among the ten works performed. According to the souvenir program, the *Légende* was performed on six of the ten dates, more often than any other ballet. Diaghilev had revolutionized ballet by importing innovations from painting, drama, design, and music into the productions, so as to visibly "cast off the burden of the nineteenth century," and the mandate was here very much in evidence.[3] For one thing, the librettists decided early on that the Joseph story was to be staged "as a

12. Souvenir program, *La Légende de Joseph*, Ballets Russes, Paris, June 14, 1914. Howard D. Rothschild Collection, Harvard Theatre Collection, Houghton Library.

13. Léon Bakst, costume design for Potiphar's wife in *La Légende de Joseph*. Howard D. Rothschild Collection, Harvard Theatre Collection, Houghton Library.

Renaissance painter would have interpreted it," or in Hofmannsthal's words, "in the costumes of Veronese and spirit of Veronese."[4] Spanish painter José-Maria Sert was commissioned to design the sets—the first non-Russian to be thus appointed.[5] Léon Bakst, famous for his historicist approach to costuming, designed the spectacular costumes (fig. 13).[6] The choreographer was Michel Fokine, choreographer also of *Petrouchka* and *Schéhérazade,* who was known for his orientalism and for an "ethnographic" approach that imported authentic styles of dance from diverse periods and countries into classical ballet.[7] Vaslav Nijinsky did not dance the part of Joseph after all; he had been abruptly dismissed from the company in 1913. Instead Léonide Massine, nineteen years old, made his debut with the Ballets in the starring role (fig. 14).

By some accounts, the involvement of so many diverse talents ended up working to the ballet's detriment. Massine's poignant recollections of the rehearsals provide a clue as to the challenges presented by this particular collaboration.

During the few weeks we spent in Monte Carlo there were continual conferences about *La Légende de Joseph.* I was present at a number of these, and although the ballet was already in rehearsal, it seemed to me that the people chiefly concerned with the story were not clear about what they were trying to do. Von Hofmannsthal would explain, in his soft, self-effacing way, that he envisaged Joseph as a noble, untamed young savage in search of

Leonid Mjäsin
als Josef
„Josefslegende."

Verl. Herm. Leiser, Berlin-Wilm.

8698
Atelier Dührkoop.

14. Léonide Massine as Joseph in *La Légende de Joseph.* Howard D. Rothschild Collection, Harvard Theatre Collection, Houghton Library.

God, and said that this, and the young man's tale of exaltation, must be implicit in his dance. Count Henry would then say, in his brooding Germanic manner, that though he agreed with Hofmannsthal, we must also remember that we were interpreting something more than a biblical story, that the legend was symbolic of the struggle between good and evil, between innocence and experience. He stressed the dark, stifling atmosphere of Potiphar's house. . . . But both Hofmannsthal and Kessler were insistent that they wanted our interpretation to explore all these many fates of the subject. Diaghilev listened patiently, but I could see that he was inwardly irritated by their philosophizing, Yes yes, he would say, "You are both right about the underlying philosophy. But you must remember that this is a ballet, and our prime concern must be with its visual impact."[8]

Massine's account provides a unique perspective on the Kessler-Hofmannsthal partnership, and in particular on Hofmannsthal's understanding of Joseph. But it also validates the assessment of some critics that the end result of this illustrious collaboration was a production as overdetermined as the heavy layers on the dress of Potiphar's wife. "The result, wrote the *Times*, was 'an extraordinarily skillful piece of artifice' that sacrificed dramatic development and metaphysical contrast to the achievement of spectacular effects. Strauss conducted the premiere before an 'auditorium crowded to its utmost capacity.' . . . With its celebrity names and proven formulas, *Legend of Joseph* came to life not from any genuine artistic impulse, but as a 'concept.' Collaboration was now a matter of business, and the business of ballet, it seemed, was the making and marketing of spectacular, saleable commodities."[9] The "genuine artistic impulse" eclipsed in the market-driven 1914 production may well correspond to Hofmannsthal's contribution.

Within Hofmannsthal studies, the libretto known as *Josephslegende* has been largely forgotten. It has not been granted the significance of the opera libretti or the Austrian-nationalistic dramas performed in Salzburg. Studies of the Hofmannsthal-Strauss collaboration tend to focus on the six operas.[10] One source of confusion is that there are different accounts of Hofmannsthal's contribution to the script and the production. The libretto was evidently coauthored, but the ballet was Kessler's dream, and it was largely due to his efforts that the production materialized. At one point early on, when the critic G. Brecher, a friend of Strauss, held Hofmannsthal accountable for the *Textbuch*, Hofmannsthal left Paris and wrote two angry letters to Strauss rehearsing his claim that he had only partially authored the work.[11] The ballet's marginal status ostensibly has something to do with its genre, since the poet's fame rests on his word artistry, and his experiments with ballet and mime—eighteen texts without texts—have resisted easy reception. Add to this the critical disregard for minor works using explicitly Jewish (biblical) material, and the conditions of neglect are in place. That this is the sole occasion on which Hofmannsthal employed a central character from the Hebrew Bible only partly denotes the ballet's significance for Viennese Jewish modernism; as in all the works in this study, the exceptional turn to a Jewish theme transpires at the very intersection of European and Jewish preoccupations.

A BIBLICAL BALLET

Its cosmopolitan origins notwithstanding, *Josephslegende* fits the mold of much of biblical theater in that it centers upon a cross-cultural encounter. Throughout Jewish history, biblical art has taken as its subject the dilemmas of Jewish existence in the diaspora—a temptation captured in the three fateful words uttered by Potiphar's wife: "Lie with me!" The tradition reaches back to first-century Alexandria, where a playwright named Ezekiel composed a drama in Greek concerning the exodus from Egypt. Hofmannsthal and his contemporaries might have known the play, since the renowned German preacher and reformer Ludwig Philippson translated it into German in the nineteenth century.[12] Whether to establish metaphysical authority or to gain ideological reinforcement, dramatists have regarded scripture as a signifier of competing identities rather than an absolute source of identity. They make the text their interlocutor, transforming the Bible from a source to be transmitted into a vehicle of transmission—from a book into what Maurice Halbwachs called a "social framework" of collective memory.[13] All biblical art imposes memory and incites forgetting, and Hofmannsthal's ballet is no exception.

Charismatic and virtuous, politically savvy and still true to his native heritage, Joseph has been a religious exemplar in the eyes of Jews, Christians, and Moslems alike. Insofar as his reputation is linked to his ability to acculturate, he may also be the most modern of biblical heroes. Hofmannsthal's most blatant *misreading* of scripture in *Josephslegende* is his disavowal of Joseph's assimilatory ability. The mythic Joseph has a pure and undivided spirit. He resembles Professor Bernhardi in that he triumphs by refraining from conflict; he is unlike the doctor in that the source of his power is mystical—religious rather than intellectual. And whereas Freud and Beer-Hofmann overstate the agon of their biblical heroes so as to highlight their relevance for a 1930s German Jewish audience, Hofmannsthal had a different heroic template in mind. Joseph is a quasidivine being who shames his Egyptian adversaries and promptly ascends to the next world in the company of a golden-winged angel. He renounces Egyptian culture and exposes its depraved materialism.

The ballet achieves this reversal much in the way that Michelangelo's Moses unbreaks the tablets of the Law—by turning scripture on its head. According to the biblical narrator,

she caught hold of him by his garment and said, "Lie with me!" But he left his garment in her hand and got away and fled outside. . . . She kept his garment beside her, until his master came home . . . saying . . . "The Hebrew slave whom you brought into our house came to me to dally with me; but when I screamed at the top of my voice, he left his garment with me and fled outside." When his master heard the story that his wife told him . . . he was furious. So Joseph's master had him put in prison, where the king's prisoners were confined. (Genesis 39:12–20)

The Bible leaves no doubt that Joseph refuses his mistress's invitation and that she is victorious in this particular confrontation. Hofmannsthal and Kessler modify the seduction scene between Joseph and Potiphar's wife by rotating the story 180 degrees; their

Joseph disrobes voluntarily before the lascivious Frau Potiphar. Hofmannsthal regarded Joseph's disrobing as the dramatic highpoint. The gesture signifies neither exorcism nor catharsis, but rather enduring self-consolidation: the retention of identity under assault.[14] It immediately places beyond reach that which a decadent culture gropes to ruin. The scene further symbolizes the nature of the memory encounter promulgated by the work as a whole. Do not resist the past, it says; behold its revelatory power, and be transformed. This is what Potiphar's wife—representing a decadent, doomed monarchy—is unable to do; she strangles herself on a string of pearls in the final act. At the core of Hofmannsthal's Joseph myth is the futility of dialogue between the artist of transcendence and a materialistic culture that attempts to appropriate his art.

Given the author's tangential relationship to Jewish culture, it is perhaps not a surprise that *Josephslegende* has not been thought comparable to other works of biblical theater in the German Jewish domain. The ballet is worth studying, however, not only because there is evidence to suggest that Joseph embodies Hofmannsthal's vision of a heroic Jew (had he been inclined to think in those terms). Much like *Der Schüler,* the ballet is an exemplary instance of minor modernism. It too is a multilayered, Jewish/non-Jewish performance, a hybrid of text and gesture, liberated dance and violent pantomime, transcendence and depravity. Here again, we are dealing with a marginalized work that reaches beyond itself by employing multiple turn-of-the-century codes. It is not entirely clear how much of the original ballet text was authored by Hofmannsthal, yet authorship is only part of the story. In point of fact, during the seven "lean" years in which *Josephslegende* was silenced—1914–21—Hofmannsthal's investment in the project only intensified.

My reading begins by contextualizing the ballet's hero and its genre. Joseph is no doubt a Hebrew, but he is at best a virtual Jew. His origins, like those of the other heroes of Viennese Jewish modernism, are carefully screened. The authors' controversial decision to represent a Jewish hero through an orientalist filter is a strategy that uncannily resembles the mythmaking practices of German Jewish intellectuals of the period, in particular those of Martin Buber and other proponents of Jewish Renaissance. Orientalism holds the first key to understanding the cultural politics of Hofmannsthal's aesthetic strategy and of thematic and stylistic decisions that point back to *Elektra* (1903) and ahead to *Die Ägyptische Helena* (1924). The mythic, epigonal message of the ballet was to be transmitted by staging the work as a scene in a late Renaissance painting by Paolo Veronese. This amalgam of artistic components— costume, music, dance, poetry—that made possible the construction of a biblical legend for the turn-of-the-century European avant-garde rendered the experiment consistent with the goals of Viennese Jewish modernism.

HOFMANNSTHAL'S JEWISH HERO

Hofmannsthal and Kessler call him "Egyptian Joseph," and he is never identified as a Hebrew, much less a Jew. Though he may be the bearer of religious authenticity, his ethnic origins fall through the cracks in the documentation pertaining to the ballet. Joseph's spirituality was to be untainted by the ideological labels dominating turn-of-the-century culture. Identifying his origins would presumably color an audience's reception of the character (or perhaps of the ballet as a whole).

The coding of Joseph's spiritual identity occurred in public and private statements, as well as on stage. In an effort to describe the disrobing scene, Kessler casts widely in search of the proper religious category. "At this moment there is no limit to his divine appearance both in musical and bodily terms. It is precisely this new (or antique), utterly unchristian (but lying close to the Renaissance) emotion, an emotion both enthusiastic and awe-struck by the dazzling divine nakedness, perhaps sacredly formulated in a culture such as that of the delphic Apollo, that I wish to have expressed here."[15] At one point, Hofmannsthal wrote to Strauss to correct the composer's impression of Joseph's spirituality, an obstacle that (as Strauss had earlier communicated) was making it difficult for him to compose the music to accompany Joseph's dance.[16] Hofmannsthal believed that the error lay in confounding the qualities *keusch* and *fromm* (chaste and pious), a distinction that was to him critical for conveying Joseph's character. "This shepherd boy," he wrote, "gifted child of a mountain tribe who got lost among a thriving river and delta people, appears to me more like a noble, untamed colt than a pious seminary student."[17] Joseph is no *Bocher*. In the tradition of Heinrich Heine and Friedrich Nietzsche, chastity does not connote scholastic asceticism, but rather the arrogant solitude of genius in tune with natural forces. The diction of this letter alone conveys that Hofmannsthal truly believed in the scenario he describes:

His search for God, moving upwards in wild strides, is nothing else but a wild leaping after the high-hanging fruits of inspiration. On mountaintops, in lucid, sparkling isolation, he is accustomed to extend himself via an Even-higher! Even-higher! into a lonely pure orgy, and to snatch out of an unattainable clarity *above him* (what kind of art can express this, if not music?) a scrap of the heavens, snatch it into himself—this transient, highest state, this trance is what he calls God, and it is the God perceived in this manner whom, with upraised hands, he forces to help him, just as the world, dark, soft, and sultry and *alien* to him, *alien* to the marrow, just as this world extends its arms to him and wants to capture him for itself—and nothing but the index finger of this God—who is light, and all that is most high, your highest—(when may you hint at it, if not in such a place?)—his index finger, a ray from him, is the angel, personified in a figure.[18]

In striving to bring the character to life for Strauss, Hofmannsthal structures Joseph's transcendental quest as a romantic one, a sublime effort to "snatch a scrap of heaven" and to make it his own. Just as Joseph seeks God by leaping higher and higher, so is Strauss's music—"your highest"—capable of representing this God, "who is light, and all that is most high" in the theater. "What kind of art can express this, if not music?" The sheer force of Hofmannsthal's rhetoric endows the ballet with a revelatory dimension. Ostensibly to flatter the composer, Hofmannsthal goes on to say that Joseph in Potiphar's house symbolizes as well the artist's isolation within a degenerate environment. He concludes the letter by reformulating the Strauss-Joseph analogy. "It is not possible that you cannot find any bridge whatsoever from this lad Joseph to the memory of your own youth—whether Potiphar or not. A higher power, sparkling, barely attainable, was above and wanted to be forced downward: that is Joseph's dance."[19] Hofmannsthal entreats Strauss, in effect, to identify with Joseph's dance by recollecting his own artistic development. That Hofmannsthal himself may have identified with Joseph warrants consideration. But it is more likely, based upon other letters, that Hofmannsthal at this time differentiates his own artistry of language from that of both the dancer and the composer.[20] It seems that the author felt only music could adequately represent the god whom Joseph was trying to reach. Music and dance would begin to purify the Joseph story of its religious and ethnic associations.

Joseph's dancing (as described in the libretto) most squarely refutes caricature. "The innermost motive of this figure is the leaping, flying, swaying, now in the dance, now in the dream, now in an intimate fusion of fantasy and movement. Joseph is a dancer and a dreamer."[21] Recall that Hofmannsthal had Nijinsky in mind for the part of Joseph; cast as a dancer, Joseph shirks his Jewish body. In turn-of-the-century Vienna, everyone knew that Jews couldn't dance. Nineteenth-century medicine had established that Jews have deformed feet; Sander Gilman has shown that Freud, for one, made extreme adjustments in order to dissociate himself from the falsehood. Joseph is thus redeemed by his "light feet," which signal to the audience that he has visibly escaped both his Jewish body and his Jewish mind. Another factor that may have enabled Hofmannsthal to mythologize a Jewish figure was that he would be mute. In his early diaries, we recall, the poet's dominant and increasingly pejorative association with Jewishness was a certain "Jewish manner of thinking."[22] While it is unclear whether these associations persist for the mature Hofmannsthal, his Joseph was as if specially crafted so as to refute any possible connection to this type of overly cerebral, anemic Jewish intellectual. Joseph's plot, which begins in scene 4, is to establish his purity before God and to retain it in the course of his Egyptian trial.

Joseph is carried onstage in a golden hammock, smiling cherubically in his sleep. He wears "a gold-blue, sun-colored silken shepherd's coat"—yellow has mystical significance for Hofmannsthal—carries a halo, and begins immediately to dance "as if in mystical ecstasy." Four solo dancers join him to enact the pantomime of Joseph's quest for God. In the first dance, "the movements enact how the pious shepherd boy steps in front of the visage of his god and shows to him all his limbs, his head, breast, hands, feet, one after the other, showing that they are pure. He seems to be saying to God: 'Lord, see: my body and my heart are innocent before you.'"[23] Joseph shows God (but perhaps more importantly the audience) that his body remains untainted. The next dancer depicts "searching and struggling for God" by leaping too high and falling too hard.[24] Here lightness and gravity rhythmically converge. But the text makes a point of calling this dance "not in the least hysterical or unhealthy," not comparable to Elektra's dance. The text stresses that Joseph's quest for God is that of a healthy, normal, childish temperament. The script mentions yet another biblical dancer: Joseph leaps "as David leaps in front of the tabernacle."[25] At last, "Joseph has found God; his movements are now a glorification of God." All impediments have been cast off: "Joseph now leaps with 'light feet.'"

Joseph's spiritual nature is then highlighted through stark contrast with his Egyptian environment, culminating in the encounter with the mistress that spans scenes 6 through 9. Hofmannsthal referred to "the pointed antithesis between the two protagonists, which finally manifests itself in a polar opposition, leading one to the bright heaven, the other to sudden death and to damnation" as one of the ballet's central aspects.[26] Two sequences prior to Joseph's arrival on stage (scenes 2 and 3) introduce this encounter plot, its erotic and violent themes pantomimed by oriental slaves. The first, a wedding dance, depicts a bride's unveiling by her bridegroom. Yet in the course of this dance, a lone figure evokes a third biblical dancer, this time from the Song of Songs, who dances "the dance of the most glowing yearning of love, the *dance of Sulamith.*"[27] Here the pantomime of consummation unfolds into illicit seduction; when the Shulamite reaches out to greet Potiphar's wife, she is promptly slapped. The second dance depicts a Turkish boxing match. Yet again a contained conflict escalates into a violent melee, as Potiphar's armed guards descend upon the boxers with whips and they are led offstage. Though the slaves appeal to their benefactress to intervene, she remains unmoved: "Potiphar's wife, who during the whole scene has sat there rigid and indifferent, does not show emotion even now; cold and completely sunk into herself, she does not feel another's suffering."[28]

Neither of these oriental pantomimes is sufficiently powerful to awaken the woman's passion, yet their hostile reception suggests that they arouse an indomitable compulsion to dominate. Joseph will be able to elude her grasp, but only because he has access to forces well beyond the trappings of earthly sovereignty. Two central episodes together explain why Joseph escapes (as Salome and other dancing daughters could not). The first is the seduction scene itself (scene 9), in which Potiphar's wife first approaches Joseph asleep in his coat. Her figure gleams, "as of ice, hard and straight," in the moonlight.[29] She frees her hair from the pearls and, after hesitating, caresses his hair maternally and kisses him. "In this moment, Joseph's rigidity slackens, he jumps up, tremblingly wrapping his coat around himself, runs past her."[30] Joseph's first impulse is to hide, which only provokes the mistress to forcibly undress him, repeating the earlier bridal pantomime. But then Joseph changes his mind and boldly lets his coat fall to the ground.

Suddenly the trembling stops, he frees himself . . . from her, whereby he lets sink the coat that he had been holding in front of his face, stares at the woman, and stretches out his left hand towards her. Naked from shoulder to hip he stands before her. She sinks to her knees, as if blinded by his nakedness . . . now she is the sinner who begs forgiveness. In vain: he does not bend down to her, harsh and boyishly unrelenting he remains standing without moving, the left hand stretched out above her head.[31]

Potiphar's wife perceives not Joseph's body, but rather his boundless spiritual fertility: the "future that he carries inside."[32] The power relation between the two is irrevocably reversed.[33] Kessler's preface further explains why Joseph's disrobing is not a self-division, but a fusing of inner powers. He too struggles to resolve competing identities: "the two faces of Joseph, the child-like one and the future one, alternate continuously in the course of the plot."[34] At the touch of Potiphar's wife's lascivious lips, "his two faces are struggling with one another." Ultimately, opting to reveal rather than conceal makes Joseph powerful. But why does disrobing empower Joseph? One clue, as Kessler wrote, is that "his mysticism is not Parsifal's"; his potency hails from another continent. "His secret is that of growing and becoming, his holiness is about creating and giving birth, his perfection is that of things that do not yet exist."[35] Though he was not Parsifal, Joseph's dancing and disrobing could not help but evoke memories of *Salome.* That Hofmannsthal and Kessler had this story in mind while composing the ballet is suggested by their attempts to convince each other, and the composer, that their work differed in its core dynamic and atmosphere from the opera of 1905.[36] Salome's dance of unveiling before Herod signifies her subversion of the extant power dynamic. Salome and Joseph both disengage from the coerced dance and activate a personal drama of escape. It is a potent metaphor, among other things, for artistic liberation from a hegemonic discourse. As elsewhere in Hofmannsthal's oeuvre, dance signals that those who have been rendered impotent by forces inundating them from the outside are reestablishing a living connection with inner sources of autonomy.

Confronted at once with the object of her desire and her own powerlessness to acquire it, Potiphar's wife moves impulsively to strangle Joseph, but she is forced to avert her gaze and adopt a penitent posture. This vacillation between violence and shame repeats itself again in the finale. In a scene that verges on kitsch, an angel descends to rescue Joseph on the brink of fire torture. Potiphar's wife, after reaching out in vain to follow the two figures, strangles herself with her pearls.[37] In the final tableau, morning has broken; the funeral procession exits stage right, as Joseph's apotheosis transpires stage left.

THE MYTH OF THE ORIENTAL JEW

Joseph's legacy is beyond the reach of the Egyptians, but the authors did not want that legend to be lost to the contemporary European audience. His imploring letters to Strauss notwithstanding, Hofmannsthal feared the music did not do justice to the abyss separating Joseph and the Egyptians; the most important artistic component for him became the costuming. He took credit from the start for a vision of how costumes would visually frame the encounter between Joseph and the Egyptians: "The Egyptians wear Venetian costumes, Joseph and the traders who bring him to Potiphar, oriental [costumes] of the sixteenth century."[38] In Hofmannsthal's orientalist allegory, the Hebrew Joseph represents the "real" Orient, whereas the Egyptians, clothed as Venetians, are the orientalists, Europeans who have fetishized the oriental image and appropriate an orientalist veneer: an oriental carpet hangs in the backdrop, African slaves and mulattoes serve them. These descriptions—"lavish, copious, sultry, filled with exotic scents and creatures like a tropical garden, but without mystery: classic, hard, heavy, a world in which even the air seemed to be loaded with gold dust"—recall Hofmannsthal's early critique of his own culture.[39] Importing the Orient-Occident polarity was a popular trend in avant-garde theater and dance, and Hofmannsthal had introduced an oriental atmosphere in *Elektra,* likewise to enhance the psychological effect. What is unusual here is that the plot symbolically reverses the classic orientalist message, whereby the European—"rational, virtuous, mature, 'normal'"—asserts his superiority over the Oriental, who is "irrational, depraved (fallen), childlike, 'different.'"[40] Here, the childlike Oriental exposes the mature European and shames her into submission, with the signature gesture of disrobing implying the rejection of the framing discourse as such. Joseph's oriental nature runs deeper than his coat; he is neither epigone nor memory individual, but a legitimate heir: pure memory personified.

In casting Joseph as an Oriental and by staging a biased confrontation between the alluring Orient and the sallow Occident, the ballet shows a striking affinity with the phenomenon of Jewish counterorientalism, or "the 'internal orientalism' of Jew versus Jew."[41] As part of the project of Jewish Renaissance, westernized, Ashkenazic Jewish intellectuals in the early twentieth century sought to persuade assimilated European Jews to reconnect with their internal, "oriental" selves. Turn of-the-century writers took advantage of the fashionable revalorization of the exotic East (in the wake of Bachofen, Nietzsche, and Schopenhauer) to deflect the anti-Jewish orientalism of European culture since the eighteenth century and to allow "the Western Jew to develop a new perception of himself, his Oriental origins, and his East European brethren."[42] The project had begun in the nineteenth century, when German Jewish writers began to internalize and articulate a dualistic or hybrid model of Jewish identity, much along the lines of minority responses to victimization theorized by Homi Bhabha and Robert Young.[43]

In the influential volume *Vom Judentum* (1913), opening essays by Karl Wolfskehl, Jakob Wassermann, and Hans Kohn grouped under the suspicious heading "Jüdisches Wesen" (Jewish Essence) convey the essentializing strategies by which the volume attempts to redefine Jewish identity. The titles—"Das jüdische Geheimnis" (The Jewish Secret), "Der Jude als Orientale" (The Jew as Oriental), and "Der Geist des Orients" (The Spirit of the Orient)—express the priorities of this modern Torah: memory, creativity, fertility are appropriated from European neo-romanticism and *Lebensphilosophie* in the effort to launch a new Jewish myth valorizing life over law and mystery over knowledge. In these pages, the only modern thinker to be named in the same breath as Moses is Henri Bergson!

It is the opposition between decay and fertility, between individuation and belonging, between anarchy and tradition. To cut oneself off from the past is the passionate ambition of the Jew who is on his own precisely because milieu, reminiscence, habit and obligations of various sorts bind him externally or internally to the past. But in this binding, he does not find the law, and thus he destroys it and becomes an individualist. He does not have enough imagination to harmonize in himself two forms of existence which only appear to be different from one another.[44]

Thus Jakob Wassermann establishes the parameters of the myth by initiating the Orient-Occident polarity. The distinction boils down to two types of remembering. European Judaism connects with the past through sterile formalism and habit, in ways accidental to human existence, rather than through the organic, intuitive pathways that are the very "law" of the organic self's unfolding—*Gerechtigkeit,* in Beer-Hofmann's vision—and only the imagination is capable of uniting these two forms. Wassermann goes on to characterize the oriental Jew: "The Jew . . . whom I call Oriental—it is naturally a symbolic figure; I could just as well have named him the fulfilled, or the legitimate heir—is sure of himself, is sure of the world and of humanity. He cannot lose himself, since a noble consciousness, blood consciousness, links him to the past, and an uncommon responsibility obligates him to the future; and he cannot betray himself, since he is at the same time a revealed being."[45] The parallels to Joseph continue: "He has everything within him that others seek outside; not in burning restlessness, but in free movement and giving he participates in the progressing lives of nations. He is free, and they are his slaves. He is true, and the others lie. He knows his sources, he lives by the mothers, he rests and creates; the others are the eternally wandering unchangeable ones."[46] These motifs comprise the central traits of the oriental Jew: his selfhood constructed freely from within, neither static nor restive, he is neither wandering Jew nor *Grübler.* He moves freely but is always at home, because home is the self. The idea that Jewish creativity is born of intimate immersion in the feminine sources of selfhood recurs in powerful ways in Beer-Hofmann's characterization of the biblical David.

Wassermann's essay is formulated as a letter to Buber, whose thought was the central inspiration behind the volume. It is worth briefly citing the main points, expressed in similarly schematic terms, of Buber's essay "Der Geist des Orients und das Judentum" (The Spirit of the Orient and Judaism), written, like *Josephslegende,* between 1912 and 1914. Buber likewise differentiates "the oriental type" from the occidental in terms of motion versus stasis, fertility versus sterility, becoming versus being.[47] Like many writers of the time, Buber challenged racial science with his own, no less racist rhetoric. Thus the occidental is represented by the Greeks of Pericles' day, the Italians of Trecento, and the modern Germans, whereas exemplars of the Asiatic type include not only "Asiatic antiquity" but modern Chinese, Indians, and Jews. Paramount is the distinction between spatial consciousness and relational, temporal perception. "Like the Oriental as such, the Jew perceives the gestures of things rather than their outlines, the *Nacheinander* rather than the *Nebeneinander,* time rather than space. . . . He experiences the world less in the atomized, varied singularity of things than in their connection, their commonality and community."[48] Buber's description of the Oriental as the "motoric man" is perhaps the best explanation of why Hofmannsthal's ideal Jew was to be depicted by Nijinsky, "the most exceptional person to grace the contemporary stage." "The basic psychic act of the motor being is centrifugal: a stimulus emanates from the soul and becomes movement. The basic psychic act of the sensory being is centripetal: an impression falls into his soul and becomes an image. . . . Both think, but for one, to think means to have an impact, for the other, thinking means form."[49] We are a long way from the image of the bearded rabbi bent over his books, and an equally long way from the image of the detached aesthete hurtling on a train through space. The oriental Jew expresses himself dynamically, unlike "the sensory person," who controls and rigidifies all inspiration by creating icons and idols. Potiphar's wife in Hofmannsthal's ballet is an obvious case in point. She "sits frozen, upright. She does not move. Her posture expresses icy pride and a brooding, almost passionate boredom."[50] The ballet foregrounds the moment when sterile decadence encounters in its midst the face of pure inspiration, awakens just long enough to recognize that which it has irrevocably banished, and, enraged, attempts to extinguish this memory once and for all. Buber goes on to stress that deciding (*sich entscheiden*) is the ultimate redemptive act; this explains why Joseph's deliberate disrobing is the work's highpoint.[51] Such an act of resolve corresponds literally to self-revelation that unifies, rather than divides, the spirit; it is at this moment that communication stands or falls. Witnessing Joseph's bold gesture (not only his nakedness) after her own attempts to seduce him through stealth engenders in Potiphar's wife a full awareness of the gulf that separates them.

Buber finally regarded the oriental "elemental force" as a "unifying impulse" in multiple senses, and here he engages in some problematic mythmaking of his own. The Oriental has the potential not only to remedy his own deracinated condition, but also to unite a divided world. "He is the bearer of the world torn asunder, he experiences the destiny of the world that . . . has fallen from unity into disunity."[52] The disunity of the European Jew signifies the broken character of the Occident as such, because the Orient once encompassed two subgroups—the Greeks and the Jews—that bifurcated. The mystical movements of sixteenth-century Spain, like the rise of Hasidism in eighteenth-century Poland, testify that the oriental impulse, exemplified by "life in the spirit," survives only as a Jewish countertradition. And yet Buber anticipates that Europe's return to Asian ways (understood as the reversion from Platonic forms to the Tao, as a release from the plastic, spatially oriented Greco-German tradition into the primacy of temporal and dynamic values) shall occur via the Jew's consciousness! In this model, geared toward promoting German-Jewish symbiosis, the German Jew as oriental Jew represents the *Urmythos* of the German soul, embodying Germany's forgotten (pre-Grecian) past. But Buber's rhetoric goes one step further. For it is not only Jews who embody the "unifying impulse," but all

Germans, "a mediating *Volk* . . . who acquired all the wisdom and art of the Occident, and have not lost their oriental primal essence."[53] If this is so, then mediation becomes the common interest of Germans and Jews, and Jewish writers can gravitate to public genres—drama, ballet—in the service of their common redemption. The oriental Jew recalls the German past and at the same time, as a European, is a living symbol of the existential German national character.

HOFMANNSTHAL'S LITERARY ORIENTALISM

Is it conceivable that the ideas expressed in the collection *Vom Judentum* influenced Hofmannsthal? Buber wrote admiringly of Hofmannsthal as early as the 1890s, and in 1906 he sent him his edition of the legends of the eighteenth-century mystic Rabbi Nachman of Bratslav. Hofmannsthal, who maintained a lifelong interest in both Eastern and Western mystical traditions, thought highly of the project.[54] Though their correspondence is sparse, the letters testify to mutual appreciation, a common literary sensibility, and intellectual kinship.[55] The most important affinity between Hofmannsthal and Buber may have been that both appropriated orientalist discourse in their quest for a genre of memory. Both wanted moderns to experience a subliminal encounter with the past that would ultimately become a redemptive self-encounter. Here we find ourselves at the heart of the phenomenon I have been calling Viennese Jewish modernism.

In his preface to the new translation of the *Thousand and One Nights* (1907), Hofmannsthal describes the impact of an oriental aesthetic on the reader: "The longer we read, the more beautifully we give ourselves to this world, lose ourselves in the medium of the most immeasurable and naïve poetry and yet rightfully possess ourselves; just as when bathing in a beautiful water, you lose your heaviness, but only then rightfully perceive the feeling of your body as an enjoying, magical one."[56] Oriental tropes are not simply a figure for memory; the medium of oriental poetry perpetrates a self-forgetting that goes hand in hand with self-affirmation; this (as we shall see) is likewise the priority of the mythic theater. The preface clarifies a further advantage in casting Joseph as an Oriental. Hofmannsthal associates oriental prose with tropes as such: media that lie between *Jugendstil* ornaments and parables, the former transmitting too little memory, the latter too much. Tropes are "unencumbered," "primal words" that freely allow the reader access into the secret weave of language, where "all [is] derivation from ancient roots, all is thinkable in manifold ways, all is floating."[57] The past signified by tropes is a mythic past of unlimited possibilities, infinite regress, and indefinite parameters. Again, the miracle occurs by way of the implied reader response: magically, as when we watch a pantomime or view a hologram, we are "liberated from every anxiety, every ignobility."[58] Subsequent to liberation, the reader is transported to a world that is archaic, dynamic, naïve. "From such an original state of the world we here are quite far away, and Baghdad and Basra are not the tents of the patriarchs. But this distance is not yet such that a language unsullied and abounding in perception would not be able to link in a thousand ways this modern state of affairs to that ancient one."[59] The oriental alienation effect brings the modern condition into focus. The quasi-mnemonic agenda of Hofmannsthal's orientalism now becomes clearer: to respond to the modern crisis of memory in an antiallegorical, antirealistic manner, not by restoring a lost legacy but by taking the modern reader on a detour through an invented, mythic past. This type of contrived memory quest is precisely what Hofmannsthal hoped to incite, on a grand scale, in his later mythological operas.

Based upon the programmatic statements in the collection *Vom Judentum*, it is tempting to speculate that the form of biblical ballet qua legend was attractive to Hofmannsthal for much the same reason that Freud preferred tradition to scripture and Schnitzler favored tragicomedy over tragedy. As Edward Said has shown, falsification of the oriental, in the very act of celebrating the oriental, is more the norm than the exception in the West. Biblical ballet frames the exotic in yet a second mask of exoticism to create a holographic effect that shields the author from identification with an ultimately facile contrast and a limited ideological stance, but it also shields the audience from any kind of direct ideological engagement. Nowhere is there mention of a lasting legacy. In this respect oriental poetry, for all its magic, has a paradoxical function vis-à-vis memory. On one hand, Hofmannsthal regards it as a virtual *Ursprache* whose naïveté surpasses even that of Homer.[60] It is rich with poetic memory; the "primal sound of the word" resonates, and even a common word opens up an ancient, secret world, "like a window."[61] Yet, as in *Der Tod Georgs*, windows to the past can be opened and shut at will; like the dancer's sheer garment, they signify an ever-present barrier separating the very domains they unite. Oriental myth replaces the Bible as a source of religious experience; thus it is altogether consistent that Hofmannsthal adds "what Stendhal said about [*The Thousand and One Nights*]. It is the book that you should forget again and again, in order to read it again with renewed joy."[62] Yet the encounter with the "Orient" provides only a temporary refuge from the past: it imposes no obligations. Like the vanishing monument in postmodern culture, it is designed to provoke an ephemeral effect. Hofmannsthal's attraction to oriental poetry in this early stage in his career reveals itself to be at bottom a version of fin de siècle orientalism that appropriates the other for specific rhetorical purposes.

MANUFACTURING MYTHS FOR LATECOMERS

In the turbulent decade following its composition, the ballet *Josephslegende* came to acquire a legendary aura in Hofmannsthal's mind. In the wake of its first German performance in Berlin in 1921, Hofmannsthal set out to explicate the ballet's significance in the first of the Vienna Letters he wrote for the American magazine the *Dial*. The prominence granted this work—he devotes roughly one-sixth of the article to it—indicates that it had become more than simply a successful international collaboration. He initially offers an account of the ballet's genesis that omits Kessler's role and gives himself full credit for the decision to turn to the Bible. It becomes clear that the hindsight of ten years (including four war years) intensified Hofmannsthal's investment in the production and led him to historicize its agenda. Most interestingly, the imaginative (orientalist) encounter no longer takes priority, but gives way to an almost pedagogical mandate, fueled by nostalgia, to craft an aesthetic befitting an epigonal culture (fig. 15).

Guiding the project (in this 1922 account) was the contest between old and new. Hofmannsthal reveals that the story of David and Bathsheba competed with that of Joseph and Potiphar's wife. In fact, both incidents conform to the Salome archetype by depicting the illicit lust of an older figure of royalty for a defenseless, beautiful youth as an allegory for the depraved attempts of powerful materialistic cultures in decline to rejuvenate themselves at the expense of the next generation. The encounter between Potiphar's wife and Joseph, in so many words, was to allegorize the confrontation between Hapsburg historicism and Viennese modernism, specifically those modernists seeking to recapture "the spiritual in art."

15. Hugo von Hofmannsthal.

What potential existed for communicating the legacy of the biblical Joseph, thus interpreted, to a European audience on the eve of World War I? According to the *Dial* essay, the priority was to lift the story out of the "pathetic and psychological" sphere and into the domain of "the imaginative and the decorative." The effect would be achieved by way of a simulacrum. The "age-old, legendary material" would be represented in the manner of the biblical paintings of Paolo Veronese, in late Renaissance style.[63] The painterly trope would free up the biblical tale from the strictures of historical accuracy, didactic purposes, and the projections of a contemporary audience and create mythic theater. The Veronesian screen reminds the viewer that the artist transmits the eternal legacies to a new generation, especially in "late times."

Along with Swinburne and Aubrey Beardsley, I consider anachronism to be a valuable element of the arts of later times, and although I am aware of the fact that the painters at the close of the seventeenth century in their naïveté clothed the biblical figures in contemporary costume, and that we, when we do the same, appear anything but naïve, I still think it infinitely more enchanting and important that in the case of a theatrical work of art, certain internal correspondences [*Übereinstimmungen*] are achieved, instead of catering to the historically educated bourgeois in the parterre.[64]

In his most visionary voice, Hofmannsthal articulates the significance of anachronism as a device befitting epigonal cultures. He also draws attention to what is perhaps one of the most central tenets governing his late work: the decision to downplay the naturalistic features of the story so as to highlight symbolic affinities between past and present, art and reality. "Correspondence" is once again the functional term. The purpose of the artistic anachronism is not to satisfy the historicist, nor is it to remove all temporal associations; rather, it can, on the basis of certain historical affinities between past and present ages, transmit a disguised past to a contemporary audience. Mythic theater, much like tradition, is able to convey the truth because of its quasidelusional character. Hofmannsthal comments that this type of aesthetic transposition reflects an awareness of history far more nuanced than the positivistic idea of historical accuracy. Like Veronese, like Strauss (and arguably like Freud in *Moses and Monotheism*), Hofmannsthal presents himself as an artist who manufactures myths for latecomers: "And such an inner correspondence in fact rules between the music of Strauss, which is very clearly the last, pompous expression of a great musical epoch, and the paintings of those Venetians who also represent a pompous, overripe finale of a great age."[65] Ten years' hindsight offers Hofmannsthal a historical perspective on the culture that generated this particular work, which he now can claim epitomizes the world of prewar Austria. The priority now is to transport an unsuspecting audience into an earlier time and place and thereby situate it squarely in its own historical moment. And it is not only Strauss's music that engenders the analogy between Baroque Italy and Vienna, 1914, it is the costuming, for which Hofmannsthal again claims credit.

Having stressed in the *Dial* article the need to remove the biblical story from its psychological context, Hofmannsthal expands this antirealist stance into a general principle in a 1928 article. This commentary on the opera *Die Ägyptische Helena*, which leads into a reported conversation between Hofmannsthal and Strauss, debates precisely the question of which aesthetic strategies are most suitable for the modern age, while serving as the librettist's de facto defense of "mythological opera" as the preferred genre. In the process, Hofmannsthal explains what myth, music, and dialogue each contribute to a theatrical production. The debate culminates with the following summation of the poet's major arguments. "Whatever it may be, this present, it is certainly mythic—I know of no other expression for an existence that unfolds before so many enormous horizons, for this being surrounded by millennia, this inundation of Orient and Occident in our self, for the enormous inner expanse, these raging inner tensions, this here and there that is the signature of our life. It is not possible to capture this in bourgeois dialogues. Let us make mythological operas: the truest of forms. Take my word for it."[66] When one's very existence resembles a mythic memory theater, a naturalist aesthetic holds little chance of influencing the status quo. It is not only the mythic aura that dialogue stands to dispel by reducing a theatrical work to "a psychological conversation-play"; "the dialectic," he comments enigmatically, "forces the I out of existence."[67] Hofmannsthal could not be further from Peter Szondi's dialectical theory of drama, or, for that matter, from Beer-

Hofmann's dialogical conception of artistic creation.[68] Hofmannsthal sees dialogue as void of redemptive power, due in part to the intrinsic nature of mythic memory, but also to the particular gullibility of late ages.

To explain how "mythological opera" employs dialogue differently from drama, Hofmannsthal distinguishes transmission (*Übermitteln*) from communication (*Mitteilen*). This distinction resonates for each of the works discussed in this book. Naturalism and psychologism both stress direct communication, to their detriment. "I claim that a writer has the choice to create either speeches or characters!"[69] Dialogue undermines the theatrical aesthetic because it is susceptible to what Hofmannsthal calls "the critique of the lower consciousness."[70] The alternative, *Übermitteln*, imparts something much more subtle: "How I construct the plot, intertwine the motifs, allow what is hidden to resonate, and what has resonated to disappear again—through similarity of the figures, through analogies of the situations—through the intonation which often says more than the word."[71] An audience must not be distracted by quotidian impressions. Transmission must occur subliminally, as a mystery disengaged from the here and now, via art, and in a fundamentally non-historical manner. "But in a 'naturally' conducted dialogue there is no room for this. The 'natural' is the projection of unfathomable life onto a very arbitrarily chosen social level. The maximum of our cosmically moved, time-and-space-embracing human nature can no longer be encompassed through naturalness."[72] Again, it is the chaos of his age that justifies the writer's approach.

These remarks provoke Strauss to respond: "But those are mine—the devices of the musician!"[73] Indeed, when Hofmannsthal writes that "the dialectic forces the I out of existence," he invokes the view of many twentieth-century intellectuals, Freud and Benjamin among them, that modern media of communication perpetrate amnesia. Walter Benjamin's 1934 essay "Der Erzähler" (The Storyteller) makes a parallel distinction between sterile and fertile genres of transmission in the modern age. Benjamin too claims that optimal transmissibility requires the omission of psychological commentary and a disregard for the informational content of the narration.[74] Benjamin's contrast of the premodern and modern prose forms story and novel resembles the opposition Hofmannsthal erects between mythic drama and modern drama.[75] The storyteller, like the allegorist, forges bridges between past and present, individual life and group memory, the physical and the metaphysical. He is the artist who reestablishes the supernatural framework for collective events. The legacy—Benjamin too names Scheherazade's tales as a prime example—is thus intrinsically ritualistic, for in it the individual merges into the collective and discrete temporal episodes can once again interconnect—in short, the plight of the memory individual is overcome. Hofmannsthal's belief that dialogue lacks all mnemonic power may have been what led him to dissociate himself from the libretto and to conceive of his contribution to *Josephslegende* in painterly, theatrical, and even musical terms. The 1912 ballet, by omitting dialogue altogether, comes even closer than opera to meeting the criteria for mythic theater.

It is important to note that Hofmannsthal, unlike Benjamin and Freud, invested in mythic art as a means of transmitting not just memory, but belief, the possibility of belief; it is an ambition that he linked to the poet's vocation even in the 1903 *Gespräch über Gedichte* (Dialogue on Poems). His closing words in the 1928 essay ("Let us make mythological operas: the truest of forms. Take my word for it") suggest that the artist's pursuit is indeed extraordinary, for he not only facilitates dialogue but creates substitute religious truths, new sources of belief that supersede past legacies. Let us recall the testimony of the very first Joseph, the young Léonide Massine: "Von Hofmannsthal would explain, in his soft, self-effacing way, that he envisaged Joseph as a noble, untamed young savage in search of God, and said that this, and the young man's tale of exaltation, must be implicit in his dance." The religious legacy that Hofmannsthal might have wished to transmit in the *Josephslegende* is embodied in the dancing Joseph, who, when stripped of all of his various disguises, represents the artist in collusion with divinity.

THE MYTHIC IMPULSE OVERCOME

As history came to have a greater impact on Hofmannsthal in the late 1920s, he moved to renounce the aesthetics of myth altogether. Michael P. Steinberg argues that as early as *Elektra,* a drama-turned-opera, Hofmannsthal felt compelled to add a musical dimension to capture the experience of the "metalinguistic, irrational." Music created the possibility for *Übermitteln,* without which, as Steinberg's argument goes, Hofmannsthal's late works (*Jedermann, Das Salzburger grosse Welttheater*) lapse into ideology-based allegory.[76] I would propose that one can nonetheless, and at the same time, regard mythological opera as a solution to the opposite problem: how to reintroduce dialogue into the mythic theater in order to tilt the balance in favor of *Mitteilen,* and thereby supplant mythic remembering with historical remembering, while avoiding the perils of naturalism. At the very least, one can say that a shift toward dialogue summarizes the trajectories—generic and thematic— from the Egyptian Joseph to *Die Ägyptische Helena.* The plot of the opera, which was composed between 1919 and 1924, along with the interpretive comments of 1928 discussed earlier, testify that it was not for aesthetic reasons alone that Hofmannsthal renounced mythic theater; personal memory compelled him as well.

Die Ägyptische Helena also conceptualizes a mythic encounter between two legendary figures as a meeting of Orient and Occident. Of Menelas and Helena, survivors of a war-torn epoch whose tangled destiny is at the center of the plot, Hofmannsthal writes: "He was for me the embodiment of the Occidental; in her, the inexhaustible strength of the Orient. He stood for law, marriage, fatherhood. She hovered above them all, uncannily intoxicating, not-to-be-bound goddess."[77] Staging a confrontation between Occident and Orient in this opera serves to illustrate not an irrevocable break, but rather the healing of the break allegorized in *Josephslegende:* to facilitate the reunion and re-marriage of Helena and Menelas, separated since her abduction ten years earlier, under *occidental* terms.[78]

After Menelas rescues Helena, an even more impenetrable barrier raises itself between husband and wife: his traumatic war memories and tortured fantasies about the years she spent in the arms of other men. At sea, the frustrated Menelas raises the knife to murder her, but at the last moment Aïthra, "an Egyptian princess and magician," stages a shipwreck and kidnaps Helena. Back at her island palace, Aïthra supplies Helena with a magic brew for Menelas: a brew of forgetfulness with which to convince him that she, "the Egyptian Helen," had actually been whisked away to spend the war primly asleep on the island. Here Hofmannsthal introduces an authentic myth that appears in *The Odyssey* and in Herodotus and that received its first dramatic treatment in Euripides' tragedy *Helen*. This magic brew, a potential refuge from history, promises continual renewal: one

can be
blissful
today as yesterday
again and again![79]

But drinking the brew of forgetfulness only disorients Menelas further. In a fit of paranoia, he kills an innocent boy whom he believes to be Paris. He suffers from more than just repetition compulsion, for he remains suspended in a private limbo between past and present, tormented by hallucinations from wartime, still unable to connect with Helena.

She is speaking to me—
(*to himself*)
and I hear the other!
My body is here,
the soul down there—doubled I live
in a twofold place!
That should not be![80]

Underlying the operatic action is the question of whether, and under what terms, Europe may resurrect classic standards of beauty and cultural icons after World War I. In the 1928 commentary, Hofmannsthal explains that Menelas is suffering from a very contemporary ailment, shell shock: "He is not a madman, but he is in that state of complete dissolution which has been observed for days and weeks in many war hospitals amongst those who returned from all-too-horrible situations."[81] In such a case, artificially induced forgetting seems to be a remedy, but in fact only perpetuates the trauma. In his graphic description of Menelas recapturing Helena from the burning palace after he murders Paris, Hofmannsthal cannot repress the association with his own war experience. "In that night, when the Greeks penetrated the burning Troy (it is easier for us to imagine this kind of night than for those who lived before 1914)—in that night Menelas had to find his wife in one of these burning palaces and carry her out amidst collapsing walls, this woman, his beloved, stolen wife . . . who was also the widow of Paris and the lover of these ten or twelve other sons of Priam! . . . What a situation for a husband!"[82] The Euripidean myth of the two Helens symbolizes for Hofmannsthal the false illusion that aesthetics are unsullied by history. This was the very philosophy that had justified mythic recollection as a form that shields one from a true encounter with the past (history) by offering instead a narcissistic self-projection—that which Potiphar's wife sees when she looks at Joseph. Euripides' myth exculpates those values, and the very function of myth itself, saying that the cause of the bloodshed was not the genuine article, but a mere effigy, a phantom. Hofmannsthal's later opera asks: can past and present enter into a dialogue without recourse to myth? Can we risk reconciling the occidental and oriental Helens? Can the artist admit history into the mythic memory theater?

Helena ultimately demands the antidote to the brew of forgetfulness, the memory brew. She renounces Aïthra's counsel and takes steps to reunite her two selves, knowing that Menelas would have to recognize both her current Egyptian self and her tainted Greek self before any lasting bond could be reestablished—before their daughter Hermione would be permitted to rejoin them. Reconciliation with history restores the future: a hopeful countermyth for a traumatized generation. Orientalism is revealed to function as a temporary asylum. The couple's foray into Aïthra's domain provides a vital refuge, and the illusion offers a new, revised memory narrative to cancel out the memory of their separation and bring them halfway together. Again, myth mediates. But myth proves to be a hazard in its own right and must be relinquished. Helena's heroism lies in her willful return to the most worldly of resources—neither magic, nor illusion, nor even beauty, but dialogue—to forge a future. In a poignant moment after her first night together with Menelas, she sings a duet with Aïthra that expresses this realization: a paean to memory.

And more and more!
And not enough
Of the dark drink
Remembrance!

The flame of past grief
flares up:
Before it, the here
becomes dire and pale.

But what once was
steps forth
spirit-filled
out of the dark gate.

And what comes back
from below
is all that
befits the hero!

And more and more!
And not enough
Of the magic drink
Remembrance![83]

6 The Forgotten Modernism of Biblical Drama

Beer-Hofmann's *Die Historie von König David* (The History of King David, 1918–33)

The Jews remember far too much. —Richard Beer-Hofmann

Richard Beer-Hofmann lived just long enough to experience the end of World War II. He had become a citizen of the United States; seen his late poems and autobiographical writings published in this country; and achieved fame as an emigré writer, having lectured at Harvard, Yale and Columbia and having been honored by the National Institute of Arts and Letters. Beer-Hofmann also willed that his *Nachlass* remain in the States, to ensure that those who would encounter him after his death would retrace the journey he had made. One wonders how he would have reacted to the memorial service held at the Burgtheater in Vienna on October 14, 1945. The ceremony included readings, music, and a performance of the first act of *Jaákobs Traum* (fig. 16). Actress Hedwig Bleibtreu, the grande dame of Viennese theater, returned to play the character of Rebekah as she had done in 1919. The complete play was staged only a few months later.

Within literary scholarship, Beer-Hofmann came into his own as a major writer in the 1990s. Signs of the revival included the publication of a critical edition of his works in eight volumes,[1] a reception history,[2] and a spate of critical studies. In 1995, the Academy of Sciences in Heidelberg held a conference, Between Aestheticism and Judaism, to mark the fiftieth anniversary of Beer-Hofmann's death;[3] and in 1999, the Jewish Museums of Amsterdam and Vienna collaborated on an exhibit about Jewish Vienna at the turn of the century that took none other than Beer-Hofmann as its centerpiece. Literally: the exhibition, called Zu Gast bei Beer-Hofmann (Visiting Beer-Hofmann), staged a virtual gathering at Richard and Paula Beer-Hofmann's fashionable villa in the eighteenth district. Visitors were introduced to the couple's family, home, and property—the villa had been designed and partly furnished by Josef Hoffmann of the *Wiener Werkstätte*—and then to the social milieu. Freud, Schnitzler, and Hofmannsthal were of course in attendance, as were Buber and Herzl, Reinhardt and Altenberg, Mahler and Schönberg, Andreas-Salomé and

Kokoschka, along with forty others. Each of these guests brought along a gift characteristic of his or her vocation or avocation.

Imagining Beer-Hofmann as the host of this gathering allows us to imagine his life as the esteemed "patriarch of Young Vienna," and it restores to him something of the aura that enveloped him especially in his early career. Above all, it was his status as an unapologetic Jew that led the curators to choose him for the role of host: "In an exhibition about this so very 'Jewish Vienna of the turn of the century,' the protagonist has to be a convinced and convincing 'homo judaicus.' Only through him was it possible to show that in the cultural world of the Viennese fin-de-siècle there existed not only a 'breadth of community,' but also a 'depth of community,' dependent on Jewish consciousness, Jewish experience, and similarities in the 'soul's deepest and most ancient corners.'"[4] What it meant to be a *homo judaicus* may be inferred from Beer-Hofmann's response to Theodor Herzl upon reading *The Jewish State* in 1896: "What appealed to me more than everything in your book was what stood behind it: finally, again, a human being who doesn't bear his Judaism like a

16. Program, memorial service for Richard Beer-Hofmann, Burgtheater, Vienna, October 14, 1945.

burden or a misfortune, but is rather proud to be a legitimate heir of an ancient, distinguished civilization."[5] Two decades later, Beer-Hofmann's drama *Jaákobs Traum* was praised in similar terms: "He who can write in this way proves that the mission that God laid out for Jacob back then lives on in his descendants, and that it continues to find men of a prophetic temper who know how to proclaim it. Beer-Hofmann has experienced Judaism in himself, a Judaism neither of submission nor of *galut* [exile], but rather a strong, self-conscious, defiant Judaism, the kind we would wish from its adherents."[6] Beer-Hofmann's philosophy of Jewish renewal had strong affinities with Herzl's vision, and his emphasis on a dialogical partnership between human beings and God is said to have inspired Martin Buber's *I and Thou*.[7]

The biblical trilogy *Die Historie von König David* is no hologram. The work can hardly be dismissed as an isolated episode in the author's career, since composition began in 1898 and continued for forty years. The chief source of disappointment for its audience was that more of the trilogy was not completed, and sooner. Beer-Hofmann managed to complete only the prologue—a play in its own right—called *Jaákobs Traum* (1919) and first of the three plays, *Der junge David* (1933), which he spent fifteen years writing (or, as he liked to stress, *not* writing).[8] Nor is there anything ambivalent about their Jewish focus. *Jaákobs Traum* is a short, expressionistic play that centers on the biblical Jacob's

17. Program, *Jaákobs Traum*, Burgtheater, Vienna, April 5, 1919.

18. Beer-Hofmann's program for *Jaákobs Traum*, Hebrew performance by the Moscow theater troupe Habima, Carltheater, Vienna, June 1, 1926. Beer-Hofmann penciled in the word "Première."

struggles with his brother Esau and with angels. Here Beer-Hofmann condenses three encounters in Jacob's life that in the Bible occur over several years into one long day's journey into night.[9] The theme of wrestling drives the prologue as a whole as well as each discrete episode. Beer-Hofmann had not planned to publish *Jaákobs Traum* independently, but his preface to the first edition suggests that the war led him to do so; the drama was welcomed as a morale-booster by Austrian and German Jews, a courageous and timely retrieval of a Jewish national legacy.[10] It was first performed in the Vienna Burgtheater in April 1919, and Max Reinhardt produced it in Berlin that same year, where it ran for over fifty performances (fig. 17). In the 1920s the play was picked up by the Russian-Jewish (now Israeli) theater group Habimah, and this Hebrew rendition, *Chalom Ya'akov*, has been part of their repertoire ever since. In 1926 and 1927, Habimah performed the play in Vienna, Berlin, Palestine, and the United States. The author attended the Viennese production at the Carltheater (fig. 18), where it was staged together with Ansky's *The Dybbuk*. The play was also performed in Germany in the 1960s.

 Jaákobs Traum takes the concluding sequence of *Der Tod Georgs* to the next level (paralleling the author's own development). In the same way, the first play of the trilogy, *Der junge David*, strives to outreason its own prologue. *Der junge David* is a drama in seven scenes (*Bilder*), designed "to fuse the customary elements of drama, particularly action, with those of the pageant and the tableau."[11] The play is cast for over eighty characters and accompanied by footnotes and copious stage directions. The young David's brief historical moment corresponds to the morning after Jaákob's dream; David must apply last night's lessons to tomorrow's problems. Fortunately, David inherits Jaákob's predisposition to wrestling, though on a more frenetic scale. Unfortunately, the conflicts that challenge Jaákob in the private sphere and in the virtual reality of his dream require a vastly different strategy when the fate of the nation hangs in the balance. God no longer plays a speaking role; the theological energy that traversed Jacob's ladder must be channeled into social and political realms, where words matter far less than action. Historical Jews—and Austrian Jews of the 1930s, to be sure—no longer have the luxury to ponder God's plans in the abstract: they need pragmatic solutions. In particular, they must negotiate between particularism and universalism, the diaspora Jew's "eternal" dilemma.

How does one sustain multiple commitments on the stage of history? To provoke some unorthodox answers, the dramatist selected a notorious interregnum chapter in biblical history, corresponding more or less to chapters 27–31 of 1 Samuel. King Saul has already officially been deposed by God, but has not yet transferred the crown to David. Saul suffers from manic depression and paranoia that lead him to persecute David, his most loyal servant, finally driving David and his followers from the land. But these events are relegated to the background. David and his troops have found asylum on foreign soil, in exchange for which he has become a vassal of King Achisch of Gat. In one month, the right to hospitality is set to expire. Yet the Philistines (led by Achisch) are fortifying and ready to attack Israel. The plot begins when David learns from Achisch's messengers of the impending war and struggles to resolve this conflict of interest. Shall he break his oath to Achisch or go to war against Israel? His best advisor is his ancestress Ruth, a figure even more revered than David himself, who supplies an indispensable counterforce to David's restive wakefulness. Midway through the play, David takes leave of his wife, Maácha, concealing from her his decision to remain faithful to his oath to Achisch. In this scene, as in the dialogues with Ruth, the tables begin to turn against David's authority and in favor of feminine wisdom: Maácha intuits that a crisis is at hand and undermines David's resolution by swearing her own oath to God to spare him at her own expense. In the penultimate scene, rapid-fire dialogue among David's captains conveys that he has entered the war and been victorious. The play culminates with David's coronation ceremony, in what is more anticlimax than celebration, given that Maácha has died a sacrificial death in the interim. While David's charisma and bold, iconoclastic discourse convey that he has all the makings of a real hero, the plot conveys that it is David's very youthfulness, his volatility, that has failed him.

The *Historie,* subtitled *A Cycle,* had all the makings of a magnum opus, a work tragically aborted by Nazism, emigration to Zurich in 1938, and the death of the author's beloved wife, to whom the project was dedicated, that same year. Beer-Hofmann wanted to produce *the* Jewish national drama of his generation.[12] Freud's *Moses and Monotheism* sought "to deprive a people of the man whom they take pride in as the greatest of their sons,"[13] but Beer-Hofmann's historical dramas sought, in a more classical vein, to reacquaint the Jewish community with its heroes, above all with the biblical David, the "hero-king" to whom German Jewish families were wont to trace their lineage.[14] Beer-Hofmann's project (like Freud's) extended from a lifelong involvement with cultural heroes—Shakespeare and Dante, Goethe and Mozart—and his commitment to staging epic dramas. He had established his reputation as a dramaturge with memorable productions of Goethe's *Iphigenie* (Vienna, 1928; Berlin, 1930) and, in one evening, Faust 1 and 2 (Vienna, 1932). He had no qualms about claiming for himself the goal of the epic poet, namely "to preserve the life of heroes, of exemplary individuals, from oblivion by reviving them, in retrospect, for later generations."[15]

Hofmannsthal relied on a visual anachronism to invent a biblical myth, keeping the sacred text pristinely out of the theater in order to promote his production, originally subtitled *Ein Mysterium,* as a surrogate.[16] Freud modeled his Moses essays on non-religious sources—paintings, sculpture, and classical epic—to counteract the Jewish fixation on the biblical Moses. Beer-Hofmann's approach to biblical theater stands out among these large-scale works as being historicist and text-based. The inclusion of Hebrew names—Isaac is called Jizchak, Jacob, Jaákob, and Saul, Schául—signals the fidelity of these dramas to the Hebrew Bible, as well as their modernism.[17] Nor did Beer-Hofmann view modern biblical scholarship as a threat to his project; source criticism was his ally, and while composing the plays he spent thirty years studying the cultural, natural, geographical history of Palestine, Babylonia, and Assyria. In a like vein, Beer-Hofmann's scriptural idiom is devoutly pluralistic. He drew upon eleven different translations as sources for his drama, ranging from the Kautsch-Bertholet of 1923, to Leopold Zunz's nineteenth-century translation, to the Latin Vulgate, the Greek Septuagint, and the Luther Bible. He does not explicitly name Jewish midrashic and Talmudic literature as sources, and statements of ideological intent are virtually absent from the *Nachlass.*[18] The scholarly apparatus left its handprints on the dramas in the form of extensive footnotes, much in the way that Hofmannsthal exaggerated the Veronesian cartoon as a frame for his *Legend.* But the difference between Beer-Hofmann's and Hofmannsthal's biblical theater could not be greater.

THE RECEPTION OF *DIE HISTORIE VON KÖNIG DAVID*

What is shortsighted about the terms in which this remembered-forgotten hero of Jewish dissimulation is being championed in our time is that his literary reputation continues to rest on *Der Tod Georgs*—Jewish, yes, but not too—while the magnum opus, so laboriously composed, remains an impossibility: fragmentary, unstaged, unread. Stefan Scherer's recent book-length study of Beer-Hofmann devotes over two hundred pages to *Der Tod Georgs,* but a mere twenty pages to the mature work. Jacques Le Rider emphasizes *Der Tod Georgs* as the work of theoretical interest, the Jewish novel that sets Beer-Hofmann apart from his more "reticent" friends Hofmannsthal and Schnitzler; he mentions *Jaákobs Traum* only briefly as a Baroque- play about divine election, intended (in Hermann Bahr's words) to "'show forth God, thank God, celebrate God.'"[19] If Beer-Hofmann is to be rehabilitated as a German Jewish writer, it should be as an unrepentant modernist and as the creator of the impossible dramas that retract, or at the very least reinterpret, the Jewish legacy of the earlier novella. Within the context of Viennese modernism and its response to the problem of memory, the *Historie* is not only highly interesting and theoretically significant, but also represents a challenge to the new image of Beer-Hofmann taking shape today—which makes it appropriate that this failed work be the concluding text of this study.

The critical reception of the *Historie* has been largely positive, even adulatory. Themes of being-chosen (*Erwähltsein*), prophecy, theodicy, dialogical theology, dual identity, and enlightened cosmopolitanism dominate the critical conversation. Beer-Hofmann's critics have occasionally accused him of apologetics, either for the Jewish God or for assimilation. In his review of *Jaákobs Traum*, Arnold Zweig claims that Beer-Hofmann "ennobled" Jacob by painting him in too-Western tones, thus turning a Titan, an Odysseus figure, into a saint.[20] Much to the author's outrage, Hofmannsthal wrote that he found *Jaákobs Traum* too chauvinistic for his taste.[21] By stressing the author's relatively affirmative Jewish identity and theological commitments, the reception history has diverted attention from the tensions within the *Historie*, in particular, from the fact that the dramas reinterpret the Jewish legacy in a counterhistorical vein. Beer-Hofmann's treatment of Jewish themes surely looks straightforward in comparison with those of Freud and even Schnitzler, and critics have not been inclined to look to him to illuminate the conundrums faced by his less identified Jewish colleagues. Just as Hofmannsthal's apathy toward his Jewish heritage (and arguably also his late Catholicism) may have preempted serious attention to his Jewish pantomime and biblical ballet, so has Beer-Hofmann's Jewish pride precluded a serious inquiry into aspects of the biblical plays as radically heterodox as those associated with *Moses and Monotheism*. At most, critics will consider *Jaákobs Traum*, but David, whom biographers have regarded as the author's spokesperson, and Ruth, a heroine in her own right, have been all but forgotten.

What deserves to be remembered in the case of Beer-Hofmann is that, as one reviewer in 1934 wrote, the dramas do not supply the expected legends, and they portray instead much that is unexpected. We do not find David slaying Goliath, seducing Bathsheba, confronting the paranoid King Saul, or singing psalms; the king of Israel is cornered in his brief tenure as a diaspora Jew, a fugitive in a foreign land who feels compelled to resist the kingship, and also the mythic status that awaits him in Jewish lore. The tensions experienced by David, Jaákob, Ruth, and others pertains not only to the meaning of Jewish identity but rather, as in the novella and throughout this study, to what makes one Jewish at all; the answer is no longer "the blood in your veins." The drama's most radical moments are those in which characters reinterpret and remix the signs of Jewish identity.

The forgotten modernism of biblical drama manifests itself in four strategies. Beer-Hofmann challenges the primal scene of Jewish suffering; he adopts an enlightened critique of chauvinism and the impulse towards mythmaking; he invents strategies of Jewish countermemory (Jacob); and he champions a return to apolitical genres of deep memory, coded feminine, in order to secure the future (David and Ruth). This final strategy encompasses the others to a certain degree and infiltrates the *Historie* in all of its dimensions. Where one spoke of a flawed hybridity in the case of *Der Weg ins Freie,* and, in the case of *Moses and Monotheism,* of a distorted tradition, Beer-Hofmann's dramas aim for counterpoint, even harmony, between male (solar) experience and female (lunar) wisdom. At almost every step, female characters step in to "supplement and contradict" the vision of their male counterparts. The dramatic idiom itself was dialectical in character, so as to highlight the interplay of the epic element and the dramatic element representing two equally compelling temporal realities: dream versus life, past versus present, the long-term vision versus the heat of the moment, memory versus history. It might even be said that the author is present in a dialectical relationship with the text: he hovers over each locution, introjects scenic and gestic descriptions at every turn, and interrupts characters' speech with dashes and stresses, all of which exacerbates emotional intensity and conveys restlessness and indecision.[22] The playwright's use of parataxis, together with his apocalyptic religious vision, suggest an affinity with Expressionist theater.[23] Yet in a letter of 1933, the dramatist spoke emphatically about the dialectical effect he hoped to create: the authorial voice would supply the reader with an epic "vaporization" to counteract the "painful, feverish poetic vision," "to force the excited reader to rest," to provide sedation from the "feverish" dramatic tempo.[24] That which the authorial voice accomplishes, line by line, vis-à-vis the dramatis personae, occurs on a large scale through the counterposing of two primal scenes, one "dramatic," patriarchal, traumatic, the other "epic," matriarchal, therapeutic.

ISAAC UNBOUND: THE PRIMAL SCENE REVISITED

Two biblical stories serve as the key texts for the *Historie,* and they implicitly rival each other as primal scenes for the modern Jewish experience. The binding of Isaac, or *Akedah,* in Genesis 22 is the trauma that gives rise to Jaákob's predicament. Yet in the David play the legend of Ruth the Moabite has an even greater impact than the *Akedah.* Isaac and Ruth are antithetical paragons of sacrifice and loyalty. The former is coerced and debilitating; the latter, freely chosen and enlightened: "For wherever you go, I will go; wherever you lodge, I will lodge; your people shall be my people, and your God my God" (Ruth 1:16).

In the second act of *Jaákobs Traum,*[25] Jaákob narrates the trauma of the *Akedah* as if he could see it from his father Isaac's perspective:

(*Bitterly and in a menacing tone*)
What there the child's eyes—wide with fear—
For once have seen, think you they can forget?

The hand—the father's hand—that shyly tender
Used to caress his fever-stricken face—
That arm which once embraced, clung so tightly
As though such nearness were not near enough—
That eye—whose look was longing, care and blessing—
And that whole countenance, that earliest childhood's home,
Whereto old age, long, weary and disheartened,
Still as to some enchanted island flies . . .
And now all this—hand, arm, eye, countenance—
Transformed into a madness filled with God,
Blind, deaf—forgetting his very self
A single outcry only: "Kill!"
(*Shuddering*)
Whose faith was thus—in childhood—crushed by God—
In whom shall he trust, where feel secure?[26]

The memory of the *Akedah*—not repressed, all too vivid—forms the matrix of Jaákob's identity as a Jew. The *Akedah* has debilitated Isaac and has made a memory individual out of his son. Jaákob has the profound insight that his father failed to become a father in his own right because his inheritance of the Abrahamic legacy was stunted at the moment he became its scapegoat. To his wife Rebekah belongs the insight that Isaac's trauma is to blame for his failing to choose the right son to receive his blessing. Though she intervenes (in an Abrahamic mode) to correct this lapse (again at her husband's expense) and reroute the blessing from Edom to Jaákob, she cannot undermine its impact. Jaákob (much like the twentieth-century authors in this book) represents the epigonal mind-set of the third generation, heir to Abraham, the proud agent of destiny, and to Isaac, the survivor whom destiny has crippled. Jaákob's trial, his *Bildung*, is to figure out how to be faithful to both grandfather and father, to the legacy and its undoing. As we have seen before, the road to individuation entails a series of progressively more intense encounters with sources of destiny.

Beer-Hofmann diminishes the aura of the *Akedah* in other ways. He dejudaizes the sacrifice and its significance by revealing it to be a Jewish *and* pagan myth. In Jaákob's dialogue with his Phoenician slave, he discovers that what is Mount Moriah to one (and recognizable to the audience as the Temple Mount in Jerusalem) is "Uru-Schalim" to the other. For the Phoenician, Moriah is the site where, in the process of creating the world, primordial monsters were suppressed and buried and a rock sealed the crevice to contain chaos.[27] The once and future *Urtopos* of Jewish suffering has universal and potentially apocalyptic implications. In the David drama, Beer-Hofmann telescopes the event into the modern psyche (much like Freud and Hofmannsthal in their biblical works). In the midst of one of David's most impassioned discourses, one of his cohorts comments that the story of the *Akedah* is pure projection: the monstrous forces lie buried not within the earth, rather "in us, it lies and lures."[28] What must be controlled in order to form lasting attachments (God to his creation, Abraham to his faith, a people to their legacy, David to the crown) are the unresolved conflicts within the self.

The view that the *Akedah* was an event with harmful consequences for Jewish national consciousness has become a topos within Jewish culture. Genesis leaves no doubt that Abraham passes the test: Isaac is spared; the promise is renewed; and the story acquires a central place in Jewish liturgy. This story, like no other, has been a vehicle for the Jewish imagination. Medieval Jews, called upon to sacrifice their children for their faith, chose to believe that Isaac was in fact killed, though resurrected later by tears of angels.[29] Postbiblical commentators and imaginative writers have been far less certain that things turned out well. Modern intellectuals regard the twenty-two verses, with their utter concision and existential directness, as fertile ground for philosophical and poetic mediation. Israeli writers such as Haim Gouri, Amir Gilboa, Yehuda Amichai, and the novelist A. B. Yehoshua (who wrote an entire novel so as to uproot the *Akedah* from Jewish consciousness) believe that the *Akedah* bestowed a knife in the Jewish heart, to paraphrase Gouri's famous poem "Yerushah" (Legacy).[30]

The *Akedah* is the traumatic past over which Beer-Hofmann's characters must prevail; the usable past, by contrast, is the heritage of Ruth, a Gentile matriarch. Ruth too has made sacrifices; we learn in the final act that she is a bereaved mother and grandmother. But she exemplifies *Treue* (loyalty) most clearly in her promise of devotion to her mother-in-law—lines that recur throughout the play and that serve as a filter of the play as a whole. For *Der junge David* opens with a recitation of the Book of Ruth. On a dark stage, light descends to reveal a narrator clad in an "undulating, sea-green, occidental garment," who proceeds to recite the entire scroll. On occasion he pauses, then the stage lights up to reveal a tableau vivant in illustration. "For only a moment the image is illumined, then retreats into darkness."[31] One sees momentary flashbacks conjured out of oblivion by the narrator's voice. Even as voice engenders the visual image, the effect highlights the stark contrast between narrative and theater, between the epic recitation of scripture and the snapshot effect of the scenes flashing before the audience. Scripture is directly incorporated into the theater, but on an equal footing; the source text and the theatrical medium appear in counterpoint, without pretense of mystification or fusion. Reading Ruth foreshadows the play's central message, namely that Jewish memory is to be learned from women, and moreover, from Gentile women. Like the Book of Ruth itself, the introductory recitation ends by recounting the genealogy leading from Ruth to David; the Book mothers the drama just as Ruth mothers David. The story of Ruth does not negate the trauma of the *Akedah* as much as heal its victims; themes of organic discontinuity, orphaning, and sacrifice continue to dominate in *Der junge David*, and Jewish suffering remains the sine qua non of Beer-Hofmann's theology.

A MODERNIST RETURNS TO THE ENLIGHTENMENT

All that we know about Beer-Hofmann's sources and composition suggests that an even deeper motive than the obvious wish to buttress Jewish national pride was, in the manner of *Moses and Monotheism,* to invent a Jewish countertradition opposed to chauvinism (as to myths of all sorts). Beer-Hofmann's dramas appeal to reason in the tradition of the German Jewish Enlightenment, whose proponents regarded the theater of Lessing, Goethe, and Schiller as the preeminent art form of the German Jewish symbiosis—poets who, through the Weimar period, were believed to be perpetuating the values of Abraham, Jacob, Moses, Moses Maimonides, and Moses Mendelssohn. Dialogue, not dance, was Beer-Hofmann's central medium, for any resolution promoted by the Enlightenment had to be rational, interpersonal, and ethical.[32] Thus, while the characters in the *Historie* wear oriental costumes, their mentality is unmistakably occidental. They use reason to counteract the seductions of their milieu, namely idealism, myth, idolatry, even art. In this regard, and to a degree that has not been noticed, the dramas are not large-scale fulfillments of the conclusion to *Der Tod Georgs.* Rather, they take a strong stand against the privileging of blood memory that that text, like the oft-cited poem "Lullaby to Miriam" (1897), seems to advocate. The drama as a whole contends with blood and myth as sources of the self. Characters who assert privilege by virtue of blood lineage alone continue to serve as straw men in *Der junge David.* As one minor character puts it: "Blood doesn't call—only the Lord calls!"[33] Claiming Jewish identity is more likely to subvert kinship than to reinforce it. To this end, the drama shows numerous examples of both the disintegration of the parent-child bond and God's forced sundering of family ties.

Equally hazardous are loyalties formed on the basis of myth, or what David calls "Bild." Jaákob and David both challenge sources of determinism by way of reason and dialogue; David's greatest adversary is not blood, but the myths that dehistoricize, fetishize, or foster idolatrous devotion. Myth, much to David's chagrin, constructs the optic of popular, communal memory and pervades the minor characters' conversations. Serujah, David's sister, calls him "You wonderful figure [*Bild*] from God's hand," and this type of sentiment infects the popular perception of the Ruth-David bond.[34]

God *lent* her beauty [*Schönheit*], and she was allowed
to transmit it in her blood—*now*—
her beauty has newly revived in David![35]

Schönheit connotes not so much beauty as the particular charismatic aura that lends itself to mythmaking. David dislikes this word above all, and he expresses his displeasure when Serujah chastens him for keeping his wife, Maácha, hidden from public view.

David: (dissatisfied with himself)
"Beautiful?"–"Shameless!" [*Schön?–Schamlos!*] Leaves a bad taste in one's mouth!
No—No! Nothing should be torn out of its secrecy

And sold and betrayed
By words: "beautiful" words![36]

David's fear of aestheticization drives his effort to deconstruct the myth of Israel as a chosen people, as well as the intention to build the temple on the threshold of primordial chaos rather than on terra firma.

But Beer-Hofmann makes clear from the start that in the popular imagination, myth has already claimed David irrevocably. Witness the child Abjathar's comment to Timnah, his nursemaid in act 1: "Whatever I ask—*David—David!* That is / Your refrain!"[37] The plot of *Der junge David,* comprised of a tight chain of events leading up to David's coronation, dramatizes his coming to terms with his legendary status. David will, in effect, step into the legend that has already been fashioned for him. Allusions to this legend-in-progress pervade the play, as when Abjathar, learning about the ways of David's ancestress Ruth, asks, "Is this a fairytale?" The reponse—"No, my child! But it *will* be *like* a fairytale, some day!" captures the mood of anticipation fueling the drama as a whole.[38] To rewrite the sequence of events that culminate in the fixing of David in the Jewish imagination is to expose the conflicted human being behind the myth, or in psychoanalytic terms, to allow the resistance, normally hidden, to come into view. This is not unlike what Freud achieves by imagining that Moses rose up to shatter the tablets, felt them spin out of his grasp, then decided he'd be better off not shattering them.

As his title indicates, Beer-Hofmann, alone among the four writers under discussion, elevates history to a central position in his art of memory. The tension, then, lies in the fact that even as Beer-Hofmann strove for historical (and religious) authenticity in constructing his stage Jews, the characters themselves are obsessed with countermemory.[39] The concept bears an affinity to what David Biale calls "counterhistory," a phenomenon associated with Walter Benjamin, Gerschom Scholem, and other German Jewish intellectuals in the early twentieth century who sought to synthesize modernity and tradition but resisted the premises of nineteenth-century Jewish historiography.[40] Counterhistory is a secular project committed to legitimizing the repressed components of the tradition on a new plane, thereby creating "a place for tradition—newly conceived—in a secular world."[41] Much like Freud's understanding of tradition, countermemory regresses beyond the originary idea at the root of metaphysical, teleological history to uncover the underlying drama in which rivals contest the right to shape the legacy. At the zenith of their defiance, David and Jaákob resemble the radical Zionists of Beer-Hofmann's time. The Russian-born Micah Joseph Berdichevski (1865–1921), who lived in Berlin and wrote in German, Yiddish, and Hebrew, quite literally applied Nietzsche's program of "Umwertung aller Werte" (Transvaluation of Values) to Judaism. As he wrote in his essay "Wrecking and Building": "To be or not to be! To be the last Jews or the first Hebrews. . . . We must cease to be tablets on which books are transcribed and thoughts handed down to us—always handed down. Through a basic revision of the very foundations of Israel's inner and outer life, our whole consciousness, our pre-dispositions, thoughts, feelings, desires, and will and aim will be transformed: and we shall live and stand fast."[42]

JAÁKOB, OR THE HEROISM OF COUNTERMEMORY

Jaákob is a religious breed of memory individual—an epigone who, like Paul in *Der Tod Georgs,* has reached an impasse (fig. 19). Jaákob struggles with a God who feels too close, too demanding, and who afflicts humanity with "too much" direction:

Great *is* the God and *is* with us!
(*Then softly, as if imparting a secret.*) Too much with us, Idnibaál, too much!—
. . . .
Too near, this God breathes round us—say what wills He?
What *wills* He that He presses round us so?[43]

Jaákob overcomes his condition by manipulating symbols and, like a true epic hero, by subverting destiny through dialogue. Indeed, dialogue is both an essential vehicle of memory and an instrument of countermemory; therein lies the critical legacy of Jaákob, ancestor of the modern European Jew. In the sequence of three exchanges with his slave, his brother, and the angels, Jaákob rewrites various narratives from the past and thereby reroutes the individual as well as the collective course. Dialogue becomes, so to speak, the legacy that humanity bequeaths to God—the ladder by which man can challenge God and induce God to go in search of man. Through dialogue, Beer-Hofmann's characters seek to import enlightened values into the core of the promise, values such as consent, justice, pluralism, and moral outrage in the face of human suffering, all of which lie beyond the confines of Jewish collective memory proper. Counter-memory serves a revolutionary purpose: not to undermine the divinely constituted collective, but rather to humanize (Europeanize) the intact (Jewish) legacy by making it consensual. Jaákob reasons that by learning to communi-

19. Alfred Gerasch as Jaákob in the Burgtheater production of *Jaákobs Traum,* April 1919.

cate with humanity in dialogue and thus secure consent, God would be able to trans-form an unendurable legacy into a true blessing:

Looking up with a frowning brow, emphatically:
Was it for this,—You God above,
You chose me? Then come, and whisper to me
How I should answer and how I, Your creature,
Can exculpate You, God! Speak, speak! Fearful
You are, when You do speak to us, more awful
In Your silence![44]

Language permits the rectification of past acts and the release from commitment. No moment articulates more vividly the power of words than that in which Jaákob challenges God to retract the ancestral promise: "What You my fathers promised— take it back! / I free You, God—You may Your vow deny!"[45] Jaákob is privileged to converse with divinity and to express grievances with impunity.

Jaákob's first independent act of countermemory is to free his slave Idnibaál from lifelong servitude by a ritualistic act of liberation with no parallel in Genesis (fig. 20). Beer-Hofmann embeds the liberating in a poignant memory narrative. Ini-tially, Idnibaál is deaf to the idea of freedom. Jaákob bequeaths freedom in the same way that Georg, the memory doctor in *Der Tod Georgs,* was said to have cured his patients. He recollects Idnibaál's native land in vivid detail, and the pathos of the description wears down the slave's resistance. He foresees the man's recuperation through marriage and fatherhood. The master then performs a pantomime of liber-ation: Jaákob clothes Idnibaál in a new garment, rents the discarded shirt with his hunting knife, tosses it behind him, and lastly, girds him anew: "Idnibaál of Gebál / Jizchak's from Beér-Scheba slave—*be free!*"[46] This sequence establishes Jaákob's char-acter as a master of countermemory, but it is also an allegory of Jaákob's own mat-uration, or of exorcism. Jaákob's gestures—dismantling, rending, girding—exorcise the slave within and create an autonomous human being.

Jaákob tampers even more graphically with the sources of selfhood in the rec-onciliation scene with his brother, an episode that contains both Christian and Ger-manic allusions. Beer-Hofmann characterizes Edom very much along traditional lines as his brother's alter ego, in close to the same way Chrysothemis challenges her sister Elektra in Hofmannsthal's play. He is the sibling who suffers from too little memory, who cries,

I do not want this God who's always near!
More insistently.
Come, Jaákob! Leave this land, where drought by day—
And frost by night consume! Leave Him this land,
Leave Him His blessing!—Jaákob, flee this God

and who is capable of renouncing the legacy altogether in the name of peace.[47] When Edom catches up to his brother, the encounter begins violently, as Edom has sworn an oath not to eat or drink before shedding his brother's blood. But his attacks prove futile: an arrow strikes the lamb Jaákob holds to his breast rather than its target (reenacting the sacrifice of Isaac, where an animal similarly died in place of an intended human victim); Jaákob refuses to raise a hand against his brother, and Edom's next assault is staved off by a flock of white-winged angels guarding Jaákob. Yet Jaákob divests himself of all advantage in the ensuing dialogue. He persuades his brother that *rejected* (*verworfen*) and *chosen* (*erwählt*) are relative terms, thus contradicting not only the essentialization of their respective identities, but also the very postulates of the Genesis account: a discriminating legacy, a single correct choice, and an irrevocable enmity between insider and outsider. To seal this dramatic revocation, Jaákob performs a stunning deed: he cuts into both their arms, stating,

20. Photograph from the Habima production of *Jaákobs Traum* in 1926: Leo Warschauer, in the role of Jaákob, sets free the slave Idnibaál, played by Czezhk-Efrati.

Thus do I engrave upon you sacred symbols!
You, brother—hostile from our mother's womb—
Of your free choice, become anew: my brother!
(*Stepping backwards, he lowers their intertwined arms towards the ground.*)
Flow—flow into the earth, you blood long-parted,
And mingle and become again as one!
Blood-brothers are now grown Edom and Jaákob.[48]

Jaákob inscribes a new sign into their flesh; blood mixed by force of will reconstitutes their bond, so as to refute the antagonistic legacy imposed upon then from the womb. The bold gesture of spilling and remixing the blood signals more than forward-looking reconciliation; it is a tactic of countermemory par excellence. But even blood brotherhood does not require that difference be erased. "God wants me *thus*, and wants you *otherwise*! / Only because you Edom are—may I be Jaákob!"[49] Affirming difference by way of a blood covenant allows them to unite freely, and renders Edom too into a source of a humanistic legacy. Jaákob is certain that God's promise to Abraham (Genesis 12:3) applies as well to the Gentile Edom.

Jaákob: Thus on Mount Moriah
He spoke to Abraham: "In your seed shall all

The nations of the earth be blessed!"

Edom: *Looking at Jaákob.* The Gentiles . . . ?

Jaákob: Yes![50]

In the climactic dream sequence that follows, the angel Samael, a Jewish Mephistopheles, descends to demonize the notion of excessive memory and unremitting vigilance regarding collective destiny (fig. 21). In a scene that some Christian reviewers found scandalous, God descends to debate with Jaákob, to reiterate the promises face to face—promises that define being-chosen excruciatingly in terms of sacrifice, ostracism, eternal homelessness, and hatred. The substance of this legacy is, if anything, anticlimactic, overly contrived to justify a lachrymose theory of Jewish history. Again, Beer-Hofmann's innovation is not so much that God concedes Samael's vision, but that God and Jaákob jointly recast a legacy for the modern Jew—repeating the Jaákob-Edom interaction—by tempering metaphysical truths and inherited beliefs with the forces of intellect, reason, and free will. God endorses Jaákob's resistance and his iconoclastic strategies. Conflict becomes the blueprint for the future struggles of Jaákob and his descendants. Having broken free of the past, Jaákob awakens from the dream with a new name, "der mit Gott rang"—"the one who strove with God—Jisro-El."

DAVID, POST-ZIONIST HERO

Were Beer-Hofmann's main goal to depict the birth pangs of the Davidic kingdom as grounding a new national myth, *Der junge David* would presumably have stayed closer to the genre of historical drama exemplified by Franz Grillparzer's *König Ottokars Glück und Ende* (1823), the monumental work of Hapsburg nationalism. In Grillparzer's play, two kings, embodying two distinct legacies, compete for sovereignty. Schaúl represents a clear throwback to the *Trauerspiel* despot exemplified by Ottokar; theirs is the pathos of the belligerent and autocratic ruler who cannot adapt to more pluralistic times and ends in melancholy and madness. Margarethe, symbol of old Austria and banished first wife of Ottokar, finds a partial parallel in Schaúl's daughter Michal (not Maácha), who is similarly banished by David when she fails to produce heirs. David, however, diverges from the prototype of Rudolf von Hapsburg, enlightened nationalist, and therein lies the stark difference between Grillparzer's Austrian mythmaking and Beer-Hofmann's counterhistorical approach to the Bible.

To convey David's relevance for modern German Jewry, Beer-Hofmann corners David in his brief tenure as a diaspora Jew. He is neither the dauntless youth slaying the giant nor the triumphalist king of Israel, just a man with two claims on his soul: a David whom all the legends have eclipsed, whom Zionist historiography disavows. During this brief chapter in the history of the Jewish nation, David promotes a Zionism rooted in humanism and distorted, as it were, by a severe distaste for idolatry of any sort. Before the threat of war materializes to test (and ultimately correct) David's vision, he is given one opportunity to articulate it in the boldest possible strokes before his followers. Scenes 1 and 2 have already created David's allure. When he arrives at the camp late at night in scene 3, anticipation is at its peak. Yet the idealistic vision announced at the Alter Burgplatz in Bethlehem (Old Castle Square in Bethlehem) proves to be controversial and even unpopular (fig. 22).

David begins by unceremoniously rejecting the Mosaic legacy on the grounds that it breeds national self-aggrandizement. He dismisses the Exodus from Egypt, the miracle at the Red Sea, and revelation at Sinai as myths that incite "slave's dreams" of power and glory, territorial expansion, and lordship over surrounding nations. In David's account, Jewish national memory must establish its primal scene in the preslavery period.

21. Photograph from the Habima production of *Jaákobs Traum* in 1926: Benjamin Zemach in the role of the angel Samael. This production also toured in Berlin, Palestine, and the United States.

Know you not, who you were and who you are?
Shepherds and farmers—Free men—you were here—
Until your fate sent you to Egypt.[51]

David goes on to note, with increasing cynicism, the sequence of miraculous events that followed the redemption: manna from heaven, a rock that gave forth water, and a mountain spewing fire. His message is that the covenantal relationship between God and Israel post-Sinai, as much as the term in Egypt, fosters a slave mentality that fuels misguided nationalism.

The Lord knows:
I want it to be *otherwise!* And I don't ask for much:
A bit of peace—a *span* of time—
To sow seeds, so that a race
Would arise—not like us—better, *purer!*
One that does not rejoice when it knows suffering surrounds it—
That cannot breathe, when hard labor pants nearby—
That craves not sovereignty—doesn't abolish itself
In the name of glory and power![52]

In his subversive nationalism, David defines the purest race as that most universal in orientation, most thoroughly purged of its chauvinistic illusions. He vociferously

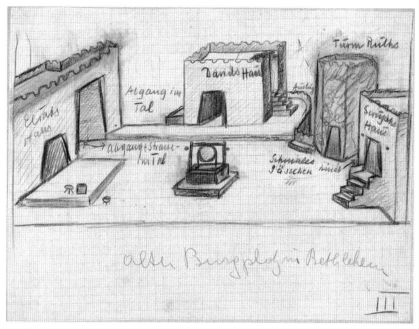

22. Sketch by Beer-Hofmann, "Old Castle Square in Bethlehem," the stage setting for scene 3 of *Der junge David*. Ruth's tower stands to the right of David's house.

dissociates his motives and ambitions from the popular view, to the outrage of his son Abischai:

Abischai, *angrily interceding:*
Why not splendor and power?
The Lord did indeed lead the children of Israel
with *his own hand* out of Egypt—
David: And lead *with his own hand* the children of Aram
out of Kir—and the Philistines out of Kaphtor—
Shouting at Abischai with unrelenting repulsion:
Like—them—and not differently—are we valued by God!
Abischai *insistent:* We are *chosen!*
David *bursting out in laughter with anger and scorn:*
Are you?!—Fool!
Threatening and menacing: Only as long as
you *alone* elect yourself to a thousand onerous tasks—
Ready to give yourself over when called—
Thus—long: "Chosen"—
Relentless, disregarding all pretensions:
—and *not* a breath longer![53]

In this dialogue with Abischai, his most zealous utterance, David puts forth two different objections to the idea of divine election. The first is the relativist position, which unmasks chosenness as an ideological construct rather than a historical reality. David rejects *Erwähltsein* as the fundamental premise of Jewish destiny; Beer-Hofmann accomplishes this by having him cite verses from the postexilic prophet Amos, whose messianic visions were grounded in egalitarianism.

To Me, O Israelites, you are just like the Ethiopians, declares the Lord. True, I
    brought Israel up
From the land of Egypt,
But also the Philistines from Caphtor
And the Arameans from Kir. (Amos 9:7)

Nonetheless, coming from David, soon to be king of Israel, such postnationalist sentiments astonish. The second objection argues that even the myth of chosenness creates an oppressive existential burden, as if the Jews were an entire nation of memory individuals! David's determination to build the temple on Mount Moriah, site of the *Akedah,* exemplifies his desire to regenerate the people of Israel in an antinationalistic mode. Such an edifice must incorporate past sacrifice, latent chaos, and imminent disruption.[54] Rather than a monument to "power, fame, glory," David's temple will be "the keeper of the abyss" ("des Abgrunds Hüter"), a reminder that uncontrollable forces threaten regardless of illusions of privilege.[55]

From a normative point of view, David's rejection of the Mosaic foundations of Jewish nationhood is ultraheretical. A third objection follows on the heels of these first two, one that lays the foundation for the new ethos Beer-Hofmann is proposing—that of the unappropriatable, nonreifiable word. "Un-ein-nehm-bar ist Wort!" The word *uneinnehmbar* can mean that which cannot be captured, cannot be taken in. This word is not "God's word" per se, but it recalls the God of Jaákob, who cannot be reduced to a prescription, banner, or slogan, but is more like a rival to be parried at every turn.

Flame, blaze with him,—and *forget* to ask,
Whether you did not also consume yourselves in the fire!
Be neither cold, nor certain, nor content with the world—
Worry, wrestle, allow yourselves again and again to be torn
Into God's spirit—his holy storm-breathing—[56]

In the course of this study, we have seen enough references to this type of language to appreciate that the wider context of David's vision is not intrinsically Jewish. It is motivated by his fear of idolatry, of "fixation," of his own (already established) iconography. The young David foresees, and foreswears, his own posthumous status in the annals of his people. At the outset, he resists uncompromisingly; by the end, he will wear the crown, and tolerate the myth, and concede the paradox that he cannot have one without the other—a reality that Ruth, his great-grandmother, has been assigned to teach him.

RUTH'S HEROISM: TOWARD A FEMININE POETICS OF JEWISH MEMORY

Passionate and idealistic as they are, both Jaákob and David prove to be ineffective in the political arena. This fact points to Beer-Hofmann's final strategy: the casting of Ruth and other female characters as the (unacknowledged) heroines of the *Historie*. Dialogue, agon, linear and historical time are the essential components of David's weltanschauung. Song, lullaby, ritual, and cyclical time frame the experience of the female characters. The men are dramatic heroes, spokesmen for modernity; the women are associated with enduring solutions and durational genres that are native to scripture. Female experience is immanently transmissible, whereas male experience, so right in the moment, lacks staying power. Within the gender codes of turn-of-the-century Vienna, Beer-Hofmann proves Otto Weininger wrong. Women represent neither discontinuous existence (Weininger's misogyny) nor mindless, corporeal memory (Bachofen's matriarchy), nor are they (as in the early works in this study) daughter-scapegoats within male plots, mere projections of male myths; they champion an alternative poetics of memory that is authentic, enlightened, and text-centered. We recall that Georg, the non-Jewish protagonist of *Der Weg ins Freie,* learns about memory and fidelity (*Treue*) from his Jewish friends, and also from his Catholic mistress, Anna. David learns about fidelity from the foreign-born women in his life: his Gentile ancestress, Ruth, and wife, Maácha. In a deeper sense, their native land is nature, and their wisdom expresses itself through organic and aesthetic tropes. Both are beyond politics, outsiders, who, because of their timeless and universal perspective, determine the true destiny of the people. The fact that neither heroine is biologically Jewish is a critical and controversial strategy that has not been given much attention by scholars. The humbling message of this drama is that (female) non-Jewish outsiders facilitate political mediation and spiritual transmission more effectively than authentic (male) Jews.

Beer-Hofmann's female characters mediate under the sign of lunarity. The use of lunar symbolism is one way the drama was constructed to reflect the multinational, multiethnic makeup of the ancient Near East. Beer-Hofmann adopts a prominent fin de siècle discourse, one most famously associated with J. J. Bachofen, whose mythology was widely accepted in Beer-Hofmann's era. The moon adjudicates or mediates between the tellurian and solar principles; it is quasiandrogynous, but finally "marries" the masculine and feminine under the sign of the feminine. In contrast to the masculine-solar principle, sublunary existence signifies becoming rather than being. It represents the cosmic priority of matriarchy or *Mutterrecht,* but also the power to intercede between earthly and heavenly realms.[57] Women in *Der junge David* consistently identify with the lunar cycles and in a complex way with transience and transmission. By dressing in female colors for his coronation, with silver laces to his armor and vestment, David makes a clear statement about the assumption of the crown.

Ruth controls David, and it is no coincidence that she functions as the primary guardian of memory for Israel. She is ageless, virtually immortal, having outlived her husband, Boas, her son Obed, and her grandson (David's father) Jischai. Ruth lives secluded in Bethlehem, gracing the stage at critical moments, when her advent is announced, "Ruth wacht!" Timnah describes her to the child Abjathar:

From a time, which to them is like the time in fairy tales, she rises,
A cautiously greeted, holy image of an ancestor,
For which one burns incense on special days, gives
Graciously and approaches with veneration, not with love.[58]

Ruth's most important function is to ensure the transmission of her legacies—of loyalty, suffering, and beauty—to David, her great-grandchild. At the end of scene 3, David faces his first test. A messenger brings word that Schaúl has declared war on the Philistines, and that King Achisch, ally of the Philistines, has assigned David's army to the border. The young David must choose between loyalty to his people and an oath sworn to a foreign king. Ruth appears, veiled as always in silver, a tall, thin column:

David: *trembling:* You don't know what to do?—You have seen so *much!*
Ruth: *impassive:* How *would* I know what to do?—
Her voice darkens somewhat: I have seen so *much!*
David: *adjuring, quiet:* Don't close yourself off from me—
Beseeching: I am *your* blood!
Ruth: *far from being moved. With each mention of the word* son, *she increases the distance between herself and David.*
Calmly, with a high-pitched voice: Yes!—son—of the son—of my son—Obed!
When he died—how *long* ago that is—, I thought
I too would die, of grief—
Taking a deep breath:—but I *lived on*
—*buried* what should have buried me—
Everything left me, went away—at last my pain too went away!
David: Speak, ancestor! Your voice is like Maácha's voice—
Cool, silver—morning air on fevered temples!
Give advice—I *need* it!
Ruth: *for the first time a slight movement of her hand releases itself from its motionlessness and—under the silver veil—feels for the leaves of the vine, which have overgrown the parapet:*
Because—the young tendril
Of the vine continues to sway at night in the wind—in the morning

it has—without eyes—true to its deepest nature
already found its hold—and does not need advice!
David: *You* give me hold! Give only *one* word!
Ruth: *already stepping back into the darkness:* Stay faithful!
She can no longer be seen . . .
David: (*throwing himself at the parapet, as if to follow her:*)
Faithful—to whom? (*He listens for a moment*)
Away!
Pondering: To my people?—To the oath?[59]

I cite this passage at length to give an impression of the visual tumult facing the reader, but also because the exchange, for all of its emotion, is extremely programmatic. The more desperate David's entreaties, the more Ruth withdraws. Though dramatically present, she will not become an instrument of political decision making. She retreats even further when David claims entitlement to her cooperation on the grounds of lineage. Her response is to lapse into recollection, moreover, to recount her own experience of sacrifice, as if to say, this is the kind of intervention that David, in the throes of conflict, requires. Ultimately, Ruth gleans her wisdom from nature: the vine is "true to its deepest nature" and need not ask others for advice. David's final question, "true—to whom?" reveals that he misses the point, for he still seeks a referent for loyalty beyond himself. By suggesting that Ruth "cools" David's feverish indecision, the exchange echoes Beer-Hofmann's claim that epos and drama temper one another; yet we see here that the two forces fail to agree, much less synthesize, in the terms of the drama. David is left with a message about sacrifice and loyalty that he must translate for himself. It is at this point that he makes the impetuous decision to go with Achisch, yet kill himself before doing battle against his people. He adopts Ruth's advice in principle, but in practice he distorts it, thus exposing his own limitations as once and future king.

The drama conveys these limitations also in the subsequent encounter with Maácha. David goes to bid his wife farewell, assuming that he will not return. Yet although he withholds news of his decision, Maácha, like Ruth, intuits that a further corrective is in order when David asserts that should he die, "your—our-life—carry it / then smiling, a bit longer, through the world."[60] David fails to hold to the standard of self-sacrifice, to submit to the finitude of his existence, and constructs Maácha (if only in his imagination) as a *Bild:* a refuge from his historical role, the instrument of his own immortality. "*This* is my self—my true one!" he cries to Maácha, convinced he is speaking to her for the last time.[61]

Into you—Maácha—I cast it—guard it—
protect it—and smile, if the others think—
I no longer exist!—
I just hid myself in you.[62]

The drama insinuates that by using the verb *bergen*, criticized earlier vis-à-vis God, David betrays his own convictions. In response, Maácha performs a single gesture that rectifies David's misguided oath and dooms herself in the process:

If it is unavoidable that over us, now, one
beats the icy, heavy, black wings—
If now there must be a sacrifice—(*tearing the wreath from her head and hurling it to the side, her head thrown back into the nape of her neck, offering herself:*) Here!—be it *I*—
Not *he!*[63]

She defies David's desire to turn her into his sanctuary through an act that at the same time cruelly literalizes his intent. Thus Maácha "teaches" David about sacrifice.

David's final trial is neither political nor personal; it cannot be resolved by a slingshot or a dramatic gesture. That he must assume the crown in the wake of his wife's death configures the coronation along the model of *Treue* (fidelity) established throughout the drama. The preordained union of David and Israel is finally, after much commotion, consummated. This achievement appears on the surface to vindicate the power of myth after all, or at the very least the subordination of individual will to blood, inheritance, political expediency, to all those things that David and Jaákob resist. David only agrees to be king at Ruth's bidding. The matriarchal rejoinder—"Du *mußt* es!" (You *must!*)—and the blessing Ruth summons from the depths of *her* blood— "One more time—you / Already distant wave of my blood—surge back to your spring!"[64]—force David into line. The final image is of David's coronation, which is of necessity a self-coronation:

David lifts the crown with outstretched hands, until it is high above his head. He leans his head back into the nape of his neck. Looking up to the crown:
Crown—heavy, you—
He lowers his head. Pressing decisively the crown onto his head with an abrupt gesture:
I *want* to wear you! . . .
David stands with sunken head, his arms spread out in devotion. Behind him towers a silver column, motionless, showered with moonlight: Ruth. Over the walls of Hebron the narrow sickle of the young moon has risen in the cloudless night sky.[65]

With music sounding and the Israelites bent prostrate before their young king, the curtains close. The triumph expresses itself not only through David's decisive gesture, nor only in his apostrophe—by which we learn that only by establishing an "I-You" connection with destiny can he bear its weight—but also in the modal "want." But we must also notice that the final tableau, like the initial one, is composite and conflicted: David stands almost as if crucified, mimicking Maácha's posture of submission; the silver-clad Ruth supports him as a pillar, and behind it all, *der junge Mond* lends cosmic confirmation to the fate of *der junge David*. Until he himself grasps hold of the crown, it is surrounded by flames; receiving the crown signals a shift from the solar to a lunar pole. The sickle moon dignifies this coronation ceremony, a rite occurring at the peak of the lunar cycle to coincide with the new-moon festivities. Why does a feminine aura envelop David's ascent to kingship? Samuel, whose death just precedes the drama's opening, is identified as the prophet who crowned Schaúl (and then dethroned him) at God's bidding. But Ruth, the prophetess of God's lunar element, officiates at the crowning of David. Beer-Hofmann evokes lunarity on account of the star's constant inconstancy. The moon reflects the only occasionally visible God with whom David has come to terms; it evokes the cycle of sacrifice and reconciliation, both personal and political, that brings him to say, "Ich will," though clearly still torn about his decision—it is only a sickle moon, not a full shining star. And only Ruth, heroic in her ability to mediate opposites, can take her place between this David and this God.

The David-Ruth collaboration epitomizes Beer-Hofmann's struggle to compromise, and even harmonize, disciplines, genres, and ideas that the other writers I have discussed set up as mutually irreconcilable. Recall Freud's rhetorical (and often prejudicial) use of scholarly and biblical citations in the Moses essays. Beer-Hofmann's plays are infused with biblical language, and what is also noteworthy, each play is followed by an appendix that lists the biblical and scholarly passages most relevant to each and every scene. Hofmannsthal's vision of mythic theater compelled him to exclude language and rely on dance, music, and costumes in rewriting Joseph's story; the fatal break between Joseph and Potiphar's wife around which *Josephslegende* revolves, symbolizing the futility of collaboration between the young and the old, couldn't contrast more sharply with the eloquent conversations between old and young that pervade the *Historie*. Professor Bernhardi, for all his good memory, insulates himself from the next generation, which may explain why he is so inept when it comes to countermemory. Beer-Hofmann's dramas of countermemory rely deeply on memory. The most potent genre of memory promoted here, coded female, is lyric. The muse of lyric memory is the matriarch Rachel, "*Urmutter* of us all."[66]

Scene 1 of *Der junge David* takes place at a "street by Rahel's tomb," and the play opens with the singing of a "lullaby": "And where the road turns towards Bethlehem, / there Rahel sank down in pain—and bore."[67] Rahel was the first to perpetuate memory in the face of loss by way of song—her *Klage* (lament) is older still than Ruth's *Liebeslied*. Rachel's legacy conjoins two charged scriptural moments: the story of her dying while giving birth to Benjamin in transit (Genesis 35), and the elegy in Jeremiah 31, in which the prophet consoles her as she stands at the roadside weeping for her exiled children.

Among the people they said, from Rahel's grave
sounds a lament, at night, when catastrophe is about to befall
Israel's children. And the ancient saying goes: "Rahel

grieves and cries bitterly
for her children—and will not be comforted."[68]

Rahel represents the dead mother and the bereaved mother, the abandoner and the abandoned; yet in translation, these traumatic experiences (unlike the *Akedah*, or the slaying of Moses) prove to be instructive, even a source of comfort. Rahel's *Klage* has become a lullaby for children, and Maácha quotes the lament again when she sings to David. Ruth's promise to her mother-in-law Naomi has likewise filtered into popular culture through song: "Ruths Liebeslied" is a children's lullaby. These oral forms of transmission are vulnerable to distortion. When a young girl refers to "Ruth's love song," David's sister corrects her:

Ruth never sang that! Not a song, no, rather,
She spoke and *did* it! And was yet so young!
To an old woman, who suffered, lonely,
And loved Ruth so, she spoke it—not to a lover!
It is not a love song!—Does this make it any less beautiful?[69]

The lyrical sensibility is by no means naïve. In a surprising reversal, the dramatist casts the dialogical as naïve, short-sighted, and "youthful," and the lyrical as mature and nuanced. The genres that Timnah, Ruth, and Maácha inhabit are ideologically complex and canny about the hazards of fetishization and aestheticization. Lyric perpetuates memory in a distinctly mortal fashion, for it acknowledges the fragility of fortune and the transience of human life. Maácha's last words before dying, "It will pass" ("Es geht vorüber"), encapsulate this lesson. Ruth memorializes Maácha in like terms—"Fortune comes—fortune goes" ("Glück kommt—Glück geht")—when commenting upon her untimely death, and repeats essentially the same wisdom in order to convince David to take the crown.

David: What will become of me?!
Ruth: What will become of us all: dung of the earth—
Perhaps a song—
—this too passes too soon!
And yet: until then—no more eternal, and
no more fleeting than HIS stars—you must,
Like them, complete—David!—your course![70]

Ruth voices the very paradox that eludes David to the end: a human life, even one privileged to enter collective memory, attains ultimate meaning only as a conjunction of the fleeting moment with one's predestined course, of immanent and long-term concerns. Like the moon, songs come and go, and though their context has been lost, they need not be icons. With this admission, the unfinished whole of *Die*

Historie von König David, by encircling David's drama with Ruth's story, justifies its curious subtitle: *A Cycle.*

EPILOGUE

Late in life, Beer-Hofmann characterized the Jews in terms familiar from the epigonal laments of the 1890s: "People that cannot forget. The most pious and burdened people. Eternal life of all ancestors in the youngest of the race. Young eyes, still inexperienced, know all that the fathers experienced and suffered—without having seen it."[71] The belief that Jews "remember far too much" and suffer as a result of an overly pious relationship to their heritage had very practical implications for the author: it shaped not only the genres of his cultural production, but also the conditions of his participation in Jewish culture. At one point, Beer-Hofmann declined an invitation by Martin Buber to participate in a meeting to design a Jewish college (what would become the Akademie für die Wissenschaft des Judentums)—one of many attempts to recruit the author in those years.[72] His response to Buber voices two qualitatively different misgivings about founding an institution of Jewish learning. The first set of reservations pertains to the challenges of constructing an authentic educational program. "It is impossible to found this college without broaching the entire complex of religious questions. . . . Should it sanctify the Sabbath and take Sunday as a workday? What, of all that constitutes tradition, should it retain? A Jewish college cannot simply be a college like any other. It must be exemplary or not exist at all. And do you know—do we know—how much of the tradition we may regard as living, and how much as extinct?"[73] Beer-Hofmann then voices apprehensions of a different order. "What we Jews do takes place upon a stage—a stage constructed by our destiny. That other nations have virtues and vices is taken for granted. But the world is allowed to sprawl in their theater seats and stare at the Jews. Gaze, voice, posture, hair color, body size—all are to be scrutinized by malicious judges—and woe if we do not stride as demigods across the stage."[74] Like Kafka and Freud, Hofmannsthal and Schnitzler, Beer-Hofmann responded to these external and internal predicaments in a series of quixotic literary experiments, works whose modernist character lies in their imperfect quest for a way out that is also a way back. An amalgam of epos and lyric, memory and countermemory, solar power and lunar reflection, *Die Historie von König David* reads like a novel, and perhaps should have been a novel: the work contains too many formal and thematic contradictions, and at its center, David and Ruth: characters from works barely read outside of religious circles. Beer-Hofmann's *Historie* may have been eclipsed by the Holocaust, but its distinct post-Zionist agenda and conscientious interweaving of masculine and feminine poetics confirm its relevance, beyond history, into the twenty-first century.

Conclusion

I began this book with two passages that capture the challenges facing the Viennese Jewish writer in the early twentieth century. The first was the question Freud posed to himself in anticipation of seeing his prose translated into Hebrew. *What is still Jewish about you?* Freud asked. Indeed, what can be said to be Jewish about a writer, plot, character, or genre, once the visible trappings of Judaism—and in some cases even Judaism itself—have been given up? In the second passage, Schnitzler described the feeling of being besieged on all sides. *It is not only the "others" who are against him, no, it is above all the Jew, the Viennese.* But what single strategy could combat anti-Semitism joined with the pervasive typing of Jews by Jews? These are questions of identity and language, racial politics and religious survival. My argument has been that these questions also capture the internal and external factors that motivated Freud, Hofmannsthal, Schnitzler, and Beer-Hofmann to invent new forms of Jewish writing. They chose not to respond in *klare Worte*, but rather creatively, elusively, by situating the crisis of Jewish identity within their larger preoccupations with memory and the place of art in modern life. Most of their contemporaries could not help but misconstrue their intentions. But Freud foretold that scholars would someday be in a position to understand him, and Schnitzler likewise imagined a "purer atmosphere" in which his works could find a proper reception.

To convey the apparitional character of Viennese Jewish modernism, I invoked the metaphor of the hologram: a kind of image that changes depending on your standpoint. I offered readings of texts that were holographic before their time. I highlighted the negative reception they received, their indeterminate Jewish character, and, in certain cases, their lack of visibility within the received historiographies of the period. I refrained from locating the authors and their literary subjects on a spectrum from less to more Jewish, since this would have been to predetermine the question I wanted to explore. Yet, while the image of holographic writing conveys the extent to which Viennese Jewish modernism was a strategy of resistance, the metaphor fails to do justice to the positive aspirations of these writers and their legacy. What exactly did Freud and Hofmannsthal, Schnitzler and Beer-Hofmann hope to gain by writing the ways they did? Were these writers, like the Rabbi in Hofmannsthal's pantomime, merely crossing their hands so as to deliberately baffle their readers? Can one charge them, as the Minister does Professor Bernhardi, with perpetrating a "tragicomedy of stubbornness"? In my introduction I raised similar questions about the postmodern holograms in the new Jewish Museum in Vienna. Beyond making a political statement about the reluctance of the Austrian State to confront its Jewish past, what did the curators hope to gain by staging Austrian Jewish history as twenty-one ephemeral holograms?

Hofmannsthal's phrase "saying much without speaking" might stand for all of the works discussed here. They make profound statements about living and writing as Jews in Vienna, even as they try to be European and modernist. What Freud called "die Hauptsache," the principal thing, refers to their collective effort to create a *Rückweg,* a way back to authentic Jewish experience—to what Buber called "religiosity," in contrast to religion. These writers and thinkers sought to replace the inherited lessons about Jewish identity with Jewishness as lived experience: something creative and life-enhancing. They wanted the Jewish past—personal memories, Hebrew scripture, cultural and religious legacies—to appear as an *Erlebnis,* immediately experienceable, not as an *Ergebnis,* information processed by scholars.[1] The *Erlebnis* would provide an antidote to deterministic models of identity, to aestheticism, and to the lure of ultimate answers. The desire for such an experience, and in particular for experiential memory, is a defining characteristic of modernism.

The concept of *Erlebnis* became popular at the turn of the century in the context of the *Lebensphilosophien* of Nietzsche and Bergson, of Georg Simmel and Max Scheler. *Erleben* as an epistemological concept was first introduced by German philosophers in the early nineteenth century, although Wilhelm Dilthey was the first to put forth a theory of the *Erlebnis* as a psychological and hermeneutical category. A philosophical concept with immediate poetic force, an *Erlebnis* was understood as an oasis of presentness within the temporal flow; as that which is immanently known and understood, without reflection or mediation; as a "transitive moment of self-forgetting" in which one experiences the unity of subject and object, reality and life.[2] From a psychological standpoint, such experiences elude fixation; communication or mediation of any kind detracts from their integrity.[3]

The *Erlebnis* plays a critical role in Freudian psychotherapy. When Freud describes how memories vanish, ghost-like, in the process of narration, he too emphasizes an experience whose special potency dissolves when subject to reflection. Thus, he instructed his patients to say "whatever comes to mind" without reflection, and therapists as well are warned against listening in an overly directed manner. Similarly, it was in the interest of *Erlebnis* that Hofmannsthal opted to reject naturalistic drama in favor of mythic theater. He viewed direct communication (*Mitteilung*) as sterile, powerless to affect the modern spectator. For him, the ideal memory encounter had to occur through a subliminal channel. In the museum of the twenty-first century, by the same logic, virtual media have become the ideal counterforce to "historical comprehensiveness" because they allow us to experience the past as present.[4] The commemorative priority to encounter the past by way of an artistic experiment instead of learning about the past through historical exposition links our own fin de siècle with the previous one.

To make possible an existential encounter with the Hebrew Bible, the writers under discussion consistently circumvented normative interpretations of scripture. Joseph does not run from Potiphar's wife, as Genesis reports: he exposes himself voluntarily, thereby damning her and redeeming his audience at the same time. Jacob and Esau overcome the tainted legacy of their birth rivalry by cutting into their arms and remixing their blood. David, the first king of Israel, is a devout antinationalist who only assumes the crown in deference to matriarchal values represented by the biblical heroines Rachel and Ruth. In place of the covenant revealed by God to the Israelites at Mount Sinai, the formative bond entails an interethnic compromise between two peoples, two gods, two Moseses. Nor is the Moses who shattered the tablets of use. Of far more relevance is the Moses who both does and does not want to shatter them, in perpetuity—Moses, as an artist or psychoanalyst might see him.

For reasons also having to do with the preference for experience, modernists made much of the role of chance, *Zufall*, in returning the past to us and us to the past. Chance became structural, controlling plot, and thematic, triggering reflection and crisis. Hofmannsthal's pantomime, Schnitzler's Jewish plots, as well as Freud's essays on the "Great Men" all highlight the role of the unexpected turn of events.

Viennese Jewish modernists took pains to stage the creative endeavor itself as an *Erlebnis:* a mysterious process transpiring beyond the artist's control. One might say of Hofmannsthal's famous obsession with *Geheimnis* (mystery) that to him, the greatest mystery of all was the birth of his own poetic imagination, the emergence of the epigone as poet.[5] Schnitzler wrote of his Jewish novel, "Even while working [on the novel] I always felt that it would turn out that way [i.e., as a flawed work],—but I could not, or did not, want to help myself. As carefully as the book was planned, it simply became what it is, as I wrote it."[6] Beer-Hofmann's pronouncements on the subject of memory follow similar lines. In an aphorism called "Form-Chaos," Beer-Hofmann likens the art of memory to sculpting a figure in stone: one can hew the bodily form, the contours of neck and shoulders, "but the full figure, the face and the soul that peers out of it, will remain forever within the stone, mute, unredeemed, hidden."[7] Freud's invention of the method of transference sought, by circumventing consciousness, to draw out the past despite itself. But as a practitioner of cultural recollection, Freud found himself subject to forces beyond his control. At the close of *Moses and Monotheism,* reflecting back on the unsystematic shape of the work, he admitted: "I found myself unable to wipe out the traces of the history of the work's origin, which was in any case unusual."[8] Freud closes the preface with another explanation: "Unluckily, an author's creative power (*Schöpferkraft*) does not always obey his will: the work proceeds as it can, and often presents itself to the author as something independent or even alien."[9]

As I have argued throughout this study, the highly experimental quality of Viennese Jewish modernism as a literary movement bears upon the writers' attempt to foreground the idea of *Erlebnis* as a problem of representation. The status of these works as transitional, "minor," and flamboyantly hybrid is not incidental; it inheres in their very conception. The Hebrew modernist S. Y. Agnon offers a potent symbol in his coming-of-age story "The Kerchief." "It was a silk brocaded kerchief adorned with flowers and blossoms. On the one side it was brown and they were white, while on the other they were brown and it was white." The kerchief's double-sided character represents the interdependence of the religious (Jewish) and universal (Oedipal) dimensions of Agnon's story. Likewise, Schnitzler questioned whether a Jew could also be a great dramatist, and whether a Jewish novel could also be a first-rate bildungsroman. The hybrid character of Jewish modernism may reach its apotheosis in Franz Kafka's description of the art of Josephine the Singer, the genre of which falls ineluctably between singing and piping. She is only piping, and piping is what we do all day; yet through Josephine's performances, one can have the sensation of being "in the warm bed of the community, for a brief while," which is just about as long as the Hunger Artist's audience is able to take pleasure in his fasting. These are the conditions of *Erlebnis*.

Taken together, these performances of Viennese Jewish writing make up a coherent Jewish countertradition. Though the authors may have disagreed about what that countertradition was, they responded similarly on the level of form—a similarity I have tried to capture by focusing on their attempts to produce genres of memory within a modernist context. Genres of memory imply continuity and discontinuity. They mark each writer's conscious effort to mediate between tradition and innovation, communal ties and individual freedom. They represent manipulations of accepted cultural codes through radical reworkings of received forms. We heed these writers' example by avoiding reductive conceptions about what constitutes an authentic legacy, as well as facile claims about Jewish self-consciousness, and by striving for a more inclusive understanding of the place of Jewish writing within the Western European tradition.

NOTES

INTRODUCTION

The quotation from Freud is from his preface to the Hebrew edition of *Totem and Taboo*, in *The Standard Edition of the Complete Psychological Works of Sigmund Freud,* ed. and trans. James Strachey, 24 vols. (London: Hogarth Press, 1953), 13:xv (*Standard Edition* hereinafter cited as *SE*); also in *Studienausgabe,* ed. Alexander Mitscherlich, Angela Richards, and James Strachey, 12 vols. (Frankfurt am Main: Fischer Taschenbuch, 1982), 9:293 (*Studienausgabe* hereinafter cited as *SA*). The translation here is my own. Subsequent citations from Freud follow *SE* and will be referenced both to *SE* and *SA*.

The quotation from Schnitzler is from *Tagebuch,* ed. Werner Welzig (Vienna: Österreichische Akademie der Wissenschaften, 1987–99), entry for January 13, 1908 (*Tagebuch* hereinafter cited as *TB*).

1 . Edward Timms, *Karl Kraus: The Apocalyptic Satirist* (New Haven: Yale University Press, 1986), 7. See Timms's illustration "The Vienna Circles: A Diagram of Creative Interaction in Vienna Around 1910," ibid., 8.

2. It was at Zuckerkandl's salon that Gustav Mahler met his future wife, Alma Schindler; Hofmannsthal gave a debut reading of one of his plays; and the Vienna Secession is said to have been born. On Zuckerkandl's role as cultural emissary for the Viennese modernists, see Emily D. Bilski and Emily Braun, *Jewish Women and Their Salons: The Power of Conversation* (New Haven: Yale University Press, 2005), 85–99.

3. Political factors also become more decisive, as Timms's second diagram, "Wiener Kreise in den späten 1920er Jahren," makes clear. Edward Timms, "Die Wiener Kreise," in *Vienna 1900: From Altenberg to Wittgenstein,* ed. Edward Timms and Ritchie Robertson (Edinburgh: Edinburgh University Press, 1990), 140. Allan Janik and Stephen Toulmin elaborate on the factors that made independent groups increasingly important after 1918 once the social and political authority of the Hapsburg Empire had been dismantled. *Wittgenstein's Vienna* (New York: Simon and Schuster, 1973), 239–62.

4. Gotthart Wunberg, ed., *Das junge Wien: Österreichische Literatur- und Kunstkritik, 1887–1902* (Tübingen: Niemeyer, 1976).

5. Schnitzler, *TB,* March 29,1891.

6. Michael Worbs discusses these parallel developments in detail in *Nervenkunst: Literatur und Psychoanalyse im Wien der Jahrhundertwende* (Frankfurt am Main: Athenäum, 1988), 62–64.

7. For the statistics pertaining to the Jewish presence in Viennese *Gymnasien* and in the professions, see Steven Beller, *Vienna and the Jews, 1867–1938* (Cambridge: Cambridge University Press, 1989), 33–70.

8. Gerson D. Cohen, "The Blessing of Assimilation in Jewish History," in *Great Jewish Speeches Throughout History,* ed. Steve Israel and Seth Forman (Northvale, N.J.: Jason Aronson, 1994).

9. Michael Stanislawski, *Zionism and the Fin de Siècle: Cosmopolitanism and Nationalism from Nordau to Jabotinsky* (Berkeley and Los Angeles: University of California Press, 2001), 9.

10. On the reception of these works, see Peter Gay, *Freud: A Life for Our Time* (New York: W. W. Norton, 1988), 645–46; and Konstanze Fliedl, *Arthur Schnitzler: Poetik der Erinnerung* (Vienna: Böhlau, 1997), 225–29.

11. For a discussion of this reception, see Michael P. Steinberg, *Austria as Theater and Ideology: The Meaning of the Salzburg Festival* (Ithaca: Cornell University Press: 2000), 164–67.

12. Julius Bab, "Hugo von Hofmannsthal," in *Jüdisches Lexicon* (Berlin: Jüdischer, 1928).

13. Robert S. Wistrich, *The Jews of Vienna in the Age of Franz Josef* (Oxford: Oxford University Press, 1989), 585–86.

14. Franz von Hofmannsthal shot himself on July 13, 1929, and Hugo von Hofmannsthal died two days later. Lili Schnitzler shot herself on June 27, 1928, and Schnitzler died on October 21, 1931.

15. Letter, May 8, 1906, in "Briefe an Arthur Schnitzler," *Die Neue Rundschau* 66, no. 1 (1955): 95.

16. Letter, May 14, 1922, ibid., 97.

17. Letter, July 10, 1936, *Fischer Almanach 77* (1963): 64.

18. Worbs, *Nervenkunst,* 259–69.

19. Ibid., 269–72. Schnitzler called Hofmannsthal's ability to render Sophoclean drama into a popular play "echt jüdisch." Letter, November 4, 1903, in *Briefwechsel,* by Hugo von Hofmannsthal and Arthur Schnitzler, ed. Therese Nickl and Heinrich Schnitzler (Frankfurt am Main: Fischer Taschenbuch, 1983), 176 (hereinafter cited as *Hofmannsthal/Schnitzler Briefwechsel*).

20. Leo A. Lensing, "Elektra 'antik u modern': Zu einem Abend der Mittwoch-Gesellschaft im Jahre 1905 (mit einem unbekannten Postkarte Freuds an Paul Federn)," *Luzifer-Amor* 19, no. 38 (2006): 46–75. On the Freud-Hofmannsthal connection, see also Bernd Urban, *Hofmannsthal, Freud und die Psychoanalyse: Quellenkundliche Untersuchungen* (Frankfurt am Main: Peter Lang, 1978).

21. In response to *Jaákobs Traum,* Hofmannsthal accused Beer-Hofmann of chauvinism. Letter, April 20, 1919, in *Briefwechsel,* by Hugo von Hofmannsthal and Richard Beer-Hofmann, ed. Eugene Weber (Frankfurt am Main: S. Fischer, 1972), 144–46 (hereinafter cited as *Hofmannsthal/Beer-Hofmann Briefwechsel*). In a postscript to a letter to Schnitzler of 1910, Hofmannsthal mentioned that he had forgotten the copy of *Der Weg ins Freie* "half accidentally, half intentionally" on a train two years earlier, and requested a replacement copy. Letter, October 29, 1910, in *Hofmannsthal/Schnitzler Briefwechsel,* 256.

22. Hugo von Hofmannsthal, *Reden und Aufsätze II: 1914–1924,* ed. Bernd Schoeller (Frankfurt am Main: Fischer Taschenbuch,1979), 195.

23. Letter, September 5, 1897. "Ich werde nie imstand sein und werde mir's auch nie verlangen, aus dem Gewebe meines Wesen die Fäden herauszuziehen, die Ihr Geschenk sind: es fiele dann alles auseinander. Ich weiss genau, dass es keinen Menschen gibt, dem ich so viel schuldig bin wie Ihnen."

24. Within the early oeuvre alone, the problem of memory is taken up in works as different as the one-act plays *Gestern* (Yesterday) and *Der Tod des Tizian* (The Death of Titian); lyric poems such as "Dein Antlitz" (Your Face) and "Terzinen: Über Vergänglichkeit" (On Transitoriness, in Terza Rima); a dialogue, *Gespräch über Gedichte* (Dialogue on Poems); and a prose poem, "Die Wege und die Begegnungen" (Paths and Encounters).

25. Jeffrey Moussaieff Masson, trans. and ed., *The Complete Letters of Sigmund Freud to Wilhelm Fliess, 1887–1904* (Cambridge, Mass.: Belknap Press of Harvard University Press, 1985), 207.

26. "*Vb* [Vorbewußtsein (preconsciousness)] is the third transcription, attached to word presentation and corresponding to our official ego." Ibid., 208.

27. "The conscious text is thus not a transcription, because there is no text *present elsewhere* as an unconscious one to be transposed or transported. . . . The unconscious text is already a weave of pure traces, differences in which meaning and force are united—a text nowhere present, consisting of archives which are *always*

already transcriptions" (emphasis in original). Jacques Derrida, *Writing and Difference,* trans. Alan Bass (Chicago: University of Chicago Press, 1978), 211.

28. Franz Kafka, "Brief an den Vater," in *Zur Frage der Gesetze und andere Schriften aus dem Nachlass* (Frankfurt am Main: Fischer Taschenbuch, 1999), 42.

29. Yosef Hayim Yerushalmi, *Zakhor: Jewish History and Jewish Memory* (New York: Schocken Books, 1989), 86.

30. Harold Bloom, foreword to Yerushalmi, *Zakhor,* xix.

31. Harold Bloom, *The Strong Light of the Canonical: Kafka, Freud, and Scholem as Revisionists of Jewish Culture and Thought,* City College Papers 20 (New York: City College, 1987).

32. Some of these debates are surveyed in "Das Gedächtnis des Jahrhunderts," special issue, *Transit* 22 (Winter 2001/2002).

33. See Susannah Radstone, introduction to *Memory and Methodology,* ed. Susannah Radstone (Oxford: Berg, 2000), 1–22; Andreas Huyssen, *Twilight Memories: Marking Time in a Culture of Amnesia* (London: Routledge, 1995); Mieke Bal, Jonathan Crewe, and Leo Spitzer, *Acts of Memory: Cultural Recall in the Present* (Hanover, N.H.: University Press of New England, 1999).

34. The AIDS quilt contains over forty-four thousand panels memorializing lives lost to AIDS. See Peter S. Hawkins, "Naming Names: The Art of Memory and the NAMES Project AIDS Quilt," *Critical Inquiry* 19, no. 4 (1993): 752–79. The Fortunoff Video Archive for Holocaust Testimonies at Yale University contains forty-two hundred videotaped testimonies of survivors and witnesses. The archive of the Survivors of the Shoah Foundation contains fifty-two thousand testimonies from Holocaust survivors and witnesses from fifty-six countries recorded in thirty-two languages. Out of a similar impulse, the German sculptor Gunther Demnig continues to install *Stolpersteine,* inscribed brass plaques, on the sidewalks outside victims' former homes—nine thousand as of the end of 2006.

35. Dennis Smith, "Memorials Without a Memory," *New York Times,* November 16, 2003, A29. The ongoing controversy over the proper way to list the victims' names—alphabetically, or by place of employment—represents the struggle to further humanize a design perceived to be out of touch with the needs of the victims' families.

36. Michael Kimmelman, "Out of Minimalism, Monuments to Memory," *New York Times,* January 13, 2002, 37.

37. I recount some of this story in "Cultural Awakening and Historical Forgetting: The Architecture of Memory in the Jüdisches Museum Wien and in Rachel

Whiteread's 'Nameless Library,'" *New German Critique* 93 (Fall 2004): 145–73.

38. Holograms are three-dimensional images created by a photographic technique involving laser beams.

39. On these contemporary predilections, see Barbara Kirshenblatt-Gimblett, *Destination Culture: Tourism, Museums, and Heritage* (Berkeley and Los Angeles: University of California Press, 1998), and Ruth Ellen Gruber, *Virtually Jewish* (Berkeley and Los Angeles: University of California Press, 2002).

40. As curator Felicitas Heimann-Jelinek states: "Perhaps it makes more sense to think about the relativity of history and historical presentations than to say this object means this, and this year was that, and this event meant such and such, and so on—because it's not true." Cited in Gruber, *Virtually Jewish*, 177.

41. Matti Bunzl, "Of Holograms and Storage Areas: Modernity and Postmodernity at Vienna's Jewish Museum," *Cultural Anthropology* 18, no. 4 (2003): 435–68.

42. http://www.jmw.at/en/museum.html.

43. See Stephen Kern, *The Culture of Time and Space, 1880–1918* (Cambridge: Harvard University Press, 1983), 36–64.

44. Hayden White, "The Burden of History," in *Tropics of Discourse: Essays in Cultural Criticism* (Baltimore: Johns Hopkins University Press, 1978), 27–50.

45. Pierre Nora, "Between Memory and History: *Les Lieux de Mémoire*," *Representations* 26 (Spring 1989): 7–25.

46. Ibid., 6.

47. See my essay "'Ich suche ein Asyl für meine Vergangenheit': Schnitzler's Poetics of Memory," in *Arthur Schnitzler: Zeitgenossenschaften/Contemporaneities*, ed. Ian Foster and Florian Krobb (Bern: Peter Lang, 2002), 141–56.

48. Kern, *Culture of Time and Space*, 64.

49. Richard Terdiman, *Present Past: Modernity and the Memory Crisis* (Ithaca: Cornell University Press, 1993), 225.

50. Radstone, "Working with Memory," 6.

51. Boncompagno da Signa (1235), cited in Frances A. Yates, *The Art of Memory* (Chicago: University of Chicago Press, 1966), 58. "The art of memory as it was traditionally conceived was based upon associations between a structure of images easily remembered and a body of knowledge in need of organization." Patrick H. Hutton, *History as an Art of Memory* (Hanover, N.H.: University Press of New England, 1993), 27.

52. Franz Kafka, *Letters to Friends, Family and Editors*, trans. Richard Winston and Clara Winston (New York: Schocken Books, 1977), 1.

53. Radstone, "Working with Memory," 6.

54. *SE*, 12:135; *SA Ergänzungsband*, 214.

55. Some examples include Shmuel Finer, *Haskalah and History* (Oxford: Littman Library of Jewish Civilization, 2002); Arnold Eisen, *Rethinking Jewish Modernity* (Tucson: University of Arizona Press, 1992); Pierre Vidal-Naquet, *The Jews: History, Memory, and the Present*, trans. and ed. David Ames Curtis (New York: Columbia University Press, 1996); Yerushalmi, *Zakhor*; Shulamit Volkov, "Die Erfindung einer Tradition: Zur Entstehung eines modernen Judentum in Deutschland," *Historische Zeitschrift* 253, no. 3 (1991): 603–28; Yael Zerubavel, *Recovered Roots: Collective Memory and the Making of Israeli National Tradition* (Chicago: University of Chicago Press, 1995); Amos Funkenstein, *Perceptions of Jewish History* (Berkeley and Los Angeles: University of California Press, 1993); James Young, *The Texture of Memory: Holocaust Memorials and Meaning* (New Haven: Yale University Press, 1993); and Dan Diner, *Gedächtniszeiten: Über jüdische und andere Geschichten* (Munich: C. H. Beck, 2003).

56. David G. Roskies, *The Jewish Search for a Usable Past* (Bloomington: Indiana University Press, 1999), 1.

57. Ibid., 3.

58. Yerushalmi, *Zakhor*, 44.

59. Initiating the trend in German was Heinrich Heine's *Der Rabbi von Bacherach* (1824; continued 1848), and in Hebrew, Abraham Mapu's *Love of Zion* (1824). This first modern Hebrew novel was also a historical novel. On Jewish historical fiction in Germany, see Florian Krobb, *Selbstdarstellungen: Untersuchungen zur deutsch-jüdischen Erzählliteratur im neunzehnten Jahrhundert* (Würzburg: Königshausen and Neumann, 2000).

60. Asher Biemann, "The Problem of Tradition and Reform in Jewish Renaissance and Renaissancism," *Jewish Social Studies* 8, no. 1 (2001): 64.

61. Martin Buber, "Die Erneuerung des Judentums," in *Der Jude und sein Judentum: Gesammelte Aufsätze und Reden* (Gerlingen: L. Schneider, 1993), 28.

62. Martin Buber, "Jewish Religiosity" (1912–14), in *On Judaism*, ed. Nahum M. Glatzer (New York: Schocken Books, 1987), 81. Originally published in *Vom Geist des Judentums* (Leipzig: K. Wolff, 1916).

63. For an analysis of this phenomenon, see Chana Kronfeld, *On the Margins of Modernism* (Berkeley and Los Angeles: University of California Press, 1996).

64. Mendele Mocher Sforim (Mendele the Book Peddler), "Of Bygone Days," trans. Raymond P. Sheindlin, in *A Shtetl and Other Yiddish Novellas*, ed. Ruth R. Wisse (Detroit: Wayne State University Press, 1986), 270.

65. Dagmar Lorenz, *Wiener Moderne* (Stuttgart: J. B. Metzler, 1995), 1–8. See also Timms and Robertson, *Vienna 1900*; and Jens Rieckmann, *Aufbruch in die Moderne: Die Anfänge des jungen Wien* (Königstein: Athenäum, 1985).

66. "Die Vergangenheit war groß, oft lieblich. Wir wollen ihr feierliche Grabreden halten. Aber wenn der König bestattet ist, dann lebe der andere König!" Hermann Bahr, "Die Moderne" (1890), in *Die literarische Moderne: Dokumente zum Selbstverständnis der Literatur um die Jahrhundertwende*, 2nd ed., ed. Gotthart Wunberg and Stephan Dietrich (Freiburg im Breisgau: Rombach, 1998), 100.

67. Lorna Martens's sustained study of how dualistic thinking pervaded Austrian literature of the period emphasizes texts that rhetorically "antithesize" the past and the present. Lorna Martens, *Shadow Lines: Austrian Literature from Freud to Kafka* (Lincoln: University of Nebraska Press, 1996).

68. Gotthart Wunberg, "Fin de siècle in Wien," *Text + Kritik* 138/139 (April 1998): 9–11; and Carl E. Schorske, "The Ringstrasse and the Birth of Urban Modernism," in *Fin-de-Siècle Vienna* (New York: Vintage Books, 1981), 24–115.

69. Rieckmann, *Aufbruch in die Moderne*, 190–92.

70. Thomas A. Kovach, *Hofmannsthal and Symbolism: Art and Life in the Work of a Modern Poet* (New York: Peter Lang, 1985), 74–89.

71. The tendency to divide up the topic of memory in this way occurs in Claudio Magris's study of Hapsburg national memory. Magris regards the proponents of "modern culture" (including champions of psychoanalysis, logical positivism, language philosophy, and Expressionism) as adventurous Odysseus figures who left behind the siren song of "Hapsburg culture, saturated with tradition and the past." Claudio Magris, *Der habsburgische Mythos in der österreichischen Literatur*, 2nd ed. (Salzburg: Otto Müller, 1988), 20–21.

72. Thomas A. Kovach, "Traditionalist Modernism or Modernist Traditionalism: The Case of Hugo von Hofmannsthal, *Philological Papers* 39 (1993): 57–61.

73. Jacques Le Rider, *Modernity and Crises of Identity: Culture and Society in Fin-de-Siècle Vienna*, trans. Rosemary Morris (New York: Continuum, 1993), 23.

74. Ibid., 24.

75. Steven Beller, ed., *Rethinking Vienna 1900* (New York: Berghahn Books, 2001), 40.

76. Ibid., 8.

77. See Steven Beller, "Was bedeutet es, 'Wien um 1900' als eine jüdische Stadt zu bezeichnen?" *Zeit-geschichte* 23, nos. 7–8 (1996): 274–80, and Ernst Gombrich, *The Visual Arts in Vienna Circa 1900; and Reflections on the Jewish Catastrophe* (London: Austrian Cultural Institute, 1997).

78. Beller, *Vienna and the Jews*, 244.

79. Letter, April 17, 1907, in *Briefe, 1875–1912*, ed. Therese Nickl and Heinrich Schnitzler (Frankfurt am Main: S. Fischer, 1981), 555 (hereinafter cited as *Briefe I*). Cited in Iris Bruce, "Which Way Out? Schnitzler's and Salten's Conflicting Responses to Cultural Zionism," in *A Companion to the Works of Arthur Schnitzler*, ed. Dagmar C. G. Lorenz (Rochester: Camden House, 2003), 107.

80. Matti Bunzl, "The Poetics of Politics and the Politics of Poetics: Richard Beer-Hofmann and Theodor Herzl Reconsidered," *German Quarterly* 69, no. 3 (1996): 277–304.

81. Steinberg, *Austria as Theater and Ideology*, 173.

82. See Sander L. Gilman, *Jewish Self-Hatred: Anti-Semitism and the Hidden Language of the Jews* (Baltimore: Johns Hopkins University Press, 1986); *The Jew's Body* (New York: Routledge, 1991); and *Freud, Race, and Gender* (Princeton: Princeton University Press, 1993).

CHAPTER 1

1. Sigmund Freud, *The Psychopathology of Everyday Life*, 6:278. *Gesammelte Werke*, 4:309.

2. Yosef Yerushalmi, *Freud's Moses* (New Haven: Yale University Press, 1991); Jacques Derrida, *Mal d'Archive: Une impression freudienne* (Paris: Galilée, 1995); Cathy Caruth, *Unclaimed Experience: Trauma, Narrative, and History* (Baltimore: Johns Hopkins University Press, 1996); Jan Assmann, *Moses the Egyptian: The Memory of Egypt in Western Monotheism* (Cambridge, Mass.: Harvard University Press, 1997); and Richard Bernstein, *Freud and the Legacy of Moses* (Cambridge: Cambridge University Press, 1998). Of these works, three are particularly relevant in this context. Yerushalmi reads Freud's Moses essays in connection with "the various modalities of modern Jewish historicism, of that quest for the meaning of Judaism and Jewish identity through an unprecedented examination of the Jewish past which is itself the consequence of a radical break with that past"—the "break" being Freud's lapsed Jewish observance, perhaps also that implicit in the enterprise of Jewish history as such. Yerushalmi, *Freud's Moses*, 2. Caruth argues that a different break—Freud's exile—controls the form and substance of *Moses and Monotheism*, which she calls "one of the first works of trauma in this century." Freud's "seeming fictionalization of the Jewish past" can moreover "help us understand our own cata-

strophic era, as well as the difficulties of writing history within it." Caruth, *Unclaimed Experience,* 11–12. Bernstein explains how and why the concept of tradition developed in the Moses essays differs from "'traditional' accounts of tradition, which restrict themselves to the conscious mental processes," and thus "fail to shed any light on the *unconscious* dynamics involved in receptivity and resistance to tradition." Bernstein emphasizes: "Traditions are not simply continuous; they involve ruptures and reversals. They may seem moribund—only to come to life again with renewed psychological vigor." He takes issue with Yerushalmi (as does Derrida), arguing that Freud's Lamarckism—his references to genetic memory—is far less central than the concepts of unconscious memory and tradition (Bernstein, *Freud and the Legacy of Moses,* 50–51).

3. "For centuries, Leonardo was venerated beyond comparison in German culture. Winckelmann, Goethe, Kant, the Romantics, and more recently Jacob Burkhardt and Heinrich Wölfflin had marveled at his vast talents and enormous range of scientific studies." Jutta Birmele, "Strategies of Persuasion: The Case of *Leonard da Vinci,*" in *Reading Freud's Reading,* ed. Sander L. Gilman, Jutta Birmele, Jay Geller, and Valerie D. Greenberg (New York: New York University Press, 1994), 134.

4. See Louis Rose, *The Freudian Calling: Early Viennese Psychoanalysis and the Pursuit of a Cultural Science* (Detroit: Wayne State University Press, 1998).

5. Oscar Wilde, "The Critic as Artist," in *The Artist as Critic: Critical Writings of Oscar Wilde,* ed. Richard Ellmann (Chicago: University of Chicago Press, 1982), 342.

6. See Conrad Alberti, "Das Milieu," in Wunberg and Dietrich, *Die literarische Moderne,* 83–95.

7. Rational thinking in itself is not necessarily a sign that the past has been forsaken, however. Eugene Weber shows that this same judgment is the overt basis of Freud's criticism of Adler's systematic theory. Systematizing thought is suspect because it seeks coherence and unity in a naïve or misguided way. Eugene Weber, *The Legend of Freud* (Stanford: Stanford University Press, 2000), 17–21.

8. The comment recalls the frustration of Kafka's country doctor: "That is what people are like in my district. Always expecting the impossible from the doctor. They have lost their ancient beliefs; the parson sits at home and unravels his vestments, one after another; but the doctor is supposed to be omnipotent with his merciful surgeon's hand." Franz Kafka, "A Country Doctor," in *The Complete Stories,* ed. Nahum N. Glatzer (New York: Schocken Books, 1995), 204.

9. See Meyer Schapiro, "Leonardo and Freud: An Art-Historical Study," *Journal of the History of Ideas* 17, no. 2 (1956): 147–78; Robert S. Liebert, *Michelangelo: A Psychoanalytic Study of His Life and Images* (New Haven: Yale University Press, 1983); Bradley I. Collins, *Leonardo, Psychoanalysis, and Art History: A Critical Study of Psychobiographical Approaches to Leonardo da Vinci* (Evanston: Northwestern University Press, 1997); and Wayne Anderson, *Freud, Leonardo Da Vinci, and the Vulture's Tail: A Refreshing Look at Leonardo's Sexuality* (New York: Other Press, 2001).

10. These writers were responsible for turning the Mona Lisa into a *Kultbild,* and all influenced the Viennese authors. Hofmannsthal, who refers to *La Gioconda* in *Der Tor und der Tod* (The Fool and Death), includes a translation of Pater's description of the portrait from *The Rennaissance* in his essay "Über moderne englische Malerei" (On Modern English Painting) of 1894, and in the same year he wrote an essay titled "Walter Pater." Worbs, *Nervenkunst,* 104–17. Ursula Renner notes the existence of an unpublished Hofmannsthal poem, "Madonna Lisa." According to Renner, the combination of a "woman without qualities" and the lack of a "plot" made possible the quintessential aesthetic encounter, in which the observer could connect, from a distance, to a woman who was unreachable yet, as Gautier wrote, who also prompted a sense of deja vu, "as if one had seen her before, in an earlier life." Ursula Renner, "Mona Lisa— Das 'Rätsel Weib' als 'Frauenphantom des Mannes' im Fin de Siècle," in *Lulu, Lilith, Mona Lisa: Frauenbilder der Jahrhundertwende,* ed. Irmgard Roebling (Pfaffenweiler: Centaurus, 1989), 141.

11. Renner, "Mona Lisa," 139.

12. Freud mentions Pater's essay in a letter to Ernest Jones of April 15,1910. Worbs, *Nervenkunst,* 117.

13. Ibid., 107.

14. Ibid., 108.

15. For a comprehensive discussion of Freud's method in relation to the history of art and photography, see Mary Bergstein, "Freud's *Moses of Michelangelo:* Vasari, Photography, and Art Historical Practice," *Art Bulletin* 88, no. 1 (2006): 158–76.

16. "Der Moses des Michelangelo," *Imago* 3, no. 1 (1914): 15.

17. Bluma Goldstein, *Reinscribing Moses* (Cambridge, Mass.: Harvard University Press, 1992), 66–136. Goldstein claims that Freud "conquers" the biblical Moses, in that his interpretation effects a transformation "from Freud's idea of the traditional biblical Moses into a civilized and controlled hero, from the overwhelming threat

of a figure of commanding, even physical, power into one of constrained quiescence—a transformation that is the result of Moses' mental decision" (81).

18. Letter from Sigmund Freud to Carl Jung, January 17, 1909, in *The Freud/Jung Letters: The Correspondence Between Sigmund Freud and C.G. Jung,* ed. William McGuire, trans. Ralph Mannheim and R. F. F. Hull (Princeton: Princeton University Press, 1974), 196–97.

19. "He had not returned to the Bible and the teachings of the father. He feels guilty, singled out under the rebuking stare of the statue. Unable to bear the full weight of it, he suddenly sees something no one else had ever seen—that Moses-Jakob contains his anger, that the wrath will not burst forth upon him" (Yerushalmi, *Freud's Moses,* 76).

20. Bergstein, "Freud's *Moses of Michelangelo,*" 161.

21. Ken Frieden, "Sigmund Freud's Passover Dream Responds to Theodor Herzl's Zionist Dream," in *Yale Companion to Jewish Writing and Thought in German Culture, 1096–1996,* ed. Sander L. Gilman and Jack Zipes (New Haven: Yale University Press, 1997), 240.

22. The formulation appears in the twenty-third introductory lecture, "Die Wege der Symptombildung" (The Paths to the Formation of Symptoms, 1916–17): "For there is a path that leads back [*Rückweg*] from fantasy to reality—the path, that is, of art" (*SE* 16:376; *SA,* 1:366).

23. Yerushalmi makes this connection. "He and the great sculptor have one thing in common: both are, in effect, biblical exegetes who radically violate the plain sense of the text—Michelangelo by presenting a Moses who contains his anger and does not shatter the Tablets, Freud by making him an Egyptian and having him killed by the Jews" (Yerushalmi, *Freud's Moses,* 22).

24. Carlo Ginzburg, "Morelli, Freud, and Sherlock Holmes: Clues and Scientific Method," *History Workshop Journal* 9 (1980): 11.

25. On the possible reasons for these suppressions, see Goldstein, *Reinscribing Moses,* 87–89.

26. Bergstein speculates, "these illustrations all have the ungrounded look of contour-line drawings made from (perhaps traced from) photographs, and, in fact, the pose of his figure 3 corresponds precisely to Alinari photograph number 6205, in which the *Moses* is viewed from 30 degrees to the left, a view in which the tablets and prophet's hand intertwined with his beard are most prominently featured" (Bergstein, "Freud's *Moses of Michelangelo,*" 165).

27. Ibid.

28. The discussion can be linked to the only other appearance of Hebrew *Fremdwörter* in the text, Freud's quotation of the *Shema Yisrael* (Hear O Israel) prayer in Hebrew. There, playing the poet, he expresses a wish that the acoustic similarity Aton-Adonai would indicate the identity of the two Gods, but admits that he has "no confirmation from other sources" of this conjecture.

29. The phrase is repeated several times, as in "it was this one man Moses who created the Jews" (Es war der eine Mann Moses, der die Juden geschaffen hat) (*SE,* 23:107; *SA,* 9:553). "Now the man Moses was a very humble man, more so than any other man on earth" (Numbers 12:3).

30. "Freud emerges as an intermediate sphere between ancient and modern Judaic commentary, despite his efforts to forestall such associations. He never acknowledges the pseudorabbinic elements of his work, and his silence forms a resonant space in which his repressed precursors echo." Ken Frieden, *Freud's Dream of Interpretation* (Albany: SUNY Press, 1990), 7.

31. "In Cicero's version of the Simonides legend, the disfigured, mutilated dead stand for the past; they stand for the order of signs that existed before the catastrophe and is no longer decipherable. The catastrophe consists in the experience of forgetting." Renate Lachmann, *Memory and Literature,* trans. Roy Sellars and Anthony Wall (Minneapolis: University of Minnesota Press, 1997), 7.

32. "Circumcision is the symbolic substitute for the castration which the primal father once inflicted upon his sons in the plenitude of his absolute power, and whoever accepted that symbol was showing by it that he was prepared to submit to the father's will, even it if imposed the most painful sacrifice on him" (*SE,* 23:122; *SA,* 9:567).

33. Masson, *Freud/Fliess Correspondence,* 208.

34. Neurosis is a compromise with respect to two more extreme reactions to trauma. Traumatic experiences can "stamp character" in two ways, one "positive" and one "negative." Either the adult compulsively repeats the behavior in his or her adult life ("fixation") or develops defenses, avoidances (inhibitions and phobias) to preempt such repetition. Freud admits that both of these are "fixations to the trauma," "except that they are fixations with a contrary purpose" (*SE,* 23:75–76; *SA,* 9:524). Too much memory and too little memory are revealed to have a common etiology. A third possible response is neurosis. Neurosis is not a fixation: it is a type of reaction that falls midway between compulsive repetition and compulsive avoidance. "The symptoms of neurosis in the narrower sense are compromises [*Kompromißbildungen*] in which both the trends proceeding from traumas come together, so that the share, now of

one and now of the other tendency, finds preponderant expression in them. This opposition between the reactions sets up conflicts which in the ordinary course of events can reach no conclusion" (*SE,* 23:75; *SA,* 9:524). A neurotic symptom, like a fossil, is a hardened domain within the mind, "a State within a State, an inaccessible party, with which cooperation is impossible" and which is "insufficiently or not at all influenced by external reality" (*SE,* 23:76; *SA,* 9:525).

35. Letter to Arnold Zweig, September 30, 1904, in *The Letters of Sigmund Freud and Arnold Zweig,* ed. Ernst L. Freud, trans. Elaine Robson-Scott and William Robson-Scott (New York: Harcourt Brace and World, 1970), 91.

36. Letter to Lou Andreas-Salomé, January 6, 1935, in *Sigmund Freud and Lou Andreas-Salomé: Letters,* ed. Ernst Pfeiffer, trans. William Robson-Scott and Elaine Robson-Scott (New York: W. W. Norton, 1966), 204.

37. Cited in Yerushalmi, *Freud's Moses,* 17.

38. "One may say that a phantasy at one and the same moment hovers between three periods of time—the three periods of our ideation. The activity of phantasy in the mind is linked up with some current impression, occasioned by some event in the present, which had the power to rouse an intense desire. From there it wanders back to the memory of an earlier experience, generally belonging to infancy, in which this wish was fulfilled. Then, it creates for itself a situation which is to emerge in the future [*Zukunftsbild*], representing the fulfillment of the wish—this is the day-dream or phantasy, which now carries in it traces both of the occasion which engendered it and of some past memory. So past, present and future are threaded, as it were, on the string of the wish that runs through them all" (*SE,* 9:147). "Man darf sagen: eine Phantasie schwebt gleichsam zwischen drei Zeiten, den drei Zeitmomenten unseres Vorstellens. Die seelische Arbeit knüpft an einen aktuellen Eindruck, einen Anlaß in der Gegenwart an, der imstande war, einen der großen Wünsche der Person zu wecken, greift von da aus auf die Erinnerung eines früheren, meist infantilen, Erlebnisses zurück, in dem jener Wunsch erfüllt war, und schafft nun eine auf die Zukunft bezogene Situation, welche sich als die Erfüllung jenes Wunsches darstellt, eben den Tagtraum oder die Phantasie, die nun die Spuren ihrer Herkunft vom Anlasse und von der Erinnerung an sich trägt. Also, Vergangenes, Gegenwärtiges, Zukünftiges wie an der Schnur des durchlaufenden Wunsches aneinandergereiht" (*SA,* 10:174).

39. The image of "filling in gaps" recurs in the opening pages of the third and final essay. Referring to the account provided in the first two essays, Freud comments, "All this, however, is still history, an attempt to fill up the gaps in our historical knowledge" (*SA,* 9: 510; *SE,* 23:61).

40. "Freud is acutely aware (even near the end of his life) of how ignorant we still remain about the dynamics of our conscious and unconscious mental processes—including the complex ways in which unconscious mental processes and memory-traces are transmitted and shape our conscious lives. Unconscious mental processes are not *totally* sealed off from our conscious lives; they are always affecting and shaping them, albeit in devious and complex ways" (Bernstein, *Freud and the Legacy of Moses,* 53).

41. "Religions owe their compulsive power to the *return of the repressed;* they are reawakened memories of very ancient, forgotten, highly emotional episodes of human history. I have already said this in *Totem and Taboo;* I express it now in the formula: the strength of religion lies not in its *material,* but in its *historical* truth." Letter to Lou Andreas-Salomé, January 6, 1935, in *Freud/Andreas-Salomé Letters,* 205.

42. Sigmund Freud, "Postscript (1935)," in *An Autobiographical Study,* trans. and ed. James Strachey (New York: W. W. Norton, 1989), 83.

43. Yerushalmi, *Freud's Moses,* 35.

44. "What we should most expect would be that it would be crushed by the written account [*daß sie von der Niederschrift erschlagen wird*], would be unable to stand up against it, would become more and more shadowy and would finally pass into oblivion" (*SE,* 23:69; *SA,* 9:518).

CHAPTER 2

The quotation from Hofmannsthal is from "Über die Pantomime," in *Reden und Aufsätze I, 1891–1913,* ed. Bernd Schoeller (Frankfurt am Main: Fischer Taschenbuch, 1979), 504.

1. Hugo von Hofmannsthal, letter to Willy Haas, June 4, 1922, in *Ein Briefwechsel,* by Hugo von Hofmannsthal and Willy Haas (Berlin: Propyläen, 1968), 46–47.

2. Willy Haas, "Hugo von Hofmannsthal," in *Juden in der deutschen Literatur,* ed. Gustav Krojanker (Berlin:Welt, 1922), 139–64. Krojanker was the editor of the first Zionist press in Europe. This volume included twenty-four essays on writers including Alfred Döblin, Franz Kafka, Alfred Ehrenstein, Peter Altenberg, and Carl Sternheim.

3. See also Ernst Simon, "Hugo von Hofmannsthal:

Seine jüdischen Freunde und seine Stellung zum Judentum," *Mitteilungsblatt* 38 (14 October 1977): 3–5; and John Milfull, "Juden, Osterreicher und andere Deutsche," *Geschichte und Gesellschaft* 7, nos. 3–4 (1981): 582–89.

4. Peter Pfeifer, "Hugo von Hofmannsthal Worries About His Mixed Ancestry," in *Yale Companion to Jewish Writing and Thought in German Culture, 1096–1996*, ed. Sander L. Gilman and Jack Zipes (New Haven: Yale University Press, 1997), 212–18. A more recent piece of biographical (bad) news about Hofmannsthal's negative associations with Jewishness is found in Martin Stern, "Verschwiegener Antisemitismus: Bemerkungen zu einem widerrufenen Brief Hofmannsthals an Rudolf Pannwitz," *Hofmannsthal Jahrbuch* 12 (2004): 243–53.

5. Jens Rieckmann, "Zwischen Bewußtsein und Verdrängung: Hofmannsthals jüdisches Erbe," *Deutsche Vierteljahrsschrift für Literaturwissenschaft und Geistesgeschichte* 67, no. 3 (1993): 466–83.

6. It is of his future brother-in-law that Hofmannsthal observes, "ohne Vergnügen . . . den gewissen Hang zur Reflexion, zur 'kritischen' 'historischen' 'objectiven', nach- und anempfundenen gebildeten jüdischen Denkungsweise . . . die so etwas blutloses fürs Leben untüchtiges, ja mit der Zeit die Fähigkeit zum Erleben aufhebendes in sich hat" (ibid., 476–77).

7. See also Jens Rieckmann, "(Anti-)Semitism and Homoeroticism: Hofmannsthal's Reading of Bahr's Novel *Die Rotte Kohras*," *German Quarterly* 66, no. 2 (1993): 212–21.

8. Steinberg, *Austria as Theater and Ideology*, 172.

9. Ibid., 170.

10. Ibid., 173.

11. Wolfram Mauser, "Hofmannsthals 'Triumph der Zeit': Zur Bedeutung seiner Ballett- und Pantomimen-Libretti," in *Hofmannsthal und das Theater*, ed. Wolfram Mauser (Vienna: Karl M. Halosar, 1981), 141–48.

12. *Neue deutsche Rundschau* 3 (November 1901): 1204–11.

13. These editions were not destroyed, and they can be found in private collections. Martin Stern surmises that they were withdrawn in deference to the family of Hofmannsthal's new wife. Martin Stern, "Ein Brief Hofmannsthals an Samuel Fischer," *Hofmannsthal Blätter* 5 (Fall 1970): 339. Karin Wolgast concurs, noting that the periodical version had been fully corrected, whereas the book retained the name "Rabbi" on two occasions. It remains unclear whether Hofmannsthal would also have withdrawn the text from *Neue deutsche Rundschau* if he had had the option to do so. Karin Wolgast, "*Scaramuccia non parla, et dice gran cose*: Zu Hofmannsthals Pan-

tomime *Der Schüler*," *Deutsche Vierteljahrsschrift für Literaturwissenschaft und Geistesgeschichte* 71, no. 2 (1997): 245–63. According to Horst Weber, there exists an unpublished score composed by Erich Julius Wolff. *Hugo von Hofmannsthal: Bibliographie* (Berlin: Walter de Gruyter, 1972), 281.

14. Wolgast does not accord the Jewish version a place in her interpretation, beyond noting that Hofmannsthal encountered Eastern European Jews and attended performances of Yiddish theater, during his year of military service in Galicia; neither does Gotthart Wunberg, who devotes a chapter to *Der Schüler* in *Der frühe Hofmannsthal: Schizophrenie als dichterische Struktur* (Stuttgart: W. Kohlhammer, 1965), 92–105, or Donald G. Daviau, "Hugo von Hofmannsthal's Pantomime 'Der Schüler': Experiment in Form—Exercise in Nihilism," *Modern Austrian Literature* 1, no. 1 (Spring 1968): 4–30. Martin Stern ("Ein Brief," 339) discusses the pantomime in light of its publishing history in his commentary on an unpublished letter to Samuel Fischer. Hofmannsthal mentions *Der Schüler* in passing in a letter to Schnitzler of February 1902, and in a letter of December 22, 1901, to Ria Schmujlow-Claassen.

15. The comment was made by a prince about the Roman actor Tiberio Fiorelli. Wolgast, *Scaramuccia non parla*, 245–46.

16. Rieckmann, *Zwischen Bewußtsein und Verdrängung*, 466. "Wenn meine ganzen inneren Entwickelungen und Kämpfe nichts wären als Unruhen des ererbten Blutes, Aufstände der jüdischen Blutstropfen (Reflexion) gegen die germanischen und romanischen, und Reactionen gegen diese Aufstände."

17. Hugo von Hofmannsthal, *Dramen VI: Ballette; Pantomimen; Bearbeitungen; Übersetzungen*, ed. Bernd Schoeller (Frankfurt am Main: S. Fischer 1979), 55. All subsequent references are to this edition and are noted parenthetically. Translations are my own.

18. "Nun bin ich groß. Nun ich bin imstande, Odem des Lebens über meine Lippen zu blasen. Meinem Schatten, der hinter mir kauert, der hier hinter meinem Stuhl liegt und lauert, dem vermag ich Leben einzublasen."

19. "Ich bin kein Mensch mehr, seit ich dies getan habe."

20. "Ein ganzes Vlies, sich darein zu hüllen, wenn es draußen kalt ist."

21. "Ich liebe dich, ich, mich verlangts nach dir, mich!" "Ihr? Ihr—mich? Narr!" "Warum nicht mich? Warum nicht mich?" "Euer Haar ist widrig. Eure Augen haben so rote Ränder. Eure Hände sind zu schmutzig. . . . Eure Gestalt ist mir zu häßlich!"

22. "Noch ein Zeichen will ich abwarten. *Sieht in schauerlicher Erwartung um sich. Plötzlich bleibt die Pendeluhr stehen. In seinem Gesicht bricht dämonische Freude hervor.* Ich vollstrecke nur sein Schicksal. Und sie wird mir gehören!"

23. "Den stummen Leser zurücklassend."

24. Stéphane Mallarmé, "The Mime," trans. Barbara Johnson, in *Selected Poetry and Prose,* ed. Mary Ann Caws (New York: New Directions, 1982), 69.

25. Jacques Derrida, *Dissemination,* trans. Barbara Johnson (Chicago: University of Chicago Press, 1981), 206.

26. *Ballets* is the preceding piece in Mallarmé's *Crayonné au Théatre* sequence. Stéphane Mallarmé, *Oeuvres Complétes* (Paris: Gallimard, 1945), 304.

27. In Derrida's reading of Mallarmé, "The Mime is *acting* from the moment he is ruled by no actual action and aims toward no form of verisimilitude. The act always plays out a difference without reference, or rather without a referent, without any absolute exteriority, and hence, without any inside. The Mime mimes reference. He is not an imitator; he mimes imitation" (Derrida, *Dissemination,* 219).

28. Worbs, *Nervenkunst,* 269–303. Hofmannsthal's essay appeared first in a periodical and was later published together with the pantomimes *Das fremde Mädchen* (1910) and *Amor und Psyche* (1911).

29. Hofmannsthal, *Reden und Aufsätze I,* 502.

30. Ibid., 505.

31. Ibid., 504–5. "Es ist ein Mensch wie wir, der sich vor uns bewegt, aber freier, als wir jemals uns bewegen, und dennoch spricht die Reinheit und Freiheit seiner Gebärden das Gleiche aus, das wir aussprechen wollen, wenn wir gehemmt und zuckend uns innerer Fülle entladen."

32. "In der Pantomime werde nicht gesprochen, weil sie jede Begebenheit auf die 'Grundgefühle' zurückführe, für deren Ausdruck der bloße Gestus genüge, ja deren Mitteilung das Wort nur erschwere." Hermann Bahr, *Rezensionen: Wiener Theater, 1901–1903* (Berlin: S. Fischer, 1903), 161.

33. Robert Storey, *Pierrot: A Critical History of a Mask* (Princeton: Princeton University Press, 1978), 11–12.

34. "In an alienated society, all the alienations, no matter what their structural level, symbolize one another." Jean-Paul Sartre, cited in Hélène Cixous and Catherine Clément, *The Newly Born Woman,* trans. Betsy Wing (Minneapolis: University of Minnesota Press, 1986), 7.

35. My reading will venture to make a case for the centrality of the daughter figure rather than the student. The alternative reading, represented by Daviau, stresses the symmetry between teacher and student: both are "students" who try to force the hand of higher authorities and unleash their power upon Taube. If we concentrate on this double triangulation in the story (Student-Alchemist-Taube, Alchemist-God-Taube), the forgotten player is Taube, whose role in both scenarios is that of passive victim. Taube too acts on her own behalf to escape destiny; moreover, she is the critical arbitrator in this text, the "third term," as signified in part by the critical role of dance in the pantomime.

36. "Gekleidet im gewöhnlichen Gaze- und Trikot-Kostüme und umhergaukelnd in den banalsten Pirouetten." Heinrich Heine, *Der Doktor Faust,* ed. Joseph A. Kruse (Stuttgart: Philipp Reclam, 1991), 14.

37. Jeffrey L. Sammons, *Heinrich Heine* (Princeton: Princeton University Press, 1980), 290.

38. Mephistophela overcomes Faust's resistance by conjuring forth an ape who metamorphoses into a slender ballet dancer. When the beautiful woman in the mirror reaches out her arms to that man, arousing Faust's jealous horror, he hastily agrees to sign the pact in blood.

39. Heinrich Heine, "Atta Troll," st. 6, in *Heines Werke,* vol. 2 (Berlin: Aufbau, 1974), 27.

40. See Sammons, *Heine,* 290, and Joseph A. Kruse's afterword to Heine, *Der Doktor Faust,* 110–12.

41. Dancing is an even more compelling symbol of social membership given the fact that Jews were believed to have deformed feet. See Sander L. Gilman, "The Jewish Foot," in *The Jew's Body,* 38–59.

42. The character configuration of *Der Schüler*—father, daughter, suitor, golem—denotes its status as a variant golem text. In Rudolf Lothar's version of 1899, the daughter must overcome her repulsion toward the ugly creature to perceive that he embodies the soul of her bridegroom; in Arthur Holitscher's *Der Golem* (1908), the father is vicariously punished for controlling life and death by his daughter's suicide.

43. The small notice appears under the headline "Literarisches." "Hugo v. Hofmannsthal has written a pantomime for the Young-Vienna Theater 'Zum lieben Augustin' that plays in the Prague ghetto. From what we have heard, one of our own Jewish actors will be chosen for the part. *Die Welt* 5, no. 42 (1901): 10. "Das Jung-Wiener Theater Zum lieben Augustin" was a literary cabaret started by Felix Salten that opened in November 1901 and closed after only a few performances.

44. Beate Rosenfeld's 1934 study traces the reception of the golem legend in German literature. Referring

specifically to Pernath, the hero of Meyrink's *Golem*, Rosenfeld comments: "Jeder Schritt zur Erkenntnis bedeutet zugleich einen Schritt weiter in der Erinnerung; Wissen und Erinnerung . . . sind nach Meyrink dasselbe, und die Erlösung ist nichts anderes als ein Zurück-findung des Menschen in der Ursprung seines Seins." Beate Rosenfeld, *Die Golemsage und ihre Verwertung in der deutschen Literatur* (Breslau: Hans Priebatsch, 1934), 165.

45. In Hasidic folklore, a dybbuk, from the Hebrew word meaning "to cleave," is a disembodied spirit forbidden to transmigrate on account of past sins.

46. "Dauer / Zeit, Sein / Werden," "Das ich als Sein und das Ich als Werden"

47. Peter Szondi elaborates: "Wichtig ist der Gegensatz Sein und Zeit, es könnte auch heißen Sein und Werden oder Dauer und Zeit. Hofmannsthal hat darin eine der Grundantinomien des Daseins gesehen . . . und gesagt, diese beide seien in seinem Werk zu lösen gewesen. . . . Das Über-ich, die präexistentielle Ich-form ist dem Sein untertan und über die Zeit erhaben, das heißt: es lebt in der zeitlosen Dauer, in einer Welt ohne Geschichte." *Das lyrische Drama des Fin de Siècle* (Frankfurt am Main: Suhrkamp Taschenbuch Wissenschaft, 1975), 345.

48. In traditional kinship systems and the cultural and social codes that grew out of them, daughters pose a threat to the certainty of lineage that is wholly absent in the case of sons. They represent a potential disruption of filiation should they "marry out" or otherwise stray from the patriarchal domain. A father will confine his daughter, then render her an extension of himself by treating her as property to be exchanged or sacrificed according to his will. Daughters' behaviors fall on a continuum from rebellion to victimization. By marrying, daughters only confirm or renounce their origins; in other cases, daughters are called upon to "redeem" the father by undergoing a test of loyalty, often at cost of their lives. Fictional daughters—here Antigone is an important prototype—are frequently depicted at the moment when they engage with "daughterliness" as such, a liminal moment when they must choose compliance or disobedience. Linda E. Boose, "The Father's House and the Daughter in It: The Structures of Western Culture's Daughter-Father Relationship," in *Daughters and Fathers*, ed. Linda E. Boose and Betty S. Flowers (Baltimore: Johns Hopkins University Press, 1989), 19–74.

49. This is one of five novellas comprising *Erzählungen aus dem jüdischen Familienleben* [Tales from Jewish Family Life], in *Gesammelte Werke*, vol. 1 (Stuttgart: Eduard Hallberger, 1878).

50. "'Gott der Allmächtige!' stammelte er, 'wenn ich lebendig durchkomm', so bin ich menadder (gelobe ich), daß ich Wolf Breitenbach mein Kind geb' und ihm anbiet' und ihn um Verzeihung bitt'.". . ."Er hatte gethan, was er zu thun nur vermochte; wie die Verlobten im Tempel hatte er dem Herrn ein Täubchen geopfert" (ibid., 147).

51. The English translation is by Caitlin Zacharias. "Es war eine alte Jüdin / Ein grimmig gelbes Weib; / Sie hatt' eine schöne Tochter; / Ihr Haar war schön geflochten; / Mit Perlen, so viel sie mochte / Zu ihrem Hochzeitskleid. // "Ach liebste, liebste Mutter, / Wie tut mir's Herz so weh;— / In meinem geblümten Kleide / Ach laß mich eine Weile / Spazieren auf grüner Heide, / Bis an die blaue See.'" // "'Gut Nacht! Gut Nacht Herz Mutter, / Du siehst mich nimmermehr; / Zum Meere will ich laufen / Und sollt ich auch ersaufen; / Es muß mich heute taufen; / Es stürmet gar zu sehr!'" This is the shortest version of the ballad by Albert Ludwig Grimm that appeared in *Des Knaben Wunderhorn*, and it was abridged by Achim von Arnim for inclusion in his novella *Die Majoratsherren*. Achim von Arnim, *Sämtliche Erzählungen, 1818–1830*, ed. Renate Meoring (Frankfurt am Main: Deutscher Klassiker, 1992), 1055–56.

52. "Die Mutter wandt den Rücken / Die Tochter sprang in die Gaß, / Wo alle Schreiber saßen: / 'Ach liebster, liebster Schreiber! / Was thut mir mein Herz so weh!'" // "'Wenn du dich lässest taufen, / Luisa sollst du heißen, / Mein Weibchen sollst du seyn.' / 'Eh ich mich lasse taufen, / Lieber will ich mich versaufen / Ins tiefe, tiefe Meer.'" Clemens Brentano, *Sämtliche Werke und Briefe*, vol. 6, no. 1 (Stuttgart: W. Kolhammer, 1975), 237; see also critical notes in vol. 9, no. 1, 432–33.

53. "'Ach Jüdin, liebste Jüdin, / daß kann fürwahr nicht sein! / Hättest du dich lassen taufen, / Ein Ringlein wollt ich dir kaufen, / Sollst mir die Liebste sein.'" // "'Ach Schreiber, liebster Schreiber, / Schreib meiner Mutter 'nen Brief, / Schreib mich und dich zusammen, / Schreib ihr in Gottes Namen, / Eine Christin wollt ich sein.'" // "'Ach Jüdin, liebste Jüdin, / Das kann fürwahr nicht sein! / Das wär mir eine Schande / Im ganzen Christenlande, / Wollt ich 'ne Jüdin frein.'" Author unknown; poem found in an anonymously edited volume in the Gershom Scholem Library, Hebrew University of Jerusalem.

54. William Shakespeare, *The Merchant of Venice* (Cambridge: Cambridge University Press, 1987), 2.5.34–36.

55. Ibid., 51, 53–55.

56. Ibid., 56–57.

57. In the same scene, Shylock likens himself to the biblical Jacob, who became rich through cunning: Jacob crosses his father-in-law by strategically cross-breeding cattle (Genesis 30). Jacob is the correct prototype here—the hairless, daughterly son who "dwells in tents" (Genesis 25:27) and who resorts to cunning, in alliance with his mother, to challenge the patriarchy. In another respect, when Jacob dons Esau's hairy garb to trick his blind father, he is acting out the daughter plot. In this respect, Jessica is the truer Jacob figure in the play, as is Taube, who must beard herself to pass the inspection of the father's blind maid.

58. The dancing Mademoiselle Laurence of Heine's second Florentine Night articulates how dancing facilitates recollection. Referring to the story of her origins as a "death child" (*Totenkind*) she comments: "These words, which seemed to ascend from the earth, mingled together fearful tales—tales which I never understood in their connection, and which later on I gradually forgot; but when I danced they would again come into my mind with living power. Yes, when I danced a singular remembrance seized me; I forgot myself, and I seemed to be quite another person, and as if all the sorrows and secrets of this person were poisoning me, and as soon as I left off dancing it was all extinguished in my memory.'" *The Prose Writings of Heinrich Heine*, ed. Havelock Ellis (London: W. Scott, 1887; repr., New York: Arno Press, 1973), 238.

59. Oscar Wilde, *Salomé* (Boston: John W. Luce, 1903), 5.

60. *Taubes Gesicht verklärt sich, sie wiegt sich in den Hüften, setzt die Füße im Tanz, spielt mit ihrem aufgelösten Haar wie mit einem Schleier. / . . . Meister: Nun ist es genug. / Taube steht, wie zu sich gekommen, purpurrot, mit gesenkten Augen, stark atmend. / Der Schüler, an der Tür, verschlingt sie mit den Blicken. / Meister: Nein geh, mein Kind, ruh dich aus. / Taube schwankt wie aufgelöst in ihre Kammer.*

61. Maximilian's response to Mademoiselle Laurence's dance in the Florentine Night is a case in point. He obsessively quests, in vain, after its "significance." "There was an intoxicated absence of will about her dance, something gloomy and inevitable; it was like the dance of fate. Or was it a fragment of some venerable forgotten pantomime? Or was she dancing her personal history?" *Prose Writings*, 218–19. She dominates his thoughts: "But I could not forget Mademoiselle Laurence; she danced in my memory for a long time." Ibid., 221. His final account of her dance shows him to be as haunted and mystified by this memory dance as ever.

"This dance with closed eyes in the silent nocturnal chamber gave this sweet being so ghostly an appearance that a disagreeable feeling seized me; I shuddered, and was heartily glad when she finished her dance." Ibid., 242. Arnim's Majoratsherr responds in a similar way to the mad Esther's nightly pantomimes he observes from his window. Only later is his attraction explained: Esther is his parents' true daughter, who was given away to Jews in order to create a space for him, an illegitimate son.

62. Christine Froula voices this criticism in reference to several texts, including *Studies on Hysteria*, in "The Daughter's Seduction: Sexual Violence and Literary History," in Cixous and Clément, *The Newly Born Woman*. A more radical condemnation of the male "filter"—the doctor, judge, or writer positioned to "cure" the woman (of her femininity)—can be found in Cixous and Clément's identification of "hysteric and sorceress" in the same volume.

63. The two original titles of this text, *Der Mirza Hochzeitsnacht* and *Die junge Frau, eine orientalische Erzählung dramatisiert*, confirm Sobeide's oriental heritage. Hofmannsthal's orientalism represented a fertile model of memory, as his ballet *Josephslegende* confirms.

64. In notable contrast to *Der Schüler*, this daughter remarks as she nurses her father, "It is too dark to read in her. I want to dance for you. Shall I?" Then, "The daughter dances a gavotte, with noiseless steps and deep bows, when there is a knock on the door. She pauses. Enter the suitor, roses in hand." Like the Bocher, this petulant suitor is rejected, much to the relief of the father. Later, by the light of the moon, the rival suitor, or "the daughter's secret lover," makes his appearance, causing a violent disruption. The daughter's dancing and the loosening of her hair in the third act, "Hour of Remembering," symbolize her liberation from the father's will and new power of self-determination (Hofmannsthal, *Dramen VI*, 35–42).

65. Hugo von Hofmannsthal, *Erzählungen, Erfundene Gespräche und Briefes: Reisen,* ed. Bernd Schoeller (Frankfurt am Main: Fischer Taschenbuch, 1979), 577. "Die [Furcht] hält oben die Fäden, die Mitten in unserem Leib befestigt sind, und reißt uns hierhin und dorthin und macht unsre Glieder fliegen."

66. Ibid., 574–75. "Bist du nur einen Augenblick glücklich? . . . Kannst du dich vergesssen, ganz alle Furcht loswerden, jeden Schatten loswerden, der das Blut in deinen Adern verdüstert?"

67. Gabriele Brandstetter, "Der Traum vom anderen Tanz: Hofmannsthals Ästhetik des Schöpferischen im Dialog 'Furcht,'" in "Hugo von Hofmannsthal: Dichtung

als Vermittlung der Künste," ed. Gottfried Schramm, special issue, *Freiburger Universitätsblätter* 112 (June 1991): 37–58.

68. "Du springst hin und wieder: flüchtest du vor dir selber? . . . Du äffst die Gebärden der Tiere und Bäume: wirst du eins mit ihnen? Du steigst aus deinem Gewand. Steigst du aus deiner Furcht?"

69. Lorna Martens, "The Theme of Repressed Memory in Hofmannsthal's *Elektra*," *German Quarterly* 60 (1987): 38–51; Reinhold Schötterer, "Elektras Tanz in der Tragödie Hugo von Hofmannsthals," *Hofmannsthal Blätter* 33 (1986): 56.

70. "Eifersüchtig sind / die Toten: und er schickte mir den Haß, den hohläugigen Haß als Bräutigam. / Da mußt ich den Gräßlichen, der atmet / wie eine Viper, über mich in mein / schlafloses Bette lassen, der mich zwang, / alles zu wissen, wie es zwischen Mann / und Weib zugeht." Hugo von Hofmannsthal, *Dramen II, 1892–1905*, ed. Bernd Schoeller (Frankfurt am Main: S. Fischer, 1979), 63.

71. "Diese süßen Schauder / hab ich dem Vater opfern müssen" (ibid., 63).

72. "Ein namenloser Tanz, in welchem sie nach vorwärts schreitet" (ibid., 74).

73. See aphorism 52, "Mit dem Fusse schreiben" (Writing with One's Feet). "Not with my hand alone I write / My foot wants to participate" (Ich schreib nicht mit der Hand allein / der Fuss will stets mit schreiber sein). Friedrich Nietzsche, *The Gay Science*, 2nd ed., trans. Walter Kaufmann (New York: Vintage Books, 1974), 62–63.

74. "Eine Sprache . . . in welcher ich vielleicht einst im Grabe vor einem unbekannten Richter mich verantworten werde."

CHAPTER 3

1. Werner Vordtriede, "Gespräche mit Beer-Hofmann," *Die Neue Rundschau* 63 (April 1952): 132.

2. "Da ist nämlich eben jene Frage des Mittuns im Leben. Einer hat das Gefühl, daß er nicht mehr weiter mitgehen könne, weil mit jedem Schritt, den er mache, so vieles, so viele Möglichkeiten und Keime zu andrem Leben zerstört würden. Aber dann: wenn er stehenbleibt, so verdorrt das, was ihm unmittelbar unter den Füßen wächst. Aus diesem unlösbaren Problem heraus kommt das Buch." Ibid.

3. "Wenn er sprach, meinte er das Antlitz seiner Worte zu sehen, die der mühevolle Dienst des Alltags verzerrt und kraftlos und niedrig gemacht." Richard Beer-Hofmann, *Der Tod Georgs*, ed. Alo Allkemper, vol.

3 of *Grosse Richard Beer-Hofmann-Ausgabe*, ed. Günter Hermes, Michael M. Schardt, and Andreas Thomasberger (Paderborn: Igel-Verlag Literatur, 1994), 26. All references to *Der Tod Georgs* are to this edition, and will be noted by page number in the text. English translations are my own.

4. "Der graue Schutt gleich verrinnender Tage."

5. The novella was composed over a critical period in the author's personal development. He began writing the work, which he originally titled "Der Götterliebling" (The Gods' Favorite), after the publication in Berlin of his first two stories, "Camelias" and "Das Kind," in 1893, but the writing did not progress. The impasse was breached in 1895 when Beer-Hofmann met sixteen-year-old Paula Lissy. By all accounts, the relationship with Paula catalyzed the creative process. The bulk of the novella was written in 1897–98. A daughter, Mirjam, was born in 1897. Richard and Paula married in 1898, and a second daughter, Naemah, was born that same year. See Sarah Fraiman, *Judaism in the Works of Beer-Hofmann and Feuchtwanger* (New York: Peter Lang, 1998), 18–21; and Ulrike Peters, *Richard Beer-Hofmann: Zum jüdischen Selbstverständnis im Wiener Judentum um die Jahrhundertwende* (Frankfurt am Main: Peter Lang, 1993).

6. Bahr unreservedly praises the work as a hard-won linguistic accomplishment—"In it, our hard and grand language has been so hewn and carved and chiseled and smoothened and straightened out that it has acquired a completely alien sheen and new sharpness, [to the point] that you often don't even recognize [the language] anymore"—while judging the cumulative effect to be not one of poetic escalation but rather of formal dissipation resulting in the "suppression" of meaning. *Neues Wiener Tagblatt,* March 24, 1900.

7. Letter to Beer-Hofmann, March 2, 1900, in *Briefwechsel, 1891–1931*, by Arthur Schnitzler and Richard Beer-Hofmann, ed. Konstanze Fliedl (Vienna: Europaverlag, 1992), 144 (hereinafter cited as *Schnitzler/Beer-Hofmann Briefwechsel*). The fact that the novella's development is "arbitrary" leads Lukács to conclude: "Therefore what beauty is contained in these novellas can only be of a purely *lyrical character.*" Georg von Lukács, "Der Augenblick und die Formen," in *Die Seele und die Formen* (Berlin: Egon Fleischel, 1911), 253. One contemporary reviewer separated form from content, designating the novella "a psychological analysis in poetic language." Another found, however, a middle ground between prose and lyric: "the whole is neither philosophy or poetry: it's actually music." Alexander von Welien, *Beilage zur Allgemeine Zeitung,* January 1, 1901.

8. Alfred Gold, "Aesthetik des Sterbens," *Die Zeit,* February 24, 1900, 122.

9. Letter to Beer-Hofmann, March 2, 1900, in *Schnitzler/Beer-Hofmann Briefwechsel,* 144. See also Oskar Baum's essay on Beer-Hofmann in Krojanker, *Juden in der deutschen Literatur,* 200–201.

10. Hartmut Scheible, *Literarischer Jugendstil in Wien* (Munich: Artemis, 1984), 148–49.

11. Rainer Hank, *Mortifikation und Beschwörung: Zur Veränderung ästhetischer Wahrnehmung in der Moderne am Beispiel des Frühwerkes Richard Beer-Hofmanns* (Frankfurt am Main: Peter Lang, 1984), 166.

12. Ibid.,192–93, and Scheible, *Literarischer Jugendstil,* 166.

13. Undocumented citation, Beer-Hofmann Collection, Houghton Library, Harvard University.

14. Walter Sokel, "Narzißmus und Judentum: Zum Oeuvre Richard Beer-Hofmanns," in *Zeitgenossenschaft: Zur deutschsprachigen Literatur im 20. Jahrhundert: Festschrift für Egon Schwartz zum 65. Geburtstag,* ed. Paul Michael Lützeler (Frankfurt am Main: Athenäum, 1987), 33–47.

15. See Judith Ryan, "The New Psychologies," in *The Vanishing Subject: Early Psychology and Literary Modernism* (Chicago: University of Chicago Press, 1991), 6–22.

16. The fluid effects of narrated monologue as Dorrit Cohn has analyzed them converge precisely with the challenge this narrator has lined up for Paul. The technique discreetly fuses the unconscious and conscious dimensions of the mind, and moreover, can convey "a fictional mind suspended in an instant present, between a remembered past and an anticipated future." Dorrit Cohn, *Transparent Minds: Narrative Modes for Presenting Consciousness in Fiction* (Princeton: Princeton University Press, 1978), 126; see also 99–140.

17. "Wie mondhell das Zimmer war! Und das da an der Wand war der schwarze Schatten des Fensterkreuzes. Georg schlief da drinnen. Wie ein Gitter von schwarzen Herzen sah das Laub der Linde vor dem Fenster aus.— Was das für ein Duft war, den der Wind da durchs offene Fenster trug? Kam der aus dem Garten? Oder waren das frischgemähte Wiesen auf den Bergen?—Er schlief."

18. "Nichts sah er ahnenlos."

19. "Greisenhaft verzerrt und beladen mit der Last von Erinnerungen, und sich schleppend mit Ketten, die es an Gewesenes schmiedeten."

20. "Eigensinn folgte er den Spuren aller Dinge nach rückwärts, bis ihre Wege mit den Wegen alles Lebens unlöslich sich verschlangen."

21. "Vergangenes, und was um ihn täglich sich erfüllte, war ihm gleich nahe gewesen. Längst kalt gewordene Taten, von denen nur ein matter Schein, verblassend, durch Jahrhunderte zu den Lebenden herüberdämmerte, hatte er mit fiebernden Händen an sich herangerückt, und noch zuckende Schicksale lebendiger Menschen, die um ihn gedrängt, mit ihm zugleich die Erde traten, solange mit abwehrend sich spreizenden Fingern von sich ferne gehalten, bis beides—Totes und Lebendiges—gleich weit von ihm, wie auf derselben Bühne, schattenhaft sich selbst zu spielen schien."

22. Walter Benjamin, *Das Passagen-Werk,* vol. 1, ed. Rolf Tiedemann (Frankfurt am Main: Suhrkamp, 1982), 465.

23. On the question of Mach's reception by the Young Vienna authors, see Claudia Monti, "Mach und die österreichische Literatur: Bahr, Hofmannsthal, Musil," in *Akten des Internationalen Symposiums: "Arthur Schnitzler und seine Zeit,"* ed. Giuseppe Farese (Bern: Peter Lang, 1985), 263–83; and Martens, *Shadow Lines,* 237–39.

24. Hermann Bahr, *Dialog vom Tragischen* (Berlin: S. Fischer, 1904), 113.

25. Henri Bergson, *Matter and Memory,* 3rd ed., trans. N. M. Paul and W. S. Palmer (New York: Zone Books, 1991), 134.

26. Impressionism, for example, relies on the *Vergessenszwang* by requiring the eye to perceive nothing more than surface reality. It originates, according to Wunberg, in a sociohistorical condition related to the problem of "too much memory," discussed in the introduction. "The thesis that an aesthetics of modernity can be deduced from the historically determined, specific dialectics of forgetting and remembering, relies completely on proving that for this modernity something specifically new, or at least not previously seen in this form, exists: an excess of information [*Informationsüberschuss*]." Gotthart Wunberg, *Wiedererkennen: Literatur und Ästhetischer Wahrnehmung in der Moderne* (Tübingen: Gunter Narr, 1983), 78. See also 75–112.

27. "Vor einer der großen sandsteinernen Urnen, die den Platz umsäumten, standen sie still, unschlüssig, in welche Allee sie einbiegen sollten. In der sonnenlosen nebeligen Luft schienen ihre Gestalten körperlos, nur Schatten, von unsichtbaren Leibern an die graue steinerne Masse der Urne geworfen. Sie lösten sich von ihr, wurden von breiten Stämmen gedeckt, glitten hinter ihnen hervor, und schienen, wie gefangen hinter dem schwarzen starren Netz dürrer Hecken, immer weiter zu irren."

28. "Dann glitten die Ringe, die sonst ängstlich einen

Gedanken an den andern ketteten, von einander—und über kühne pfeilerlose Brücken, die sich schwindelnd wölbten, schritten nachtwandelnd seine Gedanken."

29. The architectonic of Paul's escapist imagination also incorporates what Mikhail Bakhtin terms the "adventure chronotope . . . characterized by a *technical, abstract connection between space and time,* by the *reversibility* of moments in a temporal sequence, and by their *interchangeability* in space." Mikhail Bakhtin, *The Dialogic Imagination: Four Essays,* ed. Michael Holquist, trans. Caryl Emerson and Michael Holquist (Austin: University of Texas Press, 1981), 100.

30. "In gewundenen labyrinthischen Wegen lief ihr Leben, mit dem Anderer seltsam verkettet. Was einem Irrweg glich, führte ans Ziel."

31. Mach too employs the topos of the labyrinth to convey the degree to which memory traces become unmoored from their unique place in time and adjoin to an infinite number of new associations. "Now since ideas [*Vorstellungen*] have their roots in very different realms of emotion, and since these realms of emotion are related to different memories which were acquired individually and can therefore also be lost individually— human memory does consist of a bundle of individual memories—the reciprocal awakening of ideas via the biological interest leads man through the strangest labyrinths." "Psychisches und organisches Leben," in *Populärwissenschaftliche Vorlesungen,* 5th ed. (Vienna: Böhlau, 1987), 556.

32. Letter to Schnitzler, June 18, 1898, in *Schnitzler/Beer-Hofmann Briefwechsel,* 120; letter to Hofmannsthal, August 5, 1898, in *Hofmannsthal/Beer-Hofmann Briefwechsel,* 81.

33. Windows play a central role in *Sterben* as well as in Hofmannsthal's *Die Frau im Fenster.* See Rainer Hank's exposition of this and other window intertexts in *Mortifikation und Beschwörung,* 89–94; see also Werner Kraft, "Das Fenster," in *Wort und Gedanke* (Bern: Francke, 1959).

34. "Das frühere Bild war verloren."

35. Critics have noted a number of details that stylize the deathbed scene after the Passion, with Paul as Judas and his wife as Jesus—a reading that bears little relation to the larger plot (see Jens Malte Fischer, "Richard Beer-Hofmann, 'Der Tod Georgs': Sprachstil, Leitmotiv und Jugendstil in einer Erzählung der Jahrhundertwende," *Sprachkunst* 2, nos. 2–3 (1971): 221–22). The exclaimed "Jesus," like the omnipresent *Fensterkreuz,* invokes a death experience whose mythic, and hence semiotic, relevance exceeds its Christian meaning. It refers, rather, to

a reconception of temporality wherein each moment becomes a juncture of time and infinity.

36. "Keine leeren Stunden, die nur die Brücken zu erhofften reicheren waren; und nichts, das wertlos am Wege stand und an dem man fremd vorüberging. Ihm hatten alle Dinge ihr Antlitz zugewandt—er konnte nicht an ihnen vorüber; um seinetwillen waren sie da, und ihr Schicksal vermochte er nicht von dem seinen zu lösen. Er stand auf und tratt ans Fenster."

37. "Woher er nur kam? Von ganz nah schien er zu kommen; in unregelmäßigen Zwischenräumen klang er immer wieder in sein Schläfern und machte ihn wach. Er setzte sich aufrecht."

38. "Einen Augenblick lang nur folgte er dem grünlichen Schillern der Flasche, die hin- und herrollte, dann waren seine Gedanken weit weg von ihr, und er mußte an Georgs Sarg denken, der allein im Gepäckwagen stand, geschüttelt vom Stoßen des Zuges oder vielleicht zur Seite geschleudert, wenn der Zug holpernd über Weichen fuhr—."

39. "Starr und wehrlos . . . wie in einer Kiste, nur viel schlechter und nachlässiger als ein Ding gepackt."

40. Nets symbolize the way in which both dreaming and dying entrap us, in Paul's way of thinking: "Or had death tied together the net that had cast dreams over Georg, and, trapped under it, had he lived the life that dreams commanded?" (Oder hatte der Tod das Netz zusammengeschnürt, das Träume über Georg geworfen, und, gefangen unter ihm, hatte er das Leben gelebt, das Träume befahlen?) (100).

41. "Alles Zufällige und Launenhafte der Landstraße schien von seinem Weg entfernt. Unabweichbar lief sein Weg."

42. Claudio, Hofmannsthal's "fool," is a baroque-style aesthete who recovers his will to live while standing on death's threshold. Death appears in person to grant Claudio a chance to reencounter his life in retrospect, inviting the shades of his mother, lover, and best friend to recapitulate the episodes of his misspent life. To him belongs the famous resolution "Da tot mein Leben war, sei du mein Leben, Tod!" (Because my life was dead, you, death, be my life!). Schnitzler's *Sterben* narrates, in a painfully protracted manner, a writer's decline over several months while tended by his very much alive, younger lover. When Felix first falls ill and announces to Maria that his illness is terminal, she vows to die together with him. The plot surrounds Felix's growing determination to hold her to that promise as his condition worsens, while much to her own consternation, her will to live intensifies. In this way Schnitzler details the

stages of psychological rebirth as a direct if involuntary response to death; he depicts the growing rift between the two figures as it transpires internally via a blend of two narrative styles, *erlebte Rede* and internal monologue. The novella is structured by numerous motifs and symbols that found their way into *Der Tod Georgs*.

43. The affinities, contrasts, and common influences that mark the oeuvres of these three friends have been explored by Dorrit Cohn, who locates this novella within a different triadic configuration. Dorrit Cohn, "A Triad of Dream Narratives: *Der Tod Georgs, Das Märchen der 672. Nacht, Traumnovelle,*" in *Focus on Vienna: Change and Continuity in Literature, Music, Art, and Intellectual History,* ed. Erika Nielson (Munich: Fink, 1982), 58–71.

44. Peter Brooks, *Reading for the Plot: Design and Intention in Narrative* (Cambridge, Mass.: Harvard University Press, 1984), 22.

45. Benno von Wiese's introduction to *Die deutsche Novelle von Goethe bis Kafka,* ed. Benno von Wiese (Düsseldorf: August Bagel, 1971), 11–32. I concur with Georg von Lukács's assessment, along with the general thrust of his reading (though not his conclusions), which assumes a far greater connection between the formalistic dynamics, the plot, and the hermeneutic dilemmas that arise in the act of reading than do most interpreters (Lukács, "Der Augenblick und die Formen").

46. Umberto Eco, "An *Ars Oblivionalis?* Forget It!" *PMLA* 103, no. 3 (1988): 254–61. See also Renate Lachmann, "Text als Mnemotechnik—Panorama einer Diskussion," in *Gedächtniskunst: Raum—Bild—Schrift: Studien zur Mnemotechnik,* ed. Anselm Haverkamp and Renate Lachmann (Frankfurt am Main: Suhrkamp, 1991), 20.

47. "Wie Kostbarkeiten in verschütteten Schatzhäusern geflohener Könige, hatte es lange geruht, bis Georgs Wort es gehoben. . . . Heiß und süß und duftend wie ein Schlaftrunk bot sich dem Sterbenden dies alles; und sie standen da, diese Dinge, mit offenen Augen, das Antlitz ihm zugewandt, als hätten die letzten Stunden sie mit ihrem wahren Namen angerufen."

48. Ewald Hering's metaphor: the one who stands behind the stages needs to take advantage of the spectator's vantage point to watch the action from outside as well as inside. Ewald Hering, *Über das Gedächtnis als eine allgemeine Funktion der organisierten Materie* (Leipzig: Wilhelm Engelmann, 1905), 5.

49. "Wie die Augen der Künstler an allen Dingen tasten und die Form um ihr Schicksal fragen—woher sie geworden und wohin sic wird—so hätten seine Augen voll Frage auf leidenden Menschen geruht."

50. "Aus dem eigenen Leben der Kranken, das hinter ihnen versank, holte Georg Linderung für sie. Kinder, die sie gezeugt, ließ er an ihrem Bett sitzen—und Kindeskinder. . . . Erinnerungen, die das Leben lange verscheucht, lockte Georg mit seinen Worten, bis sie wieder mit lichten stillfächelnden Flügeln heranglitten, und rastend auf dem Bettrand niedersaßen."

51. Ewald Hering, *Über das Gedächtnis,* 12.

52. Hering challenged the empiricism of Helmholtz in the name of a post-Lamarckian school of thought that identified memory as the "Urvermögen" (primal capability) of organized matter, broadly defining memory as the ability to retain, reproduce, and organically transmit acquired characteristics. For a discussion of Hering and his influence, see Laura Otis, *Organic Memory: History and the Body in the Late Nineteenth and Early Twentieth Centuries* (Lincoln: University of Nebraska Press, 1994).

53. Ernst Mach, *Die Analyse der Empfindungen und das Verhältnis des Physischen zum Psychischen,* 9th ed. (Darmstadt: Wissenschaftliche Buchgesellschaft, 1985), 141.

54. "So now the behavior of the living being becomes more complicated, as it is now constantly *changed* by the residual traces of its experiences. The more primitive the animal is, the more its behavior is innate, machine-like. The more developed it is, the more powerful becomes his memory, the richer its experience and influence on his behavior." Ernst Mach, "Leben und Erkennen," in *Populärwissenschaftliche Vorlesungen,* 5th ed. (Leipzig: J. A. Barth, 1923; repr., Vienna: Böhlau, 1987), 490.

55. Mach, *Analyse der Empfindungen,* 192.

56. Ibid.

57. "Because the organic beings are not rigid material systems, but essentially dynamic balanced forms of streams of 'matter' and 'energy.' Once they have been rerouted, the deviations of these streams from the dynamic state of balance recur always in the same manner" (ibid., 194).

58. "The memory traces [*Erinnerungsspuren*] of previous sensation-experiences which are crucial in determining the fate of newly entering sensation-complexes, and which inconspicuously weave themselves together with the latter and, spinning these further, connect themselves with the sensation-experience—we shall call these memory traces representations" (ibid.).

59. "And he lived as in dreary overcrowded rooms. . . . But windowless and locked, the room contracted, and all that crowded around him in oppressive disarray seized his breath and stole the air he needed to live" (Alles war mit allem unlösbar verknotet, Gewesenes stand neben ihm aufrecht wie Lebendiges, und er lebte wie in dumpfen menschenüberfüllten Räumen. . . . Aber

fensterlos und versperrt engte sich der Raum, und alles was in gepreßtem Gewühl sich um ihn drängte, nahm ihm selbst den Atem und stahl ihm seine Lebensluft).

60. "Wie das Korn in trockenen Speichern."

61. Wolfgang Schivelbusch, *Geschichte der Eisenbahnreise* (Munich: Carl Hanser, 1977), provides a fascinating discussion of the numerous physiological and psychological issues raised by this redefinition of the travel experience.

62. "Später vielleicht erst würde er um ihn trauern können."

63. Sigmund Freud, *Mourning and Melancholia, SE,* 14:245; *SA,* 3:199.

64. William James, *The Principles of Psychology,* vol. 1 (New York: Dover, 1950), 654–55.

65. George Poulet, *L'espace Proustien* (Paris: Gallimard, 1963), 92.

66. Bergson, *Matter and Memory,* 138.

67. The empiricist equivalent to the fusion of past and present is called "Verzögerung" (delay), the moment when two sensations overlap and retention occurs. "Something . . . is either wholly or in part still in that place which it should already have left in the case of an undisturbed flow to make room for the next thing. Delay here means: at the *same* time *two* are there." Sommer, *Evidenz im Augenblick,* 167.

68. Henri Bergson, *Creative Evolution* (1907), trans. Arthur Mitchell (New York: Modern Library, 1944; repr., Westport, Conn.: Greenwood Press, 1975), 7.

69. Bergson, *Matter and Memory,* 135.

70. As Paul says: "Georg arrived today—he is staying with me; . . . before he moves to Heidelberg he wants to spend a few quiet weeks here" (Georg ist heute gekommen—er wohnt bei mir. . . . bevor er nach Heidelberg geht, will er noch ein paar Wochen hier in Ruhe verbringen) (7). When the novella begins, each has already begun to affect the other's rhythm. Paul puts Georg "to sleep," whereas Georg stimulates Paul to go out into the night. Yet walking proves to be only temporarily restorative. Georg pays lip service to the idea that Georg's fortune, his "Glück," lies in his mobility in all spheres of life: professional accomplishment ("Georg has been appointed a professor in Heidelberg" [Georg ist als Professor nach Heidelberg berufen worden] [7]); thriving health and virility ("You would barely recognize him . . . he has gotten such a tan, and he has grown a full beard, and he has gotten stronger" [Sie würden ihn kaum erkennen . . . so braun hat ihn die Sonne gebrannt; und einen Vollbart trägt er, und stärker ist er geworden] [8]); and progress by way of intention rather than chance

("that determination, that sheer determination and faith in what he wanted!" [und den Willen, den starken Willen, und den Glauben an das was er wollte] [8]). Despite a momentary flash of envy, Paul formulates his own ideal of *Glück* in contradistinction, and in so doing rejects all that Georg represents in the name of his own, passive equilibrium.

71. In reviewing the trying events of previous days, Paul mentions "the argument with the coffin maker who had wanted to squeeze Georg's corpse into a too short coffin" (der Streit mit dem Sargtischler, der Georgs Leichnam in einen zu kurz geratenen Sarg hineinzwängen wollte) (69).

72. "Und später, viel später, wenn seine Augen, die dann nicht mehr viel erhofften, den suchen würden, der dieselben Sommer wie er 'Jugend' nannte und in dessen kühlem Altern Erinnerungen sich heiß und süß emporsogen, wenn er zu ihm sagte: 'Weißt du noch?'"

73. "Was dazwischen lag, war nur leerer Weg gewesen, und erst an den Zielen stand man still, und in Erreichtem empfand man mit Gefallen den Inhalt seines Lebens?"

74. "Oder war er von denen, die wußten, daß ihr Leben floß, und das Wasser nicht stillstand, um sich selber zu besehen? Und die wußten, daß man es nicht in Krüge fassen konnte, um in die gefangene Flut zu starren und ihr zu sagen: '*Du* bist mein Leben.'. . . und daß verborgenes Denken in uns, Hauch und Schall und Worte ward, die sich zitternd von unseren Lippen schwangen, und hallend zu uns zurückkamen und, Antlitz an Antlitz mit unseren Gedanken, wie schreckerstarrte Doppelgänger standen."

75. "Georg hatte dem Fenster den Rücken gewandt, und das Licht umrandete hell seine Wangen die braun gebrannt von der Sonne waren. Voll und ruhig ausschwingend klang Georgs tiefe Stimme, leise umschwirrt von dem laurieselnden Regen, wie von einem fernen Flügelrauschen endlos hinziehender Vogelschwärme. Ein Jahr lang hatten sie einander nicht gesehen; sie sprachen von fast gleichgültigen Dingen, und ihre Reden reihten sich eintönig und gleich aneinander, wie in den dumpf dämmernden Sälen alter Paläste die hohen mit Läden geschlossenen Fenster; aber sie wußten: wenn eines sich öffnete, lag draußen hell vor ihnen wie leuchtendes weit sich dehnendes Land, ihre Freundschaft. Und jetzt war das vorbei; rasch vergangen wie die Zeichen, die einer flüchtig mit dem Finger in angehauchtes trübes Glas schreibt."

76. "Und er fühlte, daß unter aller Trauer, tief in ihm, geweckt durch Georgs Tod, die Freude am eigenen

Lebendigsein schamlos aufjubelte."

77. "Weit über die Brüstung des Fensters lehnte er sich, und bog sich dem Wind entgegen. . . . Einen Augenblick fühlte er sich Antlitz an Antlitz, wie in stummem Ringen, mit dem Wind, dann mußte er reden, und er hörte seine eigene Stimme hell das Rasseln des Zugs durchschneiden. 'Wind,' rief er, 'Wind,' und fühlte es wie Glück, daß Atem über seine Lippen wehte und dem Wind seinen Namen gab, und ihn, den Starken, zwang, den Hall seines eigenen Namens ein Stück weit mit sich zu tragen."

78. "Jedes Ding ist für uns erst da, wenn es benannt ist." "Form-Chaos," in *Gesammelte Werke* (Frankfurt am Main: S. Fischer, 1963), 628.

79. "Paul schloß das Fenster, dann trat er zurück ins Coupé."

80. "Wie der Zug in eine Kurve einbog, sah er den letzten Wagen. Da drinnen lag Georg. Paul dachte daran, wie er ihn zuletzt gesehen."

81. "Grauenhaft verzerrt waren hier die Häßlichkeiten des Alters gehäuft."

82. "Denn Mund und Augen waren nur Löcher, unfähig, die Spuren von Erlebtem in sich aufzubewahren."

83. "Im Wiederholen hatte sich das Lächeln verzerrt; weil ihm Dauer gegeben ward, am Leben selbst, war es häßlich geworden."

84. Such a conception of life grounds itself, writes Bergson, in phenomena of material destruction, disregarding the fact that evolution determines old age no less than embryonic development. "Here calculation touches, at most, certain phenomena of organic *destruction.* Organic *creation,* on the contrary, the evolutionary phenomena which properly constitute life, we cannot in any way subject to a mathematical treatment" (Bergson, *Creative Evolution,* 24; see also 20–25).

85. "Was, *was* war aus ihrem Besitz geworden?" "Aber jeder Tag hatte von ihrem Besitz gestohlen."

86. "Flüchtig war er an manchen vorübergegangen, aber ohne seinen Willen hatte sein Gedächtnis sie aufbewahrt."

87. Le Rider, *Viennese Modernity,* 12.

88. Rieckmann, "(Anti-)Semitism and Homoeroticism," 212.

89. "Welches Zeichen war ihm denn gegeben, daß dies nicht vergänglich in ihm war, daß es ihn nicht verlassen konnte. . . ?"

90. "Aber, was diese Abendstunde ihm gegeben, blieb; immer in ihm und nur in ihm; dem Blut in seinen Adern nicht bloß vergleichbar—sein Blut selbst, das zu

ihm geredet hatte; und darauf zu horchen, hatte diese Stunde gelehrt."

91. "Denn über dem Leben derer, deren Blut in ihm floß, war Gerechtigkeit wie eine Sonne gestanden, deren Strahlen sie nicht wärmten, deren Licht ihnen nie geleuchtet, und vor deren blendendem Glanz sie dennoch mit zitternden Händen, ehrfürchtig ihre leidenerfüllte Stirne beschatteten.

"Vorfahren, die irrend . . . wanderten; Alle gegen sie. . . .

"Und hinter ihnen Allen ein Volk, um Gnaden nicht bettelnd, im Kampf den Segen seines Gottes sich erringend; durch Meere wandernd, von Wüsten nicht aufgehalten, und immer vom Fühlen des gerechten Gottes so durchströmt, wie vom Blut in ihren Adern: ihr Siegen—Gottes Sieg, ihr Unterliegen—Gottes Gericht, sie selbst sich bestimmend von seiner Macht zu zeugen, ein Volk von Erlösern, zu Dornen gesalbt und auserwählt zu Leiden. Und langsam ihren Gott von Opfern und Räucherungen lösend, hoben sie ihn hoch über ihre Häupter, bis er, kein Kampfesgott von Hirten mehr—ein Wahrer allen Rechtes—über vergänglichen Sonnen und Welten, unsichtbar, Allem leuchtend, stand.

"Und von ihrem Blute war auch er."

92. Rainer Hank attempts quite comprehensively to situate this novella within the various discourses and socio-political ideologies available to Viennese Jews at the time, though straying far from the text in the process (*Mortifikation und Beschwörung,* 159–92).

93. Le Rider, *Viennese Modernity,* 329. Along Le Rider's model too, Paul, who at last hears nothing more than "das Schlagen seines eigenen Bluts" (the pulsing of his own blood), must fall short. Fischer and Hank likewise see the conclusion as foreshadowed by the orgiastic Syrian dream segment. Fischer's reading of the work as a whole appears to be strongly influenced by *Death in Venice* (1913), a text that has prominence in his article. I have not read the Syrian orgy as vital to the memory theme; it is to my mind an even more unintegrated segment than the Jewish conclusion. When Paul recalls his dream in chapter 4, he recollects only the death scene, the fish, and the woman; not once does he return to this part of the dream. Hank argues that this is due to repression of a matriarchal, Dionysian model in favor of a patriarchal, judicial model. But though both symbolize reintegration, I find scant textual evidence that the Astarte cult and Jewish heritage are to be read as parallel episodes in the text.

94. An extreme case was Martin Buber's 1909 address to the Prague student Zionist association. Buber, whose ultimate goal was not all that different than that of Beer-

Hofmann, strove to inspire a Jewish reawakening by evoking the (historically suppressed) essence of *Judentum*—a discourse that met with enthusiastic approval. See Stephen M. Poppel, *Zionism in Germany, 1897–1933: The Shaping of Identity* (Philadelphia: Jewish Publication Society of America, 1977), 127; also 123–35.

95. "Als wäre es vom Himmel herab, schwer und eisern, gefallen und läge nun, ein Fremdes, in mitten seiner Gedanken."

96. "Gerechte Wege ging alles, ein jedes Gesetz erfüllend . . . das in seinem Samen schlief, keimend erwachte."

97. *Gerechtigkeit* applies equally to the natural world and to human existence. "And nothing unjust occurred. Not towards the stream, blocked by cliffs, and not towards the cliffs, against which, gnawing at it incessantly, waves hurled themselves" (Und es geschah nicht Unrecht. Nicht dem Strom, dem Felsen den Weg versperrten, und den Felsen nicht, gegen die, rastlos sie zernagend, Fluten sich warfen) (127); "And he who sensed this was able, a just person, to move through life, not looking at himself, his gaze pointed in the distance" (Und der dies ahnte, vermochte, ein Gerechter, durchs Leben zu schreiten; nicht sich betrachtend, sein Blick ins Weite gerichtet) (130); "He knew no fear; because whatever he hit upon—things more reticent than cliffs—law broke out of it for him like gushing water, and justice like an unceasing stream" (Angst war ihm fremd; denn woran er schlug—an Verschlosseneres als Felsen—Recht brach für ihn daraus hervor wie sprudelndes Wasser, und Gerechtigkeit wie ein nicht versiegender Bach) (131).

98. "Ein großes, von Urbeginn gemessenes feierliches Kreisen"

99. Walter Sokel's claim that *Gerechtigkeit* is primarily an ethical category seems misleading in light of the text's persistent association of the term with natural law (Sokel, *Narzißmus und Judentum,* 37).

100. "Wasn't it appropriate, also before the veiled possibility of just destinies, to lower one's eyes in respect, as the stone woman—there, in front of him, on the dolphin—lowered her eyes before the luminous rays of a sun, which—even if unseen—stood dazzlingly in the sky?" (Ziemte es sich nicht, auch vor der verhüllten Möglichkeit gerechter Lose, ehrfürchtig seine Augen zu beschatten, so wie die steinerne Frau—da, vor ihm, auf dem Delphin—ihre Augen vor den leuchtenden Strahlen einer Sonne beschattete, die—wenn auch ungesehen—blendend am Himmel stand?) (118).

101. "Der strengen Ordnung zeitlichen Ablaufes sich nicht unterwerfend, sind diese Erinnerungen oft eigen-

willig—und doch vielleicht, unbewußt, verhülltem Gesetz gehorsam—aufeinander gereiht" (Beer-Hofmann, *Gesammelte Werke,* 678).

CHAPTER 4

First epigraph: "Ich trete für niemanden ein, weil er zufällig derselben Familie entstammt wie ich. . . . Ich war niemals der Kamerad von irgendwem, weil er zufällig dieselbe Charge bekleidet hat, nie der Kollege von jemandem, weil er auf derselben Schulbank saß wie ich. . . . Ich fühle mich mit niemandem solidarisch, weil er zufällig derselben Nation, demselben Stand, derselben Rasse, derselben Familie angehört wie ich. Es ist ausschließlich meine Sache, mit wem ich mich verwandt zu fühlen wünsche." Arthur Schnitzler, "Bekenntnis" (1904), in *Aphorismen und Betrachtungen II: Der Geist im Wort und der Geist in der Tat,* ed. Robert O. Weiss (Frankfurt am Main: Fischer Taschenbuch, 1993), 109.

Second epigraph: "Zum erstenmal begann ihm die Bezeichnung Jude, die er selbst so oft leichtfertig, spöttisch und verächtlich im Mund geführt hatte, in einer ganz neuen gleichsam düstern Beleuchtung aufzugehen. Eine Ahnung von dieses Volkes geheimnisvollem Los dämmerte in ihm auf, das sich irgendwie in jedem aussprach, der ihm entsprossen war; nicht minder in jenen, die diesem Ursprung zu entfliehen trachteten wie einer Schmach, einem Leid oder einem Märchen, das sie nichts kümmerte,—als in jenen, die mit Hartnäckigkeit auf ihn zurückwiesen, wie auf ein Schicksal, eine Ehre oder eine Tatsache der Geschichte, die unverrückbar feststand." Arthur Schnitzler, *Der Weg ins Freie* (Frankfurt am Main: Fischer Taschenbuch, 1998), 108 (hereinafter cited as *Weg*). All German citations are from this edition. The English translation is from *The Road into the Open,* trans. Roger Byers (Berkeley and Los Angeles: University of California Press, 1992), 21 (hereinafter cited as *Road*).

1. "Ich bin Jude, Oesterreicher, Deutscher. Es muss wohl so sein—denn beleidigt fühl ich mich im Namen des Judentums, des Oesterreichertums und des Deutschlands, wenn man einem von den Dreien was Schlimmes nachsagt." Letter to Elisabeth Steinrück, December 22–26, 1914, in *Briefe, 1913–1931,* by Arthur Schnitzler, ed. Peter Michael Braunwarth, Richard Miklin, Susanne Pertlik, and Heinrich Schnitzler (Frankfurt am Main: S. Fischer, 1984), 69 (hereinafter cited as *Briefe II*).

2. "Wir . . . empfinden das Schicksal dieses Landes so tief wie andre, tiefer vielleicht. Wie verwurzelt ist man doch mit dem Land, das einen geboren! Was gehn uns am

Ende die Mitbürger, die Diplomaten, die Monarchen an? Das Land! Die Heimat!" (Schnitzler, *TB,* May 20, 1915).

3. On this contrast, see Bruce, "Which Way Out?"

4. Schnitzler responded with dismay to the news that the director of a Jerusalem museum was having his portrait painted. "Because I am . . . did you suspect it? a Jewish writer. And from the fact that that is also correct, to some extent, one can observe the condition of boundless confusion in which the world finds itself" (weil ich nemlich—haben Sie das geahnt, ein jüdischer Dichter bin. Und auch daraus, d[a]ss auch das richtig ist, gewissermaßen, läßt sich der Zustand grenzloser Verwirrung erkennen, in dem die Welt sich befindet). Letter to Dora Michaelis, November 11, 1920, in Schnitzler, *Briefe II,* 218.

5. Wistrich, *The Jews of Vienna,* 610–11.

6. Egon Schwarz, "Arthur Schnitzler und das Judentum," in *Im Zeichen Hiobs: Jüdische Schriftsteller und deutsche Literatur im 20. Jahrhundert,* ed. Gunter E. Grimm and Hans-Peter Bayerdörfer (Königstein: Athenäum, 1985), 82. For a revaluation of Schnitzler's approach to politics in the interwar period, see Felix W. Tweraser, *Political Dimensions of Arthur Schnitzler's Late Fiction* (Rochester: Camden House, 1998).

7. Letter to Schnitzler, December 14, 1912, cited in Schnitzler, *Briefe II,* 824n.

8. Schnitzler, *TB,* June 12, 1908.

9. Ibid., May 21, 1908.

10. "Dr. Bettelheim . . . bemängelte [an meinem Roman], dass die 'Judenfrage'—mit nicht genügender Courage angepackt sei. Ich erwiderte, bisher hätte ich nur das Gegentheil gehört—im übrigen sei ich gar nicht dazu da 'Fragen' anzupacken, sondern Gestalten darzustellen, die sich so oder so zu Fragen stellten. Da er fühlte, wie dumm er gewesen, kam B. wieder, nach einer Abschweifung zurück und sagte, was er gemeint: 'ich hätte die "heroischen" Juden nicht dargestellt.' Wer— z.B.—z.B. erwiderte er . . . Friedjung. Ich: 'Ja, hochbegabter Mensch, aber, inwiefern ein heroischer Jude—?' . . .'Er hält an Judentum fest—ist nicht getauft—'—'Und solche vermissen Sie in meinem Roman?—Und Leo Golowski ist weniger heroisch als Friedjung—?!!' Zu solchen Albernheiten führt Krittelsucht und Mißgunst und Partei einen leidlich klugen Menschen" (ibid., December 2, 1908).

11. For a detailed look at the novel's reception, see Konstanze Fliedl, *Arthur Schnitzler: Poetik der Erinnerung* (Vienna: Böhlau, 1997), 225–29.

12. Schnitzler, *TB,* February 25, 1905.

13. Ibid., January 6, 1906.

14. Ibid., April 7, 1906, October 22, 1909.

15. Ibid., January 8, 1907.

16. Ibid., November 29, 1907. The phrase "security is nowhere" also appears in Schnitzler's early one-act play *Paracelsus.*

17. Letter to Max Brod, June 1921, in *Letters to Friends, Family, and Editors,* by Franz Kafka, trans. Richard and Clara Winston (New York: Schocken Books, 1977), 289.

18. W. E. Yates, "The Tendentious Reception of *Professor Bernhardi.* Documentation in Schnitzler's Collection of Press Cuttings," in Timms and Robertson, *Vienna 1900¸* 111. See also Werner Willhelm Schnabel, "*Professor Bernhardi* und die Wiener Zensur: Zur Rezeptionsgeschichte der Schnitzlerschen Komödie," *Jahrbuch der Deutschen Schillergesellschaft* 28 (1984): 349–83.

19. *Österreichische Volkspresse,* January 8, 1915.

20. *Neue Freie Presse,* January 4, 1913.

21. Schnitzler personally collected some 850 reviews of this play alone, and thanks to W. E. Yates's examination of this collection, we can envision the playwright, crayon in hand, angrily underscoring the same slur, the same objection, time and again.

22. Schnitzler, *TB,* December 5, 1912.

23. "Theater und Schauspiel in Deutschland," *Der Merkur* 4, no. 3 (1913): 95–99.

24. Cited in Schnitzler, *Briefe II,* 832n.

25. Letter to Georg Brandes, February 27, 1913, in Schnitzler, *Briefe II,* 12–13.

26. Letter to Georg Brandes, December 9, 1915, in Schnitzler, *Briefe II,* 100.

27. Letter to Ludwig Hirschfeld, February 22, 1919, in Schnitzler, *Briefe II,* 175–76.

28. Karl Schönherr, Austrian playwright and "Heimat" writer, wrote *Familie* in 1905.

29. Schnitzler, *Der Ruf des Lebens* (The Call of Life) (1905).

30. Beer-Hofmann, *Der Graf von Charolais* (The Count of Charolais) (1904).

31. "Anläßlich Schönherrs 'Familie' mit O. Gespräch übers dramatische. Es ist mir (wahrscheinlich allen Juden) versagt, ein absolut gutes Drama zu schreiben. Dazu gehört eins: 'sich innerhalb des gegebenen zu beruhigen'. Weltanschauungen wie sie im 3. Akt des Ruf (und auch im 5. Des Charolais) zum Ausdruck kommen, heben das dramatische auf. Der Held des Dramas muss innerhalb der bestehenden Gesetze weiterlaufen. Kerr findet gerade (nur) den 3. Akt des Ruf gut ('Zukunftsträchtig'). Der Dramatiker mag von Vergangenheiten schwer sein; zukunftsträchtig soll er nie und nimmer sein" (Schnitzler, *TB,* April 7, 1906).

32. Yates, "The Tendentious Reception," 117.

33. Schwarz, "Arthur Schnitzler," 75. The name "Esoi" comes from the Yiddish "azoi," meaning "thus" or "so."

34. "Es war nicht möglich, insbesondere für einen Juden, der in der Öffentlichkeit stand, davon abzusehen, daß er ein Jude war, da die andern es nicht taten, die Christen nicht und die Juden noch weniger. Man hatte die Wahl, für unempfindlich, zudringlich, frech oder für empfindlich, schüchtern, verfolgungswahnsinnig zu gelten." Arthur Schnitzler, *Jugend in Wien,* ed. Therese Nickl and Heinrich Schnitzler (Frankfurt am Main: Fischer Taschenbuch, 1996), 322.

35. "Und auch wenn man seine innere und äußere Haltung so weit bewahrte, daß man weder das eine noch das andere zeigte, ganz unberührt zu bleiben war so unmöglich, als etwa ein Mensch gleichgültig bleiben könnte, der sich zwar die Haut anaesthesieren ließ, aber mit wachen und offenen Augen zusehen muß, wie unreine Messer sie ritzen, ja schneiden, bis das Blut kommt" (ibid.).

36. Franz Kafka, *The Collected Stories,* ed. Nahum N. Glatzer (New York: Schocken Books, 1971), 157.

37. Gilles Deleuze and Félix Guattari, *Kafka: Toward a Minor Literature,* trans. Dana Polan (Minneapolis: University of Minnesota Press, 1986), 18.

38. The creative paralysis plaguing both Georg and Heinrich dominates their relationship, and it is the common plight of Berthold, Anna, Nürnberger (including both his sister and the hero of *his* novel), as well as Therese.

39. Deleuze and Guattari, *Kafka,* 17.

40. Letter dated "Ende Juni," in *Ein Briefwechsel,* by Georg Brandes and Arthur Schnitzler, ed. Kurt Bergel (Bern: Francke, 1956), 95.

41. Russell A. Berman, introduction to Schnitzler, *The Road into the Open,* ix.

42. Russell Berman claims that the novel "never lets us fully determine which material is central and which is merely background—private desire and public life—on the contrary, the perspective constantly shifts, neither realm is entirely stable, each contaminates the other " (ibid., viii). Martin Swales, who sees only the agonizing struggles common to both two plots, sees the Jews as the novel's main victims: "They are socially and psychologically rootless: hence, they have little or no plot to represent the bind enactment of themselves in practical activity, hence there is no judgment to interpret and evaluate their precarious state from the standpoint of a reliably informed and understanding onlooker." Martin Swales, "Nürnberger's Novel: A Study of Arthur Schnitzler's 'Der Weg ins Freie,'" *Modern Language Review* 70 (1975): 570. David Low writes: "In terms of its critical reception we may summarize the fate of the novel over the last seventy-five years generally as a mixture of praise for the parts . . . and reservations about the whole, particularly in respect of its moral framework and its narrative structure." David Low, "Questions of Form in Schnitzler's *Der Weg ins Freie,*" *Modern Austrian Literature* 19, nos. 3–4 (1986): 21.

43. Bruce, "Which Way Out?" 111.

44. Wistrich, *The Jews of Vienna,* 609.

45. Georg and Felician resemble the brothers Clemens and Georg von Franckenstein; Anna Rosner, the author's deceased lover, Marie Reinhardt; Leo Golowski is modeled upon Theodor Herzl; Heinrich Bermann resembles Jakob Wassermann, or in other readings, the author himself. See Wolfgang Nehring, "Zwischen Identifikation und Distanz: Zur Darstellung der jüdischen Charaktere in Arthur Schnitzlers *Der Weg ins Freie,*" in *Jüdische Komponente in der deutschen Literatur—die Assimilationskontroverse,* ed. Walter Röll and Hans Peter Bayerdörfer (Tübingen: Max Niemeyer, 1986), 162–70.

46. Harry Zohn, cited in Krobb, *Selbstdarstellungen,* 148.

47. Schnitzler may not have used the term *bildungsroman,* but he placed *Der Weg ins Freie* in "the great line of German novels," and the works he names—*Wilhelm Meister, Der grüne Heinrich,* and *Buddenbrooks*—leave no doubt that the German tradition was that of the bildungsroman (Schnitzler, *TB,* January 6, 1906).

48. J. M. Hawes, "The Secret Life of Georg von Wergenthin: Nietzschean Analysis and Narrative Authority in Arthur Schnitzler's *Der Weg ins Freie,*" *Modern Language Review* 90, no. 2 (1995): 386.

49. "Verehrtester Herr Brandes, Sie haben wohl recht, daß in meinem Buch zwei Romane enthalten sind, und daß künstlerisch genommen, der Zusammenhang kein absolut notwendiger sein mag. . . . Schon während meiner Arbeit hab ich immer gefühlt, daß es so kommen wird—aber ich konnte—oder wollte mir nicht helfen. Denn so sorgfältig das Buch componirt war, es ist doch erst so recht *geworden,* während ich es schrieb. . . . Mir war das Verhältnis Georgs zu seiner Geliebten immer geradeso wichtig wie seine Beziehung zu den verschiedentlichen Juden des Romans—ich habe eben ein Lebensjahr des Freiherrn von Wergenthin geschildert, in dem er über allerlei Menschen und Probleme und über sich selbst ins Klare kommt." Letter, July 4, 1908, in Schnitzler, *Briefe I,* 578–79.

50. Scheible, *Literarischer Jugendstil*, 91.

51. "*Der Weg ins Freie* ist aber kein Bildungsroman: diese Begegnung mit der eigenen entfremdeten Vergangenheit führt nicht etwa zu einer Erneuerung der Lebensmöglichkeiten. Dieser Text läßt daran zweifeln, ob die Selbstanalyse . . . tatsächlich von Nutzen ist." J. M. Hawes, "'Als käme er von einer weiten Reise heim': Fremderfahrung als Erfahrung des eigenen entfremdeten Ichs in Arthur Schnitzlers Roman *Der Weg ins Freie*," in *Reisen im Diskurs: Modelle der literarischen Fremderfahrung von den Pilgerberichten bis zur Postmoderne*, ed. Anne Fuchs and Theo Harden (Heidelberg: C. Winter, 1995), 514.

52. Franco Moretti, "'A Useless Longing for Myself': The Crisis of the European Bildungsroman, 1898–1914," in *Studies in Historical Change*, ed. Ralph Cohen (Charlottesville: University of Virginia Press, 1992), 57. This latter category applies as well to Schnitzler's own experimental *Bildungsnovelle, Fräulein Else* (1923).

53. Following Barthes and Chatman, contemporary narratology distinguishes two basic classes of episodes: "kernels," abrupt, irreversible choices among widely different options, and "satellites," slower, subordinate events that qualify and enrich the chosen course. Satellites belong to the narrative "background" (to use Harald Weinrich's terms), embodying social regularity, whereas the "foreground" is occupied by kernels, which are typically the hero's doing and therefore enjoy a structural centrality in most narrative forms, from epos to tragedies and short stories. In the bildungsroman, the distance "between these two aspects diminishes, to the point where homogeneity between subject and world is achieved, where 'socialization' and 'subjective growth' are one and the same" (ibid., 47).

54. Ibid., 49.

55. "Ich konnte nicht. Die Gestalt der Anna stand vom Anfang an eben so unwidersprechlich als katholisch da. Und es kam mir ja schließlich nicht darauf an, irgendwas nachzuweisen: weder daß Christ und Jude sich nicht vertragen—oder daß sie sich doch vertragen können—sondern ich wollte, ohne Tendenz, Menschen und Beziehungen darstellen—die ich gesehen habe (ob in der Welt draußen oder in der Phantasie bliebe sich gleich)." Letter, July 4, 1908, in Schnitzler, *Briefe I*, 580.

56. Another option would have been to include a Jewish male protagonist, as in *Professor Bernhardi* (1912). Several contemporaneous works pair Jewish male protagonists with Christian women. Beer-Hofmann's novella *Das Kind* (1892), Jacobowski's *Werther der Jude* (1892), and David Vogel's Hebrew Vienna novel *Chaye*

Nisuim (Married Life, 1929) depict illicit love affairs involving a Jewish man and a Christian woman; in each case, the child born of the couple dies.

57. Marc Weiner and Konstanze Fliedl draw attention to just this aspect of Schnitzler's editorial habits. For example, when Georg moves from Vienna to Detmold, Schnitzler originally has him be privy to a far more pernicious "Germanic" anti-Semitism, rather than to the softer Austrian variety. Wiener, in analyzing the role of Wagnerism in the text, points out another intriguing omission on Schnitzler's part: the conductor of the two performances of *Tristan und Isolde* that Georg attends, and with whom he identifies in the final chapter, was Gustav Mahler. Omitting this detail is consistent with Georg's own mindset, in this case, with a detail he would likely have repressed. Marc Wiener, "Parody and Repression: Schnitzler's Response to Wagnerism," *Modern Austrian Literature* 19, nos. 3–4 (1986): 129–48. Georg was conceived as neither anti-Semitic nor a defender of the Jews—a testimony (in Fliedl's view) to the author's discretion and self-discipline (Fliedl, *Arthur Schnitzler*, 224).

58. Fliedl, *Arthur Schnitzler*, 227.

59. Nürnberger crosses the destinies of Therese and Else by regarding both womens' fates to be determined by their fathers. "I was just thinking how easily it could have happened that Fräulein Else might have had to languish for two months in prison and that Fräulein Therese had given parties in an elegant salon as daughter of the house" (Ich denke eben, wie leicht es sich hätte fügen können, daß Fräulein Else zwei Monate im Gefängnis hätte schmachten müssen, und daß Fräulein Therese in einem eleganten Salon als Tochter des Hauses Cercle hielte) (*Road*, 59–60; *Weg*, 79).

60. "'Ich bewundere überhaupt alle Leute, die imstande sind, für etwas, was sie im Grunde nichts angeht, so viel zu riskieren. Und wenn das nun gar ein junges Mädchen tut, ein hübsches junges Mädchen wie Therese . . . so imponiert mir das noch mehr" (*Weg*, 30).

61. "Mit dem festen Entschluß, alle Seligkeit und alles Leid hinzunehmen, das ihr bevorstehen mochte" (*Weg*, 95).

62. Though as Hartmut Scheible argues, the impact of social conventions on the Georg-Anna plot is substantial. Scheible, *Literarischer Jugendstil*, 96.

63. Schnitzler himself condoned and even participated in psychological interpretations of the work. See Theodor Reik's analysis of Georg's dream following his infidelity—an analysis originally undertaken together with the author. Theodor Reik, *Arthur Schnitzler als Psycholog* (1913), ed. Bernd Urban (Frankfurt am Main: S. Fischer, 1993).

64. The significance of family in the Jewish domain is articulated twice, in very different contexts. The first comment comes early in chapter 1, where we hear almost in passing that the novel's three most prominent Jewish families (the Staubers, the Ehrenbergs, and the Golowskis) are distantly related, as all come from Eastern Europe. The elder Dr. Stauber comments, "'All Jews are related to one another'" (alle Juden [sind] miteinander verwandt) (*Road*, 26; *Weg*, 37). The notion that all Jews are related surfaces again, though indirectly, by way of Heinrich's self-deprecating Jewish joke, to suggest that these are two sides of one coin. By presenting the same fact of Jewish identity in two such different ways, Schnitzler describes how the role of family devolves from a fact of identity into a tragicomedy over the course of a generation.

65. Abigail Gillman, "Failed Bildung and the Aesthetics of Detachment: Schnitzler's *Der Weg ins Freie*," in *Confrontations/Accommodations: German-Jewish Literary and Cultural History from Heine to Wassermann*, ed. Mark Gelber (Tübingen: Niemeyer, 2004), 209–36.

66. "Von allen seinen Beziehungen zu der geliebten Kunst blieb in solchen Augenblicken nur die eine übrig, sie mit tieferem Verstehen aufnehmen zu dürfen, als irgend ein anderer Mensch. Und er fühlte, daß Heinrich die Wahrheit gesprochen hatte, als sie zusammen durch einen von Morgentau feuchten Wald gefahren waren: nicht schöpferische Arbeit,—die Atmosphäre seiner Kunst allein war es, die ihm zum Dasein nötig war; kein Verdammter war er wie Heinrich, den es immer trieb zu fassen, zu formen, zu bewahren, und dem die Welt in Stücke zerfiel, wenn sie seiner gestaltenden Hand entgleiten wollte" (*Weg*, 293).

67. "Seiner Empfindung nach bestand durchaus keine Notwendigkeit, daß auch der alte Doktor Stauber ihm offizielle Mitteilung von seiner Zugehörigkeit zum Judentum machte. Er wußte es ja, und er nahm es ihm nicht übel. Er nahm es überhaupt keinem übel; aber warum fingen sie denn immer selbst davon zu reden an? Wo er auch hinkam, er begegnete nur Juden, die sich schämten, daß sie Juden waren, oder solchen, die darauf stolz waren, und Angst hatten, man könnte glauben, sie schämten sich" (ibid., 37).

68. "Diese ekelhafte Duellkomödie . . . dieses grauenvolle, vom Staat konzessionierte Hazardspiel um Leben und Tod" (ibid., 355).

69. "Ein andrer hat einfach seine Individualität zu vertheidigen—Unsereiner muss zuerst das Vorurtheil gegen Wien—dann das gegen Judentum besiegen, dann kommt man erst selber daran. Und gerade wie beim

Juden, auch beim Wiener: Nicht nur die andern hat er gegen sich, auch, nein vor allem den Juden, den Wiener" (Schnitzler, *TB*, January 13, 1908).

70. Norbert Elias diagnoses the sociological implications of the duel in German culture. See Norbert Elias, "Die satisfaktionsfähige Gesellschaft," in *Studien über die Deutschen*, ed. Michael Schröter (Suhrkamp: Frankfurt am Main, 1998), 61–158. On the dueling practices of Jewish fraternities in Vienna, see Marsha L. Rozenblit, "The Assertion of Identity: Jewish Student Nationalism at the University of Vienna Before the First World War," *Leo Baeck Yearbook* 27 (1982): 171–86; Julius H. Schoeps, *The Vienna Kadimah, Leo Baeck Yearbook* 27 (1982): 164–67; and Wistrich, *The Jews of Vienna*, 348–80.

71. Arthur Schnitzler, *Professor Bernhardi*, in *Das weite Land: Dramen, 1909–1912* (Frankfurt am Main: Fischer Taschenbuch, 1999), 268 (hereinafter cited as *PB*). All subsequent references to *Professor Bernhardi* are to this edition; translations are my own.

72. For a detailed discussion of the duel in the texts under discussion, see Andrew C. Wisely, *Arthur Schnitzler and the Discourse of Honor and Dueling* (New York: Peter Lang, 1996), 189–203.

73. "Es wird bald wieder Zeit, die Tragödie der Juden zu schreiben." Letter to Olga Waissnix, March 29, 1897, in *Liebe, die starb vor der Zeit: Ein Briefwechsel*, by Arthur Schnitzler and Olga Waissnix, ed. Therese Nickl and Heinrich Schnitzler (Vienna: Molden, 1970), 319.

74. "Zum erstenmal begann ihm die Bezeichnung Jude, die er selbst so oft leichtfertig, spöttisch und verächtlich im Mund geführt hatte, in einer ganz neuen gleichsam düstern Beleuchtung aufzugehen. Eine Ahnung von dieses Volkes geheimnisvollem Los dämmerte in ihm auf" (*Weg*, 108).

75. "Daß Heinrich, der darauf bestand, hier daheim zu sein, in Figur und Geste einem fanatischen, jüdischen Priester glich, während Leo, der mit seinem Volk nach Palästina ziehen wollte, in Gesichtsschnitt und Haltung ihn an die Bildsäule eines griechischen Jünglings erinnerte, die er einmal im Vatikan oder im Museum von Neapel gesehen hatte" (ibid.).

76. Florian Krobb sums up the almost unanimous view of recent critics that Georg is no more than a filter (Krobb, *Selbstdarstellungen*, 158).

77. "'Nie in Ihrem Leben wär Ihnen etwas Derartiges eingefallen, wenn Sie nicht mit einem Subjekt meiner Art verkehrten und es nicht zuweilen Ihre Art wäre, nicht Ihre Gedanken zu denken, sondern die von Menschen, die stärker—oder auch schwächer sind als Sie" (*Weg*, 380).

78. "Die Leute wußten alles früher als er selbst" (ibid., 361).

79. "Er war mir nicht nur ein Freund, er war mir auch der 'christliche Mitbürger', der gern mit mir verkehrte. Es war so schmeichelhaft—wir haben ja doch immer was vom Ghetto in uns. Dankbarkeit, wenn man uns wie andere Menschen behandelt. Dafür wollte ich ihm dankbar sein, indem ich mich nach ihm modelte, seine Gewohnheiten annahm, soweit ich es vermochte, seine Sprache redete, seine Gedanken dachte. . . . Und er läßt mich stehen, er läßt mich einfach stehen." Theodor Herzl, *Das neue Ghetto* (Vienna: R. Loewit, 1920), 52.

80. In 1908, a scholar of canon law at the University of Innsbruck named Ludwig Wahrmund was transferred to Prague after the clerics protested his critical examination of Catholic dogma.

81. Elizabeth Loentz, "The Problem and Challenge of Jewishness in the City of Schnitzler and Anna O.," in *A Companion to the Works of Arthur Schnitzler*, ed. Dagmar C. G. Lorenz (Rochester: Camden House, 2003), 88.

82. "Meine Angelegenheit ist eine rein persönliche"; "daß ich mit den Leuten absolute nichts zu tun haben will, die eine politische Affäre aus meiner Angelegenheit machen wollen."

83. "Es ist ja wirklich schrecklich, dass bei uns in Österreich alle Personalfragen auf politischem Gebiete endigen."

84. "Manche persönliche Affären tragen eben den Keim von politischen in sich."

85. "'Denn du wirst hoffentlich nicht glauben, daß dein Märtyrtum mir besonders imponiert. Ja, wenn du für irgend was Großes, für eine Idee, für dein Vaterland, für deinen Glauben all die verschiedenen Unannehmlichkeiten auf dich genommen hättest, die nun durch allerlei kleine Triumphe schon längst aufgewogen sind, dann vermöchte ich Respekt vor dir zu empfinden. Aber ich sehe in deinem ganzen Benehmen,—als alter Freund darf ich es dir wohl sagen—, nichts als eine Tragikomödie des Eigensinns, und erlaube mir überdies zu bezweifeln, daß du sie mit der gleichen Konsequenz durchgeführt hättest, wenn heute noch in Österreich die Scheiterhaufen gen Himmel lohten.'

"Bernhardi *sieht ihn eine Weile an, dann beginnt er zu applaudieren.*"

86. "Ich habe eine Charakterkomödie geschrieben, die in ärztlichen und zum Teil in politischen Kreisen spielt, kein Tendenzstück, das den Konflikt zwischen Wissenschaft und Kirche oder gar, wie Sie meinen, den Streit zwischen zwei Religionen darzustellen oder am Ende in irgend einer Richtung zu entscheiden sucht. Es war nicht meine Absicht (und liegt wohl auch kaum im Bereich künstlerischer Möglichkeiten) eine *Frage* zu lösen. . . . Denn ich empfinde es als meinen Beruf Menschen zu gestalten und habe nichts zu beweisen als die Vielfältigkeit der Welt." Letter to Richard Charmatz, January 4, 1913, in Schnitzler, *Briefe II*, 1–2.

87. His virtues—paternal intuition (we seem him being affectionate with son Oskar), muted charisma, and the kind of wisdom that invites the sharing of confidences—resemble those of many of Schnitzler's doctors (thought to have been modeled on Ibsen's doctors): Dr. Stauber in *Der Weg ins Freie*, Dr. Mauer in the bleak landscape of *Das weite Land*, Dr. Adler in *Ruf des Lebens*, Alfred in *Therese*. Like these doctors, Bernhardi is naturally a bystander rather than a player, and he ultimately fails to save his charge from her tragic fate. Yet unlike them, Bernhardi is forced into the role of protagonist, pushed to adopt a public stance, to play a role that goes against his nature. In this respect he is of a kind with the eponymous heroes of Hugo von Hofmannsthal's *Der Schwierige* (The Difficult Man) and G. E. Lessing's *Nathan der Weise*, both of whom are introverted, ironic, and egotistical. In spatial terms, these characters stay put as others come to attack them, seek their counsel, or advise them. Their difficulty with language is part limitation, part conviction that the truth can be uttered only before those who are able to hear it—a motif that leads Nathan to contrive the fable of the three rings in order to communicate with Saladin about tendentious matters. Bernhardi is less successful in locating an effective idiom with which to speak truth to power, symbolic of Schnitzler's own quest for a third term.

88. Michaela L. Perlmann, *Arthur Schnitzler* (Stuttgart: J. B. Metzler, 1987), 99.

89. "Es gibt Sachen von mir, die ich lieber habe,— aber mich hab ich nirgends lieber als im Bernhardi" (Schnitzler, *TB*, March 7, 1918).

90. "Wird mich nicht zu einer Rolle verführen, die mir nicht behagt, zu der ich mich gar nicht tauglich fühle, weil es eben nur eine Rolle wäre."

91. "Und um ganz deutlich zu sein, daß kein Mensch den Versuch machen würde, wenn Bernhardi nicht zufällig ein Jude wäre."

92. "Bernhardi: . . . 'Meine Angelegenheit is eine rein persönliche . . .'

"Löwenstein: 'Aber—'

"Kulka: 'Manche persönliche Affären tragen eben den Keim von politischen in sich. Die Ihrige—'

"Bernhardi: 'Das ist ein Zufall, für den ich keine Verantwortung üb[e]rnehme. Ich gehöre keiner Partei an und wünsche von keiner als der ihrige in Anspruch genommen zu werden.'"

93. "Ich fühle mich mit niemandem solidarisch, weil er *zufällig* derselben Nation, demselben Stand, derselben Rasse, derselben Familie angehört wie ich. Es ist ausschließlich meine Sache, mit wem ich mich verwandt zu fühlen wünsche" (emphasis added). "Bekenntnis" (1904), in Schnitzler, *Aphorismen und Betrachtungen II*, 109.

94. "Der Zufall nichts anders ist, als die Notwendigkeit, die außerhalb der von uns hauptsächlich beobachteten Linie liegt" (ibid., 100).

95. "Nicht weniger stark als Sie glaube ich zu empfinden, was ich dem deutschen Volke danke. Aber selbst wenn ich, unter völliger Vernachlässigung meiner Rassenzugehörigkeit, (was mir anfechtbar erschiene) *alles,* was ich besitze, dem Deutschtum zu danken glaubte, so drängte sich mir doch manchmal die Überlegung auf, wie vieles das Deutschtum selbst den kulturellen und ethischen Leistungen des Judentums, so weit seine Geschichte zurückreicht, zu verdanken hat, und würde mich immerhin auch einigermaßen in der Schuld meiner Ahnen fühlen." Letter to Richard Charmatz, January 4, 1913, in Schnitzler, *Briefe II*, 4.

96. A common tendency in Schnitzler criticism; see Wistrich's extended discussion in *The Jews of Vienna in the Age of Franz Joseph* (Oxford: Oxford University Press, 1990), 583–611; and Andrew C. Wisely, *Arthur Schnitzler and Twentieth-Century Criticism* (Rochester: Camden House, 2004), 93–121.

97. Freud's uneasy response took the form of a dream known to posterity as "My son, the myop" in *The Interpretation of Dreams*—a dream that Ken Frieden renames "the Passover dream." See Ken Frieden, "Sigmund Freud's Passover Dream Responds to Theodor Herzl's Zionist Dream," in *Yale Companion to Jewish Writing and Thought in German Culture, 1096–1996,* ed. Sander L. Gilman and Jack Zipes (New Haven: Yale University Press, 1997), 240–48.

98. Letter to Herzl, January 1, 1895, in Schnitzler, *Briefe I,* 248.

99. "Am meisten hab ich in diesem Sinne gegen den Schlußsatz des Stücks einzuwenden, den eigentlichen Schlußsatz, den der sterbende Jacob Samuel zu sprechen hat. Lassen sie ihn lieber wortlos sterben—dieser Tod sagt mehr, besseres, ich glaube selbst, was ganz anders als der Sterbende selbst. Der Sterbende sagt: 'Juden, Brüder, man wird euch erst wieder leben lassen, wenn ihr zu sterben wißt."—Sein Tod aber spricht: Dieser arme Teufel und edle Mensch muß sich von einem erbärmlichen Haderlumpen einfach deshalb niederschießen

lassen—weil er als Jude geboren ist!—Es gab eine Zeit, wo die Juden zu tausenden auf den Scheiterhaufen verbrannt wurden. Sie haben zu sterben gewußt. Und man hat sie nicht leben lassen—deswegen.—So fährt Ihr Drama, nachdem es sicher u. schön seinen Weg hingebraust ist,—auf einem falschen Geleise ein." Letter of November 17, 1894, in Schnitzler, *Briefe I,* 237.

100. Auch 'der Jude mit dem wunden Ehrgefühl' will mir nicht gefallen—geben Sie ihrem Jacob etwas mehr innere Freiheit—der Grundgedanke leidet nicht darunter, und die Person wird sympathischer. Glauben Sie nicht? . . . Und vor allem lassen Sie Ihren Helden nicht so ergeben sterben" (ibid., 239).

101. "Es ist ein Stück Judenpolitik—und wofür ich Ihren Beistand aufrufe, das ist nicht das Stück, sondern die Judenpolitik." Letter, May 19, 1895, in *Briefe und Tagebücher,* by Theodor Herzl, vol. 4, *Briefe, Anfang Mai 1895–Anfang Dezember 1898,* ed. Barbara Schäfer (Berlin: Propyläen, 1990), 41.

102. "Werden Sie standhaft sein, sich vom Pöbel der Theater u. von den Hengeln der Kritik nicht beirren lassen, werden Sie—was ich leider nicht that—sich selber treu bleiben, so werden Sie der Alkandi werden, dessen Lied Alle singen müssen, ob sie wollen oder nicht. Sie haben ein sehr süsses Lied in der Kehle, mein lieber Schnitzler, vergröbern Sie es um Gotteswillen nicht. Bleiben Sie nur sich treu." Letter to Schnitzler, July 29, 1892, in *Briefe und Tagebücher,* vol. 1, *Briefe und autobiographische Notizen, 1866–1895,* ed. Johannes Wachten (Berlin: Propyläen, 1983), 500.

103. "Das seltsamste (nicht neue): Dieser Mensch (wohl bedeutend zu nennen, Weltruhm, Staaten gründen wollend, von Millionen beweint, da er starb—Juden in Odessa sperrten die Geschäfte, wie die Todesnachricht kam—wurden von Kosaken aus der Synagoge getrieben)—dieser Mensch sprach an diesem Sonntag, eigentlich mit dem Tod vor Augen, hauptsächlich davon wie ungerecht es sei, dass er, ein Künstler 1. Ranges, als Künstler 2. Ranges gelte" (Schnitzler, *TB,* August 7, 1904).

CHAPTER 5

1. "Ich habe, zusammen mit Kessler, dem eine wahrhaft produktive, speziell malerische Phantasie eigen ist, ein kurzes Ballet für did Russen gemacht, 'Joseph in Ägypten,' de Episode mit der Frau des Potiphar, den Knabenhaften Joseph natürlich für Nijinsky, den außerordentlichsten Menschen, den die heutige Bühne besitzt." Letter, June 23, 1912, in *Briefwechsel,* by Richard Strauss and Hugo von Hofmannsthal, ed. Willi Schuh (Zürich: Atlantis, 1964), 187 (hereinafter cited as

Strauss/Hofmannsthal Briefwechsel).

2. See Kessler's accounts in his diary, *Das Tagebuch,* vol. 4, *1906–1914,* ed. Jörg Schuster (Stuttgart: Cotta, 2005), entries for June 5–6, 1912; and in the magazine *Berliner Schallkiste* 3 (June 1928): 7. The latter account likely condenses several days' events into a single evening. See also Laird McLeod Easton, *The Red Count: The Life and Times of Harry Kessler* (Berkeley and Los Angeles: University of California Press, 2002), 203–6.

3. Lynn Garafola, *Diaghilev's Ballets Russes* (Oxford: Oxford University Press, 1989), viii.

4. Léon Bakst, cited in Militsa Pozharskaya and Tatiana Volodina, *The Art of the Ballets Russes: The Russian Seasons in Paris, 1908–1929* (New York: Abbeville Press, 1990), 139; letter, June 23, 1912, in *Strauss/Hofmannsthal Briefwechsel,* 187.

5. Alexander Schouvaloff, *The Art of Ballets Russes* (New Haven: Yale University Press, 1997), 131.

6. Bakst's artistry "rested upon solid knowledge—of museum artifacts, architectural reproductions, fashion plates and illustrations, portraits, historical costume studies, design portfolios—enriched, as in 1912, when he spent several weeks in the Caucasus making preparatory studies for *Thamar,* by direct observation. Such historicizing was not an empty academic exercise. . . . Shorn of its progressive ideology, naturalism was a step to the future, a way of seeing that was radically new" (Garafola, *Diaghilev's Ballets Russes,* 17).

7. Ibid., 9–13.

8. Leonide Massine, *My Life in Ballet,* ed. Phyllis Hartnoll (London: Macmillan, 1968), 56.

9. Garafola, *Diaghilev's Ballets Russes,* 311.

10. Joanna Bottenberg, "The Hofmannsthal-Strauss Collaboration," in *A Companion to the Works of Hugo von Hofmannsthal,* ed. Thomas A. Kovach (Rochester: Camden House, 2003), 117–37.

11. Letters of May 20, 1914, and July 4, 1914, in *Strauss/Hofmannsthal Briefwechsel,* 267–68, 274.

12. Ludwig Philippson, *Auszug aus Ägypten.* Philippson (1811–89) was an extraordinarily prolific preacher and writer who not only wrote literary works but also published essays on religious thought, a Bible translation, a prayer book, a "confirmation book," and a collection of sermons, all while editing the *Allgemeine Zeitung des Judentums* for over sixty years.

13. Maurice Halbwachs, *On Collective Memory,* ed. and trans. Lewis A. Coser (Chicago: University of Chicago Press, 1992).

14. Whereas elsewhere in the ballet there are strong suggestions that Joseph draws upon supernatural sources—a halo encircles his head when he enters (scene 4), and an angel guards his bed when he goes to sleep (scene 8)—these are omitted at this stage of the encounter (Hofmannsthal, *Dramen VI,* 107, 113).

15. "Er kann körperlich und musikalisch in diesem Moment nicht *groß überirdisch* genug erscheinen. Gerade dieses neue (oder antike) ganz unchristliche, (aber der Renaissance naheliegende) vielleicht im Kultus wie dem des delphischen Apoll gottesdienstlich formulierte, enthusiastische aber zugleich ehrfurchtsvolle Gefühl vor der strahlenden göttlichen Nacktheit, möchte ich hier musikalisch gefaßt haben." Letter, August 25, 1912, in *Briefwechsel, 1898–1929,* by Hugo von Hofmannsthal and Harry Graf Kessler, ed. Hilde Burger (Frankfurt am Main: Insel, 1968) 357 (hereinafter cited as *Hofmannsthal/Kessler Briefwechsel*).

16. Letter, September 11, 1912, in *Strauss/Hofmannsthal Briefwechsel,* 198.

17. "Dieser Hirtenknabe, geniales Kind eines Bergvolkes, der sich unten in üppiges Fluß- und Deltavolk verirrt hat, sieht für mich einem edlen, ungebändigten Füllen viel eher ähnlich, als einem frommen Seminaristen." Letter, September 13, 1912, in *Strauss/Hofmannsthal Briefwechsel,* 199. Kessler confirms this in his plot description. "But his piety is not Christian, not ascetic and intellectual as in the case of Jochanaan. Because the tradition alive to him is the shepherd's tradition." Hofmannsthal, *Dramen VI,* 92.

18. "Sein Gottsuchen, in wilden Schwüngen nach aufwärts, ist nichts anderes als ein wildes Springen nach der hochhängenden Frucht der Inspiration. Auf Bergeshöhen, in klarer funkelnder Einsamkeit ist er gewohnt, sich durch ein Noch-höher! Noch-höher! in einer einsamen reinen Orgie emporzuwerfen und aus einer unerreichbaren Klarheit *ober ihm* (welche Kunst, wenn nicht die Musik, kann dies ausdrücken?) einen Fetzen des Himmels herabzureißen, in sich hineinzureißen—diesen flüchtigen, höchsten Zustand, diese Trance nennt er Gott,—und der so erschaute Gott ist es, den er mit emporgereckten Armen sich zu Hilfe zwingt, wie die Welt, dunkel, weich und schwül und ihm *fremd, fremd* bis ins Mark der Knochen, wie diese Welt die Arme nach ihm ausreckt und ihn sich einfangen will—und nichts als den Zeigefinger dieses Gottes—der Licht ist, und alles Höchste, Ihr Höchstes—(wann dürften Sie es andeuten, wenn nicht an einer solchen Stelle?)—, sein Zeigefinger, ein Strahl von ihm, ist der Engel, verleiblicht in eine Figur." Letter, September 13, 1913, in *Strauss/Hofmannsthal Briefwechsel,* 199.

19. "Es ist nicht möglich, dass Sie gar keine Brücke von diesem Knaben Joseph zur Erinnerung an die eigene Jugend fänden—ob Potiphar oder nicht: ein Höheres,

funkelnd, schwer erreichbar, war *oben* und wollte herabgezwungen sein: das ist Josephs Tanz" (ibid., 200). Earlier he had made a similar appeal: "The way I see the figure, you should search for the appropriate music not in an atavistic ornament of the appendix, but in the purest region of your brain, there, where striving upwards, pure, clear glacier air, height, unconditional pungent spiritual freedom are to be found—a region, I think, to which you ascend readily and well" (Wie ich die Figur sehe, so müßten Sie aber die Musik dafür nicht in einem atavististischen Schnörkel des Blinddarms, sondern in der reinsten Region Ihres Gehirns zu suchen haben, dort, wo Aufschwung, reine, klare Gletscherluft, Höhe, unbedingte scharfe geistige Freiheit zu finden ist—einer Region, zu der Sie, meine ich, gern und gut auffliegen) (ibid., 199).

20. Later, Hofmannsthal posits himself as unequal to Strauss' enterprise in explaining why, when visiting Strauss, he could not bring himself to request even a few bars of the score for the ballet: "I'm always inhibited to ask directly. It is my 'unmusicality' that interferes, the thought that it can't be worth your effort to play something for my mediocre understanding" (Direkt aber zu bitten, fühlte ich mich immer gehemmt. Es ist mein "Unmusikalisches," was sich dazwischenstellt, der Gedanke, daß es Ihnen nicht der Mühe wert sein kann, für mein geringes Verständnis etwas zu spielen). Letter, January 24, 1914, in *Strauss/Hofmannsthal Briefwechsel*, 260.

21. "Das innerste Motiv dieser Figur ist das Springen, Fliegen, Schweben, bald im Tanz, bald im Traum, bald in einer intimen Verquickung von Phantasie und Bewegung. Joseph ist ein Tänzer und ein Träumer" (Hofmannsthal, *Dramen VI*, 92).

22. "Jüdische Denkungsweise."

23. "Die Bewegungen stellen dar, wie der fromme Hirtenknabe vor das Antlitz seines Gottes tritt und ihm nacheinander alle seine Gliedmaßen, Haupt, Brust, Hände, Füße zeigt, daß sie rein sind. Er scheint zu Gott zu sprechen: 'Herr, sieh: mein Leib und mein Herz sind vor dir unschuldig'" (Hofmannsthal, *Dramen VI*, 107–8).

24. "Suchen und Ringen nach Gott" (ibid., 108).

25. "So wie David vor der Bundeslade 'springt'" (ibid.). The reference is to David's wanton dance at the ceremony marking the installation of the Ark of the Covenant in Jerusalem (2 Samuel 6:12–16).

26. "Die scharfe Antithese der zwei Hauptfiguren, die zum Schluß in polarem Gegensatz, die eine zum lichtem Himmel hinauf, die andere zum jähen Tod und zur Verdämmnis führt." Letter to Strauss, June 23, 1912, in *Strauss/Hofmannsthal Briefwechsel*, 187.

27. "Den Tanz der glühendsten Liebessehnsucht, den *Tanz der Sulamith*" (Hofmannsthal, *Dramen VI*, 103). The reference is to Song of Songs 7:1: "Turn back, turn back / O maid of Shulem! / Turn back, turn back, /That we may gaze upon you."

28. "Potiphars Weib, die während der ganzen Szene starr und teilnahmslos dagesessen hat, regt sich aber auch jetzt nicht, kalt und ganz in sich versunken fühlt sie kein fremdes Leid" (Hofmannsthal, *Dramen VI,* 106).

29. "Wie aus Eis, hart und grade" (ibid., 114).

30. "Da löst sich Josephs Starre; er springt auf, rafft schauernd seinen Mantel um sich, läuft an ihr vorbei" (ibid.).

31. "Plötzlich hört das Zittern auf, er macht sich . . . von ihr frei, wobei er den Mantel, den er bis dahin vor das Gesicht gehalten hat, sinken läßt, blickt die Frau an und streckt . . . die linke Hand gegen sie aus. Nackt von der Schulter bis zur Hüfte steht er vor ihr. Sie sinkt, wie geblendet von seiner Nacktheit, in die Knie . . . jetzt ist sie die Sünderin, die um Verzeihung fleht. Vergeblich: er beugt sich nicht nieder zu ihr; herb und knabenhaft unerbittlich bleibt er regungslos stehen, die linke Hand über ihren Kopf ausgestreckt" (ibid., 115).

32. "[Die] Zukunft, die er in sich trägt."

33. In Kessler's paraphrase: "In this moment the woman sees that she can never own what she desires, because she wants to grasp something ungraspable: a mystery that cannot be solved, something divine that cannot be comprehended" (In diesem Augenblicke sieht das Weib, daß sie das, was sie begehrt, nie besitzen kann, weil sie etwas Ungreifbares greifen will: ein Geheimnis, das sich nicht ergründen, ein Göttliches, das sich nicht fassen läßt) (Hofmannsthal, *Dramen VI,* 95).

34. "Die beiden Gesichter Josephs, das kindliche und das künftige, wechseln im Laufe der Handlung beständig mit einander ab" (ibid., 94).

35. "Seine zwei Gesichter ringen mit einander" (ibid., 95).

36. Kessler wrote to Hofmannsthal that the interaction of Salome and John is intellectual—thus he must pay with his head—but that the encounter with the mindless Potiphar's wife is "something purely sensual, purely sexual." To compare the atmosphere of *Salome* ("sultry") with that of *Josephslegende* is like comparing Strauss and Bach or *Elektra* and *Der Rosenkavalier*. Letter, June 21, 1912, in *Hofmannsthal/Kessler Briefwechsel,* 347. Hofmannsthal in turn writes to Strauss only five days after sending him the proposal (he had already received an affirmative response from the composer): "The similarity with Salome-Jochanaan is really only a

superficial similarity" (Die Ähnlichkeit mit Salome-Jochanaan ist wirklich eine Scheinähnlichkeit). Letter, June 28, 1912, in *Strauss/Hofmannsthal Briefwechsel*, 189.

37. "The wife of Potiphar, in whose features ever deeper terror and despair have shown themselves during these events, convulsively stretches out both arms, as if she wants to follow the angel and Joseph, then she hastily takes off her pearl strands and strangles herself by pulling them around her neck. She falls back dead into the arms of her women" (Das Weib des Potiphar, auf dessen Gesicht während dieser Vorgänge sich immer tiefer Entsetzen und Zerknirschung abgemalt haben, streckt beide Arme krampfhaft vor, als ob sie dem Engel und Joseph folgen wollte; dann nimmt sie rasch ihre Perlenstränge ab und erwürgt sich, indem sie sie um den Hals zuzieht. Tot fällt sie in die Arme ihrer Weiber zurück) (Hofmannsthal, *Dramen VI*, 122).

38. Ibid., 98.

39. "Prunkhaft, üppig, schwül, voll von seltsamen Düften und Geschöpfen wie ein tropischer Garten, aber ohne Geheimnis, in sich ausgeglichen, klassisch, hart, schwer, eine Welt, in der selbst noch die Luft mit Goldstaub geladen scheint" (ibid., 92).

40. Edward W. Said, *Orientalism* (New York: Random House, 1979), 40.

41. Ivan Davidson Kalmar and Derek Jonathan Penslar, introduction to *Orientalism and the Jews,* ed. Ivan Davidson Kalmar and Derek Jonathan Penslar (Waltham, Mass.: Brandeis University Press, 2005), xviii–xx.

42. Paul R. Mendes-Flohr, "Fin de Siècle Orientalism, the *Ostjuden,* and the Aesthetics of Jewish Self-Affirmation," in *Divided Passions: Jewish Intellectuals and the Experience of Modernity* (Detroit: Wayne State University Press, 1991), 83.

43. Homi K. Bhaba, *The Location of Culture* (London: Routledge, 1994); and Robert Young, *Colonial Desire: Hybridity in Theory, Culture, and Race* (London: Routledge, 1995). On the importation of these paradigms into German Jewish literature see Krobb, *Selbstdarstellungen,* 171–85. For a historical perspective, see Ismar Schorsch, "The Myth of Sephardic Supremacy," in *From Text to Context: The Turn to History in Modern Judaism* (Hanover, N.H.: University Press of New England for Brandeis University Press, 1994), 71–92.

44. "Es ist der Gegensatz zwischen Verwelkung und Fruchtbarkeit, zwischen Vereinzelung und Zugehörigkeit, zwischen Anarchie und Tradition. Sich von der Vergangenheit abzuschneiden, ist das leidenschaftliche Bestreben des auf sich selbst gestellten Juden, gerade weil ihn Milieu, Reminiszenz, Gewöhnung und Verpflichtung mancherlei Art äußerlich oder innerlich an die Vergangenheit binden. Aber er findet in der Bindung das Gesetz nicht, und so zerstört er sie und wird Einzelner, Individualist. Er hat nicht Phantasie genug, um zwei nur dem Scheine nach verschiedene Formen der Existenz in seinem Gemüt zum Einklang zu bringen." *Vom Judentum: Ein Sammelbuch*, 3rd ed., ed. Verein jüdischer Hochschüler Bar Kochba in Prag (Leipzig: Kurt Wolff, 1914), 6.

45. "Der Jude hingegen, den ich den Orientalen nenne,—es ist natürlich eine symbolische Figur; ich könnte ihn ebensowohl den Erfüllten nennen, oder den legitimen Erben,—ist seiner selbst sicher, ist der Welt und der Menschheit sicher. Er kann sich nicht verlieren, da ihn ein edles Bewußtsein, Blutbewußtsein, an die Vergangenheit knüpft und eine ungemeine Verantwortung der Zukunft verpflichtet; und er kann sich nicht verraten, da er gleichsam ein offenbares Wesen ist" (*Vom Judentum,* 7).

46. "[Er] hat alles innen, was die andern außen suchen; nicht in verbrennender Rastlosigkeit, sondern in freier Bewegung und Hingabe nimmt er teil am fortschreitenden Leben der Völker. Er ist frei, und jene sind seine Knechte. Er ist wahr, und jene lügen. Er kennt seine Quellen, er wohnt bei den Müttern, er ruht und schafft, jene sind die ewig wandernden Unwandelbaren" (ibid.).

47. Martin Buber, "Der Geist des Orients und das Judentum," in *Vom Geist des Judentums* (Leipzig: Kurt Wolff, 1916), 11.

48. "Wie der Orientale überhaupt, so wird ganz besonders der Jude mehr der Gebärde der Dinge als ihres Umrisses inne, mehr des Nacheinander als des Nebeneinander, mehr der Zeit als des Raumes. . . . Er erfährt die Welt weniger in dem gesonderten vielfältigen Einzeldasein als der Dinge in ihrer Verbindung, ihrer Gemeinsamkeit und Gemeinschaft" (ibid., 23).

49. "Der psychische Grundakt des motorischen Menschen ist zentrifugal: ein Antrieb geht von seiner Seele aus und wird zur Bewegung. Der psychische Grundakt des sensorischen Menschen ist zentripetal: ein Eindruck fällt in seine Seele und wird zum Bilde. . . . Beide denken; aber des einen Denken meint Wirken, des andern Denken meint Form" (ibid., 12).

50. "Potiphars Weib sitzt starr aufgerichtet da. Sie regt sich nicht. Ihre Haltung drückt eisigen Hochmut und eine brütende, fast leidenschaftliche Langeweile aus" (Hofmannsthal, *Dramen VI,* 100).

51. Buber, "Der Geist des Orients," 25.

52. "Er ist der Träger der Weltentzweiung, er erlebt an sich selber das Schicksal der Welt, die . . . aus der Einheit in die Entzweiung gefallen ist" (ibid., 25).

53. "Ein Mittlervolk . . . das alle Weisheit und Kunst des Abendlands erworben und sein orientalisches Urwesen nicht verloren hat" (ibid., 47).

54. Herbert Silberer, *Probleme der Mystik und ihrer Symbolik* (Vienna: H. Heller, 1914), for example, is quoted in Hofmannsthal's autobiographical sketch *Ad me Ipsum,* as is Bachofen.

55. Martin Buber, *Briefwechsel aus sieben Jahrzehnten* (Heidelberg: Lambert Schneider, 1972). Buber particularly admired Hofmannsthal's plays *König Ödipus* and *Der Turm* (The Tower).

56. "Je länger wir lesen, desto schöner geben wir dieser Welt uns hin, verlieren uns im Medium der unfaßlichsten und naivsten Poesie und besitzen uns erst recht; wie man, in einem schönen Wasser badend, seine Schwere verliert, das Gefühl seines Leibes aber als ein genießendes, zauberisches erst recht gewahr wird" (Hofmannsthal, *Reden und Aufsätze I,* 364). Hofmannsthal uses water imagery on several occasions to represent this type of magical transformation. In *Elektra* (1903), Chrysothemis yearns to submerge and thereby cleanse herself of her paternal legacy and the harsh obligation it imposes; in *Die Frau ohne Schatten,* the Kaiserin would procure a shadow if only she drank (1915); lastly, the Egyptian Helen, at the urging of the goddess Aïthra, gives Menelas to drink from the brew of forgetfulness to wash away the memories of the bloody years of war (1924).

57. "Alles [ist] Ableitung aus uralten Wurzeln, alles mehrfach denkbar, alles schwebend" (Hofmannsthal, *Reden und Aufsätze I,* 364–65).

58. "Von jeder Beklemmung, jeder Niedrigkeit entlastet" (ibid., 364).

59. "Von einem solchen urtümlichen Weltzustand sind wir hier weit entfernt, und Bagdad und Basra sind nicht die Gezelte der Patriarchen. Aber noch ist die Entfernung keine solche, daß nicht eine unverwüstete, von Anschauung strotzende Sprache diesen modernen Zustand an jenen uralten tausendfach zu knüpfen vermöchte" (ibid., 365–66).

60. "Here we find dazzling colors and depth, rapture of fantasy and cutting worldly wisdom; here we find infinite occurrences, dreams, wisdom speeches, jokes, obscenities, mysteries; here we find the most daring spirituality and total sensuality woven into one. There is no faculty in us that doesn't stir, from the highest to the lowest; all that is in us is brought to life here and called to enjoyment" (Hier ist Buntheit und Tiefsinn, Überschwang der Phantasie und schneidende Weltweisheit; hier sind unendliche Begebenheiten, Träume, Weisheitsreden, Schwänke, Unanständigkeiten, Mysterien; hier ist die kühnste Geistigkeit und die vollkommenste Sinnlichkeit in eins verwoben. Es ist kein Sinn in uns, der sich nicht regen müßte, vom obersten bis zum tiefsten; alles was in uns ist, wird hier belebt und zum Genießen aufgerufen) (ibid., 363).

61. "Urklang des Wortes" (ibid., 366).

62. "Es ist, was Stendhal davon sagte. Es ist das Buch, das man immer wieder völlig sollte vergessen können, um es mit erneuter Lust immer wieder zu lesen" (ibid., 369).

63. Paolo Veronese (1528–88) painted numerous scenes from both the Hebrew Bible and the New Testament. These were "narrative paintings . . . using complex and dramatic scenic devices" that often included his contemporaries; "his art was always mnemonic, the daughter of mannerism." *The Encyclopedia of World Art* (1967), s.v. "Paolo Veronese." In his initial letter to Strauss, Hofmannsthal singled out the Veronesean screen as one of the libretto's two best features. Letter, June 23, 1912, in *Strauss/Hofmannsthal Briefwechsel,* 187.

64. "Ich halte, mit Swinburne und Aubrey Beardsley, den Anachronism für ein kostbares Element der Kunst später Zeiten, und wenn ich auch weiß, daß die Maler des endenden 17. Jahrhunderts aus Naivetät ihre biblischen Figuren in das Kostüm der eigenen Zeit steckten und daß wir, wenn wir das Gleiche tun, alles andere eher als naiv in unserem Handeln sind, so scheint es mir doch unendlich reizvoller und wichtiger, daß bei einem theatralischen Kunstwerk gewisse innere Übereinstimmungen erzielt werden, als daß man dem historisch gebildeten Spießbürger im Parterre genugtut" (Hofmannsthal, *Reden und Aufsätze II,* 283).

65. "Und eine solche innere Übereinstimmung herrscht tatsächlich zwischen der Musik von Richard Strauss, der in sehr deutlicher Weise der pompöse letzte Ausdruck einer großen Musikepoche ist, und der Malerei jener Venezianer, die auch ihrerseits ein pompöses überreifes Finale einer ganz großen Zeit darstellen" (ibid.).

66. "Denn wenn sie etwas ist, diese Gegenwart, so ist sie mythisch—ich weiß keinen anderen Ausdruck für eine Existenz, die sich vor so ungeheuren Horizonten vollzieht—für dieses Umgebensein mit Jahrtausenden, für dies Hereinfluten von Orient und Okzident in unser Ich, für diese ungeheure innere Weite, diese rasenden inneren Spanungen [sic], dieses Hier und Anderswo, das die Signatur unseres Lebens ist. Es ist nicht möglich, dies

in bürgerlichen Dialogen aufzufangen. Machen wir mythologische Opern, es ist die wahrste aller Formen. Sie können mir glauben." Hugo von Hofmannsthal, "Zur 'Ägyptischen Helena'" [On "The Egyptian Helen"], in *Dramen V: Operndichtungen* (Frankfurt: Fischer Taschenbuch, 1979), 512. The article appeared on April 8, 1928, concurrently in the Berlin *Vossische Zeitung* and the *Neue Freie Presse*.

67. "Der Dialektik drängt das Ich aus der Existenz" (Hofmannsthal, *Dramen V*, 511).

68. According to Peter Szondi, drama's essence corresponds to "the again and again achieved and itself again destroyed resolution of the human dialectic, which in the dialogue becomes language." Peter Szondi, *Theorie des modernen Dramas, 1880–1950* (Frankfurt am Main: Suhrkamp, 1963), 19. As theater director, Beer-Hofmann sought every means to centralize speech—"to intensify the word to its utmost concision and force" (Beer-Hofmann, *Gesammelte Werke*, 878).

69. "Ich behaupte, ein Dichter hat die Wahl, Reden zu schaffen, oder Gestalten!" (Hofmannsthal, *Dramen V*, 511).

70. "Die Kritik des Unterbewußseins [*sic*]" (ibid., 510).

71. "Wie ich die Handlung führe, die Motive verstricke, das Verborgene anklingen lasse, das Angeklungene wieder verschwinden—durch Ähnlichkeit der Gestalten, durch Analogien der Situationen—durch den Tonfall, der oft mehr sagt als die Worte" (ibid., 512).

72. "In einem 'natürlich' geführten Dialog aber ist dafür kein Raum. Das 'Natürliche' ist die Projektion des ungreifbaren Lebens auf eine sehr willkürlich gewählte soziale Ebene. Das Maximum unserer kosmisch bewegten, Zeiten und Räume umspannenden Menschennatur läßt sich nicht durch die Natürlichkeit einfangen" (ibid., 511).

73. "Aber das sind ja meine—das sind ja die Kunstmittel des Musikers!" (ibid., 512).

74. Benjamin too considers (short-term) communication and (enduring) transmission to be antithetical. Thus, the journalist (Benjamin mentions Karl Kraus) stands opposed to the storyteller, and sterile "information" is counterposed to the lived story (not *die Geschichte* but *das Geschehene*). The storyteller "lowers the pure occurrence into the life of the teller, in order to hand it to the listeners as experience." A story embedded in the artist's own subjectivity will merge as such into the personal depths of all listeners, but "information" never enters into "tradition." Walter Benjamin, *Gesammelte Schriften,* vol. 1, bk. 2, ed. Rolf Tiedemann and Hermann Schweppenhäuser (Frankfurt am Main: Suhrkamp, 1980), 611.

75. Benjamin displays precisely the same bias against the novel. Novels appeal to the individual rather than the common (in a threefold sense: the reader of novels sits alone; the novelistic plot is determined by the death of the subject, isolated from the ritual community; the work as a whole is void of resonance). Moreover, too much emphasis is placed upon content that does not lend itself to retention and is eminently forgettable.

76. Steinberg, *Austria as Theater and Ideology,* 152.

77. "Er war mir die Verkörperung des Abendländischen, in ihr die nie erschöpfte Stärke des Morgenlandes. Er stand ein für die Satzung, die Ehe, die Vaterschaft. Sie schwebte über dem allen, unheimlich bezaubernde, nicht zu bindende Göttin" (Hofmannsthal, *Dramen V*, 502).

78. A 1926 entry in *Ad me Ipsum* reads: "The mythical in higher sphere is realized in 'Helena.' . . . Menelas as representative of the Occident . . . resolution between Orient and Occident" (Das Mythische in höherer Sphäre realisiert in "Helena." . . . Menelas als Vertreter des Abendlandes . . . Ausgleich zwischen Orient und Abendland). Hugo von Hofmannsthal, *Reden und Aufsätze III: 1925–1929: Aufzeichnungen,* ed. Bernd Schoeller (Frankfurt am Main: Fischer Taschenbuch, 1979), 623.

79. "Selig / heute wie gestern / immer aufs neue!" (Hofmannsthal, *Dramen V*, 485).

80. "Sie spricht zu mir— / (*vor sich*) / und ich höre die andre! / Mein Leib ist hier, / die Seele drunten— / gedoppelt leb ich / am zweifachen Ort! / Das darf nicht sein!" (ibid., 480–81).

81. "Er ist kein Wahnsinniger, aber er ist in dem Zustand völliger Zerrüttung, den man in so vielen Kriegslazaretten bei denen, die, die aus allzu furchtbaren Situationen kamen, tage- und wochenlang beobachtet hat" (ibid., 506).

82. "In jener Nacht, als die Griechen in das brennende Troja eindrangen (es liegt uns einigermaßen näher, uns die Schrecken einer solchen Nacht vorzustellen, als den Menschen vor 1914)—in jener Nacht muß Menelas in einem dieser brennenden Paläste seine Frau gefunden und zwischen einstürzenden Mauern herausgetragen haben, diese Frau, die seine geliebte gestohlene Gattin . . . und nebenbei noch die Witwe des Paris und die Freundin von zehn oder zwölf anderen Söhnen des Priamos. . . . Welche Situation für einen Ehemann!" (ibid., 499).

83. "Und noch und noch! / und nicht genung / vom dunklen Trank / Erinnerung! Aufzuckt die Flamme / alter Qual: / vor ihr das Hier / wird öd und fahl. / Doch was dahin, / das tritt hervor / geistmächtig aus / dem

dunklen Tor. / Und was von drunten / wiederkommt, / ist einzig, was / dem Helden frommt! / Und noch und noch! / und nicht genung /vom Zaubertrank / Erinnerung!" (ibid., 474).

CHAPTER 6

1. Günter Hermes, Michael M. Schardt, and Andreas Thomasberger, eds., *Große Richard Beer-Hofmann-Ausgabe* (Paderborn: Igel-Verlag Literatur, 1993–2002). I will be referring to vol. 5, *Die Historie von König David und andere dramatische Entwürfe* (1996).

2. Sören Eberhardt and Charis Goer, eds., *Über Richard Beer-Hofmann: Rezeptionsdokumente aus 100 Jahren* (Paderborn: Igel-Verlag Wissenschaft, 1996).

3. Dieter Borchmeyer, ed., *Richard Beer-Hofmann: "Zwischen Ästhetizismus und Judentum"* (Paderborn: Igel-Verlag Wissenschaft, 1996).

4. Felicitas Heimann-Jelinek, *Zu Gast bei Beer-Hofmann: Eine Ausstellung über das jüdische Wien der Jahrhundertwende* (Vienna: Jüdisches Museum, 1998), 145.

5. Letter to Herzl, March 13, 1896, in *Briefe: Anfang Mai 1895–Anfang Dezember 1898*, by Theodor Herzl, ed. Barbara Schäfer (Berlin: Propyläen, 1990), 585.

6. W. Cohn (1920), cited in Peters, *Richard Beer-Hofmann,* 268.

7. Ulrike Peters, "Richard Beer-Hofmann—ein jüdischer Dichter?" in Borchmeyer, *Richard Beer-Hofmann,* 50–51. Buber edited the first collection of Beer-Hofmann's works.

8. Individual scenes from two unfinished plays were published in the *Jüdische Rundschau:* the prologue to the second play, "Vorspiel auf dem Theater zu *König David*" (1936), two scenes from *König David* (King David), and two from *Davids Tod* (David's Death, 1934). The "Vorspiel" takes up David's history after a twenty-five-year hiatus. In classical form, the prologue figure speaks with various unnamed individuals, conjures David's presence, and deconstructs the aesthetic illusion by commenting on his artistic task. The prologue and unpublished notes suggest that Beer-Hofmann's plan was to depict the "re-emergence of David the man from the myth that encompassed him." Esther Elstun, *Richard Beer-Hofmann: His Life and Work* (University Park: Pennsylvania State University Press, 1983), 179.

9. The first—Jaákob's conversation with his Phoenician slave Idnibáal—has no scriptural counterpart; the second and third, the encounter with Edom and the dreamed council with the angels, occur in reverse order. As a result of the inversion, each scene becomes a stepping-stone to an even more momentous encounter. The most significant change applies to the final scene, which conflates Jacob's two divine encounters: the dream vision of ascending and descending angels, which occurs on the road shortly after he flees his parent's house (Genesis 28), and the twilight wrestling match with an unidentified divine figure, which occurs twenty years later en route back home (Genesis 32). In the biblical account of Jacob's dream, "a stairway was set on the ground and its top reached to the sky, and angels of God were going up and down on it" (Genesis 28:12). The author of *Jaákobs Traum* reads this ladder as a signal of discord and theological insecurity even among those in closest proximity to the divine legacy; he imagines a council of white-winged, gold-clad angels debating the precise nature of God's legacy to the Jewish people. Moreover, he opts to script a role for Samael, the Satan or Mephistopheles of traditional Jewish lore.

10. See Elstun, *Richard Beer-Hofmann,* 21, also Kathleen Harris, "Richard Beer-Hofmann: Ein großer Wiener jüdischer—und deutscher—Dichter: Am Beispiel von 'Jaakobs Traum'," in *Kontroversen, alte und neue: Akten des VII. Internationalen Germanisten-Kongresses, Göttingen 1985,* vol. 5, *Auseinandersetzungen um jiddische Sprache und Literatur: Jüdische Komponenten in der deutschen Literatur—die Assimilationskontroverse,* ed. Albrecht Schöne, Walter Röll, and Hans-Peter Bayerdörfer (Tübingen: Niemeyer, 1986), 172–73.

11. Elstun, *Richard Beer-Hofmann,* 171.

12. Oskar Baum, cited in Krojanker, *Juden in der deutschen Literatur,* 204.

13. Freud, *SE,* 23:7; *SA,* 9:459.

14. Bertha Badt-Strauss, Review of *Die Historie von König David,* by Richard Beer-Hofmann, *Jüdische Rundschau* 39, no. 6, cited in Eberhardt and Goer, *Über Richard Beer-Hofmann,* 154.

15. Vordtriede, "Gespräche," 134.

16. This title appears in the typed draft version, though it is crossed out and replaced by *Legende.* See the Hugo von Hofmannsthal Collection, Houghton Library, manuscript 404.

17. Beer-Hofmann commented that he gave his daughter a biblical name, Mirjam, because the name Gisela was too Jewish.

18. Hans-Gerhard Neumann, *Richard Beer-Hofmann: Studien und Materialien zur "Historie von König David"* (Munich: Wilhelm Fink, 1972), 17.

19. Le Rider, *Viennese Modernity,* 288.

20. Zweig moreover suggests that Beer-Hofmann had to tame Jacob, for reasons that further illuminate the discourse problem I refer to in chapter 2. "Zu 'Jaakobs

Traum," *Der Jude* 1, no. 4 (1919–20), reprinted in *Der Jude* (Vaduz, Liechtenstein: Topos, 1979), 425.

21. Letter, April 20, 1919, in *Hofmannsthal/Beer-Hofmann Briefwechsel,* 144–46.

22. Ritchie Robertson, *The"Jewish Question" in German Literature, 1749–1939* (Oxford: Oxford University Press, 1999), 455; Otto Oberholzer, *Richard Beer-Hofmann* (Bern: Francke, 1947), 164. In Beer-Hofmann's verse, unlike that of Goethe, Schiller, Hebbel, and Grillparzer, unsplit lines of verse are the exception; cola, elision, and defiance of the iambic blank verse impede over 50 percent of the lines. Neumann, *Richard Beer-Hofmann,* 182–90.

23. See the comments on Beer-Hofmann as a theater director in Eugene Weber, "Richard Beer-Hofmann's Translation of Shakespeare's *Richard II,*" in *Essays in Honor of James Edward Walsh* (Cambridge, Mass.: Goethe Institute of Boston and Houghton Library, 1983), 95–99.

24. "Der Leser aber braucht—je wortschärfer, je wortwirbelnder, je wortverschwendender ein Werk ist—umsomehr ein dämpfendes, ein episches Element, das die schmerzlich fiebernde dichterische Vision in glückhaft-milderes Traumerleben hinüberdämmern läßt." Letter to Erich von Kahler, 1933, in Beer-Hofmann, *Gesammelte Werke,* 879.

25. Act 1 consists of an imagined exchange between Edom and his mother Rebekah after Jaákob has snared the patriarchal blessing and fled.

26. Richard Beer-Hofmann, *Jacob's Dream,* trans. Ida Bension Wynn (New York: Johannespresse, 1946), 85 (hereinafter cited as *JD*). In quoting from this edition, I have modernized Wynn's use of "thy" and "thou." "Was dort des Kindes Augen—schreckgeweitet— / Einmal gesehn—glaubst du—vergißt sich das?! / *Die* Hand—des Vaters Hand—die schamhaft zärtlich / Sonst, bebend, über Fieberwangen strich . . . / Der Arm, der sonst umschlang und *an* sich preßte, /Als wäre Nähe *noch* nicht nah *genug! / Dies* Auge—nichts als Sehnsucht, Sorge, Segnen— / Dies ganze Antlitz—früher Kindheit Heimat, / Wohin Erinnerungen müdenttäuschten Alters / Noch, wie auf eine selige Insel, flieht . . . / Und nun dies alles: Hand, Arm, Auge, Antlitz— / Verwandelt, gottestoll, sein Selbst vergessend, / Blind, taub—ein einziger Aufschrei nur mehr: '*Mord!'* (*Erschauernd.*) Wem Gott—als Kind—Vertrauen so zertrat— / Wo darf der trauen noch und sicher fühlen?!" (Beer-Hofmann, *Historie,* 44).

27. "Who there brings offering, honors that which is / And *was!* To joyful gods the smoke ascends, / The blood drips downwards to that mourning mass, / Pining in rage and darkness, comfortless, / And tells that it is honored still, and softens / The hard defiance that is not yet crushed, / And watches, ever sleepless, for the chance / To burst its fetters in a sudden rage— / Should it succeed, my Lord—(*Shuddering in barely restrained horror*) then in revolt / 'T will raise its fearful head up towards the light— / And *all* you see and do not see—ourselves, / Earth, Heaven, Gods—(*shaking with emotion*) shall be engulfed by old / Primeval night" (Beer-Hofmann, *JD,* 83–84). "Wer *dorten* opfert, ehrt, was *ist* und *war! /* Zu frohen Göttern steigt des Opfers Rauch— / Das Blut träuft abwärts, zu dem Traurigen, / Das, trostlos siechend, dort im Düster grollt, / Und sagt ihm, daß man es noch ehrt, und sänftigt / Den Trotz, der drunten unzertreten lauert / Und schlaflos wacht, ob es ihm nicht gelänge, / In jähem Ansturm, Fesseln zu zerreißen! / Gelingt es, Herr—(*in verhaltenem Grauen bebend.*) / Dann—schwillt es, sich empörend, / Furchtbar empor ans Licht—und *was* du siehst— / Und *nicht* siehst, Herr—uns, Erde, Himmel, Götter . . . / *Von Schauern geschüttelt./* Schlingt wieder ein der alten Urnacht Schlund!" (Beer-Hofmann, *Historie,* 43).

28. "In uns liegts und lauerts!" (Beer-Hofmann, *Historie,* 301).

29. See the classic study by Shalom Spiegel, *The Last Trial: On the Legends and Lore on the Command to Abraham to Offer Isaac as a Sacrifice,* trans. Judah Goldin (New York: Pantheon, 1967).

30. See Gouri's "Legacy," Gilboa's "Isaac," Amichai's "The Real Hero of the *Akedah.*"

31. Beer-Hofmann, *Historie,* 125.

32. Michael A. Meyer, *The Origins of the Modern Jew: Jewish Identity and European Culture in German, 1749–1824* (Detroit: Wayne State University Press, 1967), 43; Moshe Pelli, *The Age of Haskalah: Studies in Hebrew Literature of the Enlightenment in Germany* (Leiden: E. J. Brill, 1979), 61–62, also 48–72; Jacob Katz, *Out of the Ghetto: The Social Background of Jewish Emancipation, 1770–1870* (New York: Schocken Books, 1978), 128–29; George Mosse, *German Jews Beyond Judaism* (Bloomington: Indiana University Press, 1985), 1–21; Sidney M. Bolkowsky, *The Distorted Image: German Jewish Perceptions of Germans and Germany* (New York: Elsevier, 1975), 91–108.

33. "Geblüt beruft nicht—nur der Herr beruft!" This rhetoric also echoes the conclusion to *Der Tod Georgs,* where the pressure to obey the voices of one's blood is likewise mitigated by metaphysical tropes of *Geheimnis.*

34. "Du wundervolles Bild aus Gottes Hand" (Beer-Hofmann, *Historie,* 315).

35. "Gott lieh ihr Schönheit! Und sie durfte / in ihrem Blut sie weitergeben—nun— / Stand ihre Schönheit—neu—in David auf!" (ibid., 143).

36. "'Schön?'—'Schamlos!' Übel schmeckt's nun auf der Zunge!/Nein—Nein! Man soll aus seiner Heimlichkeit/ Nichts reißen—und verkaufen und verraten/ An Worte: 'schöne'!" (ibid., 290).

37. "Was ich auch frage—David—David! Das ist / Dein Kehrreim!" (ibid., 43).

38. "Ist dies ein Märchen?" "Nein, Kind! / Doch einmal wird es wie ein Märchen sein!" (ibid., 142).

39. The term was coined by Michel Foucault to connote a Nietzschean model of investigating origins. Michel Foucault, Language, Counter-Memory, Practice, ed. Donald F. Bouchard, trans. Donald F. Bouchard and Sherry Simon (Ithaca: Cornell University Press, 1977), 139–64.

40. David Biale, Kabbalah and Counter-History, 2nd ed. (Cambridge: Harvard University Press, 1982), 6–8.

41. Ibid., 152–53. The counterhistorian looks back and sees a "dialectic struggle" between mainstream and subterranean traditions (ibid., 6–8). Foucauldian countermemory likewise resists placing a premium on recognition, continuity and knowledge, concepts which inform historical inquiry in the Platonic and Christian metaphysical framework. Divorced from these values, history "introduces discontinuity into our very being— as it divides our emotions, dramatizes our instincts, multiplies our body and sets it against itself. . . . It will uproot its traditional foundations and relentlessly disrupt its pretended continuity" (Foucault, Language, 154). What this conception of history (guided by Nietzsche's notion of genealogy) offers is often divisive, parodic, even carnevalesque.

42. Cited in The Zionist Idea, ed. Arthur Hertzberg (New York: Atheneum, 1959) 293–95.

43. Beer-Hofmann, JD, 88. "Groß—ist der Gott! Und ist mit uns! / (Leiser, als vertraue er Geheimes an:) Zu viel mit uns—Idnibaál—zu viel— / . . . / Zu nah umweht uns dieser Gott—was will Er? / Was will Er—daß Er also uns umdrängt?!" (Beer-Hofmann, Historie, 46).

44. Beer-Hofmann, JD, 121–22. "Wählst Du—Du Gott da droben— / Dazu mich aus? Dann komm zu mir und raune / Ins Ohr mir, wie ich Rede stehen, wie ich— / Ich—Dein Geschöpf—Dich Gott entschulden soll! / Von Schauern geschüttelt / Sprich, sprich—Furchtbarer Du, wenn Du uns redest— / Schrecklicher Du, wenn Du uns schweigst!" (Beer-Hofmann, Historie, 71–72).

45. Beer-Hofmann, JD, 159. "Was Vätern Du gelobt hast—nimm es wieder / Ich löse Dich—Du Gott—aus Deinem Eid!" (Beer-Hofmann, Historie, 98).

46. Beer-Hofmann, JD, 106. "Idnibaál aus Gebál, / Des Jizchaks aus Beér-Scheba Knecht—sei frei!" (Beer-Hofmann, Historie, 61).

47. Beer-Hofmann, JD, 122. "Ich will nicht diesen Gott, der immer nahe! / (Drängender) Jaákob komm! Laß Ihm dies Land, darinnen / Man tags vor Glut—und nachts vor Frost verschmachtet! / Laß Ihm dies Land und laß Ihm seinen Segen! / Mit mir, Jaákob, komm! Flieh diesen Gott" (Beer-Hofmann, Historie, 72).

48. Beer-Hofmann, JD, 127. "So—schneid' ich in euch ein, heilige Zeichen! / Feindlicher Bruder du, vom Mutterleib her— / Aus freier Wahl sei mir von neuem Bruder! / (Einen Schritt zurücktretend, neigt er ein wenig die Arme zur Erde.) Ström'—ström' entzweites Blut zur Erde nieder / Und mische dich—und werde wieder eins! / Blutbrüder wurden Edom und Jaákob" (Beer-Hofmann, Historie, 75).

49. Beer-Hofmann, JD, 130. "Gott braucht mich so— und anders dich! Nur weil / Du, Edom bist—darf ich, Jaákob sein!" (Beer-Hofmann, Historie, 77).

50. Beer-Hofmann, JD, 119. "Jaákob: So—sprach Er auf Moriah zu Abráham: 'Durch deinen Samen sollen alle Völker / Gesegnet sein!' Edom: (ihn anblickend:) Die Fremden . . . ? Jaákob: Ja!" (Beer-Hofmann, Historie, 70).

51. "Wißt ihr nicht, wer ihr wart und wer ihr seid?! / Hirten und Bauern—Freie—wart ihr hier— / Bis nach Mizrajim euch Geschick verschlug!" (Beer-Hofmann, Historie, 298).

52. "—der HERR weiß:/ Ich will es anders! Und nicht viel erbitt ich: / Ein wenig Frieden—eine Spanne Zeit— / Die Saat zu werfen nur, daß ein Geschlecht /Aufgehe— nicht uns gleichend—besser, reiner! / Eins, das nicht froh wird, wenn es Qual ringsum weiß— / Nicht atmen kann, wenn Fron daneben keucht— / Das nicht nach Herrschaft giert—sich nicht verwirft /An Glanz und Macht" (ibid., 301).

53. "Abischai zornig dreinfahrend: / Warum nicht Glanz und Macht?! / Der Herr hat doch mit eigener Hand die Kinder / Jisróels aus Mizrajim ausgeführt— / David: Und hat mit eigener Hand die Kinder Arams / Aus Kir geführt—aus Kaphtor die Pelischtim— / In unerbittlicher Abweisung, Abischai anherrschend: / Wie—sie—nicht anders gelten wir vor Gott! / Abischai hartnäckig: / Wir sind erwählt! / David in Zorn und Hohn auflachend: / Bist dus?!—Narr! / Drohend und warnend: Nur, solang du / Zu tausend schweren Pflichten selbst dich wählst- / Bereit, dich hinzugeben, wenn es ruft— / So—lang: 'Erwählt'— / Allen Anspruch erbarmungslos hinwegfegend: / —und keinen Atem länger!" (ibid., 301–2).

54. "Moriah heißt der Fels des tiefsten Leidens! / Drum wählt ihn David! Heilger ist kein Ort."

55. Beer-Hofmann, *Historie*, 300.

56. "Flammt, lodert mit ihm,—und *vergeßt* zu fragen, / Ob ihr im Brand nicht auch euch selbst verzehrt! / Nicht kalt, nicht sicher seid, nicht welt-zufrieden— / Bangt, ringt, laßt immer neu *hinein* euch reißen / In Gottes Braus—sein heilges Sturmeswehen) (ibid., 303).

57. Johann Jakob Bachofen, *Der Mythus von Orient und Occident: Eine Metaphysik der alten Welt*, ed. Manfred Schroeter (Munich: Beck, 1926), 256.

58. "Aus Zeit, die ihnen ist wie Zeit der Märchen, ragt sie, / Ein scheu gegrüßtes, heiliges Ahnenbild, / Dem man an seltnen Tagen räuchert, spendet, / Geneigt nur naht in Ehrfurcht, nicht in Liebe" (Beer-Hofmann, *Historie*, 139–40).

59. "David: *bebend:* Weißt du nicht Rat?—Du hast so *viel* gesehn! / Ruth: *unbewegt:* Wie *wüßt* ich Rat?— / *Die Stimme dunkelt ein wenig:* Ich hab so *viel* gesehn! / David: *beschwörend, leise:* Verschließ dich nicht von mir— / *Hilfe-suchend:* ich bin *dein* Blut! / Ruth: *entrückt allem Ergriffen-werden. Mit dem Worte / 'Sohn' jedesmal immer weitere / Ferne zwischen sich und / David legend. Ruhig. Hell:* Ja!— Sohn—des Sohnes—meines / Sohnes, Obed! / Da er mir starb—wie ist das *lang* her—, meint ich / Vor Weh, ich stürbe mit— / *Tief Atem holend:* —und hab doch *weiter* / Gelebt—begrub, was mich begraben sollte— / Alles verließ mich, ging—zuletzt ging auch mein Weh! / David: Sprich, Ahne!—Wie Maáchas Stimme ist die deine— / Kühl, silbern—Morgenluft auf Fieberschläfen! / Gib Rat—ich *brauch* ihn! / Ruth: *zum erstenmal löst sich aus ihrer Regungslosigkeit eine leichte Bewegung der Hand, die—unter dem Silberschleier—nach dem Laub der Rebe tastet, das die Brüstung überwächst:* Da—die junge Ranke / Der Rebe schwankt noch nachts im Wind—am Morgen / Hat—augenlos—treu ihrer tiefsten Art / Sie *schon* sich Halt gefunden—braucht nicht Rat! / David: Gib *du* mir Halt! *Ein* Wort nur gib! / Ruth: *schon ins Dunkel zurücktretend:* Sei treu! / *Sie ist nicht mehr zu sehen. . . . / David sich an die Brüstung werfend, als wollte er ihr nach:* Treu— wem? / *Er horcht einen Augenblick.* Fort!— / *Nachsinnend:* Meinem Volk?—Dem Eid?" (ibid., 319–20).

60. "Dein—*unser*-Leben,—trags / Dann lächelnd noch ein Weilchen durch die Welt" (ibid., 350).

61. "Dies ist mein Ich—mein wahres!" (ibid.).

62. "In dich hinein—Maácha—warf ichs,—hüt es— / Bewahrs—und lächle, wenn die andern meinen—/ Ich wär nicht mehr!— / . . . Ich barg mich nur in dich." (ibid.).

63. "*Wenn* unabwendbar über uns jetzt einer / die eisigen schweren schwarzen Flügel schlägt— / *Wenn* jetzt ein Opfer sein muß—(*Den Kranz sich vom Kopf reißend und zur Seite schleudernd, den Kopf in den Nacken geworfen, sich darbietend:*) Hier!—sei *ich* es— / Nicht er!" (ibid., 351).

64. "Noch einmal—du / Schon ferne Welle meines Blutes—woge zurück zum Quell!" (ibid., 471).

65. "*David hebt mit gestreckten Händen die Krone, bis sie hoch über seinem Haupt ist. Er lehnt den Kopf in den Nacken. Zur Krone aufblickend:* / Krone—schwere *du* — / Er senkt den Kopf. Mit jähem Ruck die Krone entschlossen sich aufs Haupt drückend: ich *will* dich tragen! . . . David steht gesenkten Hauptes, die Arme ergeben gebreitet. Hinter ihm ragt regungslos, vom Mondlicht überrieselt, eine silberne Säule: Ruth. Über den Mauern Hebrons ist am unbewölkten Nachthimmel die schmale Sichel des jungen Mondes aufgestiegen*" (ibid., 474).

66. "Urmutter von uns allen" (ibid., 135).

67. "Und wo der Weg sich wendet nach Beth-Lechem, / Da sank in Wehen Rahel—und gebar" (ibid., 134).

68. "Im Volke sagten sie, aus Rahels Grab / Ertöne Klage, nachts, wenn Unheil sich / Jisróels Kindern vorbereite. Und / der Spruch geht so, von alter Zeit her: 'Rahel / Erhebet Klage laut und weinet bitter / Um ihre Kinder—und ihr wird kein Trost!'" (ibid., 161).

69. "Das sang Ruth nie! Kein Lied wars—nein, viel mehr: / Sie sprach und *tat* es! Und war noch so jung! / Zu einer alten Frau, die einsam litt / Und Ruth sehr liebte, sprach sie's—*nicht zum Liebsten!*" *Kopfschüttelnd, lächelnd:* "Kein Liebeslied!—Scheints nun nicht mehr so schön?" (ibid., 262).

70. "David: Was soll jetzt aus mir werden?!/ Ruth: Was aus uns *allen* einst wird: Dung der Erde!— / Vielleicht ein Lied— / —auch *dieses* bald verweht! Und doch: bis dahin—ewiger nicht, und nicht / Vergänglicher als SEINE Sterne—mußt du, / Wie sie, vollenden—David!—deine Bahn!" (ibid., 471).

71. Cited in Peters, *Richard Beer-Hofmann*, 309.

72. Buber first sent him a copy of the *Reden über das Judentum* (1911), the lectures that had exerted such powerful influence in the Zionist youth movement. In December 1912, he invited Beer-Hofmann to contribute to the volume *Vom Judentum* (discussed in chapter 5).

73. Letter, April 13, 1913, in *Briefwechsel aus sieben Jahrzehnten*, by Martin Buber, vol. 1, 1897–1918, ed. Grete Schaeder (Heidelberg: Lambert Schneider, 1972), 327.

74. Buber, *Briefwechsel*, 327–28. Buber's response both grants and respectfully challenges Beer-Hofmann's concern: "Aber das von Grund aus Verkehrte daran ist nicht die Tatsache, sondern daß wir so lange die Tatsache für

unser Tun und Nichttun bestimmend sein ließen. . . .
Wenn Gott mir zusieht, kann ich mich seines Blickes nicht
würdiger erweisen, als wenn ich mich darum nicht bekümmere; und wenn Satan mir zusieht, kann ich seinen Blick
nicht vollkommener zuschanden machen, als wenn ich
mich darum nicht bekümmere. Aber ich weiß, daß ich gerade Ihnen das nicht zu sagen brauche." Letter, May 16,
1913, in Buber, *Briefwechsel,* 332.

CONCLUSION

1. Hans Blumenberg, *Lebensthemen* (Stuttgart:
Philipp Reclam, 1998), 13–14. The *Ergebnis/Erlebnis* distinction first appeared in W. T. Krug's *Encyklopädisches
Lexikon in bezug auf die neuste Literatur und Geschichte
der Philosophie* (Leipzig: Brockhaus, 1838).

2. "Was so im Fluß der Zeit eine Einheit in der
Präsenz bildet, weil es eine einheitliche Bedeutung hat,
ist die kleinste Einheit, die wir als Erlebnis bezeichnen
können." Wilhelm Dilthey, *Der Aufbau der Geschichtlichen Welt in den Geisteswissenschaften,* 4th ed., in
Gesammelte Schriften, vol. 7 (Stuttgart: B. G. Teubner,
1965), 194–95.

3. Dilthey writes that "observation destroys the act of
experiencing," and that such observed moments become
instead "remembered moments" that are no longer fluid
but objectified.Ibid., 195.

4. Kirshenblatt-Gimblett, *Destination Culture,* 194.

5. Hofmannsthal wrote, "Wie das Geistige, das in uns
lebt, von jenen durch diese zu uns gelangen konnte, ist
uns der dunkelste aller Prozesse" (How the spiritual that
lives within us was able to reach us, from those ones by
way of these, appears to us as the darkest process of all).
"Vom dichtersichen Dasein" (1907), in Hofmannsthal,
Reden und Aufsätze I, 84.

6. Schnitzler, *Briefe I,* 578.

7. Beer-Hofmann, *Gesammelte Werke,* 679. Gotthart
Wunberg described it: "Der Gegenstand der Erinnerung
ist aber nicht anzuschauen, er ist nur zu erinnern. . . .
Die wiedergewonnene Erinnerung ist zwar dieselbe wie
die verlorene, reale, bedarf aber einer anderen Auf-
nahme, einer anderen Rezeption als die erste. . . . Der
Mythos von Orpheus und Eurydike jedenfalls erklärt,
daß es zwar möglich ist, unsere Erinnerungen ihrem
Vergessen zu entreißen, daß sie aber ihre eigene Behand-
lung fordern, wenn sie bleiben sollen" (Wunberg,
Wiedererkennen, 114; see also 112–20).

8. Sigmund Freud, *The Origins of Religion,* trans.
James Strachey (Harmondsworth: Penguin, 1990), 349.

9. Ibid., 350.

BIBLIOGRAPHY

Alberti, Conrad. "Das Milieu." In *Die literarische Moderne*, 2nd ed., edited by Gotthart Wunberg and Stephan Dietrich, 83–95. Freiburg am Breisgau: Rombach, 1998.

Anderson, Wayne. *Freud, Leonardo Da Vinci, and the Vulture's Tail: A Refreshing Look at Leonardo's Sexuality*. New York: Other Press, 2001.

Arnim, Achim von. *Die Majorats-Herren*. In *Sämtliche Erzählungen, 1818–1830*, vol. 2, edited by Renate Meoring, 363–91. Frankfurt am Main: Deutscher Klassiker, 1992.

Bab, Julius. "Hugo von Hofmannsthal." In *Jüdisches Lexicon*. Berlin: Jüdischer, 1928.

Bachofen, Johann Jakob. *Der Mythus von Orient und Occident: Eine Metaphysik der alten Welt*. Edited by Manfred Schroeter. Munich: Beck, 1926.

Badt-Strauss, Bertha. Review of *Die Historie von König David*, by Richard Beer-Hofmann. *Jüdische Rundschau* 39, no. 6 (1934).

Bahr, Hermann. *Dialog vom Tragischen*. Berlin: S. Fischer, 1904.

———. *Rezensionen: Wiener Theater, 1901–1903*. Berlin: S. Fischer, 1903.

Bakhtin, Mikhail. *The Dialogic Imagination: Four Essays*. Edited by Michael Holquist. Translated by Caryl Emerson and Michael Holquist. Austin: University of Texas Press, 1981.

Bal, Mieke, Jonathan Crewe, and Leo Spitzer. *Acts of Memory: Cultural Recall in the Present*. Hanover, N.H.: University Press of New England, 1999.

Beer-Hofmann, Richard. "Form-Chaos." In *Gesammelte Werke*, 628. Frankfurt am Main: S. Fischer, 1963.

———. *Große Richard Beer-Hofmann-Ausgabe*. Edited by Günter Hermes, Michael M. Schardt, and Andreas Thomasberger. 6 vols. Paderborn: Igel-Verlag Literatur, 1993–2002.

———. *Jacob's Dream*. Translated by Ida Bension Wynn. New York: Johannespresse, 1946.

———. Letter to Erich von Kahler. 1933. In Beer-Hofmann, *Gesammelte Werke*, 877–79. Frankfurt am Main: S. Fischer, 1963.

Beller, Steven, ed. *Rethinking Vienna 1900*. New York: Berghahn Books, 2001.

———. *Vienna and the Jews, 1867–1938*. Cambridge: Cambridge University Press, 1989.

———. "Was bedeutet es, 'Wien um 1900' als eine jüdische Stadt zu bezeichnen?" *Zeitgeschichte* 23, nos. 7–8 (1996): 274–80.

Benjamin, Walter. *Gesammelte Schriften*. Vols. 1 and 2. Edited by Rolf Tiedemann and Hermann Schweppenhäuser. Frankfurt am Main: Suhrkamp, 1980.

———. *Das Passagen-Werk*. Vol 1. Edited by Rolf Tiedemann. Frankfurt am Main: Suhrkamp, 1982.

Bergson, Henri. *Creative Evolution*. 1907. Translated by Arthur Mitchell. New York: Modern Library, 1944. Reprint, Westport, Conn.: Greenwood Press, 1975.

———. *Matter and Memory*. 1896. 3rd. ed. Translated by N. M. Paul and W. S. Palmer. New York: Zone Books, 1991.

Bergstein, Mary. "Freud's *Moses of Michelangelo:* Vasari, Photography, and Art Historical Practice." *Art Bulletin* 88, no. 1 (2006): 158–75.

Berman, Russell A. Introduction to Schnitzler, *The Road into the Open*, vii–xvi.

Bernstein, Richard. *Freud and the Legacy of Moses*. Cambridge: Cambridge University Press, 1998.

Bhaba, Homi K. *The Location of Culture*. London: Routledge, 1994.

Biale, David. *Kabbalah and Counter-History*. 2nd ed. Cambridge, Mass.: Harvard University Press, 1982.

Biemann, Asher. "The Problem of Tradition and Reform in Jewish Renaissance and Renaissancism." *Jewish Social Studies* 8, no.1 (2001): 58–87.

Bilski, Emily D., and Emily Braun. *Jewish Women and Their Salons: The Power of Conversation*. New Haven: Yale University Press, 2005.

Birmele, Jutta. "Strategies of Persuasion: The Case of *Leonard da Vinci*." In *Reading Freud's Reading*, edited by Sander L. Gilman, Jutta Birmele, Jay Geller, and Valerie D. Greenberg, 129–151. New York: New York University Press, 1994.

Bloom, Harold. Foreword to Yerushalmi, *Zakhor*.

———. *The Strong Light of the Canonical. Kafka, Freud, and Scholem as Revisionists of Jewish Culture and Thought*. City College Papers 20. New York: City College, 1987.

Blumenberg, Hans. *Lebensthemen*. Stuttgart: Philipp Reclam, 1998.

Bolkowsky, Sidney M. *The Distorted Image: German Jew-*

ish *Perceptions of Germans and Germany.* New York: Elsevier, 1975.

Boose, Linda E. "The Father's House and the Daughter in It: The Structures of Western Culture's Daughter-Father Relationship." In *Daughters and Fathers,* edited by Linda E. Boose and Betty S. Flowers, 19–74. Baltimore: Johns Hopkins University Press, 1989.

Borchmeyer, Dieter, ed. *Richard Beer-Hofmann: "Zwischen Ästhetizismus und Judentum."* Paderborn: Igel-Verlag Wissenschaft, 1996.

Bottenberg, Joanna. "The Hofmannsthal-Strauss Collaboration." In *A Companion to the Works of Hugo von Hofmannsthal,* edited by Thomas A. Kovach, 117–37. Rochester: Camden House, 2002.

Brandes, Georg, and Arthur Schnitzler. *Ein Briefwechsel.* Edited by Kurt Bergel. Bern: Francke, 1956.

Brandstetter, Gabriele. "Der Traum vom anderen Tanz: Hofmannsthals Ästhetik des Schöpferischen im Dialog 'Furcht.'" In "Hugo von Hofmannsthal: Dichtung als Vermittlung der Künste," edited by Gottfried Schramm. Special issue, *Freiburger Universitätsblätter* 112 (June 1991): 37–58.

Brentano, Clemens. *Sämtliche Werke und Briefe.* Vol. 6, no. 1. Edited by Jürgen Behrens, Wolfgang Frühwald, and Detlev Lüders. Stuttgart: W. Kolhammer, 1975.

Brooks, Peter. *Reading for the Plot: Design and Intention in Narrative.* Cambridge, Mass.: Harvard University Press, 1984.

Bruce, Iris. "Which Way Out? Schnitzler's and Salten's Conflicting Responses to Cultural Zionism." In *A Companion to the Works of Arthur Schnitzler,* edited by Dagmar C. G. Lorenz, 103–26. Rochester: Camden House, 2003.

Buber, Martin. *Briefwechsel aus sieben Jahrzehnten.* Heidelberg: Lambert Schneider, 1972.

———. "Die Erneuerung des Judentums." In *Der Jude und sein Judentum: Gesammelte Aufsätze und Reden.* Gerlingen: L. Schneider, 1993.

———. "Der Geist des Orients und das Judentum." In *Vom Geist des Judentums,* 9–48. Leipzig: Kurt Wolff, 1916.

———. "Jewish Religiosity." 1912–14. In *On Judaism,* edited by Nahum M. Glatzer, 79–94. New York: Schocken Books, 1987.

Bunzl, Matti. "Of Holograms and Storage Areas: Modernity and Postmodernity at Vienna's Jewish Museum." *Cultural Anthropology* 18, no. 4 (2003): 435–68.

———. "The Poetics of Politics and the Politics of Poetics: Richard Beer-Hofmann and Theodor Herzl

Reconsidered." *German Quarterly* 69, no. 3 (1996): 277–304.

Caruth, Cathy. *Unclaimed Experience: Trauma, Narrative, and History.* Baltimore: Johns Hopkins University Press, 1996.

Cixous, Hélène, and Catherine Clément. *The Newly Born Woman.* Translated by Betsy Wing. Minneapolis: University of Minnesota Press, 1986.

Cohen, Gerson D. "The Blessing of Assimilation in Jewish History." In *Great Jewish Speeches Throughout History,* edited by Steve Israel and Seth Forman, 183–91. Northvale, N.J.: Jason Aronson, 1994.

Cohn, Dorrit. *Transparent Minds: Narrative Modes for Presenting Consciousness in Fiction.* Princeton: Princeton University Press, 1978.

———. "A Triad of Dream Narratives: *Der Tod Georgs, Das Märchen der 672. Nacht, Traumnovelle.*" In *Focus on Vienna 1900: Change and Continuity in Literature, Music, Art, and Intellectual History,* edited by Erika Nielson, 58–71. Munich: Fink, 1982.

Collins, Bradley I. *Leonardo, Psychoanalysis, and Art History: A Critical Study of Psychobiographical Approaches to Leonardo da Vinci.* Evanston: Northwestern University Press, 1997.

Daviau, Donald G. "Hugo von Hofmannsthal's Pantomime 'Der Schüler': Experiment in Form—Exercise in Nihilism." *Modern Austrian Literature* 1, no. 1 (1968): 4–30.

Deleuze, Gilles, and Félix Guattari. *Kafka: Toward a Minor Literature.* Translated by Dana Polan. Minneapolis: University of Minnesota Press, 1986.

Derrida, Jacques. *Dissemination.* Translated by Barbara Johnson. Chicago: University of Chicago Press, 1981.

———. *Writing and Difference.* Translated by Alan Bass. Chicago: University of Chicago Press, 1978.

Dilthey, Wilhelm. *Der Aufbau der Geschichtlichen Welt in den Geisteswissenschaften.* 4th ed. In *Gesammelte Schriften,* vol. 7. Stuttgart: B. G. Teubner, 1965.

Easton, Laird McLeod. *The Red Count: The Life and Times of Harry Kessler.* Berkeley and Los Angeles: University of California Press, 2002.

Eberhardt, Sören, and Charis Goer, eds. *Über Richard Beer-Hofmann: Rezeptionsdokumente aus 100 Jahren.* Paderborn: Igel-Verlag Wissenschaft, 1996.

Eco, Umberto. "An *Ars Oblivionalis?* Forget It!" *PMLA* 103, no.3 (1988): 254–61.

Elias, Norbert. "Die satisfaktionsfähige Gesellschaft." In *Studien über die Deutschen,* edited by Michael Schröter, 61–158. Frankfurt am Main: Suhrkamp, 1998.

Elstun, Esther. *Richard Beer-Hofmann: His Life and*

Work. University Park, PA: Pennsylvania State University Press, 1983.

Fliedl, Konstanze. *Arthur Schnitzler: Poetik der Erinnerung.* Vienna: Böhlau, 1997.

Foucault, Michel. *Language, Counter-Memory, Practice.* Edited by Donald F. Bouchard. Translated by Donald F. Bouchard and Sherry Simon. Ithaca: Cornell University Press, 1977.

Fraiman, Sarah. *Judaism in the Works of Beer-Hofmann and Feuchtwanger.* New York: Peter Lang, 1998.

Freud, Sigmund. "Briefe an Arthur Schnitzler." *Die Neue Rundschau* 66, vol. 1 (1955): 95–106.

———. *A Childhood Memory of Leonardo da Vinci.* In *Standard Edition,* 11:57–137.

———. *Eine Kindheitserinnerung des Leonardo da Vinci.* In *Studienausgabe,* 10:87–159.

———. Letter, July 10, 1936. *Fischer Almanach* 77 (1963): 64.

———. *Der Mann Moses und die monotheistische Religion.* In *Studienausgabe,* 9:455–581.

———. *Moses and Monotheism.* In *Standard Edition,* 23:1–137.

———. *Der Moses des Michelangelo.* In *Studienausgabe,* 10:196–222.

———. *The Moses of Michelangelo.* In *Standard Edition,* 11:57–137.

———. *The Origins of Religion.* Translated by James Strachey. Harmondsworth: Penguin, 1990.

———. Postscript to *An Autobiographical Study.* 1935. In *Standard Edition,* 20:71–74.

———. Preface to the Hebrew Edition of *Totem and Taboo.* In *Standard Edition,* 13:xv; *Studienausgabe,* 9:293 [in German].

———. *The Psychopathology of Everyday Life.* In *Standard Edition,* 6:1–279.

———. *The Standard Edition of the Complete Psychological Works of Sigmund Freud.* Edited and translated by James Strachey. 24 vols. London: Hogarth Press, 1953.

———. *Studienausgabe.* Edited by Alexander Mitscherlich, Angela Richards, and James Strachey. 12 vols. Frankfurt am Main: Fischer Taschenbuch, 1982.

Freud, Sigmund, and Wilhelm Fliess. *The Complete Letters of Sigmund Freud to Wilhelm Fliess, 1887–1904.* Edited and translated by Jeffrey Moussaieff Masson. Cambridge, Mass.: Belknap Press of Harvard University Press, 1985.

Freud, Sigmund, and C. G. Jung. *The Freud/Jung Letters: The Correspondence Between Sigmund Freud and C. G. Jung.* Edited by William McGuire. Translated by Ralph Mannheim and R. F. C. Hull. Princeton: Princeton University Press, 1974.

Freud, Sigmund, and Lou Andreas-Salomé. *Sigmund Freud and Lou Andreas-Salomé: Letters.* Edited by Ernst Pfeiffer. Translated by William Robson-Scott and Elaine Robson-Scott. New York: W. W. Norton, 1966.

Freud, Sigmund, and Arnold Zweig. *The Letters of Sigmund Freud and Arnold Zweig.* Edited by Ernst L. Freud. Translated by Elaine Robson-Scott and William Robson-Scott. New York: Harcourt Brace and World, 1970.

Frieden, Ken. *Freud's Dream of Interpretation.* Albany: SUNY Press, 1990.

———. "Sigmund Freud's Passover Dream Responds to Theodor Herzl's Zionist Dream." In *Yale Companion to Jewish Writing and Thought in German Culture, 1096–1996,* edited by Sander L. Gilman and Jack Zipes, 240–248. New Haven: Yale University Press, 1997.

Garafola, Lynn. *Diaghilev's Ballets Russes.* Oxford: Oxford University Press, 1989.

Gay, Peter. *Freud: A Life for Our Time.* New York: W. W. Norton, 1988.

"Gedächtnis des Jahrhunderts, Das." Special issue, *Transit* 22 (Winter 2001/2002).

Gillman, Abigail. "Cultural Awakening and Historical Forgetting: The Architecture of Memory in the Jüdisches Museum Wien and in Rachel Whiteread's 'Nameless Library.'" *New German Critique* 93 (Fall 2004): 145–73.

———. "Failed Bildung and the Aesthetics of Detachment: Schnitzler's 'Der Weg ins Freie.'" In *Confrontations/Accommodations: German-Jewish Literary and Cultural History from Heine to Wasserman,* edited by Mark Gelber, 209–36. Tübingen: Niemeyer, 2004.

———. "'Ich suche ein Asyl für meine Vergangenheit': Schnitzler's Poetics of Memory." In *Arthur Schnitzler: Zeitgenossenschaften/Contemporaneities,* edited by Ian Foster and Florian Krobb, 141–56. Bern: Peter Lang, 2002.

Gilman, Sander L. *Freud, Race, and Gender.* Princeton: Princeton University Press, 1993.

———. *Jewish Self-Hatred: Anti-Semitism and the Hidden Language of the Jews.* Baltimore: Johns Hopkins University Press, 1986.

———. *The Jew's Body.* New York: Routledge, 1991.

Ginzburg, Carlo. "Morelli, Freud, and Sherlock Holmes: Clues and Scientific Method." *History Workshop Journal* 9, no. 1 (1980): 5–36.

Goldstein, Bluma. *Reinscribing Moses.* Cambridge, Mass.: Harvard University Press, 1992.

BIBLIOGRAPHY

Gombrich, Ernst. "Le langage et l'inhumain." *Revue d'esthétique* 9 (1985): 65–70.

———. *The Visual Arts in Vienna Circa 1900; and Reflections on the Jewish Catastrophe.* London: Austrian Cultural Institute, 1997.

Gruber, Ruth Ellen. *Virtually Jewish.* Berkeley and Los Angeles: University of California Press, 2002.

Haas, Willy. "Hugo von Hofmannsthal." In *Juden in der deutschen Literatur,* edited by Gustav Krojanker, 139–64. Berlin:Welt, 1922.

Halbwachs, Maurice. *On Collective Memory.* Edited and translated by Lewis A. Coser. Chicago: University of Chicago Press, 1992.

Hank, Rainer. *Mortifikation und Beschwörung: Zur Veränderung ästhetischer Wahrnehmung in der Moderne am Beispiel des Frühwerkes Richard Beer-Hofmanns.* Frankfurt am Main: Peter Lang, 1984.

Harris, Kathleen. "Richard Beer-Hofmann: Ein großer Wiener jüdischer—und deutscher—Dichter: Am Beispiel von 'Jaakobs Traum.'" In *Kontroversen, alte und neue: Akten des VII. Internationalen Germanisten-Kongresses, Göttingen 1985,* vol. 5, edited by Albrecht Schöne, Walter Röll, and Hans-Peter Bayerdörfer, 171–75. Tübingen: Niemeyer, 1986.

Haverkamp, Anselm, and Renate Lachmann. "Text als Mnemotechnik—Panorama einer Diskussion." In *Gedächtniskunst: Raum—Bild—Schrift: Studien zur Mnemotechnik,* edited by Anselm Haverkamp and Renate Lachmann, 7–22. Frankfurt am Main: Suhrkamp, 1991.

Hawes, J. M. "'Als käme er von einer weiten Reise heim:' Fremderfahrung als Erfahrung des eigenen entfremdeten Ichs in Arthur Schnitzlers Roman *Der Weg ins Freie.*" In *Reisen im Diskurs: Modelle der literarischen Fremderfahrung von den Pilgerberichten bis zur Postmoderne,* edited by Anne Fuchs and Theo Harden, 509–20. Heidelberg: Winter, 1995.

———. "The Secret Life of Georg von Wergenthin: Nietzschean Analysis and Narrative Authority in Arthur Schnitzler's *Der Weg ins Freie.*" *Modern Language Review* 90, no. 2 (1995): 377–87.

Hawkins, Peter S. "Naming Names: The Art of Memory and the NAMES Project AIDS Quilt." *Critical Inquiry* 19, no. 4 (1993): 752–79.

Heimann-Jelinek, Felicitas, ed. *Zu Gast bei Beer-Hofman: Eine Ausstellung über das jüdische Wien der Jahrhundertwende.* Vienna: Jüdisches Museum, 1998.

Heine, Heinrich. "Atta Troll." In *Heines Werke,* vol. 2. Berlin: Aufbau, 1974.

———. *Der Doktor Faust.* Edited by Joseph A. Kruse. Stuttgart: Philipp Reclam, 1991.

———. *The Prose Writings of Heinrich Heine.* Edited by Havelock Ellis. London: W. Scott, 1887. Reprint, New York: Arno Press, 1973.

Hering, Ewald. *Über das Gedächtnis als eine allgemeine Funktion der organisierten Materie.* Leipzig: Wilhelm Engelmann, 1905.

Hertzberg, Arthur, ed. *The Zionist Idea.* New York: Atheneum, 1959.

Herzl, Theodor. *Briefe und Tagebücher.* Vol. 1, *Briefe und autobiographische Notitzen, 1866–1895.* Edited by Johannes Wachten. Berlin: Propyläen, 1983.

———. *Briefe und Tagebücher.* Vol. 4, *Briefe, Anfang Mai 1895–Anfang Dezember 1898.* Edited by Barbara Schäfer. Frankfurt am Main: Ullstein, 1990.

———. *Das neue Ghetto.* Vienna: R. Loewit, 1920.

Hofmannsthal, Hugo von. *Dramen II: 1892–1905.* Edited by Bernd Schoeller. Frankfurt am Main: Fischer Taschenbuch, 1979.

———. *Dramen V: Operndichtungen.* Edited by Bernd Schoeller. Frankfurt am Main: Fischer Taschenbuch, 1979.

———. *Dramen VI: Ballette; Pantomimen; Bearbeitungen; Übersetzungen.* Edited by Bernd Schoeller. Frankfurt am Main: Fischer Taschenbuch, 1979.

———. *Erzählungen, Erfundene Gespräche und Briefe. Reisen.* Edited by Bernd Schoeller. Frankfurt am Main: Fischer Taschenbuch, 1979.

———. *Reden und Aufsätze I: 1891–1913.* Edited by Bernd Schoeller. Frankfurt am Main: Fischer Taschenbuch, 1979.

———. *Reden und Aufsätze II: 1914–1924.* Edited by Bernd Schoeller. Frankfurt am Main: Fischer Taschenbuch Verlag, 1979.

———. *Reden und Aufsätze III:1925–1929: Aufzeichnungen.* Edited by Bernd Schoeller. Frankfurt am Main: Fischer Taschenbuch Verlag, 1979.

———. *Papers.* Houghton Library, Harvard University.

Hofmannsthal, Hugo von, and Richard Beer-Hofmann. *Briefwechsel.* Edited by Eugene Weber. Frankfurt am Main: S. Fischer, 1972.

Hofmannsthal, Hugo von, and Willy Haas. *Ein Briefwechsel.* Berlin: Propyläen, 1968.

Hofmannsthal, Hugo von, and Harry Graf Kessler. *Briefwechsel, 1898–1929.* Edited by Hilde Burger. Frankfurt am Main: Insel, 1968.

Hofmannsthal, Hugo von, and Arthur Schnitzler. *Briefwechsel.* Edited by Therese Nickl and Heinrich Schnitzler. Frankfurt am Main: Fischer Taschenbuch, 1983.

Hofmannsthal, Hugo von, and Richard Strauss. *Briefwechsel.* Edited by Willi Schuh. Zürich: Atlantis, 1964.

Hutton, Patrick H. *History as an Art of Memory.* Hanover, N.H.: University Press of New England, 1993.

Huyssen, Andreas. *Twilight Memories: Marking Time in a Culture of Amnesia.* London: Routledge, 1995.

James, William. *The Principles of Psychology.* Vol. 1. New York: Dover Publishing, Inc., 1950.

Janik, Allan, and Stephen Toulmin. *Wittgenstein's Vienna.* New York: Simon and Schuster, 1973.

Kafka, Franz. "Brief an den Vater." In *Zur Frage der Gesetze und andere Schriften aus dem Nachlass.* Frankfurt am Main: Fischer Taschenbuch, 1999.

———. *The Complete Stories.* Edited by Nahum N. Glatzer. New York: Schocken Books, 1995.

———. *Letters to Friends, Family, and Editors.* Translated by Richard Winston and Clara Winston. New York: Schocken Books, 1977.

Kalmar, Ivan Davidson, and Derek Jonathan Penslar, eds. *Orientalism and the Jews.* Waltham, Mass.: Brandeis University Press, 2005.

Katz, Jacob. *Out of the Ghetto: The Social Background of Jewish Emancipation, 1770–1870.* New York: Schocken Books, 1978.

Kern, Stephen. *The Culture of Time and Space, 1880–1918.* Cambridge, Mass.: Harvard University Press, 1983.

Kessler, Harry. *Berliner Schallkiste* 3 (June 1928).

———. *Das Tagebuch.* Vol. 4, *1906–1914.* Edited by Jörg Schuster. Stuttgart: Cotta, 2005.

Kirshenblatt-Gimblett, Barbara. *Destination Culture: Tourism, Museums, and Heritage.* Berkeley: University of California Press, 1998.

Kovach, Thomas A. *Hofmannsthal and Symbolism: Art and Life in the Work of a Modern Poet.* New York: Peter Lang, 1985.

———. "Traditionalist Modernism or Modernist Traditionalism: The Case of Hugo von Hofmannsthal." *West Virginia University Philological Papers* 39 (1993): 57–61.

Kraft, Werner. *Wort und Gedanke.* Bern: Francke, 1959.

Krobb, Florian. *Selbstdarstellungen: Untersuchungen zur deutsch-jüdischen Erzählliteratur im neunzehnten Jahrhundert*. Würzburg: Königshausen and Neumann, 2000.

Kronfeld, Chana. *On the Margins of Modernism.* Berkeley and Los Angeles: University of California Press, 1996.

Kruse, Joseph A. Afterword to Heine, *Der Doktor Faust.*

Lachmann, Renate. *Memory and Literature.* Translated by Roy Sellars and Anthony Wall. Minneapolis: University of Minnesota Press, 1997.

Lensing, Leo A. "Elektra 'antik u modern': Zu einem Abend der Mittwoch-Gesellschaft im Jahre 1905 (mit einem unbekannten Postkarte Freuds an Paul Federn)." *Luzifer-Amor* 19, no. 38 (2006): 46–75.

Le Rider, Jacques. *Modernity and Crises of Identity: Culture and Society in Fin-de-Siècle Vienna.* Translated by Rosemary Morris. New York: Continuum, 1993.

Liebert, Robert S. *Michelangelo: A Psychoanalytic Study of His Life and Images.* New Haven: Yale University Press, 1983.

Loentz, Elizabeth. "The Problem and Challenge of Jewishness in the City of Schnitzler and Anna O." In *A Companion to the Works of Arthur Schnitzler,* edited by Dagmar C. G. Lorenz, 79–102. Rochester: Camden House, 2003.

Lorenz, Dagmar. *Wiener Moderne.* Stuttgart: J. B. Metzler, 1995.

Low, David. "Questions of Form in Schnitzler's *Der Weg ins Freie.*" *Modern Austrian Literature* 19, nos. 3–4 (1986): 21–32.

Lukács, Georg von. *Die Seele und die Formen.* Berlin: Egon Fleischel, 1911.

Mach, Ernst. *Die Analyse der Empfindungen und das Verhältnis des Physischen zum Psychischen.* 9th ed. Darmstadt: Wissenschaftliche Buchgesellschaft, 1985.

———. *Populärwissenschaftliche Vorlesungen.* 5th ed. Leipzig: J. A. Barth, 1923. Reprint, Vienna: Böhlau, 1987.

Magris, Claudio. *Der habsburgische Mythos in der österreichischen Literatur.* 2nd ed. Salzburg: Otto Müller, 1988.

Mallarmé, Stéphane. "The Mime." Translated by Barbara Johnson. In *Selected Poetry and Prose,* edited by Mary Ann Caws. New York: New Directions, 1982.

———. "Mimique." In *Oeuvres Complétes.* Paris: Gallimard, 1945.

Martens, Lorna. *Shadow Lines: Austrian Literature from Freud to Kafka.* Lincoln: University of Nebraska Press, 1996.

———. "The Theme of Repressed Memory in Hofmannsthal's *Elektra.*" *German Quarterly* 60 (1987): 38–51.

Massine, Leonide. *My Life in Ballet.* Edited by Phyllis Hartnoll. London: Macmillan, 1968.

Mauser, Wolfram. "Hofmannsthals 'Triumph der Zeit': Zur Bedeutung seiner Ballett- und Pantomimen-Libretti." In *Hofmannsthal und das Theater,* edited by Wolfram Mauser, 141–48. Vienna: Karl M. Halosar, 1981.

BIBLIOGRAPHY

Mendes-Flohr, Paul R. *Divided Passions: Jewish Intellectuals and the Experience of Modernity*. Detroit: Wayne State University Press, 1991.

Meyer, Michael A. *The Origins of the Modern Jew: Jewish Identity and European Culture in German, 1749–1824*. Detroit: Wayne State University Press, 1967.

Milfull, John. "Juden, Osterreicher und andere Deutsche." *Geschichte und Gesellschaft* 7, nos. 3–4 (1981): 582–89.

Monti, Claudia. "Mach und die österreichische Literatur: Bahr, Hofmannsthal, Musil." In *Akten des Internationalen Symposiums: "Arthur Schnitzler und seine Zeit,"* edited by Giuseppe Farese, 263–83. Bern: Peter Lang, 1985.

Moretti, Franco. "'A Useless Longing for Myself': The Crisis of the European Bildungsroman, 1898–1914." In *Studies in Historical Change*, edited by Ralph Cohen, 43–59. Charlottesville: University of Virginia Press, 1992.

Mosenthal, S. H. "Jephthas Tochter." In *Gesammelte Werke*, vol. 1, 111–62. Stuttgart: Eduard Hallberger, 1878.

Mosse, George. *German Jews Beyond Judaism*. Bloomington: Indiana University Press, 1985.

Nehring, Wolfgang. "Zwischen Identifikation und Distanz: Zur Darstellung der jüdischen Charaktere in Arthur Schnitzlers *Der Weg ins Freie*." In *Jüdische Komponente in der deutschen Literatur—die Assimilationskontroverse*, edited by Walter Röll und Hans-Peter Bayerdörfer, 162–70. Tübingen: Max Niemeyer, 1986.

Neumann, Hans-Gerhard. *Richard Beer-Hofmann: Studien und Materialien zur "Historie von König David."* Munich: Wilhelm Fink, 1972.

Nietzsche, Friedrich. *The Gay Science*. 2nd ed. Translated by Walter Kaufmann. New York: Vintage Books, 1974.

Nora, Pierre. "Between Memory and History: *Les Lieux de Mémoire*." *Representations* 26 (Spring 1989): 7–25.

Oberholzer, Otto. *Richard Beer-Hofmann*. Bern: Francke, 1947.

Otis, Laura. *Organic Memory: History and the Body in the Late Nineteenth and Early Twentieth Centuries*. Lincoln: University of Nebraska Press, 1994.

Pelli, Moshe. *The Age of Haskalah: Studies in Hebrew Literature of the Enlightenment in Germany*. Leiden: E. J. Brill, 1979.

Perlmann, Michaela L. *Arthur Schnitzler*. Stuttgart: J. B. Metzler, 1987.

Peters, Ulrike. *Richard Beer-Hofmann: Zum jüdischen Selbstverständnis im Wiener Judentum um die Jahrhundertwende*. Frankfurt am Main: Peter Lang, 1993.

Pfeifer, Peter. "Hugo von Hofmannsthal Worries About His Mixed Ancestry." In *Yale Companion to Jewish Writing and Thought in German Culture, 1096–1996*, edited by Sander L. Gilman and Jack Zipes, 212–18. New Haven: Yale University Press, 1997.

Poppel, Stephen M. *Zionism in Germany, 1897–1933: The Shaping of Identity*. Philadelphia: Jewish Publication Society of America, 1977.

Poulet, George. *L'espace Proustien*. Paris: Gallimard, 1963.

Pozharskaya, Militsa, Tatiana Volodina, eds. *The Art of the Ballets Russes: The Russian Seasons in Paris, 1908–1929*. New York: Abbeville Press, 1990.

Radstone, Susannah, ed. *Memory and Methodology*. Oxford: Berg, 2000.

Reik, Theodor. *Arthur Schnitzler als Psycholog*. 1913. Edited by Bernd Urban. Frankfurt am Main: S. Fischer, 1993.

Renner, Ursula. "Mona Lisa—Das 'Rätsel Weib' als 'Frauenphantom des Mannes' im Fin de Siècle." In *Lulu, Lilith, Mona Lisa: Frauenbilder der Jahrhundertwende*, edited by Irmgard Roebling, 139–59. Pfaffenweiler: Centaurus, 1989.

Rieckmann, Jens. "(Anti-)Semitism and Homoeroticism: Hofmannsthal's Reading of Bahr's Novel *Die Rotte Kohras*." *German Quarterly* 66, no. 2 (1993): 212–21.

———. *Aufbruch in die Moderne: Die Anfänge des jungen Wien*. Königstein: Athenäum, 1985.

———. "Zwischen Bewußtsein und Verdrängung: Hofmannsthals jüdisches Erbe." *Deutsche Vierteljahrsschrift für Literaturwissenschaft und Geistesgeschichte* 67, no. 3 (1993): 466–83.

Robertson, Ritchie. *The "Jewish Question" in German Literature, 1749–1939*. Oxford: Oxford University Press, 1999.

Rose, Louis. *The Freudian Calling: Early Viennese Psychoanalysis and the Pursuit of a Cultural Science*. Detroit: Wayne State University Press, 1998.

Rosenfeld, Beate. *Die Golemsage und ihre Verwertung in der deutschen Literatur*. Breslau: Hans Priebatsch, 1934.

Roskies, David G. *The Jewish Search for a Usable Past*. Bloomington: Indiana University Press, 1999.

Rozenblit, Marsha L. "The Assertion of Identity: Jewish Student Nationalism at the University of Vienna Before the First World War." *Leo Baeck Yearbook* 27 (1982): 171–86.

Ryan, Judith. *The Vanishing Subject: Early Psychology and Literary Modernism*. Chicago: University of Chicago Press, 1991.

Said, Edward W. *Orientalism*. New York: Random House, 1979.

Sammons, Jeffrey L. *Heinrich Heine*. Princeton: Princeton University Press, 1980.

———. "The Mystery of the Missing Bildungsroman." *Genre* 14, no. 2 (1980): 229–46.

Schapiro, Meyer. "Leonardo and Freud: An Art-Historical Study." *Journal of the History of Ideas* 17, no. 2 (1956): 147–78.

Scheible, Hartmut. *Literarischer Jugendstil in Wien*. Munich: Artemis, 1984.

Schivelbusch, Wolfgang. *Geschichte der Eisenbahnreise*. Munich: Carl Hanser, 1977.

Schnabel, Werner Willhelm. "*Professor Bernhardi* und die Wiener Zensur: Zur Rezeptionsgeschichte der Schnitzlerschen Komödie." *Jahrbuch der Deutschen Schillergesellschaft* 28 (1984): 349–83.

Schnitzler, Arthur. "Bekenntnis." *Aphorismen und Betrachtungen II, Der Geist im Wort und der Geist in der Tat*. Edited by Robert O. Weiss. Frankfurt am Main: Fischer Taschenbuch Verlag, 1993.

———. *Briefe, 1875–1912*. Edited by Therese Nickl and Heinrich Schnitzler. Frankfurt am Main: S. Fischer, 1981.

———. *Briefe, 1913–1931*. Edited by Peter Michael Braunwarth, Richard Miklin, Susanne Pertlik, and Heinrich Schnitzler. Frankfurt am Main: S. Fischer, 1984.

———. *Jugend in Wien*. Edited by Therese Nickl and Heinrich Schnitzler. Frankfurt am Main: Fischer Taschenbuch, 1996.

———. *Professor Bernhardi*. In *Das weite Land: Dramen, 1909–1912*. Frankfurt am Main: Fischer Taschenbuch, 1999.

———. *The Road into the Open*. Translated by Roger Byers. Berkeley and Los Angeles: University of California Press, 1992.

———. *Tagebuch*. Edited by Werner Welzig. Vienna: Österreichische Akademie der Wissenschaften, 1987–99.

———. *Der Weg ins Freie*. Frankfurt am Main: Fischer Taschenbuch, 1998.

Schnitzler, Arthur, and Richard Beer-Hofmann. *Briefwechsel, 1891–1931*. Edited by Konstanze Fliedl. Vienna: Europaverlag, 1992.

Schnitzler, Arthur, and Olga Waissnix. *Liebe, die starb vor der Zeit: Ein Briefwechsel*. Edited by Therese Nickl and Heinrich Schnitzler. Vienna: Molden, 1970.

Schorsch, Ismar. "The Myth of Sephardic Supremacy." In *From Text to Context: The Turn to History in Modern Judaism*, 71–92. Hanover, N.H.: University Press of New England for Brandeis University Press, 1994.

Schorske, Carl E. *Fin-de-Siècle Vienna*. New York: Vintage Books, 1981.

Schötterer, Reinhold. "Elektras Tanz in der Tragödie Hugo von Hofmannsthals." *Hofmannsthal Blätter* 33 (1986): 47–58.

Schouvaloff, Alexander. *The Art of Ballets Russes*. New Haven: Yale University Press, 1997.

Schwarz, Egon. "Arthur Schnitzler und das Judentum." In *Im Zeichen Hiobs: Jüdische Schriftsteller und deutsche Literatur im 20. Jahrhundert*, edited by Gunter E. Grimm and Hans-Peter Bayerdörfer, 67–83. Königstein: Athenäum, 1985.

Sforim, Mendele Mocher (Mendele the Book Peddler). "Of Bygone Days." Translated by Raymond P. Sheindlin. In *A Shtetl and Other Yiddish Novellas*, edited by Ruth R. Wisse, 249–358. Detroit: Wayne State University Press, 1986.

Shakespeare, William. *The Merchant of Venice*. Cambridge: Cambridge University Press, 1987.

Silberer, Herbert. *Probleme der Mystik und ihrer Symbolik*. Vienna: H. Heller, 1914.

Simon, Ernst. "Hugo von Hofmannsthal: Seine jüdischen Freunde und seine Stellung zum Judentum." *Mitteilungsblatt* 38 (14 October 1977): 3–5.

Sokel, Walter. "Narzißmus und Judentum: Zum Oeuvre Richard Beer-Hofmanns." In *Zeitgenossenschaft: Zur deutschsprachigen Literatur im 20. Jahrhundert: Festschrift für Egon Schwartz zum 65. Geburtstag*, edited by Paul Michael Lützeler, 33–47. Frankfurt am Main: Athenäum, 1987.

Spiegel, Shalom. *The Last Trial: On the Legends and Lore on the Command to Abraham to Offer Isaac as a Sacrifice*. Translated by Judah Goldin. New York: Pantheon, 1967.

Stanislawski, Michael. *Zionism and the Fin de Siècle: Cosmopolitanism and Nationalism from Nordau to Jabotinsky*. Berkeley and Los Angeles: University of California Press, 2001.

Steinberg, Michael P. *Austria as Theater and Ideology: The Meaning of the Salzburg Festival*. Ithaca: Cornell University Press: 2000.

Stern, Martin. "Ein Brief Hofmannsthals an Samuel Fischer." *Hofmannsthal Blätter* 5 (Fall 1970): 336–45.

———. "Verschwiegener Antisemitismus: Bemerkungen zu einem widerrufenen Brief Hofmannsthals an Rudolf Pannwitz." *Hofmannsthal Jahrbuch* 12 (2004): 243–53.

Storey, Robert. *Pierrot: A Critical History of a Mask.* Princeton: Princeton University Press, 1978.

Swales, Martin. "Nürnberger's Novel: A Study of Arthur Schnitzler's *Der Weg ins Freie.*" *Modern Language Review* 70 (1975): 567–75.

Szondi, Peter. *Das lyrische Drama des Fin de Siècle.* Frankfurt am Main: Suhrkamp Taschenbuch Wissenschaft, 1975.

———. *Theorie des modernen Dramas, 1880–1950.* Frankfurt am Main: Suhrkamp, 1963.

Terdiman, Richard. *Present Past: Modernity and the Memory Crisis.* Ithaca: Cornell University Press, 1993.

Timms, Edward. *Karl Kraus: The Apocalyptic Satirist.* New Haven: Yale University Press, 1986.

Timms, Edward, and Ritchie Robertson, eds. *Vienna 1900: From Altenberg to Wittgenstein.* Edinburgh: Edinburgh University Press, 1990.

Tweraser, Felix W. *Political Dimensions of Arthur Schnitzler's Late Fiction.* Rochester: Camden House, 1998.

Urban, Bernd. *Hofmannsthal, Freud und die Psychoanalyse: Quellenkundliche Untersuchungen.* Frankfurt am Main: Peter Lang, 1978.

Verein jüdischer Hochschüler Bar Kochba in Prag, ed. *Vom Judentum: Ein Sammelbuch.* Leipzig: Kurt Wolff, 1914.

Vordtriede, Werner. "Gespräche mit Beer-Hofmann." *Die Neue Rundschau* 63 (April 1952): 122–51.

Weber, Eugene. *The Legend of Freud.* Stanford: Stanford University Press, 2000.

———. "Richard Beer-Hofmann's Translation of Shakespeare's *Richard II.*" In *Essays in Honor of James Edward Walsh,* 95–118. Cambridge, Mass.: Goethe Institute of Boston and Houghton Library, 1983.

Weber, Horst. *Hugo von Hofmannsthal: Bibliographie.* Berlin: Walter de Gruyter, 1972.

White, Hayden. *Tropics of Discourse: Essays in Cultural Criticism.* Baltimore: Johns Hopkins University Press, 1978.

Wiener, Marc. "Parody and Repression: Schnitzler's Response to Wagnerism." *Modern Austrian Literature* 19, nos. 3–4 (1986): 129–48.

Wiese, Benno von, ed. *Die deutsche Novelle von Goethe bis Kafka.* Düsseldorf: August Bagel, 1971.

Wilde, Oscar. "The Critic as Artist." In *The Artist as Critic: Critical Writings of Oscar Wilde,* edited by Richard Ellmann, 340–432. Chicago: University of Chicago Press, 1982.

———. *Salomé.* Boston: John W. Luce, 1903.

Wisely, Andrew C. *Arthur Schnitzler and the Discourse of Honor and Dueling.* New York: Peter Lang, 1996.

———. *Arthur Schnitzler and Twentieth-Century Criticism.* Rochester: Camden House, 2004.

Wistrich, Robert S. *The Jews of Vienna in the Age of Franz Joseph.* Oxford: Oxford University Press, 1989.

Wolgast, Karin. "*Scaramuccia non parla, et dice gran cose.* Zu Hofmannsthals Pantomime *Der Schüler.*" *Deutsche Vierteljahrsschrift für Literaturwissenschaft und Geistesgeschichte* 71, no. 2 (1997): 245–63.

Worbs, Michael. *Nervenkunst: Literatur und Psychoanalyse im Wien der Jahrhundertwende.* Frankfurt am Main: Athenäum, 1988.

Wunberg, Gotthart. "Fin de siècle in Wien." *Text + Kritik* 138/139 (April 1998): 3–24.

———. *Der frühe Hofmannsthal: Schizophrenie als dichterische Struktur.* Stuttgart: W. Kohlhammer, 1965.

———, ed. *Das junge Wien: Österreichische Literatur- und Kunstkritik, 1887–1902.* Tübingen: Niemeyer, 1976.

———. *Wiedererkennen: Literatur und Ästhetischer Wahrnehmung in der Moderne.* Tübingen: Gunter Narr, 1983.

Wunberg, Gotthart, and Stephan Dietrich, eds. *Die literarische Moderne: Dokumente zum Selbstverständnis der Literatur um die Jahrhundertwende.* 2nd ed. Freiburg im Breisgau: Rombach, 1998.

Yates, Frances A. *The Art of Memory.* Chicago: University of Chicago Press, 1966.

Yates, W. E. "The Tendentious Reception of *Professor Bernhardi:* Documentation in Schnitzler's Collection of Press Cuttings." In Timms and Robertson, *Vienna 1900,* 108–25.

Yerushalmi, Yosef Hayim. *Freud's Moses.* New Haven: Yale University Press, 1991.

———. *Zakhor: Jewish History and Jewish Memory.* New York: Schocken Books, 1989.

Young, Robert. *Colonial Desire: Hybridity in Theory, Culture, and Race.* London: Routledge, 1995.

Zweig, Stefan. "Zu 'Jaakobs Traum." *Der Jude* 1, no. 4 (1919–20). Reprinted in *Der Jude.* Vaduz, Liechtenstein: Topos, 1979.

INDEX

ABIGAIL GILLMAN is Associate Professor of German and
Hebrew in the Department of Modern Languages and Comparative
Literature at Boston University.